ASIAN DEVELOPMENT
OUTLOOK

SEPTEMBER 2023

ASIAN DEVELOPMENT BANK

ADB

© 2023 Asian Development Bank
6 ADB Avenue, Mandaluyong City, 1550 Metro Manila, Philippines
Tel +63 2 8632 4444; Fax +63 2 8636 2444
www.adb.org

Some rights reserved. Published in 2023.

ISBN 978-92-9270-338-7 (print); 978-92-9270-339-4 (electronic); 978-92-9270-340-0 (ebook)
ISSN 0117-0481 (print), 1996-725X (electronic)
Publication Stock No. FLS230370-3
DOI: http://dx.doi.org/10.22617/FLS230370-3

The views expressed in this publication are those of the authors and do not necessarily reflect the views and policies of the Asian Development Bank (ADB) or its Board of Governors or the governments they represent.

ADB does not guarantee the accuracy of the data included in this publication and accepts no responsibility for any consequence of their use. The mention of specific companies or products of manufacturers does not imply that they are endorsed or recommended by ADB in preference to others of a similar nature that are not mentioned.

By making any designation of or reference to a particular territory or geographic area, or by using the term "country" in this publication, ADB does not intend to make any judgments as to the legal or other status of any territory or area.

Corrigenda to ADB publications may be found at http://www.adb.org/publications/corrigenda.

Notes:
In this publication, "$" refers to United States dollars.
ADB recognizes "China" as the People's Republic of China; "Korea" as the Republic of Korea; and "Vietnam" as Viet Nam.

Cover design by Anthony Victoria.

Cover artwork by lofranco/2018.

CONTENTS

FOREWORD

Asia and the Pacific is continuing its solid economic recovery. Growth is holding up, supported by strong domestic demand, rebounding tourism, and stable financial conditions, even as export demand remains weak. Inflation is slowing, thanks to lower food and energy prices as well as timely action by central banks across the region.

Asian Development Outlook September 2023 forecasts that economies in developing Asia and the Pacific will expand 4.7% this year. However, the report notes that the recovery is still fragile. This year's El Niño climate pattern increases drought risks in some parts of the region and flooding in others, which could threaten agricultural production. Along with the possibility of increased supply-chain disruptions from the Russian invasion of Ukraine, as well as restrictions on food exports, this could reignite food inflation and exacerbate food insecurity. Continued weakness in the People's Republic of China's property sector could slow growth in Asia's largest economy. Policymakers across the region will need to remain vigilant against financial stability risks in this era of high debt and high interest rates.

More frequent and severe climate events are yet another stark reminder that the region must work together to address the threat that climate change poses to livelihoods, economic growth, safety, and well-being. As part of this, social safety nets need to be strengthened to protect the most vulnerable, and measures taken to improve agricultural productivity and food security. No single economy can tackle these challenges alone. Stronger regional cooperation and integration is essential to build resilience and ensure long-term, sustainable growth.

I hope this edition of the *Asian Development Outlook* will provide helpful insights to support the region's economies as they chart the path ahead.

MASATSUGU ASAKAWA
President
Asian Development Bank

ACKNOWLEDGMENTS

Asian Development Outlook (ADO) September 2023 was prepared by staff of the regional departments and resident missions of the Asian Development Bank (ADB) under the guidance of the Economic Research and Development Impact Department (ERDI). Representatives of these departments met regularly as the Regional Economic Outlook Task Force to coordinate and develop consistent forecasts for the region.

ERDI economists, led by Abdul Abiad, director of the Macroeconomics Research Division, coordinated the production of this report, assisted by Edith Laviña and Priscille Villanueva. Emmanuel Alano, Shiela Camingue-Romance, David Keith De Padua, Christian Regie Jabagat, Nedelyn Magtibay-Ramos, Elyssa Mariel Mores, Jesson Pagaduan, Homer Pagkalinawan, Pilipinas Quising, Ana Francesca Rosales, Divya Sangaraju, Dennis Sorino, Michael Timbang, Mai Lin Villaruel, and Priscille Villanueva provided technical and research support. Economic editorial advisors Robert Boumphrey, Eric Clifton, Joshua Greene, Richard Niebuhr, and Reza Vaez-Zadeh made substantial contributions to the country chapters.

The support and guidance of ADB Chief Economist Albert Park, Deputy Chief Economist Joseph E. Zveglich Jr., and Deputy Director General Chia-Hsin Hu are gratefully acknowledged.

Authors who contributed the sections are bylined in each chapter. The subregional coordinators were Lilia Aleksanyan and Rene Cris Rivera for the Caucasus and Central Asia, Dorothea Ramizo for East Asia, Rana Hasan for South Asia, James Villafuerte and Dulce Zara for Southeast Asia, and Cara Tinio and Remrick Patagan for the Pacific.

In addition to the contributors named in the byline, the special topic benefitted from inputs from Yothin Jinjarak, Safdar Parvez, Wen Qi, Akiko Terada-Hagiwara, and Yajing Wang of the PRC resident mission.

Peter Fredenburg and Alastair McIndoe edited *ADO September 2023*. Alvin Tubio and Jonathan Yamongan did the typesetting and graphics, assisted by Heili Ann Bravo, Dyann Buenazedacruz, Fermirelyn Cruz, Elenita Pura, and Rhia Bautista-Piamonte. Art direction for the cover was by Anthony Victoria, with artwork from Joseph Lofranco. Kevin Nellies designed the *ADO* landing page. Fermirelyn Cruz provided administrative and secretarial support. A team from the Department of Communications and Knowledge Management, led by David Kruger and Terje Langeland, planned and coordinated the dissemination of *ADO September 2023*.

DEFINITIONS AND ASSUMPTIONS

The economies discussed in *Asian Development Outlook September 2023* are classified by major analytic or geographic group. For the purposes of this report, the following apply:

- **Association of Southeast Asian Nations** (ASEAN) comprises Brunei Darussalam, Cambodia, Indonesia, the Lao People's Democratic Republic, Malaysia, Myanmar, the Philippines, Singapore, Thailand, and Viet Nam. ASEAN 4 are Indonesia, Malaysia, the Philippines, and Thailand.

- **Developing Asia** comprises the 46 members of the Asian Development Bank listed below by geographic group.

- **Caucasus and Central Asia** comprises Armenia, Azerbaijan, Georgia, Kazakhstan, the Kyrgyz Republic, Tajikistan, Turkmenistan, and Uzbekistan.

- **East Asia** comprises Hong Kong, China; Mongolia; the People's Republic of China; the Republic of Korea; and Taipei,China.

- **South Asia** comprises Afghanistan, Bangladesh, Bhutan, India, Maldives, Nepal, Pakistan, and Sri Lanka.

- **Southeast Asia** comprises Brunei Darussalam, Cambodia, Indonesia, the Lao People's Democratic Republic, Malaysia, Myanmar, the Philippines, Singapore, Thailand, Timor-Leste, and Viet Nam.

- **The Pacific** comprises the Cook Islands, the Federated States of Micronesia, Fiji, Kiribati, the Marshall Islands, Nauru, Niue, Palau, Papua New Guinea, Samoa, Solomon Islands, Tonga, Tuvalu, and Vanuatu.

Unless otherwise specified, the symbol "$" refers to United States dollars.

A number of assumptions have been made for the projections in *Asian Development Outlook September 2023*. The policies of national authorities are maintained. Real effective exchange rates remain constant at their average from 3 July to 31 August 2023. The average price of oil is $83/barrel in 2023 and $86/barrel in 2024. The 6-month London interbank offered rate for dollar deposits averages 5.2% in 2023 and 2024, the European Central Bank refinancing rate averages 4.0% in 2023 and 3.9% in 2024, and the Bank of Japan's overnight call rate averages 0% in both years.

All data in *Asian Development Outlook September 2023* were accessed from 3 July to 31 August 2023.

ABBREVIATIONS

ADB	Asian Development Bank
ADO	*Asian Development Outlook*
ASEAN	Association of Southeast Asian Nations
bp	basis point
COVID-19	coronavirus disease
CPI	consumer price index
EU	European Union
FDI	foreign direct investment
FSM	Federated States of Micronesia
FY	fiscal year
GDP	gross domestic product
H	half
IMF	International Monetary Fund
IO	input-output
Lao PDR	Lao People's Democratic Republic
LNG	liquefied natural gas
mb/d	million barrels a day
NFRK	National Fund for the Republic of Kazakhstan
OPEC	Organization of the Petroleum Exporting Countries
PMI	purchasing managers' index
pp	percentage point
PRC	People's Republic of China
Q	quarter
ROK	Republic of Korea
RPC	Regional Processing Centre (Nauru)
SDR	special drawing right
US	United States
VIX	Volatility Index
yoy	year on year

ADO SEPTEMBER 2023
HIGHLIGHTS

Growth in developing Asia remained upbeat in the first half of 2023 despite a weaker global outlook. Although soft external demand weighed on export-oriented economies, the region benefited from healthy domestic demand, the reopening of the People's Republic of China (PRC), rebounding tourism, and stable financial conditions. A particularly encouraging development is that subsiding inflation pressures allowed some central banks in the region to start loosening monetary policy, which will help boost growth.

This update revises slightly down the region's growth forecast for this year to 4.7% on slower expansions in East Asia, South Asia, and Southeast Asia. The growth forecast for 2024 is unchanged at 4.8%. With price pressures in the region remaining in check, the inflation forecast is revised down to 3.6% for 2023, but is revised up slightly to 3.5% for 2024. Importantly, headline and core inflation seem to have peaked in the region, but there is some variation across economies.

Downside risks to the outlook have strengthened. A close watch is needed on the weaknesses in the PRC's property sector. Across the region, authorities will need to take policy steps to ensure that supply disruptions and the wide-ranging effects of El Niño do not raise food security challenges. Financial stability risks require continued vigilance in vulnerable economies as the era of easy money ends.

Albert F. Park
Chief Economist
Asian Development Bank

Continued Growth and Moderating Inflation, But Risks Are Rising

Healthy Domestic Demand and the Reopening of the Region's Largest Economy Supported Growth in the First Half of 2023

- **Healthy domestic demand continued to drive developing Asia's growth.** Rising consumption underpinned the PRC's post-reopening expansion. Public investment in India remains robust and will continue to drive growth there. Domestic demand is similarly strong in other economies in the region, as economic activity continues to normalize after the pandemic.

- **A slowdown in global demand is holding back exports in economies across the region, particularly for electronics and semiconductors.** Weak external demand depressed industrial production in the region's high-income technology-exporting economies in the first half of 2023. The region's exports slowed on slumping demand for electronics and garments, although the downturn in the semiconductor cycle has flattened. The manufacturing purchasing managers' index remained below 50—the index threshold indicating improvement—for some economies.

- **Tourism continues to recover, and money transfers to developing Asia remain steady.** Visitor arrivals are reaching pre-pandemic levels in many economies. In the Pacific, the tourism revival has even led to labor shortages in the sector, partly due to increased outward migration of skilled workers during the pandemic. Remittances and money transfers to the region remain stable, but money transfers to the Caucasus and Central Asia have started to decline somewhat after rising sharply last year.

- **Central banks in the region, after raising policy rates last year, have mostly held rates this year as inflationary pressures weaken.** Waning supply side pressures, as well as the tapering of hikes in the United States (US) on slowing inflation there, have given some central banks the space to cut policy rates this year. Inflation is slowing at different rates across the region and is now within the target range for some economies, suggesting that hiking and easing cycles will vary going forward.

- **Financial market conditions have improved after a rough start to 2023.** In the first quarter, banking turmoil and continued rate hikes amid persistent inflation in the US and euro area put financial markets on edge. But financial conditions globally and in developing Asia have improved since then, supported by easing inflation in the region, and expectations of less aggressive monetary policy tightening by the Federal Reserve. Equity markets in the region have strengthened, risk premiums narrowed, and portfolio inflows risen on improved market sentiment. Regional currencies have marginally depreciated so far this year.

- **This update makes a small downward revision to the region's growth forecast for 2023, now at 4.7%.** In East Asia, the PRC's forecast is marginally revised down to 4.9% in 2023, reflecting softening momentum in domestic demand, headwinds from weaker global demand, and the property sector correction. Growth forecasts for the Republic of Korea and Taipei,China are also revised downward. A small downward revision is made for South Asia for 2023, to 5.4% from 5.5%. South Asia will still be the fastest growing subregion, led by India and driven by strong investment and consumption. Growth in Southeast Asia is revised slightly down to 4.6% in 2023 and 4.8% in 2024 due to weaker global demand for the subregion's manufactured exports. The growth forecast for the Caucasus and Central Asia is revised up to 4.6% for 2023 and 4.7% for 2024 as the factors that pushed up growth in the Caucasus last year have not faded as quickly as expected. Growth in the Pacific is revised up to 3.5% for this year and 2.9% for next on the continuing recovery in tourism and infrastructure investment. This update retains the 4.8% regional growth forecast for 2024.

■ **Inflation in developing Asia is forecast to decline from 4.4% last year to 3.6% in 2023 and 3.5% in 2024.** Much of this year's decline will be driven by the PRC, where the inflation forecast is revised down to 0.7%. Excluding the PRC, average inflation in the region will also be lower, falling from 6.7% last year to 6.3% this year and 4.9% next year. Price pressures, however, remain strong and core inflation is high in the Caucasus and Central Asia and in South Asia, most notably in Pakistan.

■ **Risks to the outlook have intensified.** The PRC's property market poses a downside risk and could hold back regional growth. High interest rates are keeping financial stability risks elevated, whether from vulnerable sovereigns or a potential renewal in banking turmoil. Despite the fall in global food prices from their 2022 peaks, food security will continue to be challenged by the effects of El Niño, sporadic food supply disruptions from the Russian invasion of Ukraine, and restrictions on food exports by some economies. Other challenges include geopolitics and the fracturing of global production, which could affect trade, employment, and productivity. Inflation dynamics and the stance of monetary policy in advanced economies will also shape the global outlook over the forecast horizon.

Spillovers from a Further Weakening in the Property Market in the PRC

- **The Special Topic analyzes the risk of a further deterioration in the PRC's property market.** The property sector accounts for an estimated 21%–24% of the country's GDP. As such, further weakness in the property market could have significant consequences in the PRC and elsewhere. The Asian Development Bank's Multiregional Input-Output Tables are used to assess the potential impact of further declines in real estate investment in the PRC and the effect of this on the domestic economy, other economies in the region, and the rest of the world. The analysis evaluates how different policy responses may attenuate the effects of the PRC's property market downturn. It should be emphasized that the Special Topic is not about the baseline forecasts in *Asian Development Outlook September 2023*. This is because the year is nearly over and the various policies that the authorities have already put in place to tackle the current weakness in the property market are sufficient to reach the forecast for 4.9% growth in the PRC this year. Rather, this analysis aims to shed light on the risks in 2024 and beyond coming from the property sector.

- **The results indicate that additional policy support could soften or even erase the impact on growth from a further deterioration in the property market.** The analysis starts by assuming a hypothetical fall in real estate investment. This also generates a decline in private consumption and private investment due to wealth and confidence effects. Scenario simulations are then used to investigate the role played by policy responses. Under a moderate policy support scenario, growth in the PRC falls slightly relative to the baseline forecast. The impact would be broad-based, affecting not just construction but also other industrial sectors and services. Under a stronger policy response scenario, GDP growth actually rises slightly relative to the baseline. Importantly, the size of policy interventions considered in both scenarios is just a fraction of the stimulus enacted by the government during the 2008–2009 global financial crisis and during the COVID-19 pandemic, and well within the PRC's current policy space.

- **The impact on other economies in developing Asia is limited.** Spillovers from a further weakening in the property market in the PRC would have modest global and regional consequences. This is because most inputs in the property sector's supply chain are domestically sourced. But trading partners tightly linked to the PRC would face significant headwinds—particularly Mongolia through its mining sector. Authorities in all economies should be on guard against potential spillovers working through other channels, including heightened international investor risk aversion.

GDP Growth Rate, % per year

	2022	2023		2024	
		April	September	April	September
Developing Asia	**4.3**	**4.8**	**4.7**	**4.8**	**4.8**
Developing Asia excluding the PRC	**5.5**	**4.6**	**4.5**	**5.1**	**5.0**
Caucasus and Central Asia	**5.1**	**4.4**	**4.6**	**4.6**	**4.7**
Armenia	12.6	6.5	7.0	5.5	5.5
Azerbaijan	4.6	3.5	2.2	3.8	2.6
Georgia	10.1	4.5	6.0	5.0	5.0
Kazakhstan	3.2	3.7	4.1	4.1	4.3
Kyrgyz Republic	6.3	4.5	3.8	4.0	4.0
Tajikistan	8.0	5.5	6.5	6.5	7.0
Turkmenistan	6.2	6.5	6.2	6.0	6.0
Uzbekistan	5.7	5.0	5.5	5.0	5.5
East Asia	**2.8**	**4.6**	**4.4**	**4.2**	**4.2**
Hong Kong, China	−3.5	3.6	4.3	3.7	3.3
Mongolia	5.0	5.4	5.7	6.1	5.9
People's Republic of China	3.0	5.0	4.9	4.5	4.5
Republic of Korea	2.6	1.5	1.3	2.2	2.2
Taipei,China	2.4	2.0	1.2	2.6	2.7
South Asia	**6.7**	**5.5**	**5.4**	**6.1**	**6.0**
Afghanistan	...	...	...	...	...
Bangladesh	7.1	5.3	6.0	6.5	6.5
Bhutan	4.7	4.6	4.3	4.2	4.4
India	7.2	6.4	6.3	6.7	6.7
Maldives	13.9	7.1	7.1	6.9	6.9
Nepal	5.6	4.1	1.9	5.0	4.3
Pakistan	6.1	0.6	0.3	2.0	1.9
Sri Lanka	−7.8	−3.0	−3.0	1.3	1.3
Southeast Asia	**5.6**	**4.7**	**4.6**	**5.0**	**4.8**
Brunei Darussalam	−1.6	2.5	2.8	2.8	2.5
Cambodia	5.2	5.5	5.3	6.0	6.0
Indonesia	5.3	4.8	5.0	5.0	5.0
Lao People's Democratic Republic	2.5	4.0	3.7	4.0	4.0
Malaysia	8.7	4.7	4.5	4.9	4.9
Myanmar	2.0	2.8	2.8	3.2	3.2
Philippines	7.6	6.0	5.7	6.2	6.2
Singapore	3.6	2.0	1.0	3.0	2.5
Thailand	2.6	3.3	3.5	3.7	3.7
Timor-Leste	3.2	3.1	2.8	3.0	2.9
Viet Nam	8.0	6.5	5.8	6.8	6.0
The Pacific	**6.1**	**3.3**	**3.5**	**2.8**	**2.9**
Cook Islands	10.5	11.2	14.5	9.1	9.1
Federated States of Micronesia	2.0	4.1	4.1	0.5	0.5
Fiji	20.0	6.3	8.3	3.0	3.7
Kiribati	1.8	2.3	2.3	2.8	2.8
Marshall Islands	−0.9	1.5	2.2	2.0	2.5
Nauru	2.8	1.8	1.6	2.2	1.6
Niue	...	...	...	...	...
Palau	−1.0	3.8	3.8	6.5	6.5
Papua New Guinea	3.2	2.4	2.0	2.6	2.6
Samoa	−5.3	4.8	6.0	2.5	4.2
Solomon Islands	−4.2	3.0	3.0	2.5	2.5
Tonga	−2.2	2.5	2.8	3.2	2.6
Tuvalu	0.7	2.5	3.0	2.0	2.5
Vanuatu	2.0	1.0	1.0	4.2	4.2

... = not available, ADB = Asian Development Bank, GDP = gross domestic product, PRC= People's Republic of China.

Notes: The current uncertain situation permits no estimates or forecasts for Afghanistan over 2022–2024. ADB placed on hold its regular assistance to Afghanistan effective 15 August 2021. Effective 1 February 2021, ADB placed a temporary hold on sovereign project disbursements and new contracts in Myanmar.

Source: *Asian Development Outlook* database.

Inflation, % per year

	2022	2023		2024	
		April	September	April	September
Developing Asia	**4.4**	**4.2**	**3.6**	**3.3**	**3.5**
Developing Asia excluding the PRC	**6.7**	**6.2**	**6.3**	**4.4**	**4.9**
Caucasus and Central Asia	**12.9**	**10.3**	**10.6**	**7.5**	**8.0**
Armenia	8.6	7.0	4.0	6.2	5.5
Azerbaijan	13.9	7.0	10.0	6.5	8.5
Georgia	11.9	6.0	3.0	4.0	3.5
Kazakhstan	15.0	11.8	12.7	6.4	7.6
Kyrgyz Republic	13.9	12.0	12.0	8.6	8.6
Tajikistan	4.2	7.0	5.5	6.5	6.0
Turkmenistan	10.0	10.0	8.0	10.0	8.0
Uzbekistan	11.4	11.0	11.0	10.0	10.0
East Asia	**2.3**	**2.3**	**1.0**	**2.0**	**2.1**
Hong Kong, China	1.9	2.3	2.5	2.1	2.1
Mongolia	15.2	10.9	10.5	8.7	8.6
People's Republic of China	2.0	2.2	0.7	2.0	2.0
Republic of Korea	5.1	3.2	3.3	2.0	2.2
Taipei,China	2.9	2.0	2.0	2.0	2.0
South Asia	**8.2**	**8.1**	**8.6**	**5.8**	**6.6**
Afghanistan	13.8	...	...	...	...
Bangladesh	6.2	8.7	9.0	6.6	6.6
Bhutan	5.6	5.5	4.1	5.1	5.1
India	6.7	5.0	5.5	4.5	4.2
Maldives	2.3	4.5	3.5	2.0	2.5
Nepal	6.3	7.4	7.7	6.2	6.2
Pakistan	12.2	27.5	29.2	15.0	25.0
Sri Lanka	46.4	24.6	18.7	5.5	5.5
Southeast Asia	**5.1**	**4.4**	**4.2**	**3.3**	**3.3**
Brunei Darussalam	3.7	2.0	1.5	1.6	1.4
Cambodia	5.3	3.0	3.0	4.0	4.0
Indonesia	4.2	4.2	3.6	3.0	3.0
Lao People's Democratic Republic	23.0	16.0	28.0	5.0	10.0
Malaysia	3.4	3.1	3.0	2.8	2.7
Myanmar	18.4	10.5	14.0	8.2	8.2
Philippines	5.8	6.2	6.2	4.0	4.0
Singapore	6.1	5.0	5.0	2.0	3.0
Thailand	6.1	2.9	2.5	2.3	2.3
Timor-Leste	7.0	5.5	5.8	2.8	3.3
Viet Nam	3.2	4.5	3.8	4.2	4.0
The Pacific	**5.2**	**5.0**	**4.9**	**4.4**	**4.5**
Cook Islands	4.2	7.7	13.0	2.3	2.3
Federated States of Micronesia	5.0	3.6	3.6	0.4	0.4
Fiji	4.3	4.2	3.0	3.5	3.0
Kiribati	5.0	3.7	6.0	3.0	3.0
Marshall Islands	3.3	3.7	3.7	3.5	3.5
Nauru	1.0	2.5	5.5	1.9	4.2
Niue	...	...	...	...	...
Palau	10.2	5.0	8.0	5.5	5.0
Papua New Guinea	5.3	5.0	5.0	5.0	5.0
Samoa	8.8	10.2	12.0	2.0	5.3
Solomon Islands	5.5	4.5	5.5	3.7	3.7
Tonga	8.5	9.4	10.3	1.5	4.5
Tuvalu	12.2	3.3	6.2	2.8	3.3
Vanuatu	6.7	4.0	9.0	3.0	5.0

... = not available, ADB = Asian Development Bank, PRC = People's Republic of China.

Notes: The current uncertain situation permits no forecasts for Afghanistan over 2023–2024. ADB placed on hold its regular assistance to Afghanistan effective 15 August 2021. Effective 1 February 2021, ADB placed a temporary hold on sovereign project disbursements and new contracts in Myanmar.

Source: Asian Development Outlook database.

1

SOLID GROWTH AND FALLING INFLATION, BUT RISING RISKS

SOLID GROWTH AND FALLING INFLATION, BUT RISING RISKS

Developing Asia's growth prospects have been upbeat despite a weaker global outlook. Reopening in the People's Republic of China (PRC) and healthy consumption and investment in the broader region supported growth in the first half of 2023. External demand has weakened, but showing some signs of bottoming out. Tourism continues to recover with arrivals in many economies now back at pre-pandemic levels, and remittances to the region are robust. Regional financial conditions have improved after a rough start to the year. And with inflation pressures subsiding, some central banks in the region are already starting to loosen monetary policy, providing breathing space for policymakers.

The growth forecast for 2023 is marginally lowered to 4.7%. This is due to downward revisions to growth for East Asia, South Asia, and Southeast Asia, offsetting the upward revisions for the Pacific and the Caucasus and Central Asia. The growth projection is maintained at 4.8% for 2024. Although trends in core inflation vary across subregions, headline inflation has peaked and remains in check. The forecast for inflation is revised down to 3.6% for 2023 and to 3.5% for next year—and coming closer to rates observed before the pandemic.

Downside risks to the outlook have intensified. The PRC's weak property sector poses a risk to the country's recovery and could hold back growth in the region. High interest rates will keep financial stability risks elevated, and food security challenges are reemerging. The stance of monetary policy in advanced economies is also key in shaping the region's outlook.

This section was written by Abdul Abiad, Shiela Camingue-Romance, David Keith De Padua, Jaqueson Galimberti, Jules Hugot, Yothin Jinjarak, Matteo Lanzafame, Nedelyn Magtibay-Ramos, Yuho Myoda, Homer Pagkalinawan, Pilipinas Quising, Irfan Qureshi (lead), and Mai Lin Villaruel of the Economic Research and Development Impact Department (ERDI), Asian Development Bank, and Jesson Pagaduan, ERDI consultant.

The Recovery in Services Is Supporting Growth

The PRC's reopening was an important contributor to developing Asia's first-half growth.
This accelerated from 3.9% in the second half of 2022 to 5.1%, mainly driven by the PRC, where growth almost doubled in the first half as consumption recovered (Figure 1.1.1, panel A). The recovery comes from a rebound in growth after COVID-19 peaked at the end of 2022 and the zero-COVID policy being abandoned. High-frequency data, however, show the PRC's recovery is quickly losing steam. Domestic demand in India was strong in the first half, but economic growth slowed slightly in some other major Asian economies. Deteriorating net exports in particular pulled down growth in Taipei,China and the Republic of Korea.

The services sector is supporting regional growth.
The supply-side decomposition of growth shows that services drove first-half growth (Figure 1.1.1, panel B). Services in the PRC showed particularly strong growth. The contribution of services to growth in the rest of the region remained largely stable. Industrial growth slowed in the first half, except in India and the PRC, and the decline was particularly pronounced in Taipei,China, Singapore, and Malaysia on lower electronics manufacturing.

Figure 1.1.1 Contributions to Real GDP Growth in Developing Asia

A. Demand Side

The PRC's recovery in consumption led the region's growth in H1 2023.

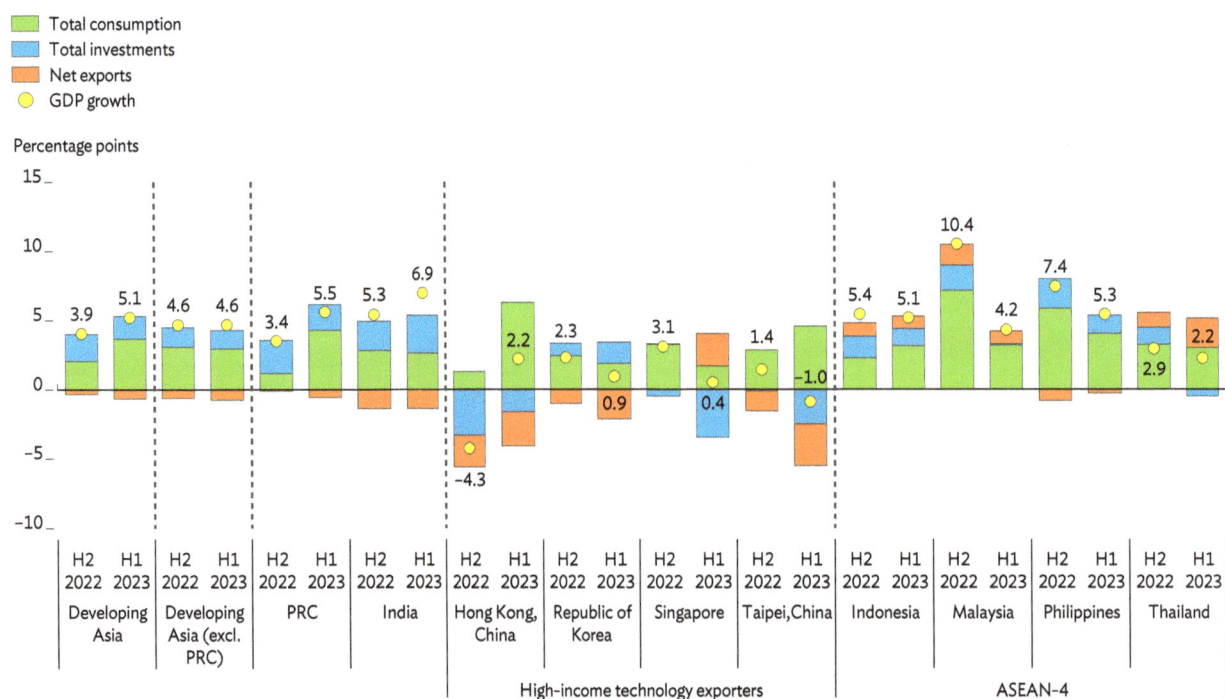

Legend:
- Total consumption
- Total investments
- Net exports
- GDP growth

Percentage points

continued on next page

Figure 1.1.1 *Continued*

B. Supply Side

Growth in the region was mostly supported by a pickup in services.

- Agriculture
- Industry
- Services
- GDP growth

Percentage points

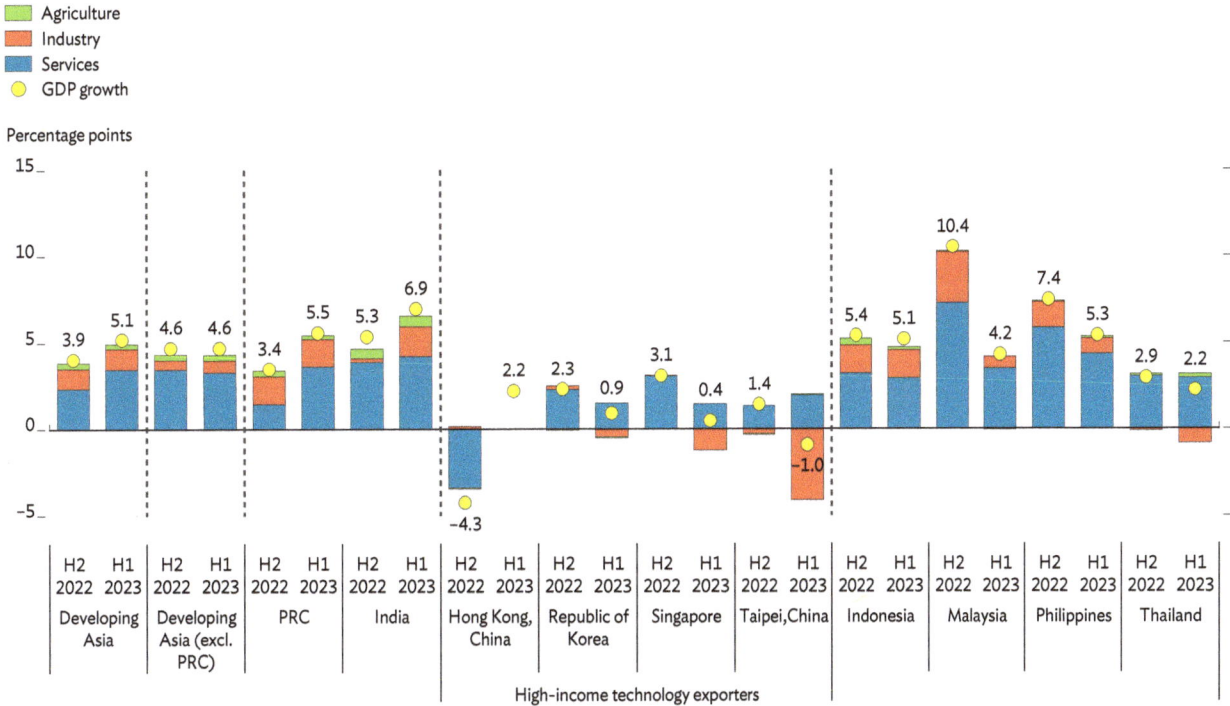

GDP = gross domestic product, H = half, PRC = People's Republic of China.

Notes: Statistical discrepancies excluded. All data in calendar years and non-seasonally adjusted terms. Regional average calculated using GDP purchasing power parity shares as weights. The supply side data for Hong Kong, China is not yet available as of 31 August 2023.

Source: Haver Analytics.

Continued weakness in demand for electronics held back manufacturing as the third quarter got underway, but services remain robust.

Industrial production continues to deteriorate in high-income technology exporters, especially Taipei,China (Figure 1.1.2). Manufacturing purchasing managers indices (PMIs) for those economies and Malaysia have remained below 50 this year, indicating the decline in demand for electronic goods has been depressing production. In Viet Nam, the slowdown in electronics has subsided, with PMIs improving in August and rising just above 50 for the first time since February. Demand for services continues to be robust. The services PMI has been mostly above 50 for economies in the region with available data—India, the PRC, Sri Lanka, and the Philippines—since the beginning of the year (Table 1.1.1).

Figure 1.1.2 Industrial Production Index, Developing Asia

Weak external demand held back industrial production.

- India
- Pakistan
- Singapore
- Viet Nam
- Indonesia
- Philippines
- Taipei,China
- Malaysia
- Republic of Korea
- Thailand

% change year on year, seasonally adjusted, 3-month moving average

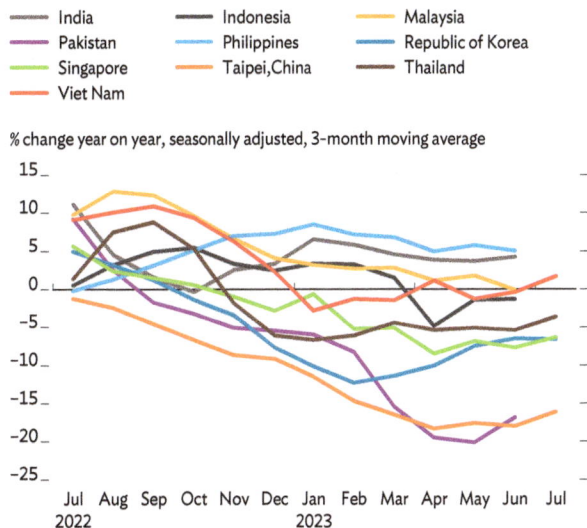

Source: CEIC Data Company.

Table 1.1.1 Purchasing Managers' Index in Developing Asia

PMI indices show continued weakness in manufacturing in some economies, but services remained strong.

Economy	2023							
	Q1			Q2			Q3	
	Jan	Feb	Mar	Apr	May	Jun	Jul	Aug
Manufacturing PMI, seasonally adjusted								
India	55.4	55.3	56.4	57.2	58.7	57.8	57.7	58.6
Indonesia	51.3	51.2	51.9	52.7	50.3	52.5	53.3	53.9
PRC	49.2	51.6	50.0	49.5	50.9	50.5	49.2	51.0
Viet Nam	47.4	51.2	47.7	46.7	45.3	46.2	48.7	50.5
Singapore	49.8	50.0	49.9	49.7	49.5	49.7	49.8	49.9
Philippines	53.5	52.7	52.5	51.4	52.2	50.9	51.9	49.7
Thailand	54.5	54.8	53.1	60.4	58.2	53.2	50.7	48.9
Republic of Korea	48.5	48.5	47.6	48.1	48.4	47.8	49.4	48.9
Malaysia	46.5	48.4	48.8	48.8	47.8	47.7	47.8	47.8
Taipei,China	44.3	49.0	48.6	47.1	44.3	44.8	44.1	44.3
Services PMI, seasonally adjusted								
India	57.2	59.4	57.8	62.0	61.2	58.5	62.3	60.1
PRC	52.9	55.0	57.8	56.4	57.1	53.9	54.1	51.8
Services PMI, not seasonally adjusted								
Sri Lanka	50.2	48.7	55.1	49.6	53.5	56.7	59.5	...
Philippines	53.7	54.9	53.4	56.9	54.0	53.0	48.2	...

... = not available, PMI = purchasing managers' index, PRC = People's Republic of China.
Notes: Pink to red indicates worsening (<50) and white to green indicates improvement (>50). Series for Singapore is not seasonally adjusted.
Source: CEIC Data Company.

Sales of semiconductors continue to decline, but the decline appears to be bottoming out.
With the slowdown in global demand, semiconductor sales fell sharply in late 2022 and the trend has largely continued this year (Figure 1.1.3). With the steeper-than-expected downturn in this market, World Semiconductor Trade Statistics expects a 10.3% contraction in global sales for this year, deeper than the 4.1% expected earlier this year. However, the uptick in the growth of global semiconductor sales averaged over 3 months suggests the downturn started to bottom out in June.

Headline inflation in developing Asia has peaked, reflecting lower energy and food prices.
The weighted average of headline inflation decelerated to 2.8% in July, close to the pre-pandemic average (Figure 1.1.4). The decline in international commodity prices since last year, alongside relatively stable exchange rates against the United States (US) dollar, helped to relieve pressure on energy and food prices in the region.

Headline and core inflation vary across subregions.
Core inflation remains well above pre-pandemic averages in the Caucasus and Central Asia, East Asia (excluding the PRC), and South Asia—and this, along with still-high food inflation, has kept headline inflation higher than the pre-pandemic average in these subregions (Figure 1.1.5). In the Pacific, headline inflation has already fallen below its historical average on lower core inflation. Data show significant variations in headline and core inflation within subregions (Table 1.1.2). In India, food inflation picked up again in July due to bad weather, which also pushed up South Asia's inflation rate.

Figure 1.1.3 Semiconductor Sales and Exports in Developing Asia's Main Technology Exporters

Global semiconductor sales appear to be bottoming out.

— Global semiconductor sales, 3-MMA
— Semiconductor (Republic of Korea)
— Parts of electronic products (Taipei,China)
— Integrated circuits (Singapore)

% change, year on year

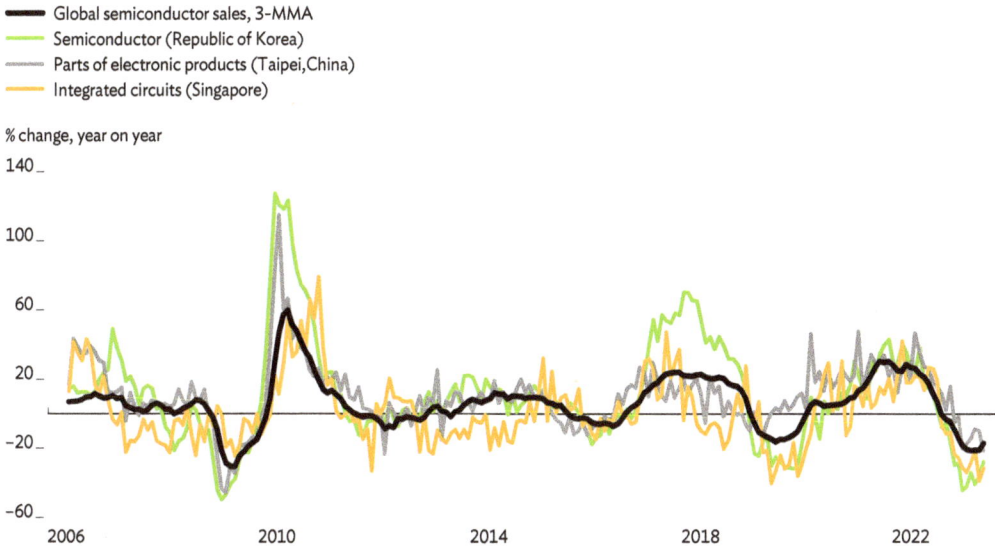

3-MMA = 3-month moving average.
Note: Data for 2023 as of 30 June.
Source: CEIC Data Company.

Figure 1.1.4 Contributions to Inflation in Developing Asia by Food, Energy, and Core Price Basket

Headline inflation fell to the pre-pandemic average on lower energy and food prices.

☐ Core
☐ Food and nonalcoholic beverages
☐ Energy related
— Headline inflation

Percentage points

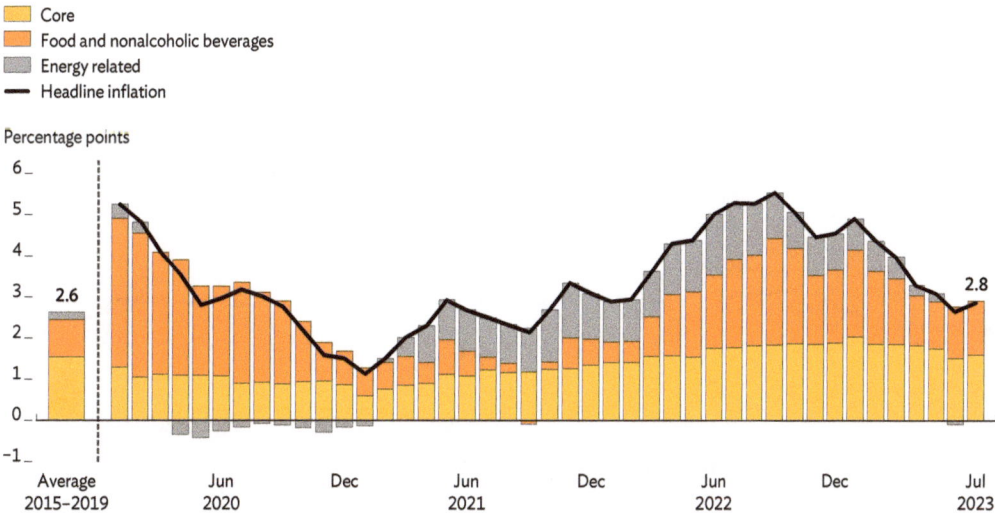

Notes: Core inflation excludes food and energy. For lack of more disaggregated data, the contribution of core inflation to the total for some economies is calculated as the difference between overall inflation and the sum of the contributions of food and nonalcoholic beverages and energy-related items. For some economies, energy-related price indices include housing, water, and nonfuel transport. Subregional averages are calculated using gross domestic product purchasing power parity shares as weights. Developing Asia in this figure covers 22 economies, comprising 94% of regional output. Caucasus and Central Asia = Armenia, Georgia, Kazakhstan. East Asia = Hong Kong, China, Mongolia, the People's Republic of China, the Republic of Korea, Taipei,China. South Asia = India, Pakistan, Maldives, Nepal, Sri Lanka. Southeast Asia = Cambodia, Indonesia, the Lao People's Democratic Republic, Malaysia, the Philippines, Singapore, Thailand. The Pacific = Fiji, Tonga.
Sources: Asian Development Bank calculations using data from Haver Analytics and official national sources.

Figure 1.1.5 Contributions to Subregional Inflation in Developing Asia by Food, Energy, and Core Price Basket

Inflation remains well above its 2015–2019 average in the Caucasus and Central Asia and South Asia, but below the average in the Pacific.

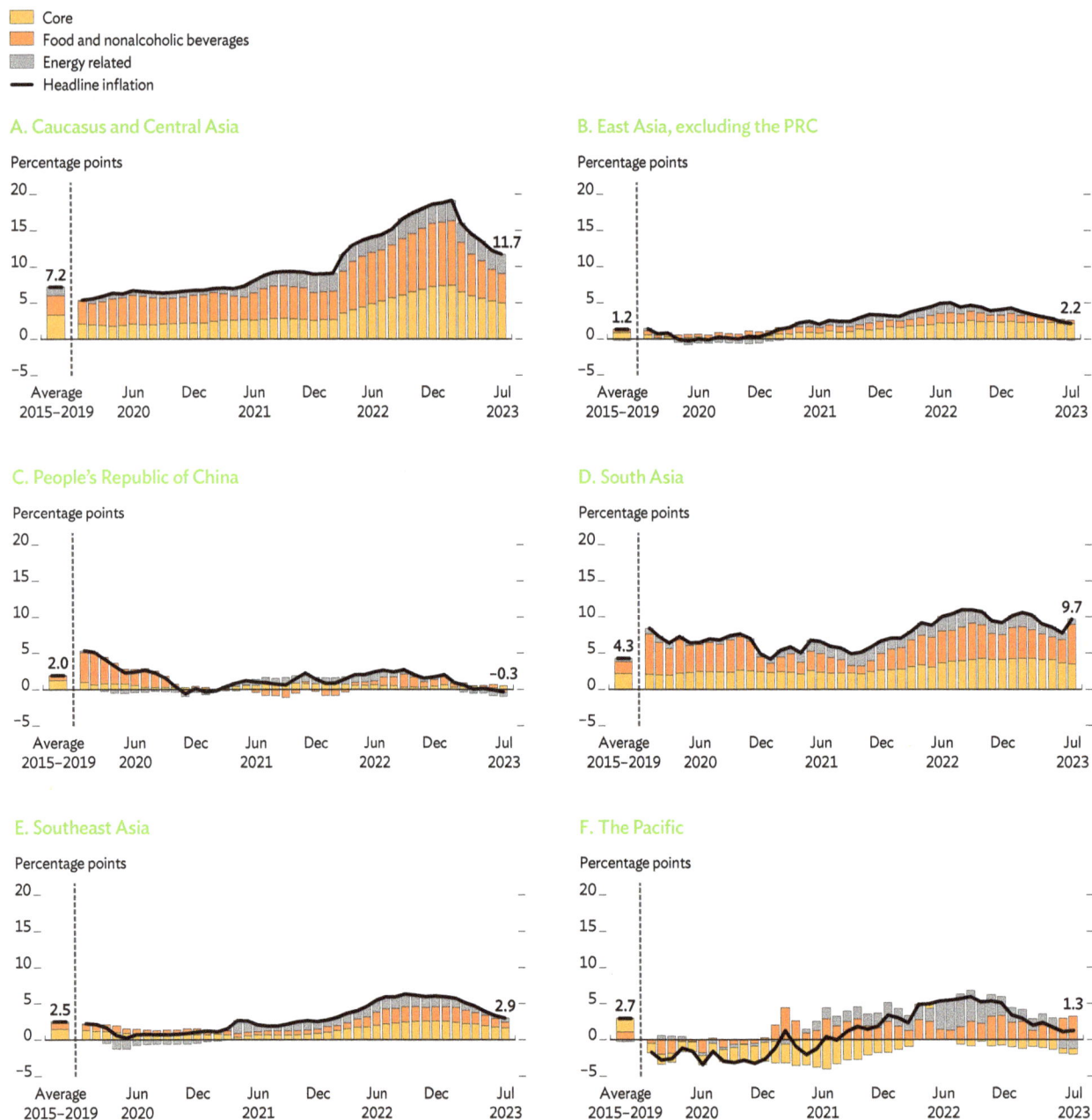

- Core
- Food and nonalcoholic beverages
- Energy related
- ▬ Headline inflation

A. Caucasus and Central Asia

B. East Asia, excluding the PRC

C. People's Republic of China

D. South Asia

E. Southeast Asia

F. The Pacific

Notes: Core inflation excludes food and energy. For lack of more disaggregated data, the contribution of core inflation to the total for some economies is calculated as the difference between overall inflation and the sum of the contributions of food and nonalcoholic beverages and energy-related items. For some economies, energy-related price indices include housing, water, and nonfuel transport. Subregional averages are calculated using gross domestic product purchasing power parity shares as weights. Developing Asia in this figure covers 22 economies, comprising 94% of regional output. Caucasus and Central Asia = Armenia, Georgia, Kazakhstan. East Asia = Hong Kong, China, Mongolia, the People's Republic of China, the Republic of Korea, Taipei,China. South Asia = India, Pakistan, Maldives, Nepal, Sri Lanka. Southeast Asia = Cambodia, Indonesia, the Lao People's Democratic Republic, Malaysia, the Philippines, Singapore, Thailand. The Pacific = Fiji and Tonga. The subregional average for the Pacific is as of June 2023.

Sources: Asian Development Bank calculations using data from Haver Analytics, CEIC Data Company, and official national sources.

Table 1.1.2 Headline versus Core Inflation in Developing Asia

Headline and core inflation varies significantly within subregions.

Economy	Headline Inflation			Core Inflation		
	2022	Jul 2023	Average, 2015–2019	2022	Jul 2023	Average, 2015–2019
Caucasus and Central Asia						
Armenia	8.6	−0.1	1.4	7.4	1.7	1.3
Georgia	11.9	0.3	3.9	6.3	3.2	3.7
Kazakhstan	15.0	13.9	8.0	15.0	14.3	8.3
Kyrgyz Republic	13.9	10.2	2.6	15.4	10.0	2.8
East Asia						
Hong Kong, China	1.9	1.9	2.4	0.7	1.4	2.1
People's Republic of China	2.0	−0.3	2.0	0.9	0.8	1.8
Republic of Korea	5.1	2.3	1.1	4.1	3.9	1.5
Taipei,China	2.9	1.9	0.7	2.6	2.7	0.9
South Asia						
India	6.7	7.4	4.2	6.1	4.9	4.8
Pakistan	19.7	28.3	5.2	11.6	18.4	5.8
Sri Lanka	46.4	4.6	4.2	43.4	6.3	4.7
Southeast Asia						
Indonesia	4.2	3.1	4.0	2.8	2.4	3.5
Malaysia	3.4	2.0	1.9	3.0	2.8	1.7
Philippines	5.8	4.7	2.5	3.9	6.7	2.5
Singapore	6.1	4.1	0.1	4.1	3.8	1.1
Thailand	6.1	0.4	0.3	2.5	0.9	0.7
Viet Nam	3.2	2.1	2.6	2.6	4.1	1.8

Note: All data in calendar years.

Sources: CEIC Data Company; Haver Analytics; official national sources.

Developing Asia's Weaker Export Trend May Have Bottomed Out

Exports remain weak in the region, reflecting softened global demand. After an initial boost from the PRC's reopening in the first quarter of 2023, exports from developing Asia declined in the second quarter (Figure 1.1.6). Average exports from the region in the year to date are 11% below last year's peak. Exports from the region's high-income technology exporters remained flat and at significantly lower levels than their peaks in the first half of 2022. To the extent that technology exports from these economies provide an early indication of trends for the region, the flat trend in the year to date suggests the softer export trend may have bottomed out.

The boost to regional exports from the PRC's reopening is fading. Although PRC exports surged in March, mostly due to the fulfillment of a backlog of orders disrupted by the pandemic, more recent data confirm a loss in momentum. In the year to date, PRC exports declined 5% relative to the same period last year. These exports accounted for 47% of developing Asia's exports and have been affected by the decline in demand for technological products, such as computers and electronics and components.

Growth has slowed in subregional merchandise exports. Merchandise exports from South Asia and Southeast Asia have stabilized at the lower levels reached by the end of 2022 (Figure 1.1.6).

Figure 1.1.6 Nominal Merchandise Exports in Developing Asia

Exports from the PRC, after an initial spike, have weakened, while exports from the region's high-income technology exporters remain flat.

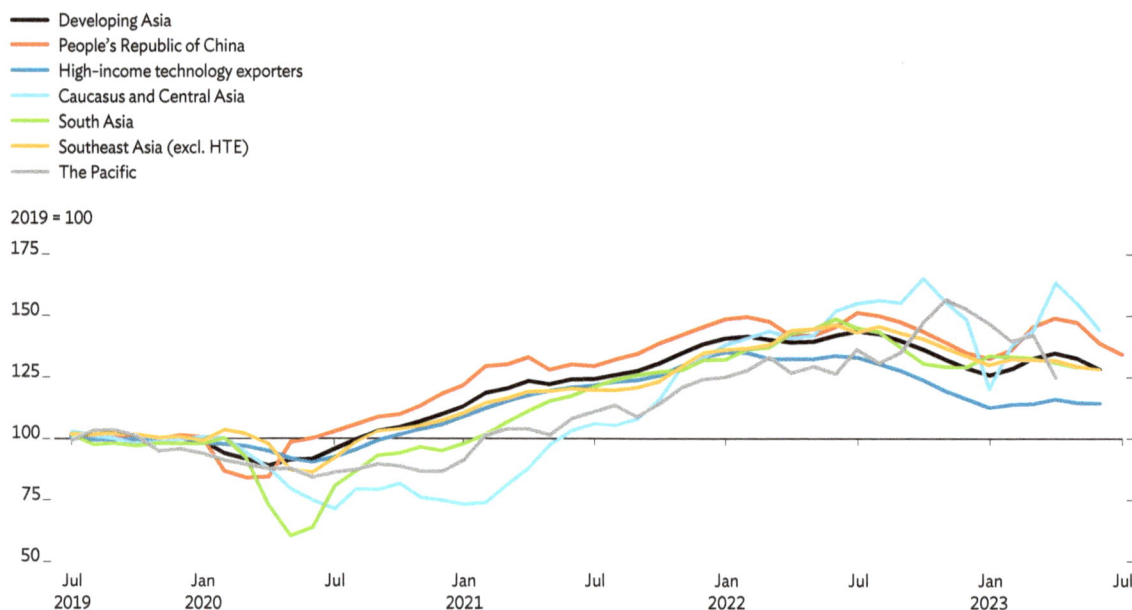

Legend:
- Developing Asia
- People's Republic of China
- High-income technology exporters
- Caucasus and Central Asia
- South Asia
- Southeast Asia (excl. HTE)
- The Pacific

2019 = 100

HTE = high-income technology exporter, PRC = People's Republic of China.

Notes: Indices based on 3-month averages of nominal merchandise exports. HTEs = Hong Kong, China; the Republic of Korea; Singapore; Taipei,China. In this figure, Caucasus and Central Asia = Armenia, Azerbaijan, Georgia, Kazakhstan, the Kyrgyz Republic, Uzbekistan; South Asia = Bangladesh, India, Nepal, Pakistan, Sri Lanka; Southeast Asia (excluding HTEs) = Cambodia, Indonesia, Malaysia, the Philippines, Thailand, Viet Nam; the Pacific = the Federated States of Micronesia, Fiji, Kiribati, the Marshall Islands, Nauru, Palau, Papua New Guinea, Samoa, Solomon Islands, Tonga, Tuvalu, Vanuatu.

Sources: CEIC Data Company; International Monetary Fund. Direction of Trade Statistics.

Export growth from the Caucasus and Central Asia remains volatile. After strong growth of 41% in 2022, exports from this subregion have stalled in the year to date on lower commodity prices. Kazakhstan's exports, which account for about half of the subregion's exports, declined by 9%. The Pacific's export growth declined to 5% in the year to date from 23% in 2022, mostly due to lower exports growth in Papua New Guinea, which accounts for 69% of the subregion's exports.

Weaker demand for goods has dented intraregional trade. The decline in exports for many economies in the region was mainly due to lower demand from the PRC and the US, which led to further declines in intraregional trade—excluding the PRC—through supply chain linkages (Figure 1.1.7, panel A). Lower exports to the PRC contributed 11 percentage points (pps) to the year-to-date contraction in the exports of Hong Kong, China; 7 pps to Taipei,China's; and 6 pps to the Republic of Korea's.

Declining demand from the US also had a significant impact on the exports of Cambodia; Taipei,China; and Viet Nam. Lower intraregional exports to other subregional economies further dented the region's export performance, except Cambodia, which offset declining exports of textiles to the US with increased exports of precious metals and electrical equipment to Singapore. Exports to the Russian Federation contributed 1 pp to the PRC's exports, while exports to the European Union contributed –1 pp to the declines in the exports of Hong Kong, China; Indonesia; Malaysia; the PRC; Singapore; and Viet Nam.

Exports of electronics and garments declined the most. Lower demand for machinery and electrical components, especially electronics, was the main contributor to the lower exports from technology exporters (Figure 1.1.7, panel B). These products account for 44% of the total exports of the economies in the figure, with the decline ranging from 5% in the PRC to 24% in the Republic of Korea.

Figure 1.1.7 Contributions to Goods Export Growth in Developing Asian Economies, 2023 to Date

A. By Destination Market

Intraregional exports declined amid weakened demand from the PRC and the US.

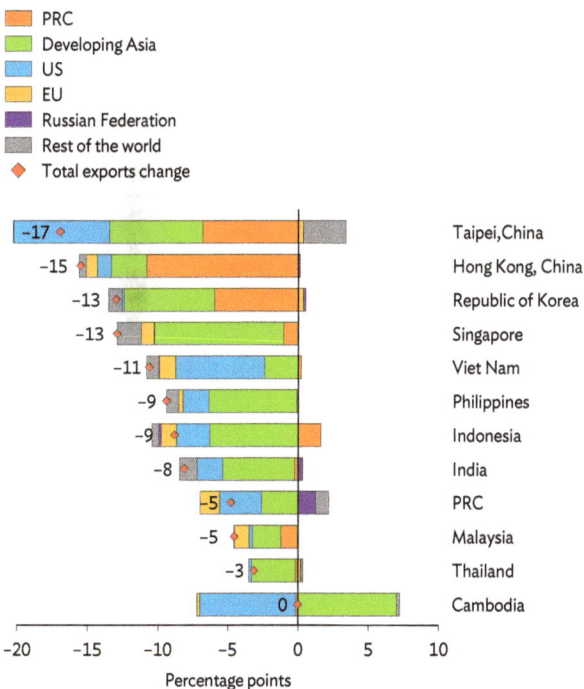

- PRC
- Developing Asia
- US
- EU
- Russian Federation
- Rest of the world
- ◆ Total exports change

B. By Product Class

Lower demand for electronics and garments are the main causes for declining exports.

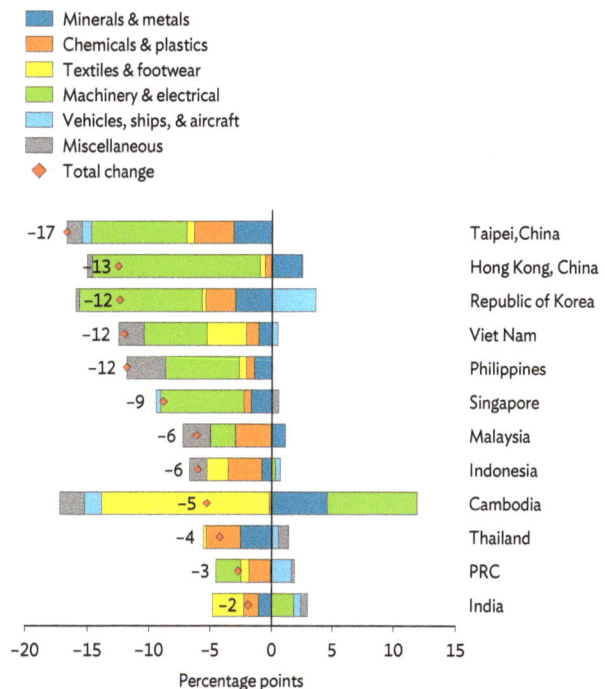

- Minerals & metals
- Chemicals & plastics
- Textiles & footwear
- Machinery & electrical
- Vehicles, ships, & aircraft
- Miscellaneous
- ◆ Total change

EU = European Union, PRC = People's Republic of China, US = United States.

Notes: Panel A: Year-to-date export growth figures are based on 2022 and 2023 total exports from January to April for Cambodia, from January to June for Hong Kong, China; India; Indonesia; Malaysia; the Philippines; and Thailand, and from January to July for the remaining economies. Panel B: Year-to-date export growth figures are based on 2022 and 2023 total exports from January to March for India, from January to May for Cambodia, Indonesia, Malaysia, the Philippines, Singapore, Thailand, and Taipei,China, and from January to June for the remaining economies. Some total change figures differ from panel A due to varying time periods and sources.

Sources: Panel A: CEIC Data Company; International Monetary Fund. Direction of Trade Statistics. Panel B: CEIC Data Company; International Trade Centre.

Cambodia and India, however, increased exports of electrical components due to their increased participation in global electronics value chains. Lower demand for textiles and footwear badly hit the exports of the region's traditional garment exporters, such as Cambodia and Viet Nam. The growth in exports of electric vehicles from the Republic of Korea and the PRC counterbalanced the overall decline in exports in these countries.

Tourism continues to recover. The revival in international travel and reopenings in many economies in the region are boosting tourism. International arrivals were at 49% of the pre-pandemic average by the last quarter of 2022 and are close to 70% in the year to date. Tourist arrivals are back to pre-pandemic

levels in the Caucasus and Central Asia, the Pacific, and South Asia, but the recovery is lagging behind in East Asia and Southeast Asia (Figure 1.1.8, panel A). The rebound in international travel is particularly welcome in tourism-dependent economies in the Pacific and South Asia. In 2019, international tourism receipts totaled 56% of gross domestic product (GDP) in Maldives, 24% each in Fiji and Samoa, and 20% each in Cambodia and Georgia. The return of international visitors has been more gradual in East Asia and Southeast Asia, regions that are heavily dependent on tourists from the PRC (Figure 1.1.8, panel B). Data from some developing Asian economies up to May this year indicate that PRC outbound tourists to the region were still only 39% of the 2018–2019 average.

Figure 1.1.8 International Tourist Arrivals in Developing Asian Economies

A. By Subregion

Tourism is back to pre-pandemic levels in most of developing Asia.

- Caucasus and Central Asia
- East Asia
- South Asia
- Southeast Asia
- The Pacific

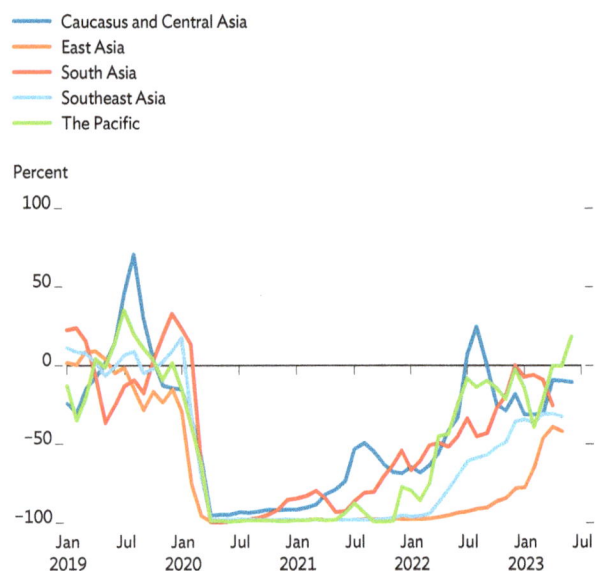

B. By Economy

The tourism recovery is still underway in East Asia and Southeast Asia.

- 2022
- 2023 ytd
- 2019

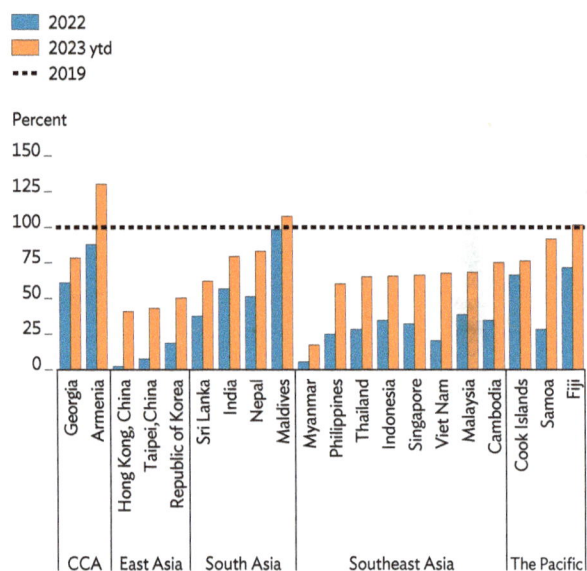

CCA = Caucasus and Central Asia, ytd = year to date.
Notes: Panel A: Caucasus and Central Asia = Armenia, Georgia; East Asia = Hong Kong, China; the Republic of Korea; Taipei,China; South Asia = India, Maldives, Nepal, Sri Lanka; Southeast Asia = Cambodia, Indonesia, Malaysia, Myanmar, the Philippines, Singapore, Thailand, Viet Nam; the Pacific = the Cook Islands, Fiji, Samoa. Panel B: Year-to-date figures based on 2019 and 2023 total arrivals from January to April for India. From January to May for Cambodia; Indonesia; Hong Kong, China; Malaysia; Myanmar; the Republic of Korea; Taipei,China. From January to June for Armenia, the Cook Islands, Georgia, Maldives, Nepal, the Philippines, Samoa, Singapore, Sri Lanka, and Thailand. From January to July for Fiji and Viet Nam.
Sources: CEIC Data Company; official national sources.

Personal money transfers to developing Asia remain robust. Regional remittances are steady and higher than their pre-pandemic level for most economies that have traditional outbound flows of migrant workers. Although money transfers associated with the Russian invasion of Ukraine have tumbled, these remain two to three times higher than pre-pandemic levels.

Personal transfers to South Asia, mostly remittances, remain steady. Money transfers to Sri Lanka doubled in the year to date, continuing a positive trend that started in early 2022 (Figure 1.1.9, panel A). However, this increase is mostly a measurement correction, as remitters returned to formal transfer channels with the narrowing of parallel exchange rates after the Central Bank of Sri Lanka relaxed controls on the official rate. Net personal transfers in the year to date increased by 13% in Nepal and 9% in Bangladesh from the same period in 2022, but decreased by 17% in Pakistan.

These changes are consistent with seasonal patterns in money transfers as well as fluctuations in the gap between official and unofficial exchange rates. Slowdowns in host economies, such as the Gulf countries where most South Asian migrant workers work, are likely to constrain growth in remittances to the region.

Personal transfers to Southeast Asia and the Pacific remain strong. Net personal transfers remain steady in the Philippines and are growing in Cambodia (Figure 1.1.9, panel B). Money transfers to Fiji ended 2022 at 73% above their pre-pandemic level. Transfers to Samoa started declining in 2023, but are still high compared to before the pandemic. The trend for transfers has been positive since borders reopened for labor migration in Australia and New Zealand, the most important destinations for migrant workers from the Pacific. Although migrant populations in both countries have surpassed pre-pandemic levels, slowing economic growth could dampen remittance growth to the Pacific.

Figure 1.1.9 Net Personal Transfers to Developing Asia

A. South Asia

Remittances to the subregion remain steady.

- Bangladesh
- Nepal
- Pakistan
- Sri Lanka

Average of the same quarter in 2018–2019 = 100

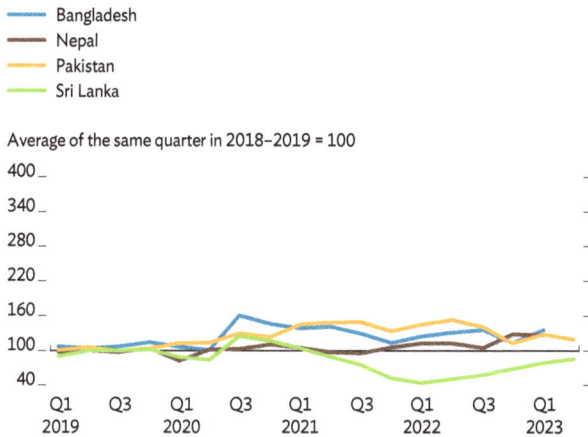

B. Southeast Asia and the Pacific

Remittances remain elevated relative to pre-pandemic.

- Cambodia
- Philippines
- Fiji
- Samoa

Average of the same quarter in 2018–2019 = 100

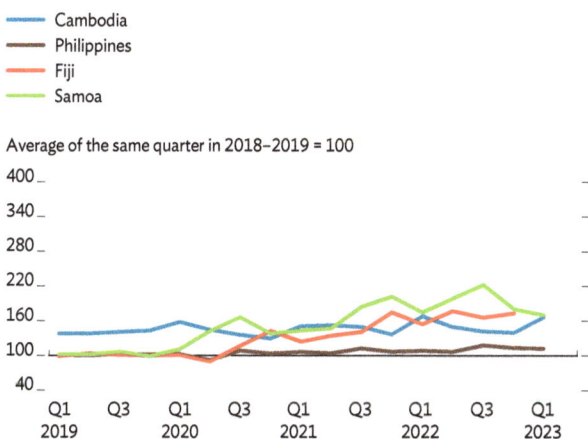

C. Caucasus and Central Asia

Money transfers started to decline, but are still at elevated levels.

- Armenia
- Georgia
- Kyrgyz Republic
- Tajikistan
- Uzbekistan

Average of the same quarter in 2018–2019 = 100

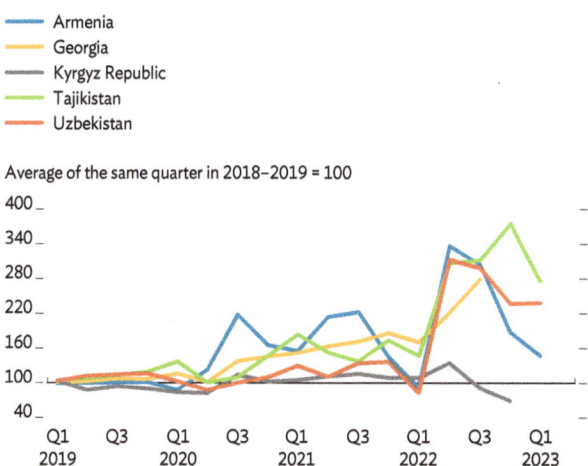

Q = quarter.
Sources: CEIC Data Company; official national sources.

The increased outflow of skilled workers from the subregion is causing labor shortages, particularly in the tourism sector (Box 1.1.1).

Money transfers to the Caucasus and Central Asia have started to decline after peaking in 2022.
In the first quarter of 2023, money transfers declined by 56% to Armenia, 62% to Tajikistan, and 55% to Uzbekistan from their 2022 peaks, but are still very high compared to pre-pandemic levels (Figure 1.1.9, panel C). These transfers reflect large inflows of Russian migrants to the subregion, corresponding transfers of savings, and possibly commercial transactions.

Financial Conditions Have Brightened, Currencies Fairly Stable

Financial conditions have improved since March after a rough start to 2023. Easing inflation in developing Asian economies, moderating monetary tightening in the US, and perceived banking sector risks in the US and Europe subsiding following the turmoil in the first quarter are behind the improvement. From April to August, equity markets rose, risk premiums narrowed, and net portfolio inflows increased in economies across developing Asia. Currencies in the region have marginally depreciated against the US dollar so far this year.

Equity markets have rallied in most markets in the region. The Chicago Board Options Exchange's Volatility Index (VIX) has fallen since the end of March on normalizing market conditions and reduced uncertainty, especially in the banking sector (Figure 1.1.10). Developing Asia's market-weighted return increased by 3.4% from 1 April to 31 August and the S&P 500 climbed by 9.7%, lifted by better-than-expected economic conditions and expectations of less hawkish monetary policy in the US. In August the VIX rose slightly, and equity markets declined after Fitch Ratings' downgrade of the US and the weak economic conditions in the PRC.

Figure 1.1.10 Developing Asia's Equity Market Performance

Markets recovered from losses from deteriorating investor sentiment during the banking turmoil in the US and Europe in March.

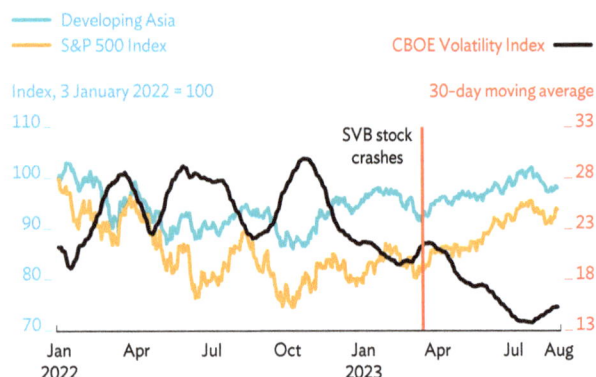

CBOE = Chicago Board Options Exchange, SVB = Silicon Valley Bank, US = United States.
Source: Bloomberg.

Figure 1.1.11 J. P. Morgan Emerging Market Bond Index Stripped Spreads in Developing Asia Subregions

Average risk premiums narrowed from April on improved sentiment.

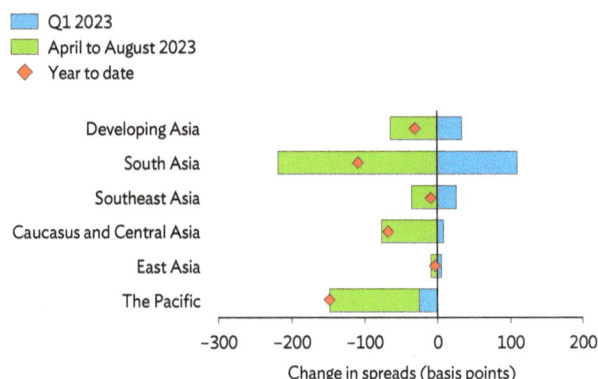

Q = quarter.
Source: Bloomberg.

Risk premiums in most regional markets have narrowed since April on improved sentiment.

The weighted average regional risk premium—as measured by J. P. Morgan Emerging Markets Bond Index Global stripped spreads—widened about 30 basis points (bps) in the first quarter on the Federal Reserve's continued monetary tightening in response to inflationary pressures and turmoil in the US and European banking sector. Bond spreads, however, have retreated since April by 64.1 bps on regained investor confidence, boosted by an improving inflation picture in the US and developing Asia's upbeat outlook. This pattern is clearly shown in South Asia, where spreads declined by 218.4 bps; in Caucasus and Central Asia, down 76.5 bps; and in Southeast Asia, down 35.1 bps. Spreads in East Asia have remained relatively stable compared to the rest of the region and spreads in the Pacific continue to decline (Figure 1.1.11).

Currencies in the region have depreciated only marginally so far this year, by 3.7% on a GDP-weighted average basis against the US dollar.

Still, large currency depreciations were seen in Pakistan given the economic and political instability there and in the Lao People's Democratic Republic due to high inflation, trade deficits, and debt concerns (Figure 1.1.12). Afghanistan's currency appreciated against the US dollar as the country continues to receive significant inflows of cash for humanitarian aid.

In the Caucasus and Central Asia, only Armenia's currency appreciated in July and August, on high labor and capital inflows from the Russian Federation. The Sri Lanka rupee, after a strong rise in the first half, has weakened against the US dollar due to relaxed import restrictions.

Net portfolio inflows increased to developing Asia.

In the first 8 months of 2023, they totaled $55.9 billion, but it was a choppy period for these inflows (Figure 1.1.13). January's large inflows slowed in February and March, reflecting a more cautious market due to uncertainty over monetary tightening in advanced economies and the turmoil in the US and European banking sector. In April, foreign portfolios had a net outflow, mainly on outflows from the PRC amid signs of a slowdown in its economic recovery. Portfolio inflows continued into the rest of developing Asia in May as economies benefited from market optimism over the easing in monetary tightening in the US and the region's continued recovery. In June and July, foreign inflows to the PRC returned on investor optimism over stimulus measures to boost the economy and monetary easing by the People's Bank of China. However, inflows turned to outflows in August following negative economic news on the region.

Figure 1.1.12 Exchange Rate Movements in Developing Asian Economies

On average, currencies in the region have marginally depreciated against the US dollar in 2023.

- ■ H1 2023
- ■ July to August
- ◆ Year to date

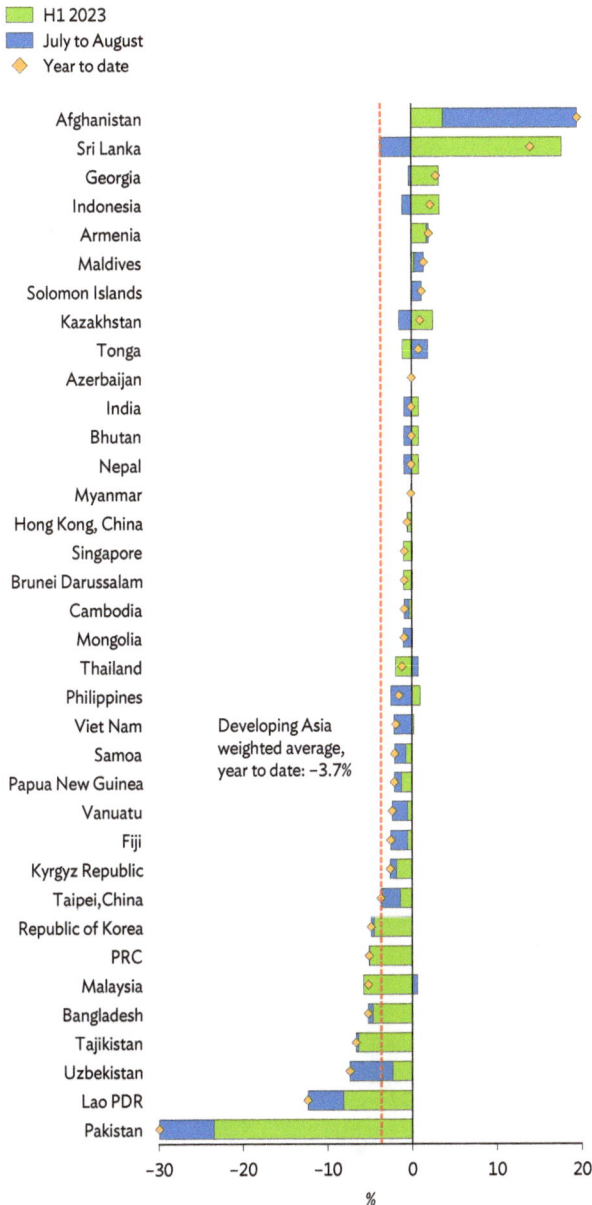

Developing Asia weighted average, year to date: −3.7%

H = half, Lao PDR = Lao People's Democratic Republic, PRC = People's Republic of China, US = United States.

Note: Developing Asia average change is calculated using gross domestic product purchasing power parity shares as weights.

Source: Bloomberg.

Figure 1.1.13 Foreign Investment Flows into Developing Asia

Foreign portfolio flows slowed on the PRC's decelerating economic recovery.

- ■ Developing Asia excluding the PRC
- ■ People's Republic of China
- ◆ Developing Asia

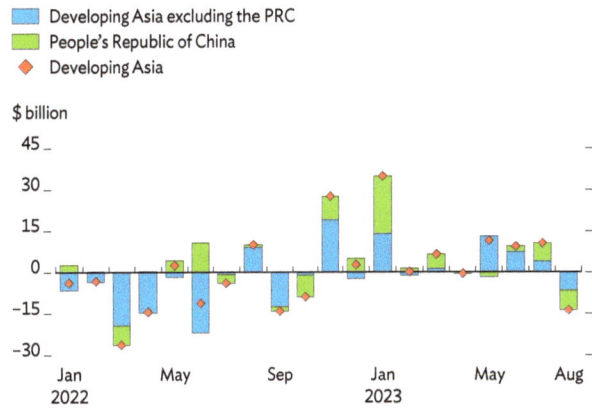

PRC = People's Republic of China.

Note: Data for August is up to 23 August.

Source: Institute of International Finance.

Foreign direct investment inflows continue, but are still off their 2021 peak. Investment flows into the region declined by 24.9% to $577.8 billion in 2022 (Figure 1.1.14). Inflows into East Asia, especially the PRC, dropped sharply in the second and third quarters of last year in a possible reflection of foreign companies lowering their exposure to the PRC and diversifying to other production locations.

Figure 1.1.14 Foreign Direct Investment into Developing Asia

FDI stabilized in Q1 2023.

- ■ Southeast Asia
- ■ South Asia
- ■ East Asia
- ■ The Pacific
- ■ Caucasus and Central Asia

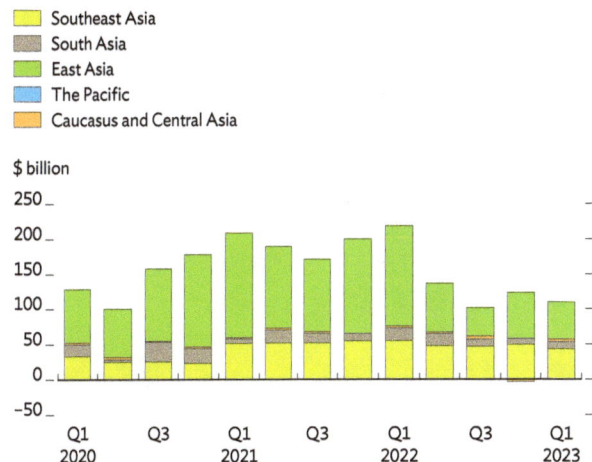

FDI = foreign direct investment, Q = quarter.

Source: Haver Analytics.

Shift Toward Monetary Easing as Fiscal Consolidation Continues

Most central banks in the region have kept policy rates on hold this year, but there are signs of easing. Inflation is slowing and has already fallen within central bank targets in several economies (Figure 1.1.15). With moderating inflation and slower tightening by the Fed, monetary authorities are turning more dovish, with some already starting to ease policy. About two-thirds of policy decisions this year have been to hold rates, and there have already been more cuts than last year (Figure 1.1.16). Central banks in Armenia, Georgia, the PRC, Sri Lanka, and Uzbekistan have cut policy rates.

Fiscal deficits in developing Asian economies are still sizable even though consolidation gathers pace. Policy support following the pandemic and shocks specific to economies widened deficits and elevated debt levels. Overall, changes in fiscal balances based on a survey of private forecasters are expected to be mixed this year, with most economies in the region continuing fiscal consolidation next year as authorities rein in deficits (Figure 1.1.17). However, deficits will remain sizable for many economies, notably in Myanmar, Pakistan, and Sri Lanka.

Figure 1.1.15 Inflation and Inflation Targets

Inflation is slowing and is within or close to central bank targets for several economies.

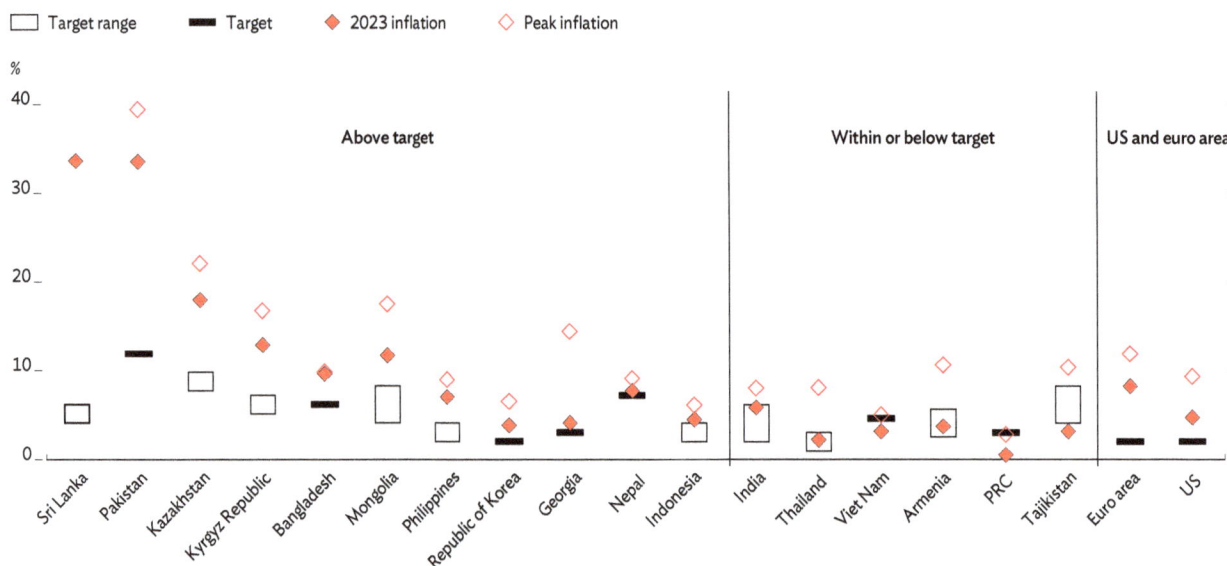

PRC = People's Republic of China, US = United States.

Notes: Figure is sorted by the size of the gap between inflation and inflation target. Peak inflation is the highest point since January 2021; Sri Lanka peak inflation was 73% and omitted for scale. Inflation refers to the average for January to July 2023. Inflation targets are the central bank point targets or target ranges.

Sources: CEIC Data Company; official national sources.

Figure 1.1.16 Policy Rate Decisions in Developing Asia

Central banks are mostly holding rates, with some starting to ease policy.

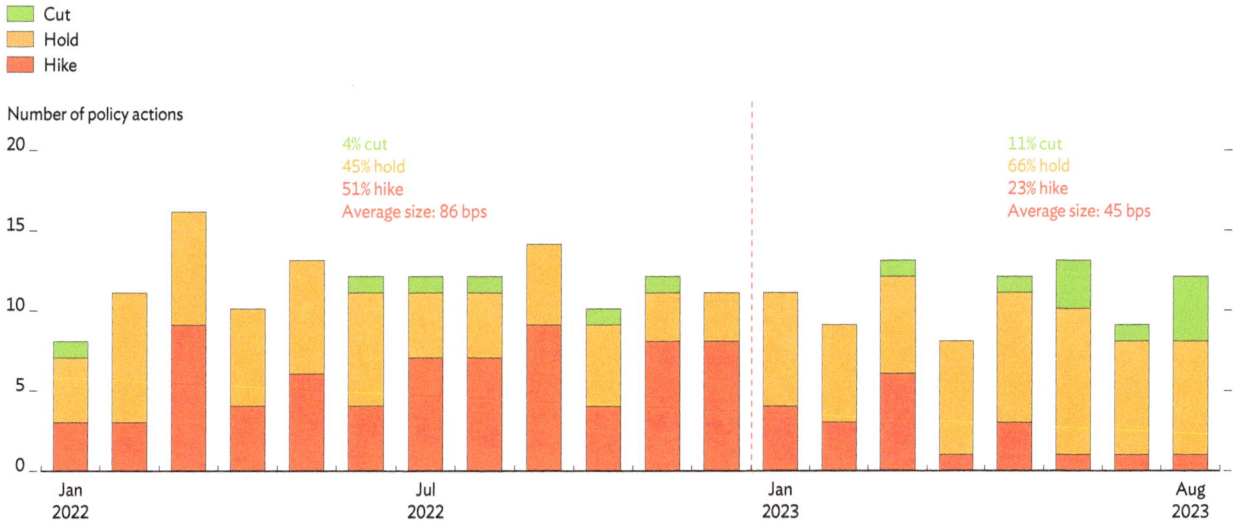

Cut
Hold
Hike

Number of policy actions

4% cut
45% hold
51% hike
Average size: 86 bps

11% cut
66% hold
23% hike
Average size: 45 bps

Jan 2022   Jul 2022   Jan 2023   Aug 2023

bps = basis points.
Note: The figure covers Armenia; Azerbaijan; Georgia; Hong Kong, China; India; Indonesia; Kazakhstan; the Kyrgyz Republic; Malaysia; Mongolia; Pakistan; the People's Republic of China; the Philippines; the Republic of Korea; Sri Lanka; Tajikistan; Taipei,China; Thailand; Uzbekistan.
Source: Trading Economics.

Figure 1.1.17 Fiscal Balances in Developing Asia Subregions

Fiscal balances are improving, but deficits will remain sizable for many economies.

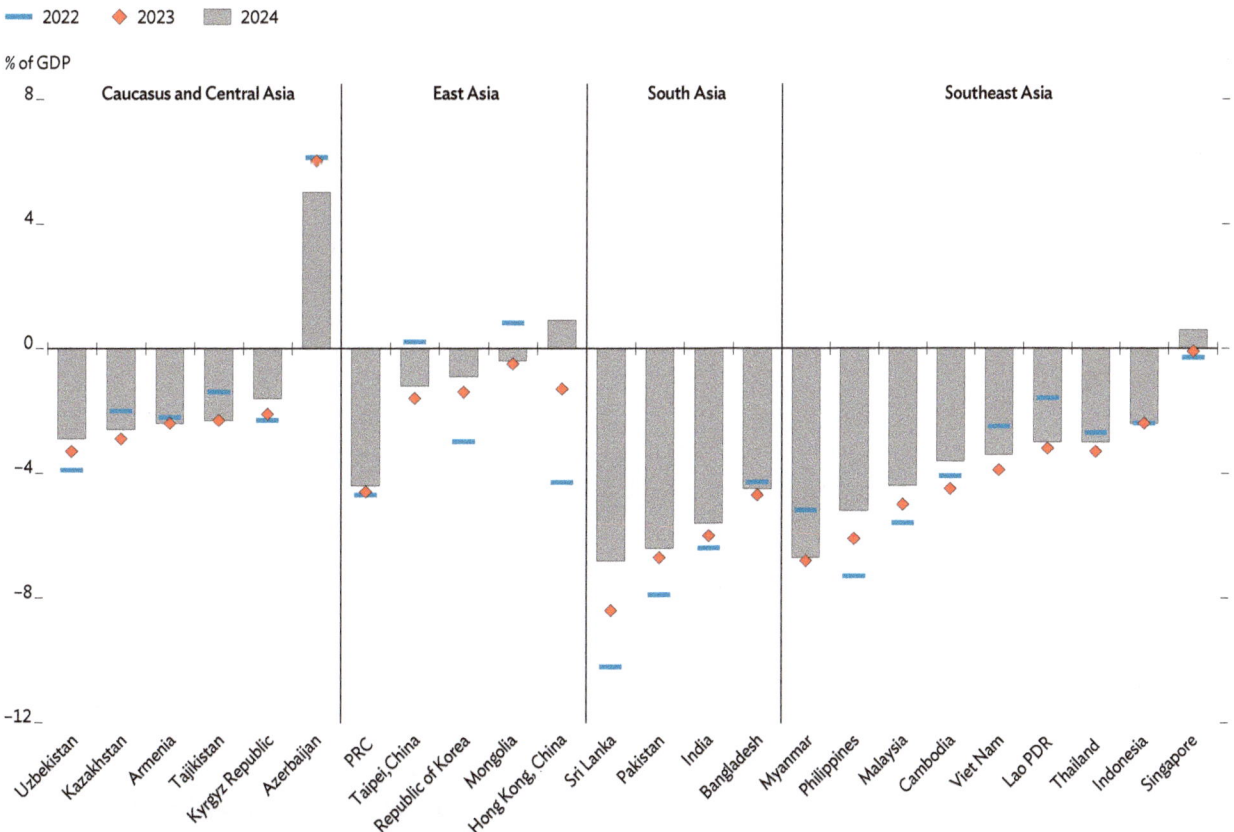

— 2022   ◆ 2023   ▢ 2024

% of GDP

Caucasus and Central Asia   East Asia   South Asia   Southeast Asia

Uzbekistan, Kazakhstan, Armenia, Tajikistan, Kyrgyz Republic, Azerbaijan, PRC, Taipei,China, Republic of Korea, Mongolia, Hong Kong, China, Sri Lanka, Pakistan, India, Bangladesh, Myanmar, Philippines, Malaysia, Cambodia, Viet Nam, Lao PDR, Thailand, Indonesia, Singapore

GDP = gross domestic product, Lao PDR = Lao People's Democratic Republic, PRC = People's Republic of China.
Source: FocusEconomics Consensus Forecasts reports.

Regional Growth and Inflation Continue Converging to Pre-Pandemic Rates

Growth this year in the major advanced economies will slow less than was forecast in *ADO April 2023*.
The sharp upward revision for 2023 in the US reflects unexpectedly strong first-half growth (Table 1.1.3). Lagged effects of interest rate hikes are expected to bite in 2024, prompting a cut in the growth forecast for the year to 0.8% (Figure 1.1.18). The euro area's growth forecast is raised to 0.7% for 2023, but trimmed to 1.1% for 2024. Japan's growth forecast is revised up to 1.7% for 2023 on strong activity in the first half and down to 0.5% in 2024. A boost in the first half is not expected to continue over the rest of the year, as the strong activity was largely driven by a backlog in car exports due to last year's chip shortage, and because domestic demand has contracted. Overall, resilience in advanced economies will mitigate the expected downturn in developing Asia as large shares of the region's exports ultimately go to advanced economies (Box 1.1.2).

Figure 1.1.18 Policy Rates in the Euro Area and United States

Monetary tightening will continue for the rest of 2023 before easing in 2024.

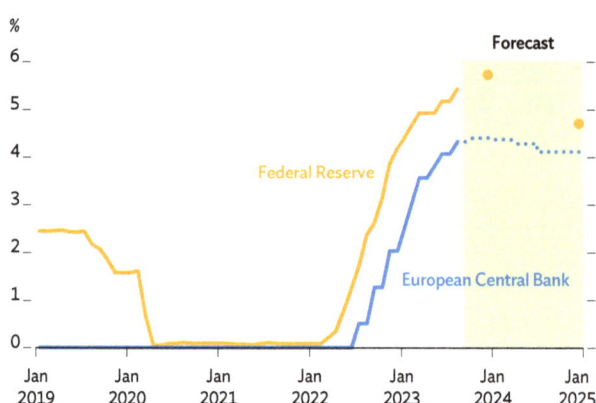

Sources: European Central Bank; Federal Open Market Committee.

Table 1.1.3 Baseline Assumptions on the International Economy

Growth for 2023 is revised up for the major advanced economies.

	2022	2023		2024	
	Actual	Apr	Sep	Apr	Sep
GDP growth, %					
Major advanced economies[a]	**2.5**	**0.7**	**1.4**	**1.3**	**0.9**
United States	2.1	0.9	1.9	1.3	0.8
Euro area	3.5	0.5	0.7	1.4	1.1
Japan	1.0	0.8	1.7	0.8	0.5
Inflation, %					
Major advanced economies	**7.5**	**4.4**	**4.5**	**2.4**	**2.3**
United States	8.0	4.0	4.0	2.4	2.4
Euro area	8.4	5.7	5.7	2.5	2.5
Japan	2.3	2.0	2.9	1.9	1.5
Brent crude spot price, average, $/barrel	100	88	83	90	86

[a] Average growth rates are weighted by GDP purchasing power parity.

Sources: Bloomberg; CEIC Data Company; Haver Analytics; International Monetary Fund. World Economic Outlook; Asian Development Bank estimates.

Oil prices will remain capped by slowing global demand. The price of Brent crude fell from about $83 in January to $75 in June on softening global demand. To halt this decline, Saudi Arabia cut output in May and July, and the Russian Federation has also reduced output since March and announced further cuts for September. These supply restrictions pushed prices to about $86 in August. But overall, slowing global demand is expected to further drive the market, prompting a downward revision to $83 on average for this year from $88 forecast in April.

Rice prices have risen to a 15-year high, and El Niño will further tense food markets. Rice prices shot up across Asia after India—which contributes more than a third of global rice exports—expanded export restrictions in July (Figure 1.1.19).

This follows erratic rainfall during the monsoon, which is expected to hurt the upcoming harvest. Price spillovers to the rest of the region are increasing the risk that key exporters, such as Pakistan, Thailand, and Viet Nam, will also restrict exports to keep domestic prices in check. In addition, El Niño is expected to result in less rainfall in the coming months, hurting the upcoming harvest, particularly in Southeast Asia (Box 1.1.3). This could dent food security and raise inflation in net rice-importing countries, such as Bangladesh, Bhutan, Maldives, Nepal, and the Philippines. Wheat prices remain in check despite the Russian Federation's withdrawal from the Black Sea Grain Initiative in July—and an abundant global wheat harvest is expected to keep prices low.

Figure 1.1.19 Commodity Prices

Oil prices are forecast averaging $83/barrel in 2023, but rice prices have risen to a 15-year high.

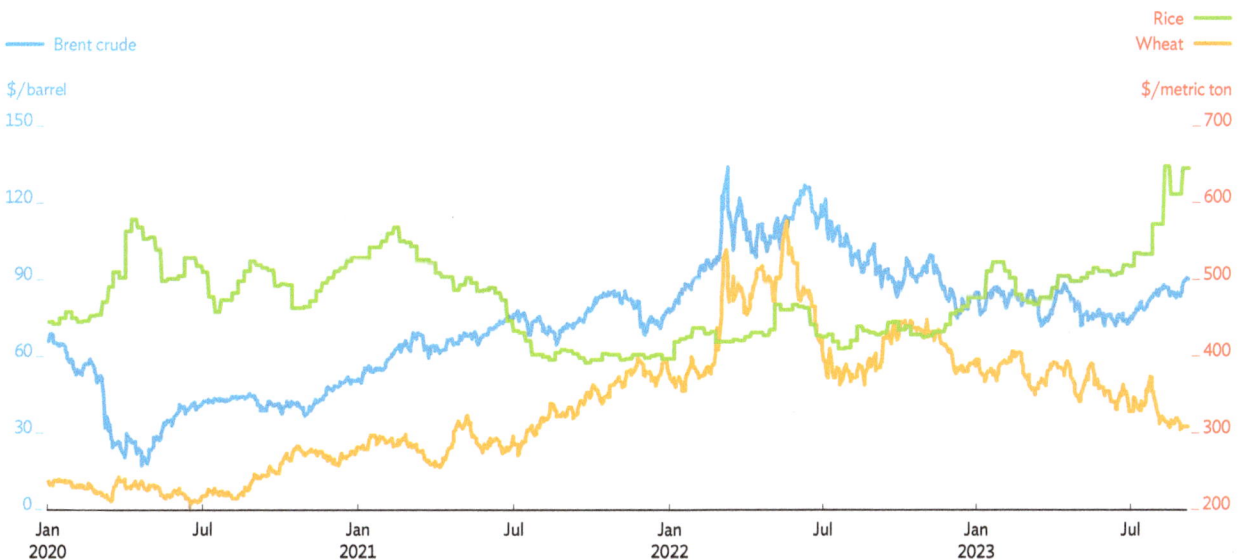

Notes: Rice refers to Thailand, 5% broken milled white rice. Wheat refers to the United States, hard red winter wheat.
Source: Bloomberg.

Regional Growth Remains Solid

The forecast for growth in developing Asia for 2023 is revised slightly down to 4.7% and kept at 4.8% for 2024 (Table 1.1.4). Downward revisions for East Asia, South Asia, and Southeast Asia largely offset upward revisions for the Caucasus and Central Asia, and the Pacific. The forecast for the PRC is revised slightly downward for 2023.

GDP growth will converge across subregions, accelerating toward pre-pandemic rates. Regional growth this year and next will be higher than average growth of 3.6% over 2020–2022, but still not at pre-pandemic levels (Figure 1.1.20). The spread between growth rates across subregions is forecast ranging from 3.2% in the Pacific to 5.7% in South Asia, with the Caucasus and Central Asia, East Asia, and Southeast Asia growing 4.3%–4.7%. This reflects the end of the global pandemic, when the outlook was shaped by the different timing of outbreaks, lockdowns, and reopenings.

The growth forecast for the PRC is revised down to 4.9% for 2023 from 5.0% projected in April, as economic activity is expected to slow in the second half of the year. The momentum from the recovery of services in the first half is waning, while headwinds from manufacturing and real estate are mounting. Growth in manufacturing is expected to moderate as external demand slows further after a 14.5% year-on-year decline in the PRC's exports in July. Investment in real estate is also expected to decline further following an 8.5% contraction over January–July. This implies weak demand for credit by property developers and industrial inputs for construction in the coming quarters. The contracting property market will also constrain local governments, whose revenues largely hinge on land value. On the upside, rising global demand for electric vehicles and batteries, and solar photovoltaic panels, will mitigate the slowdown in manufacturing, although only partly as these sectors account for less than 10% of exports. Government support is also expected to cushion the downturn using available monetary and fiscal space, notably to support the property sector. The Special Topic in this update examines the spillovers from a further weakening of the property market in the PRC.

Figure 1.1.20 Economic Growth before the Pandemic, during the Peak, and Post-Recovery in Developing Asia

GDP growth is converging across subregions and returning toward pre-pandemic rates.

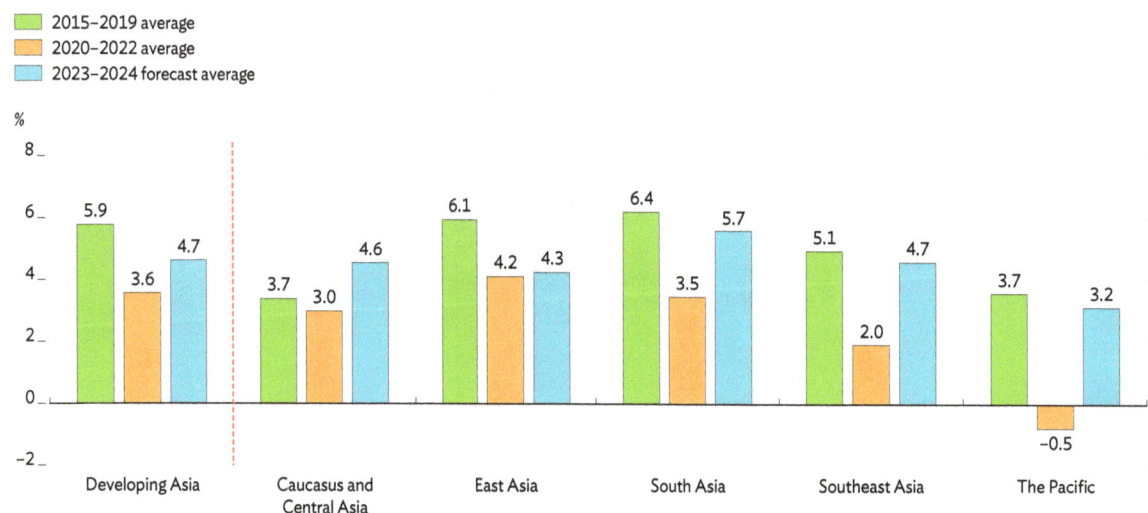

GDP = gross domestic product.
Source: *Asian Development Outlook* database.

Table 1.1.4 GDP Growth Rate and Inflation, %

Subregion/Economy	GDP Growth 2022	2023 Apr	2023 Sep	2024 Apr	2024 Sep	Inflation 2022	2023 Apr	2023 Sep	2024 Apr	2024 Sep
Developing Asia	4.3	4.8	4.7	4.8	4.8	4.4	4.2	3.6	3.3	3.5
Developing Asia excluding the PRC	5.5	4.6	4.5	5.1	5.0	6.7	6.2	6.3	4.4	4.9
Caucasus and Central Asia	5.1	4.4	4.6	4.6	4.7	12.9	10.3	10.6	7.5	8.0
Armenia	12.6	6.5	7.0	5.5	5.5	8.6	7.0	4.0	6.2	5.5
Azerbaijan	4.6	3.5	2.2	3.8	2.6	13.9	7.0	10.0	6.5	8.5
Georgia	10.1	4.5	6.0	5.0	5.0	11.9	6.0	3.0	4.0	3.5
Kazakhstan	3.2	3.7	4.1	4.1	4.3	15.0	11.8	12.7	6.4	7.6
Kyrgyz Republic	6.3	4.5	3.8	4.0	4.0	13.9	12.0	12.0	8.6	8.6
Tajikistan	8.0	5.5	6.5	6.5	7.0	4.2	7.0	5.5	6.5	6.0
Turkmenistan	6.2	6.5	6.2	6.0	6.0	10.0	10.0	8.0	10.0	8.0
Uzbekistan	5.7	5.0	5.5	5.0	5.5	11.4	11.0	11.0	10.0	10.0
East Asia	2.8	4.6	4.4	4.2	4.2	2.3	2.3	1.0	2.0	2.1
Hong Kong, China	-3.5	3.6	4.3	3.7	3.3	1.9	2.3	2.5	2.1	2.1
Mongolia	5.0	5.4	5.7	6.1	5.9	15.2	10.9	10.5	8.7	8.6
People's Republic of China	3.0	5.0	4.9	4.5	4.5	2.0	2.2	0.7	2.0	2.0
Republic of Korea	2.6	1.5	1.3	2.2	2.2	5.1	3.2	3.3	2.0	2.2
Taipei,China	2.4	2.0	1.2	2.6	2.7	2.9	2.0	2.0	2.0	2.0
South Asia	6.7	5.5	5.4	6.1	6.0	8.2	8.1	8.6	5.8	6.6
Afghanistan	...	...	...	...	...	13.8	...	...	...	...
Bangladesh	7.1	5.3	6.0	6.5	6.5	6.2	8.7	9.0	6.6	6.6
Bhutan	4.7	4.6	4.3	4.2	4.4	5.6	5.5	4.1	5.1	5.1
India	7.2	6.4	6.3	6.7	6.7	6.7	5.0	5.5	4.5	4.2
Maldives	13.9	7.1	7.1	6.9	6.9	2.3	4.5	3.5	2.0	2.5
Nepal	5.6	4.1	1.9	5.0	4.3	6.3	7.4	7.7	6.2	6.2
Pakistan	6.1	0.6	0.3	2.0	1.9	12.2	27.5	29.2	15.0	25.0
Sri Lanka	-7.8	-3.0	-3.0	1.3	1.3	46.4	24.6	18.7	5.5	5.5
Southeast Asia	5.6	4.7	4.6	5.0	4.8	5.1	4.4	4.2	3.3	3.3
Brunei Darussalam	-1.6	2.5	2.8	2.8	2.5	3.7	2.0	1.5	1.6	1.4
Cambodia	5.2	5.5	5.3	6.0	6.0	5.3	3.0	3.0	4.0	4.0
Indonesia	5.3	4.8	5.0	5.0	5.0	4.2	4.2	3.6	3.0	3.0
Lao People's Democratic Republic	2.5	4.0	3.7	4.0	4.0	23.0	16.0	28.0	5.0	10.0
Malaysia	8.7	4.7	4.5	4.9	4.9	3.4	3.1	3.0	2.8	2.7
Myanmar	2.0	2.8	2.8	3.2	3.2	18.4	10.5	14.0	8.2	8.2
Philippines	7.6	6.0	5.7	6.2	6.2	5.8	6.2	6.2	4.0	4.0
Singapore	3.6	2.0	1.0	3.0	2.5	6.1	5.0	5.0	2.0	3.0
Thailand	2.6	3.3	3.5	3.7	3.7	6.1	2.9	2.5	2.3	2.3
Timor-Leste	3.2	3.1	2.8	3.0	2.9	7.0	5.5	5.8	2.8	3.3
Viet Nam	8.0	6.5	5.8	6.8	6.0	3.2	4.5	3.8	4.2	4.0
The Pacific	6.1	3.3	3.5	2.8	2.9	5.2	5.0	4.9	4.4	4.5
Cook Islands	10.5	11.2	14.5	9.1	9.1	4.2	7.7	13.0	2.3	2.3
Federated States of Micronesia	2.0	4.1	4.1	0.5	0.5	5.0	3.6	3.6	0.4	0.4
Fiji	20.0	6.3	8.3	3.0	3.7	4.3	4.2	3.0	3.5	3.0
Kiribati	1.8	2.3	2.3	2.8	2.8	5.0	3.7	6.0	3.0	3.0
Marshall Islands	-0.9	1.5	2.2	2.0	2.5	3.3	3.7	3.7	3.5	3.5
Nauru	2.8	1.8	1.6	2.2	1.6	1.0	2.5	5.5	1.9	4.2
Niue	...	...	...	...	...	...	...	...	...	...
Palau	-1.0	3.8	3.8	6.5	6.5	10.2	5.0	8.0	5.5	5.0
Papua New Guinea	3.2	2.4	2.0	2.6	2.6	5.3	5.0	5.0	5.0	5.0
Samoa	-5.3	4.8	6.0	2.5	4.2	8.8	10.2	12.0	2.0	5.3
Solomon Islands	-4.2	3.0	3.0	2.5	2.5	5.5	4.5	5.5	3.7	3.7
Tonga	-2.2	2.5	2.8	3.2	2.6	8.5	9.4	10.3	1.5	4.5
Tuvalu	0.7	2.5	3.0	2.0	2.5	12.2	3.3	6.2	2.8	3.3
Vanuatu	2.0	1.0	1.0	4.2	4.2	6.7	4.0	9.0	3.0	5.0

GDP = gross domestic product.

Source: *Asian Development Outlook* database.

Weak global demand continues to weigh on growth in developing Asia's high-income technology-exporting economies. Despite contracting at a slower pace in the first half, exports in July were still down by 11%–16% year on year in the Republic of Korea, Singapore, and Taipei,China. This reflects the global slowdown of demand for electronics after the sharp upturn over 2020–2022. Encouragingly, the semiconductor market has likely bottomed out and is expected to bounce back in 2024. In this context, the growth forecast for Taipei,China is revised marginally up to 2.7% for next year, but revised down to 1.2% for this year. Growth in the Republic of Korea is forecast slowing to 1.3% in 2023 from 2.6% in 2022 on weakening semiconductor exports. Growth next year is forecast at 2.2%. Singapore's growth forecast is revised slightly down to 1.0% for 2023 and 2.5% for 2024. Hong Kong, China differs from this pattern, and growth there is revised up to 4.3% for this year after a sharp first-half recovery driven by the economy's post-pandemic reopening. Growth next year will be supported by normalizing external conditions, but it is nevertheless revised down to 3.3% on a higher base effect.

Growth is still expected to be strong in South Asia. The forecast for the subregion is marginally revised down to 5.4% and 6.0% for this year and next from April's 5.5% and 6.1%. This outlook is driven by India—which accounts for 80% of the subregion's economy—where growth for fiscal year (FY) 2023 will remain high at a forecast 6.3%, albeit a tad lower than April's 6.4% projection. Strong private consumption, and upticks in public and private investment, are expected to brighten India's outlook. The slight downward revision for FY2023 is due to erratic rainfall patterns during the monsoon, which will affect agriculture output in the upcoming harvest. For FY2024, India's forecast remains at 6.7%. Pakistan's growth estimate for FY2023 is revised down to 0.3% (0.6% forecast in April), because political instability and floods affected the economy. Pakistan's growth forecast for FY2024 is slightly revised down to 1.9% (2.0% in April). Bangladesh's forecast for FY2023 is raised to 6.0% (5.3% in April) on robust garment exports and healthy remittances. Sri Lanka's is kept at −3.0% for this year. The view that economic conditions will stabilize and the economy recovers is unchanged.

Domestic demand remains healthy across Southeast Asia. This update, however, revises the subregional forecast for this year down to 4.6% from April's 4.7% projection on the persisting slowdown in global demand for electronics. Viet Nam is particularly affected, with its growth forecast revised down for both 2023 and 2024, while Malaysia's is revised down for 2023. Erratic weather has already hurt agriculture in the subregion this year, and crop yields could be reduced by El Niño. Thailand's forecast, however, is revised up to 3.5% from 3.3% on strong private consumption and tourism continuing to support the recovery. In 2024, subregional growth is still expected to improve as global electronics demand picks up, but to 4.8% not the 5.0% forecast in April.

Growth forecasts for the Caucasus and Central Asia are revised up for this year and next. Government spending in Kazakhstan and resilient windfall spillovers from the Russian invasion of Ukraine underpin this revision to 4.6% for this year (4.4% in April). In Kazakhstan, the upward revision to 4.1% for this year (3.7% in April) reflects a strong fiscal stimulus. The rising volume of oil exports are cushioning declining global prices. Growth has also been stronger than expected in Uzbekistan, driven by rising exports of food and textile products to the Russian Federation, as well as investment. The forecast for Uzbekistan's growth this year is revised up to 5.5% (5.0% in April) on rising exports of food and textile products to the Russian Federation, as well as investment. Growth will also be stronger than earlier forecast in Armenia, Georgia, and Tajikistan as the windfall gains from the invasion of Ukraine are more resilient than expected. This notably reflects rising arrivals of visitors from the Russian Federation in the first full year following the invasion. For 2024, this update raises the subregion's growth forecast to 4.7% (4.6% in April). This reflects an expected continuation of fiscal stimulus and the slower-than-expected fading of the spillovers of the invasion. In fact, these gains have largely offset losses from the pandemic in the subregion. For Tajikistan, GDP levels projected for 2024 in this update even exceed forecasts for 2024 made by the International Monetary Fund in pre-pandemic 2019 (Figure 1.1.21). For the subregion's other economies. GDP in 2024 is now expected to be only marginally lower than was forecast in 2019. This is in strong contrast with developing Asia's other subregions, whose economies will remain far behind pre-pandemic growth paths.

Figure 1.1.21 Current and Pre-Pandemic GDP Forecasts for 2024 in Developing Asian Economies

GDP is expected to be close to forecasts made before the pandemic in most economies in the Caucasus and Central Asia.

△ Developing Asia
● Caucasus and Central Asia
● Other subregions

September 2023 forecast

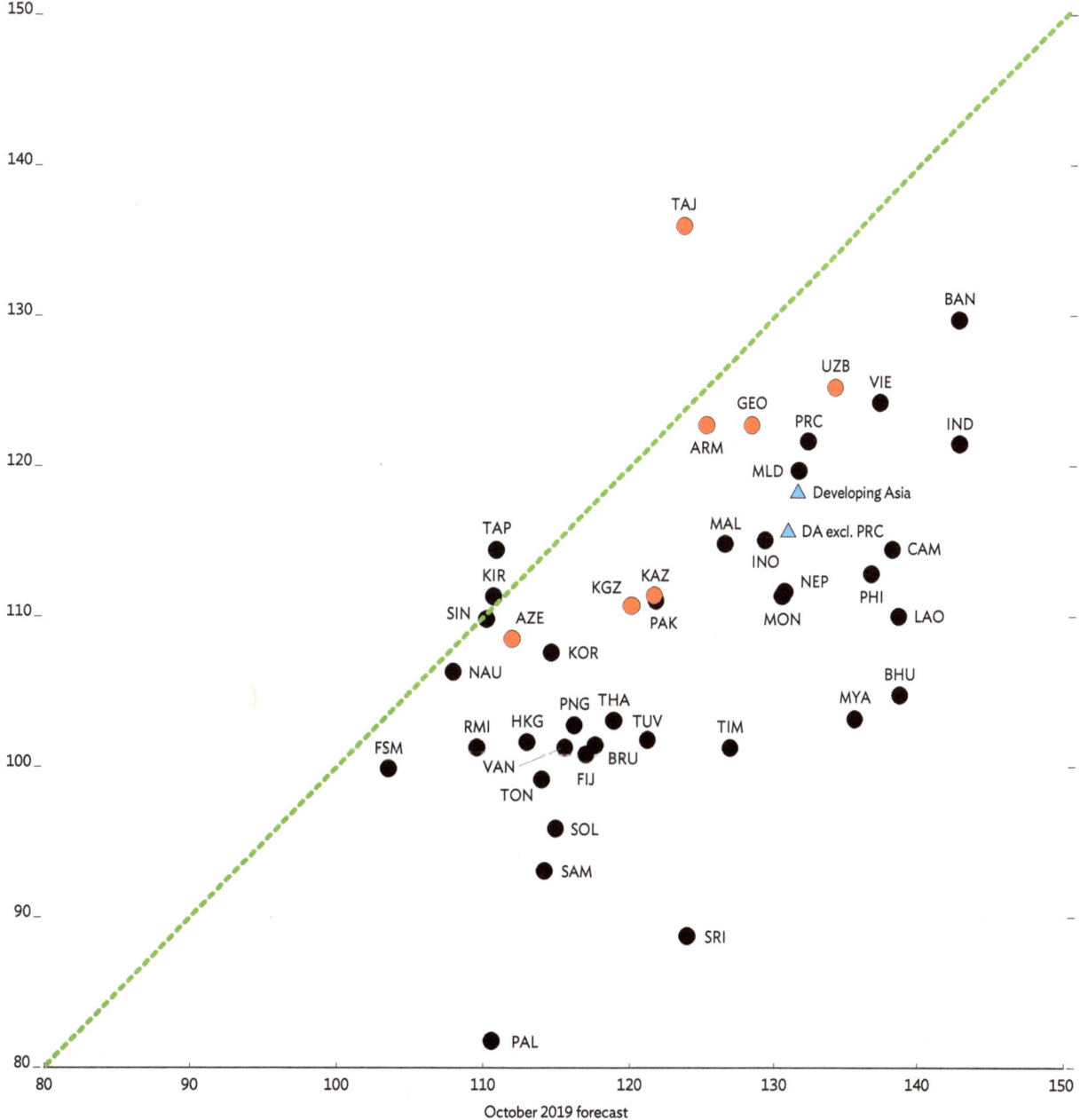

October 2019 forecast

ADO = Asian Development Outlook, ARM = Armenia, AZE = Azerbaijan, BAN = Bangladesh, BHU = Bhutan, BRU = Brunei Darussalam, CAM = Cambodia, DA = Developing Asia, GDP = gross domestic product, GEO = Georgia, HKG = Hong Kong, China, IMF = International Monetary Fund, IND = India, INO = Indonesia, KAZ = Kazakhstan, KGZ = Kyrgyz Republic, KIR = Kiribati, KOR = Republic of Korea, LAO = Lao People's Democratic Republic, MAL = Malaysia, MLD = Maldives, MON = Mongolia, MYA = Myanmar, NAU = Nauru, NEP = Nepal, PAK = Pakistan, PAL = Palau, PHI = Philippines, PNG = Papua New Guinea, PRC = People's Republic of China, RMI = Marshall Islands, SAM = Samoa, SIN = Singapore, SOL = Solomon Islands, SRI = Sri Lanka, TAJ = Tajikistan, TAP = Taipei,China, THA = Thailand, TIM = Timor-Leste, TON = Tonga, TUV = Tuvalu, UZB = Uzbekistan, VAN = Vanuatu, VIE = Viet Nam.

Notes: The GDP level on the horizontal axis are forecasts from the IMF's October 2019 forecast. The GDP levels on the vertical axis are actual outcomes in 2022 combined with *ADO September 2023* forecasts.

Sources: *ADO* database; IMF. World Economic Outlook Database.

The continued recovery in tourism and the resumption of public infrastructure projects are boosting the outlook for the Pacific. The subregional growth forecast is raised to 3.5% from 3.3% in April, prompted by a sharp increase to Fiji's growth outlook (8.3% from 6.3%) on a sustained recovery in tourism. The outlook is also raised for the Cook Islands, Samoa, and Tonga, where tourism accounts for significant shares of GDP. In the Marshall Islands and Tuvalu, the resumption of public infrastructure projects since the pandemic are behind the upward revisions. But the forecast for Papua New Guinea—which accounts for two-thirds of the subregion's GDP—is revised down to 2.0% from April's 2.4% on weaker-than-expected activity in non-resource sectors. For 2024, the subregional growth forecast is revised up a tad, to 2.9% from 2.8%. Continued growth is expected in Fiji and Samoa on the recoveries of their tourism industries and government spending. Infrastructure projects are raising expectations of higher growth in smaller island economies.

Regional Inflation on Track to Receding to Pre-Pandemic Levels Next Year

Inflation in developing Asia will continue decelerating in 2023. The region's inflation rate is forecast at a lower 3.6% (4.2% in April) and is expected to remain below the forecast average rate of 4.5% for the advanced economies (Figure 1.1.22). For 2024, the inflation forecast for the region is revised up to 3.5% from April's 3.3%. The lower forecast for 2023 is mainly due to benign inflation in the PRC, where the rates are projected at 0.7% for 2023 and 2.0% for 2024. Excluding the PRC, regional inflation is also expected to come down from last year's 6.7%, but only slightly and the forecast is revised up to 6.3% this year, which is twice as high as pre-pandemic. For next year, the forecast is also revised up, to 4.9% (4.4% in April). Across developing Asia, the deceleration in inflation is being driven by lower energy and food prices, but core inflation has also begun receding (Figure 1.1.23). In many regional economies, however, persisting inflation warrants caution in lowering interest rates.

Figure 1.1.22 Inflation Forecasts for 2023 for Developing Asian Economies

Inflation will remain high in the Caucasus and Central Asia, the Lao PDR, Pakistan, and Sri Lanka.

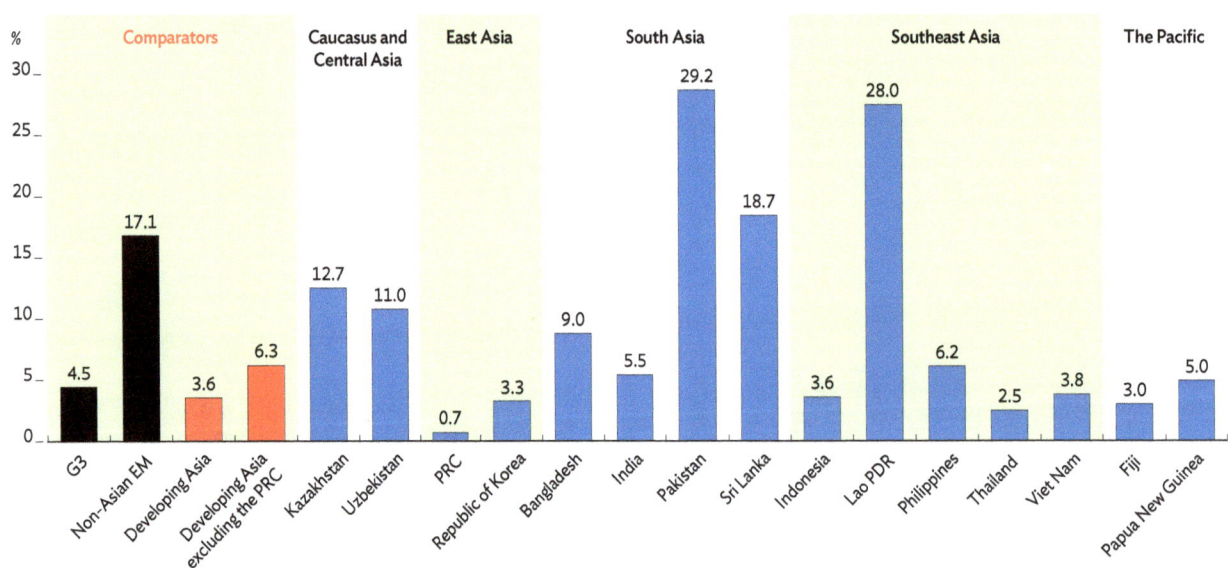

EM = emerging market; G3 = euro area, Japan, United States; Lao PDR = Lao People's Democratic Republic; PRC = People's Republic of China.
Source: *Asian Development Outlook* database.

Figure 1.1.23 Contributions to Inflation in the People's Republic of China and Developing Asia Excluding the PRC

The slowdown in headline inflation has been mostly driven by softening energy and food prices, but core inflation has also declined recently.

- Energy related
- Food and nonalcoholic beverages
- Core
- Headline inflation

A. People's Republic of China

B. Developing Asia Excluding the PRC

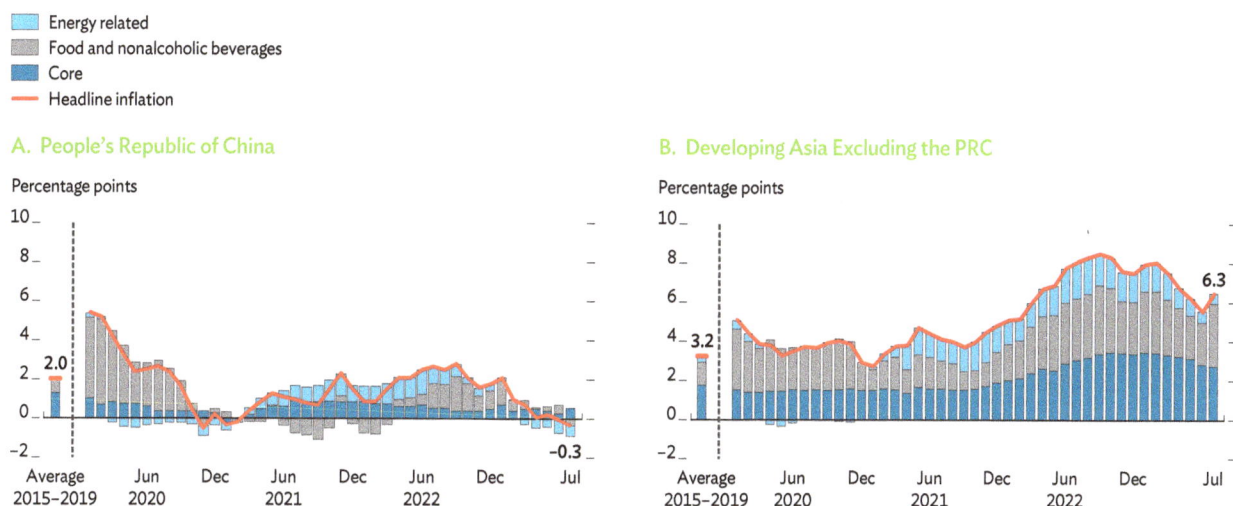

PRC = People's Republic of China.

Note: The regional average is calculated using gross domestic product purchasing power parity shares as weights and covers 22 economies.

Sources: Asian Development Bank calculations using data from CEIC Data Company, Haver Analytics, and official national sources.

Prices in the PRC have come down sharply, contracting by 0.3% in July. Services inflation in the first half of 2023 is expected to fade in the second half as the recovery in consumption slows. Producer prices continued to decline in the first half due to weaker global demand. But most significantly, energy and food prices have fallen on the high base effect from last year, particularly pork prices (Figure 1.1.23, panel A). These developments are behind the sharp downward revision for 2023's inflation, to a forecast 0.7% for this year from April's 2.2% projection. But inflation is expected to bounce back in 2024 as the low forecast for this year mostly reflects temporary factors related to energy and food. The continuation of moderate growth forecasts and low inflation should prompt the government to use its monetary policy and fiscal space to boost domestic consumption and investment, and stabilize the property market.

Inflation will continue decelerating toward pre-pandemic levels in the region's high-income technology exporters, although slightly less rapidly than expected earlier. Inflation is forecast slowing to 2.0% in Taipei,China this year from 2.9% in 2022. Inflation in Hong Kong, China is slightly revised up to 2.5% for this year on an expected pickup in demand in the second quarter. Inflation in the Republic of Korea— forecast at 3.3%—will also come in slightly higher

because of faster-than-expected inflation in the first half. Inflation in Singapore is forecast at 5.0%—down from 6.1% last year, but still far above pre-pandemic levels, reflecting persistently high costs for health care, household durables and services, transport, and housing. For 2024, inflation in these economies is expected to fully normalize to pre-pandemic levels, with the rate ranging from a forecast 2.0% in Taipei,China to 3.0% in Singapore.

Inflation is expected to remain high in South Asia. The forecast for the subregion is revised up to 8.6% for 2023 (8.1% in April) on strong demand and supply-side pressures. India's forecast is revised up to 5.5% for this year (5.0% in April), decelerating to 4.2% for 2024. Heavy monsoon rainfall pushed prices up for fruit, vegetables, and rice. To stall rising food prices, the government has restricted rice exports and increased public import procurement of pulses. This has caused rice prices to rise in Asia to levels not seen since 2008. Sri Lanka's inflation rate has fallen faster than expected due to macroeconomic adjustments. The inflation forecast for 2023 is revised down to 18.7% and kept at 5.5% for 2024. In Pakistan, inflation is estimated to have accelerated to 29.2% in FY2023, faster than April's 27.5% forecast. For FY2024, inflation is forecast at 25.0%, sharply higher than the earlier 15.0% projection.

Lower energy prices and weakening demand will continue to ease price pressures in Southeast Asia. Inflation in the subregion for 2023 is still forecast decelerating from last year's 5.1% on lower energy prices. Although inflation slowed in the first half of the year, food prices are not expected to continue moderating in the second half due to upward pressure on rice prices following India's export restrictions in July and to El Niño's expected impact on coming harvests in the subregion. Core inflation has peaked and is expected to gradually moderate. The forecast for headline inflation in the subregion is revised down to 4.2% from April's 4.4% and kept at 3.3% for 2024, with headline inflation moving toward the pre-pandemic average of 2.5%. The sharpest downward revisions in the subregion are for Viet Nam, where inflation is forecast at 3.8% for this year from 4.5% forecast in April, and Indonesia, at 3.6% from 4.2% in April.

The inflation forecasts for the Caucasus and Central Asia are revised up for this year and next. The 10.6% projected for 2023 (10.3% in April) is nevertheless lower than 2022's 12.9%. Kazakhstan is behind the upward revision, with high inflation there reflecting rising government-regulated utility and fuel prices combined with sharp fiscal stimulus. In Uzbekistan, price liberalization is still expected to contribute to inflation this year and next, although the rate is forecast edging down to 10.0% next year, the lowest level since 2015. The inflation forecasts for Armenia and Georgia are revised down for 2023 and 2024 as central banks there maintained tight policies through most of the first half of the year and because of the sharp appreciations of their currencies against the ruble.

Inflation is forecast to moderate to 4.9% in 2023 and 4.5% in 2024 in the Pacific. For 2023, this is a marginal downward revision from April's 5.0% projection as fuel prices declined faster than expected in Fiji, reducing utility prices and transport costs. However, elevated international food and petroleum prices—due partly to the lingering impacts of the Russian invasion of Ukraine—and their lagged pass-through to domestic markets are causing higher-than-expected inflation elsewhere in the subregion. Domestic factors, such as adjustments in subsidies, taxes, and utility tariffs, as well as disruptions to local food supply and supply chains caused by natural hazards, are kindling inflation in some economies. The 2024 forecast is revised slightly up to 4.5% from 4.4% as lingering impacts of high commodity prices keep inflation elevated in the smaller economies. However, the 2024 forecast for Fiji is revised down to 3.0% from 3.5% as moderating price movements are expected to continue.

Risks to Regional Growth Tilted to the Downside

Weaknesses in the PRC's property sector pose a downside risk to regional growth. The country's economy exited lockdowns much later than other parts of the world and is still regaining its footing. A further deterioration in the property sector could derail its economic recovery. The effects of declining prices, the slow recovery in investment and sales, and the ongoing debt restructuring of some property developers might spill over to other sectors, further weighing on the recovery in the second half of this year. With existing monetary and fiscal space, more stimulus measures could be used if needed in the coming quarters, which would help bolster the recovery and improve the confidence of households and businesses—and this is discussed in the Special Topic on the PRC's property market.

Higher interest rates have elevated financial stability risks. Interest rates in the US and other advanced economies have breached levels not seen since before the global financial crisis of 2008–2009. Even as inflation cools in these economies, the era of cheap credit may be over. While regional economies have fared well so far this year, the banking turmoil in advanced economies in March showed how financial strain could stress-test monetary authorities. Vulnerable sovereigns with large external debt obligations and economies with highly leveraged property markets and weaknesses in capital markets will be especially challenged.

The borrowing costs of these economies might rise if there is a sudden deterioration in global financial conditions, further worsening their fragile fundamentals.

Food security and energy challenges remain a risk. Despite the fall in global food prices from their 2022 peaks, food security will continue to be a concern, especially due to the effects of El Niño in the second half of this year (Box 1.1.3). Sporadic food and energy supply disruptions from the Russian invasion of Ukraine could rekindle inflation and commodity price risks. This happened with grain and other agricultural products following the termination of the Black Sea Grain Initiative. Restrictions on food exports by some economies are also a concern. If agricultural production in India weakens and the export ban on rice is maintained, it could add pressure to food price inflation in developing Asia.

Interest rates in the US and other advanced economies remain important to regional prospects. If disinflation proceeds more quickly than currently expected in the advanced economies, authorities there will likely adopt a less hawkish monetary policy stance, easing credit conditions further and improving external demand, which would support growth in developing Asia. Growth in the US and Japan has surprised on the upside this year and could boost developing Asia's external sector.

Box 1.1.1 Accelerating Labor Migration from the Pacific: Short-Term Blessing, Long-Term Challenge?

The economic impact of COVID-19 increased labor migration from Pacific economies.
Workers in the region have long had pathways to overseas employment through diaspora links and participating in regional temporary worker programs. This has boosted remittances to the region, a critical source of support. However, increased labor migration has also depleted local labor markets, which has serious implications for the region's economic recovery and long-term prospects.

Working abroad, even on a temporary basis, is a very attractive alternative to employment at home. World Bank (2023) estimates that seasonal workers in Australia and New Zealand can earn up to 10 times what they would have earned at home. The pandemic's impact on domestic labor markets and labor shortages abroad resulted in a dramatic increase in Pacific migrant workers, with approvals for all categories of work visas to Australia and New Zealand rising by 141.5% from 2019 to 2022 (box figure 1). Australian approvals in the first half of 2023 were 14.0% higher than those for the entire year of 2022.

The increase in migrant workers from the region has greatly boosted remittances. These play a key role in helping households in times of crisis. Across the Pacific, monthly remittances per worker are equivalent to almost 1.8 times the average earnings in the remitter's home country (World Bank 2023). Remittances cover mostly the daily living expenses of recipient households, home improvements, and education. They also support churches, civic organizations, and disaster assistance. Difficulties at home seem to motivate higher remittances, at least in the short-term, as happened during COVID-19 (box figure 2). In Samoa, many more households relied on remittances to cope with the pandemic than on government assistance. Some households even reported higher incomes during the pandemic; this was probably due to both increased remittances and government support (Webb 2022).

1 Pacific Approvals for All Categories of Work Visas to Australia and New Zealand, 2014–June 2023

Work visa approvals for Pacific workers increased sharply from 2019 to 2022.

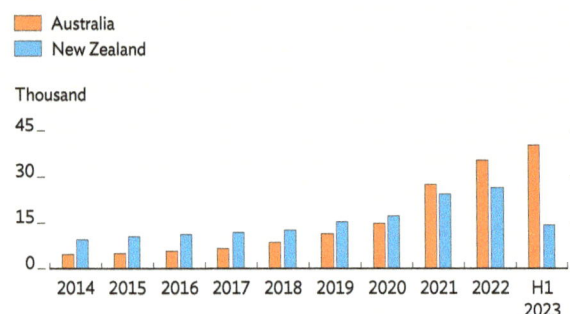

H = half.
Note: New Zealand data exclude the Cook Islands and Niue, whose citizens can freely enter and exit New Zealand under free association arrangements.
Sources: New Zealand data from Ministry of Business, Innovation and Employment. Migration Data Explorer; Australian data from Department of Home Affairs. Temporary Visa Holders in Australia.

2 Remittances to the Pacific Region and Selected Pacific Economies, 2017–2021

Remittances have increased in response to the economic impact of COVID-19.

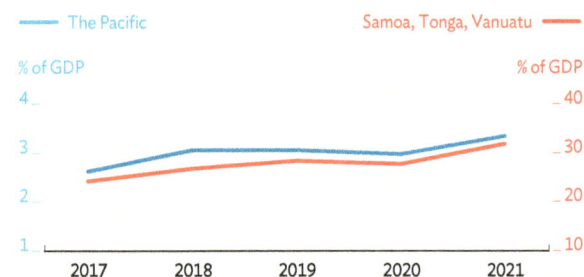

GDP = gross domestic product.
Notes:
1. Percentage of GDP is calculated as the ratio of the sum of remittances to the sum of GDP.
2. Pacific data exclude Nauru and Niue.
3. Years are fiscal years ending on 30 June for the Cook Islands, Samoa, and Tonga; 30 September for the Federated States of Micronesia, the Marshall Islands, and Palau; and 31 December elsewhere.
Sources: *Asian Development Outlook* database; International Monetary Fund. Article IV Consultation staff reports; statistics offices and central banks in Pacific countries; World Bank. World Development Indicators database; Asian Development Bank estimates.

continued on next page

Box 1.1.1 *Continued*

The main downside to increased labor migration in Pacific economies has been a dwindling supply of local labor. This is particularly worrisome in small island economies, where working-age populations are small and the pool of skilled labor is becoming insufficient to fill the gaps in the workforce. In mid-2022, Samoa, Tonga, and Vanuatu—the three major sources of migrant labor from the Pacific— had about as many temporary workers in Australia and New Zealand as government workers at home. The numbers are significant because the public sector is the largest formal employer in these and many other Pacific countries (Howes et al. 2022). Employers, both public and private, in these countries are voicing concerns over a growing scarcity of labor in agriculture, construction, health care, and tourism, among other sectors that are critical to the region's economic recovery. A particular concern is that many workers leave on short notice once they receive their work permits (Curtain 2022). Although Fiji has been open to visitors since December 2021, the increase in advertised job vacancies in 2023 has been marked, suggesting higher demand for workers well after businesses had resumed regular operations (box figure 3).

The expansion in labor mobility schemes is likely to place more pressure on the supply of local labor. The possibility of permanent residency and families of workers joining them abroad could further constrain supply. The Cook Islands is a good example of how heavy migration can affect an economy's workforce. Its citizens can migrate freely to New Zealand and Australia with their families, and this has significantly reduced the supply of local labor from an already small working-age population and caused greater dependence on migrant workers to meet labor needs. This has also reversed remittance flows from local families supporting Cook Islanders living and studying abroad and multigeneration diaspora with few immediate family remaining in the Cook Islands. Both of these factors come on top of increased outward remittances from migrant workers in the country. Similar developments have been observed in the Marshall Islands and Palau, whose citizens can migrate freely to the United States.

3 Active Job Vacancies in Fiji, Feb 2022–Aug 2023

Despite reopening borders in 2021, demand for workers remains high.

Number of job postings

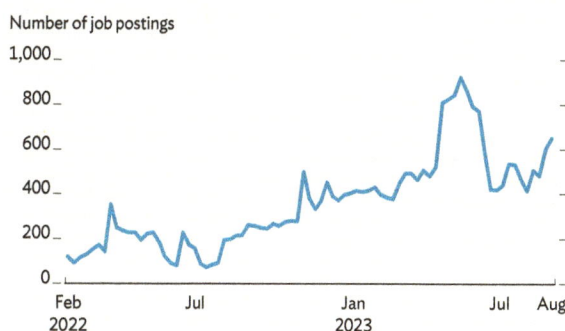

Source: CEIC Data Company.

Responses to the downsides of labor migration must strike a balance between addressing local labor shortages and sustaining remittance flows. Remittances will remain a significant source of income for many Pacific economies—but remittances alone cannot support sustainable and inclusive economic growth. Furthermore, sustaining remittances over the long term will require continued flows of new migrant workers with strong home-country ties. Tailoring domestic skills training programs to the needs of local employers, providing employment pathways through apprenticeships and placement programs, and supporting the increased labor participation of youth and women could help establish pipelines of new workers to fill local labor gaps.

References

Curtain, R. 2022. Brain Drain 1: A Growing Concern. DevpolicyBlog. 13 October.

Howes, S., et al. 2022. Labour Mobility in the Pacific: Transformational and/or Negligible? DevpolicyBlog. 10 October.

Webb, J. 2022. Far from Socially Distant: Remittances and Migration in the Time of COVID-19 in Samoa and Tonga. In *Pacific Economic Monitor*. December. Asian Development Bank.

World Bank. 2023. *Pacific Economic Update: Recovering in the Midst of Uncertainty*. August.

This box was written by Cara Tinio and Remrick Patagan of the Economic Research and Development Impact Department, Asian Development Bank, Manila.

Box 1.1.2 Global Value Chains Expose Developing Asia to Slowing Global Demand

Softer global demand is dragging economic activity in developing Asia through global value chains. The slowdown in advanced economies in particular is affecting growth in economies in the region exporting goods and services to these markets. In addition, a severe downturn in the property sector of the People's Republic of China (PRC) could further dent growth prospects for some of its main trading partners in the region.

Exposure to spillovers from slowing global demand vary across the region. Inferring exposure from total exports, however, can be misleading. This is because export data do not account for the import content of exports—that is, the portion of exported goods and services that was itself imported. This makes traditional gross trade data a poor measure to fully capture an economy's exposure to global demand.

This box uses the Asian Development Bank's Multiregional Input-Output Tables to reveal the origin of the value added in the region's exports. When value chains have many steps taking place in different economies, value-added exports reflect the exposure to foreign demand much better than total exports. In developing Asia, 17% of domestic value added is ultimately exported to foreign markets (box figure 1).[a] This is much less than the region's total exports, which are equivalent to 30% of gross domestic product (GDP). Excluding the PRC, the gap between value-added exports and gross exports is even larger. Total export data record the imported components of exports each time they cross a border—and fragmented value chains mean more border crossings. Value-added exports, however, count only the value added incorporated in the exporting country.

Value-added exports suggest that East Asia excluding the PRC and Southeast Asia are less exposed to external demand than their total exports may suggest. In both subregions, total exports are 2.2 times larger than value-added exports. But they are only 1.6 times larger than value-added exports in the Caucasus and Central Asia and 1.9 times in South Asia. The wider gap for economies in East Asia and Southeast Asia reflects a focus on downstream production stages and complex value chains—as in Singapore and Viet Nam, where the

gaps are widest in the region. Conversely, in the Caucasus and Central Asia, and in South Asia, gross exports are a better proxy for exposure to foreign demand because their exports are less complex and value chains are generally shorter in these subregions.

Southeast Asia and tourism-dependent economies are more exposed to demand from Europe and the United States. Using value-added exports instead of total exports substantially reduces the estimate of Southeast Asia's exposure. But Southeast Asia remains the most exposed subregion, with 8% of domestic value added going to Europe and the US. This is slightly higher than in East Asia excluding the PRC and the Caucasus and Central Asia (7% each), and South Asia (6%) (box figure 2). In Singapore and Viet Nam, as much as 10% of domestic value added is exported to the US, and 6%–7% to Europe. Tourism-dependent economies in the region are also largely exposed to demand from Europe and the US. In Maldives, 16% of domestic value added is exported to Europe and 5% to the US. In Fiji, 10% of GDP is exported to Europe and the US.

Southeast Asia is significantly exposed to final demand in the PRC, as is the rest of East Asia. Five economies in Southeast Asia have exposure to the PRC ranging from 6% to 9%—Cambodia, the Lao People's Democratic Republic, Malaysia, Singapore, and Viet Nam. It is in Mongolia, however, where the exposure is largest, with 36% of domestic value-added exported to the PRC. Exposure is also large in other East Asian economies, at 10% in Taipei,China, and 6% each in Hong Kong, China and the Republic of Korea. Within each economy, however, exposure varies across sectors.

Developing Asia's exposure to Europe and the US is concentrated in electronics and machinery. Value added in this sector absorbed in Europe and the US accounts for 2.3% of the region's GDP, followed by finance, trade, and business services (1.0%), and textiles and footwear (0.8%) (box figure 3). In East Asia, electronics and machinery even account for half of value-added exports to these advanced economies. The sector is also critical in Southeast Asia, alongside finance, trade, and business services. In Cambodia and Viet Nam, textiles and footwear contribute substantially to their exposure to Europe and the US.

continued on next page

Box 1.1.2 *Continued*

In South Asia, exposure is concentrated on finance, trade, and business services (led by India), as well as textiles and footwear, which are key for Bangladesh and Pakistan. In the Caucasus and Central Asia, exposure is driven by oil and metals. And in Maldives, Fiji, Cambodia, and Georgia, tourism accounts for a large share of exposure to Europe and the US.

The region's exposure to demand in the PRC is concentrated in electronics and machinery sector, and commodities. Electronics and machinery exported to the PRC account for 1.3% of the region's GDP, and commodities for 1.2% (box figure 4). In Taipei,China, electronics and machinery account for 71% of value-added exports to the PRC.

1 Developing Asia's Value-Added Exports and Total Exports Relative to GDP, 2022

Gross exports vastly exceed value-added exports, particularly in East Asia excluding the PRC and Southeast Asia.

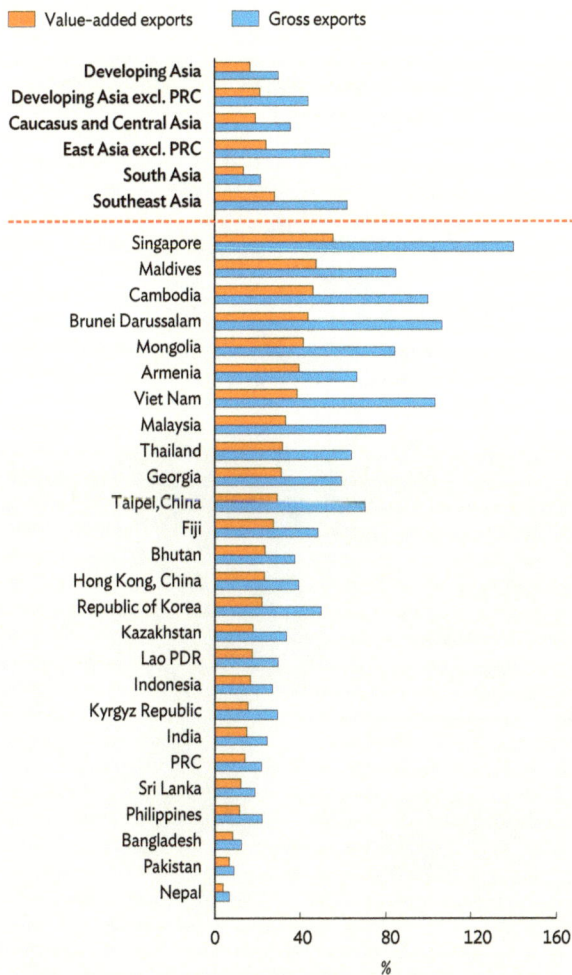

2 Developing Asia's Value-Added Exports Relative to GDP, 2022

All subregions in developing Asia export more value added to Europe and the US than to the PRC, except East Asia.

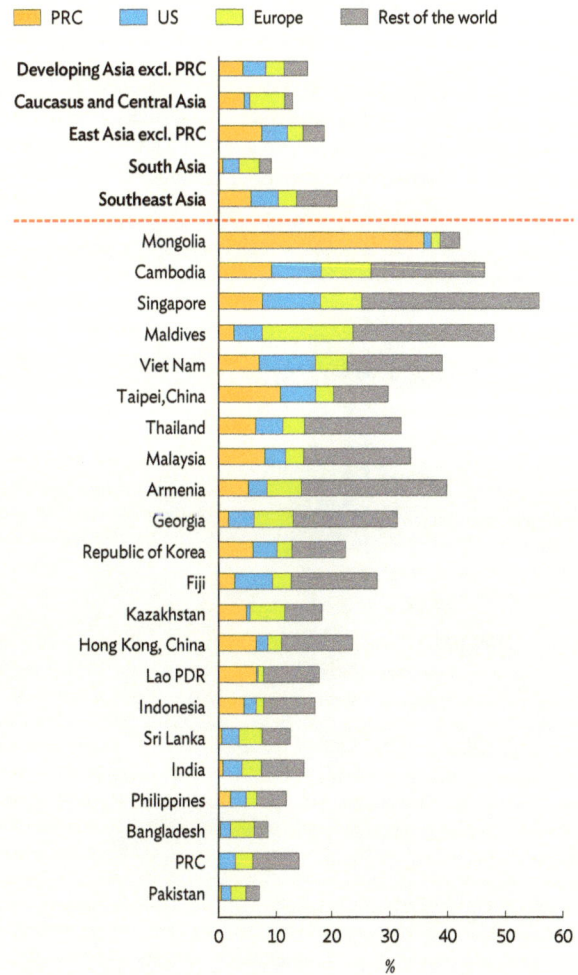

GDP = gross domestic product, Lao PDR = Lao People's Democratic Republic, PRC = People's Republic of China.
Note: Developing Asia comprises the economies listed in the chart.
Source: Asian Development Bank. Multiregional Input-Output Tables.

GDP = gross domestic product, Lao PDR = Lao People's Democratic Republic, PRC = People's Republic of China, US = United States.
Note: Europe = European Union, Norway, Switzerland, and the United Kingdom.
Source: Asian Development Bank. Multiregional Input-Output Tables.

continued on next page

Box 1.1.2 *Continued*

3 Developing Asia's Value-Added Exports to Europe and the US Relative to GDP, 2022

Electronics and machinery; finance, trade, and business services; and textiles and footwear account for the bulk of developing Asia's value-added exports to Europe and the US.

- Electronics and machinery
- Textiles and footwear
- Tourism
- Finance, trade, and business services
- Food and commodities
- Other

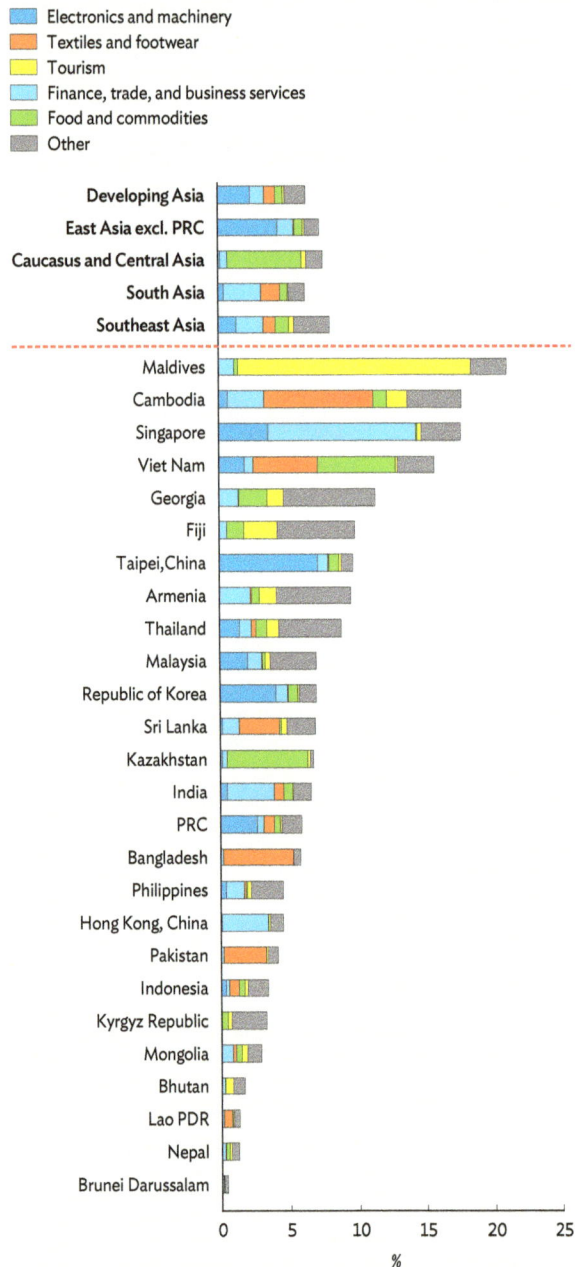

4 Developing Asia's Value-Added Exports to the PRC Relative to GDP, 2022

Electronics and machinery, and food and commodities, account for the bulk of developing Asia's value-added exports to the PRC.

- Electronics and machinery
- Food and commodities
- Tourism
- Finance, trade, and business services
- Other

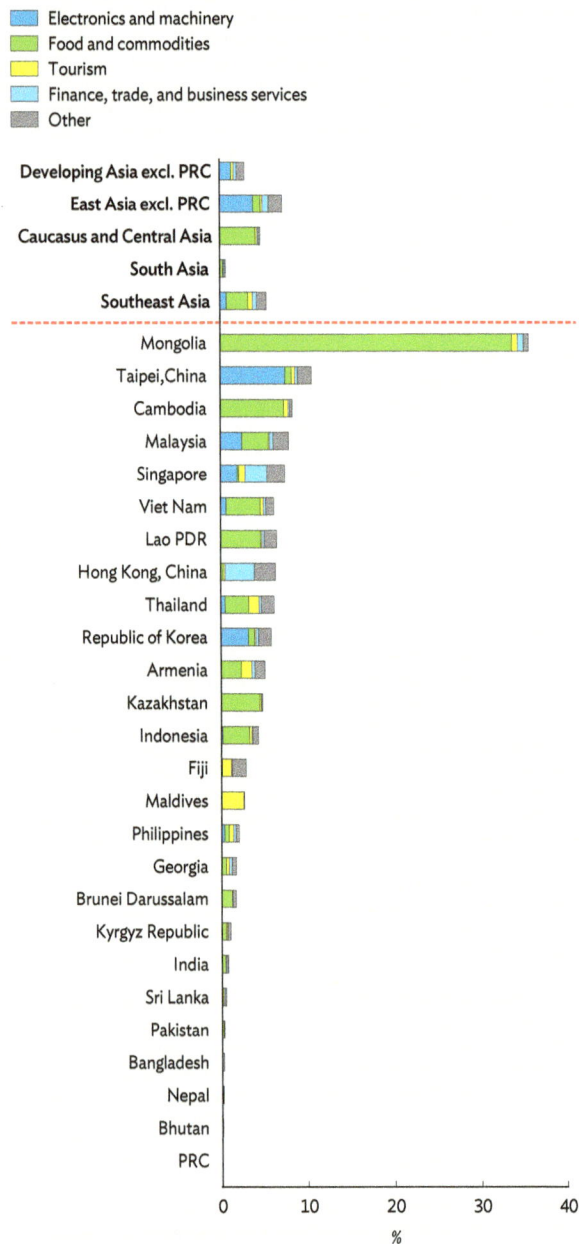

GDP = gross domestic product, Lao PDR = Lao People's Democratic Republic, PRC = People's Republic of China, US = United States.
Note: Europe = European Union, Norway, Switzerland, and the United Kingdom.
Source: Asian Development Bank. Multiregional Input-Output Tables.

GDP = gross domestic product, Lao PDR = Lao People's Democratic Republic, PRC = People's Republic of China.
Source: Asian Development Bank. Multiregional Input-Output Tables.

continued on next page

Box 1.1.2 *Continued*

Commodity exports are a critical channel of exposure to the PRC for many regional economies. They account for most of the 36% of Mongolia's GDP exported to the PRC—mostly copper, coal, and iron. Oil exports to the PRC are vital growth drivers for Brunei Darussalam, Indonesia, Kazakhstan, and Malaysia. The PRC is also a key export market for food products from Cambodia, the Lao People's Democratic Republic, and Thailand.

Southeast Asia is particularly exposed to softening demand in Europe and the US, but also from the PRC. In Cambodia, Singapore, and Viet Nam, as much as 25% of domestic value added ultimately goes to these markets (box figure 5). And for Malaysia and Thailand, the total exposure is about 15%.

The downturn in demand from Europe and the US for manufactured goods and the PRC's less promising-than-expected prospects are prompting sharp downward revisions to the growth forecasts for 2023 for Singapore and Viet Nam.

^a In this box, developing Asia comprises all the economies for which data are available in the 2022 Multiregional Input-Output Tables: Armenia; Bangladesh; Bhutan; Brunei Darussalam; Cambodia; Fiji; Georgia; Hong Kong, China; India; Indonesia; Kazakhstan; the Kyrgyz Republic; the Lao People's Democratic Republic; Malaysia; Maldives; Mongolia; Nepal; Pakistan; the Philippines; the People's Republic of China; the Republic of Korea; Singapore; Sri Lanka; Taipei,China; Thailand; and Viet Nam.

5 Developing Asia's Value-Added Exports to Europe and the United States, and the People's Republic of China, Relative to GDP, 2022

About two-thirds of developing Asian economies are more exposed to final demand in Europe and the US than in the PRC.

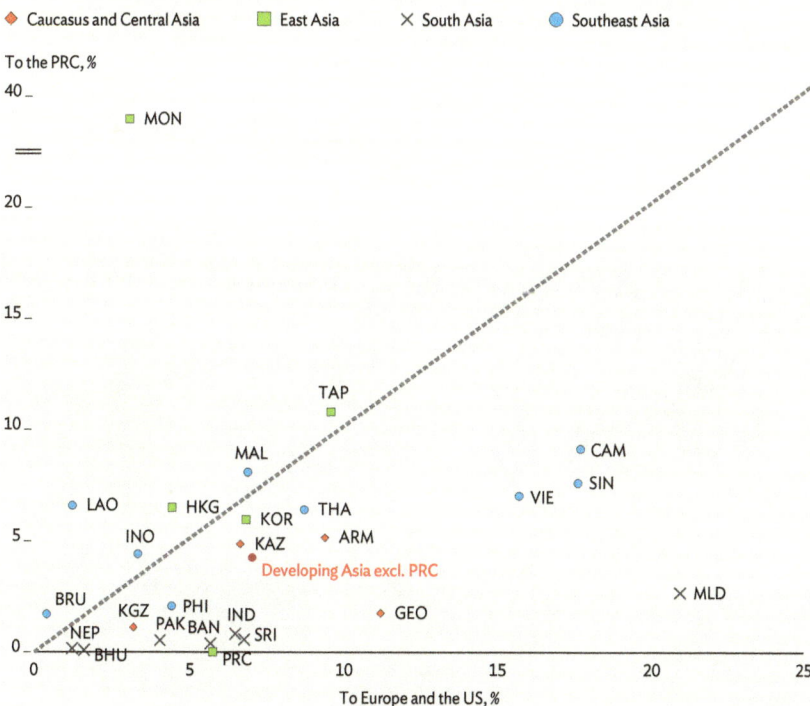

ARM = Armenia, BAN = Bangladesh, BHU = Bhutan, BRU = Brunei Darussalam, CAM = Cambodia, GDP = gross domestic product, GEO = Georgia, HKG = Hong Kong, China, IND = India, INO = Indonesia, KAZ = Kazakhstan, KGZ = Kyrgyz Republic, KOR = Republic of Korea, LAO = Lao People's Democratic Republic, MAL = Malaysia, MLD = Maldives, MON = Mongolia, NEP = Nepal, PAK = Pakistan, PHI = Philippines, PRC = People's Republic of China, SIN = Singapore, SRI = Sri Lanka, TAP = Taipei,China, THA = Thailand, US = United States, VIE = Viet Nam.

Notes: Europe = European Union, Norway, Switzerland, and the United Kingdom. For the PRC, the economy's exposure to its internal market is not shown on the vertical axis.

Source: Asian Development Bank. Multiregional Input-Output Tables.

This box was written by Jules Hugot and Homer Pagkalinawan of the Economic Research and Development Impact Department, Asian Development Bank, Manila.

Box 1.1.3 El Niño's Looming Impact on Developing Asia

El Niños can severely disrupt weather and sea conditions. This climate pattern is associated with rising surface temperatures in the central and eastern tropical Pacific Ocean (NOAA 2023). El Niño's opposite is La Niña, which is associated with cooler-than-average ocean surface temperatures. Both have the potential to significantly affect weather patterns, ocean conditions, and marine fisheries around the world. Not all El Niño (and La Niña) events are the same, and the atmosphere and oceans do not consistently follow the same pattern from one event to the next. However, based on previous events, the return of El Niño this year could cause increased rainfall in Central Asia and the southern and eastern regions of the People's Republic of China (PRC) and drier-than-average weather in Australia, India, Malaysia, northern PRC, and the Maritime Continent (Indonesia, Papua New Guinea, and the Philippines) (GEOGLAM 2023).

According to the International Research Institute for Climate and Society's August 2023 climate forecasts, the probability of below-normal precipitation has moderately to strongly increased for Australia and the Maritime Continent over September–November 2023, while above-normal precipitation is predicted over and around Central Asia (box figure 1).

The probability of El Niño affecting a substantial portion of developing Asia in 2023 and 2024 is high. El Niño does not follow a regular cycle, but occurs on average at 2- to 7-year intervals and lasts 9–12 months. The four strongest recorded El Niño episodes were 1972–1973, 1982–1983, 1997–1998, and 2014–2016. The National Oceanic and Atmospheric Administration (NOAA) advisory of 10 August 2023 says, "El Niño is anticipated to continue through the Northern Hemisphere winter, with greater than 95% chance through December 2023–February 2024."

1 Forecast Precipitation September–November 2023

El Niño shifts rainfall patterns in different parts of the world.

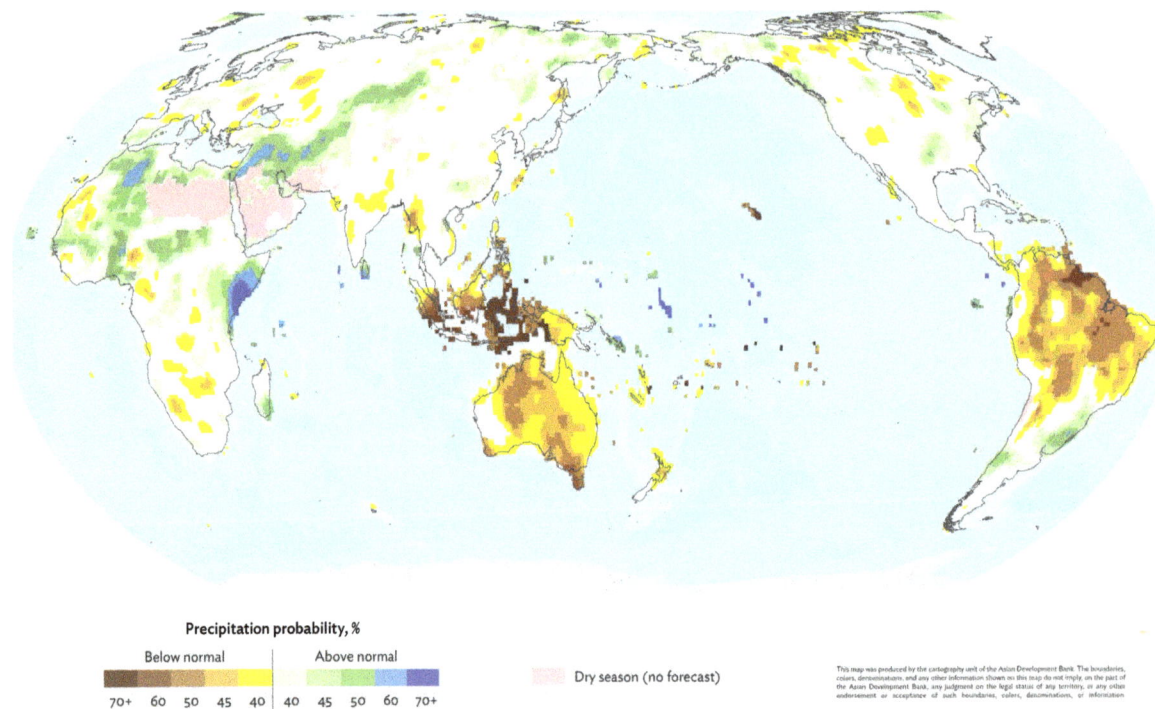

Precipitation probability, %

Below normal					Above normal				
70+	60	50	45	40	40	45	50	60	70+

Dry season (no forecast)

This map was produced by the cartography unit of the Asian Development Bank. The boundaries, colors, denominations, and any other information shown on this map do not imply, on the part of the Asian Development Bank, any judgment on the legal status of any territory, or any other endorsement or acceptance of such boundaries, colors, denomination, or information.

Note: White areas indicate grid points where all three categories are equally likely.

Source: Adapted from Columbia Climate School International Research Institute for Climate and Society. 2023. IRI Multi-Model Probability Forecast for Precipitation for September–October–November 2023. August.

continued on next page

Box 1.1.3 *Continued*

Forecasting models used by NOAA suggest this will be a strong El Niño that should peak over November 2023–January 2024, potentially lasting through the first half of 2024.

El Niño could affect economic activity.
Callahan and Mankin (2023) show the world economy incurred significant economic losses in the years following past El Niños. Global economic losses totaled $4.1 trillion in the years after the 1982–1983 El Niño and $5.7 trillion after 1997–1998's. Generoso et al. (2020), in an analysis of 75 countries linked via weather patterns over 1975–2014, show that El Niño (and La Niña) events caused total factor productivity to fall, which negatively affected output growth in subsequent years. During 2014–2016's El Niño, developing Asia experienced droughts, water shortages, land degradation, livestock losses and lower agricultural production, and lower hydropower output, resulting in slower growth in several economies in the region (ADB 2016a, UNESCAP 2017).

This El Niño might raise commodity prices.
Meteorological conditions caused by El Niño could affect commodity prices, particularly for agricultural goods. For example, the price of Asian benchmark Thai white rice 5% broken increased by nearly 60% over 1986–1988's El Niño, rising from $185.75 per metric ton at the start of El Niño to $294.00 at the end. Cashin et al. (2017), studying the effects of El Niño from the second quarter of 1979 to the first quarter of 2013 in 21 countries, find that El Niño caused inflation to increase from 0.1 to 1.0 percentage point for most of the countries, and that the larger the weight of food in a country's consumer price index basket, the greater was the spike in inflation induced by El Niño. Brunner (2002) finds that a one-standard-deviation increase in the El Niño-Southern Oscillation (ENSO) raises real commodity price inflation by 3.5–4.0 percentage points and that ENSO appears to account for almost 20% of commodity price inflation movements.

Economic disruptions from this year's El Niño may be disproportionately severe in many economies in the region. The box table shows the Asian economies identified by the Food and Agriculture Organization of the United Nations that are at risk of drought or excessive rainfall.

Developing Asian Economies at Risk from El Niño

Economies at Risk of Dry Conditions	Economies at Risk of Excessive Rainfall
Cambodia	Afghanistan
Fiji	Armenia
Indonesia	Azerbaijan
Lao People's Democratic Republic	Bhutan
Malaysia	Kazakhstan
Myanmar	Kyrgyz Republic
Papua New Guinea	Pakistan
Philippines	Tajikistan
Thailand	Turkmenistan
Timor-Leste	Uzbekistan
Viet Nam	

Source: Food and Agriculture Organization. 2023. El Niño to Return in 2023 Following a Three-Year La Niña Phase. GIEWS Update, 26 April.

In many of these economies, agriculture accounts for a significant portion of gross domestic product—more than 20% in Afghanistan, Cambodia, Myanmar, Pakistan, Tajikistan, and Uzbekistan. Many of these economies are highly dependent on hydropower (e.g., Cambodia, Fiji, the Lao People's Democratic Republic, Myanmar, and Viet Nam). These economies could face electricity shortages, with adverse spillovers on the production of goods and services. Economies in the region that are major net food exporters could see export revenue declining if production losses outweigh gains from price increases. Those that are major net food importers could face higher prices and the choice of funding wider trade deficits or cutting back imports of other goods, requiring a reduction in domestic demand.

Rice, which is strongly reliant on favorable weather and is crucial to the region's food security, has recently seen prices rise on uncertainties over El Niño's impact and India's rice export ban. The reduced availability of rice comes at an inopportune time. Because of the Russian invasion of Ukraine, wheat supplies are tight, increasing global demand for rice. India, Thailand, and Viet Nam together account for more than half of global rice exports (box figure 2). Lower production in these countries will have a significant impact on global rice supply and prices.

continued on next page

Box 1.1.3 *Continued*

2 Major Exporters of Rice, 2021

Developing Asian economies account for more than three-quarters of global rice exports.

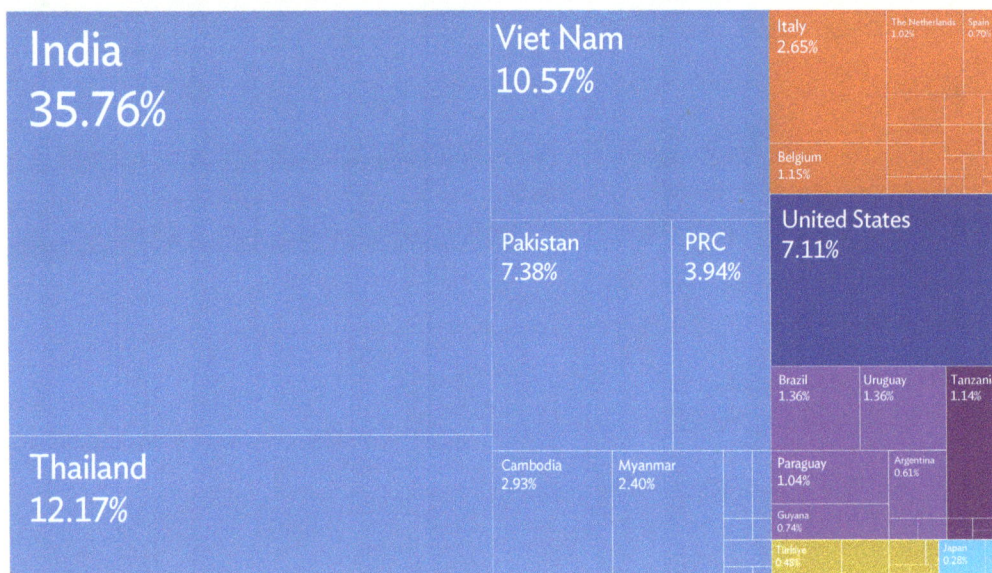

India 35.76%		Viet Nam 10.57%		Italy 2.65%	The Netherlands 1.02%	Spain 0.70%
		Pakistan 7.38%	PRC 3.94%	Belgium 1.15%		
				United States 7.11%		
				Brazil 1.36%	Uruguay 1.36%	Tanzania 1.14%
Thailand 12.17%		Cambodia 2.93%	Myanmar 2.40%	Paraguay 1.04%	Argentina 0.61%	
				Guyana 0.74%		
				Türkiye 0.48%		Japan 0.28%

PRC = People's Republic of China.
Source: Harvard Growth Lab. The Atlas of Economic Complexity.

Food and nonalcoholic beverages on average account for 30% of the CPI basket in developing Asian economies, and rice accounts for more than 10% of the food weight in several economies. Because of this, governments in developing Asia will be on high alert for El Niño's impact on inflation and trade balances.

Policy interventions can mitigate the effects of El Niño. El Niño has just started, and there is still time to take measures to mitigate its worst effects. Some of these interventions include introducing drought-tolerant crop varieties, expanding irrigation, storing and distributing grains, expanding social protection coverage, improving water management, investing in climatic early warning systems, developing national action plans, and cooperating with other economies in the region (ADB 2015; ADB 2016b; World Bank 2019). Although food trade restrictions, such as export bans and levies, have helped to stabilize domestic markets during periods of tight supply, they have also frequently impeded regional and global supply and markets. Export restrictions generate market and supply chain disruptions, resulting in broad-based food price increases, which eventually harm consumers.

References
ADB (Asian Development Bank). 2015. *Preparing for El Niño: Policy Options.*
——. 2016a. *Asian Development Outlook 2016.*
——. 2016b. *El Niño, Poor Water Management, and Climate Change Bringing Droughts to Asia and the Pacific.*
Brunner, A. 2002. El Niño and World Commodity Prices: Warm Water or Hot Air? *Review of Economics and Statistics* 84(1).
Callahan, C. W., and J. S. Mankin. 2023. Persistent Effect of El Niño on Global Economic Growth. *Science* 10.
Cashin, P., et al. 2017. Fair Weather or Foul? The Macroeconomic Effects of El Nino. *Journal of International Economics* 106.
Generoso, R., et al. 2020. The Growth Effects of El Niño and La Niña: Local Conditions Matter. *Annals of Economics and Statistics* 140.
GEO Global Agricultural Monitoring (GEOGLAM). 2023. El Niño 2023/2024 Anticipated Climate and Agricultural Yield Impacts. 24 August.
NOAA (National Oceanic and Atmospheric Administration). 2023. Understanding El Niño.
UNESCAP. 2017. *Enhancing Resilience to Extreme Climate Events: Lessons from the 2015–2016 El Niño Event in Asia and the Pacific.*
World Bank. 2019. *Striking a Balance: Managing El Niño and La Niña in the East Asia and Pacific Region's Agriculture.*

This box was written by Yothin Jinjarak of the East Asia Department and Pilipinas Quising of the Economic Research and Development Impact Department, Asian Development Bank, Manila.

Spillovers from a Further Weakening of the Property Market in the People's Republic of China

The property market in the People's Republic of China (PRC) is undergoing an adjustment as investment, sales, and prices are contracting. This Special Topic analyzes and quantifies the risk of possible further weakness in the PRC's property sector, using the Asian Development Bank's Multiregional Input-Output Tables. It examines the potential impact not just on the domestic economy but also on other economies in developing Asia and the world. The analysis shows that further property market weakness may slow the domestic economy, but policy action could soften or even erase the impact on growth. Spillovers to other developing Asian economies and to the rest of the world would be limited, with the exception of a few trading partners tightly linked to the PRC, most notably Mongolia through its mining sector.

This Special Topic considers risk scenarios for the PRC's property sector, simulating the potential impact of additional shocks in the future. It should be emphasized that this analysis is not about the baseline forecasts in *Asian Development Outlook September 2023.* The year is nearly over, and the various policies that authorities have already put in place to tackle the current weakness in the property sector are sufficient to reach the 4.9% growth forecast for the PRC this year. Rather, this analysis aims to shed light on the risks in 2024 and beyond. As the analysis shows, any further weakness in the property market next year and beyond could drag on growth—and policy would need to respond to this. The analysis examines policy packages of various magnitudes, and shows that PRC authorities have more than ample policy space to completely offset any drag on growth caused by a further weakening in the property market.

The property sector is a key component of the PRC economy. Estimates vary, but it accounts for between 21% of gross domestic product (GDP) (ADB 2022) and 23%–24% (Tilton et al. 2021; Rogoff and Yang 2021). Even at the lower range of these estimates, the importance of real estate activity for the PRC economy is larger than it is for most other economies (Figure 1.2.1). It has also been an important engine of growth in the PRC. In the 15 years before the COVID-19 pandemic, the property sector contributed on average 2 percentage points per year to GDP growth. The property market is also the most important store of wealth in the country, with 74% of household wealth held in the form of housing assets (Xie and Jin 2015). The sector is also critical for public finances—in 2021 37% of local government finances came from land- and property-based revenue (Huang 2023). The financial sector is exposed to the property sector—about a quarter of total lending is for household mortgages or lending to property developers, and indirect exposure, including lending to industries along the property sector supply chain and real estate collateral valuation changes, adds to the overall exposure.

Property market indicators suggest broad weakness. Real estate investment, sales, and housing starts have been contracting, and property prices are declining (Figure 1.2.2). Some developers are also struggling to sell properties, finish ongoing projects, and pay their bonds. Two key factors are contributing to the softening of the property market. First, since the second half of 2020, the regulatory environment was tightened to steer the economy away from property-led investment, make housing more affordable, and reduce vulnerabilities in the sector.

This section was written by Abdul Abiad, Jaqueson Galimberti, Matteo Lanzafame, Joseph Mariasingham, and Irfan Qureshi of the Economic Research and Development Impact Department (ERDI), and John Arvin Bernabe, ERDI consultant.

Figure 1.2.1 Share of Real Estate Activity to Gross
Domestic Product in Select Economies

*Real estate activity is a key component in PRC's economy, accounting
for over one-fifth of GDP.*

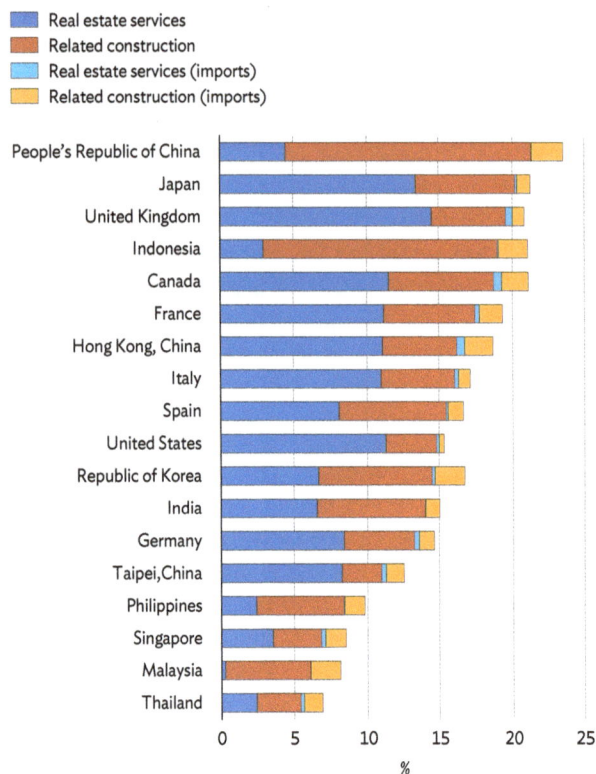

GDP = gross domestic product.
Notes: Real estate activity refers to the sum of economy-wide value-added
embodied in the final demand for real estate construction and real estate
services. Values are calculated using current price tables in US dollars.
Source: ADB (2022).

Second, subdued demand during the pandemic
has squeezed property developers' balance sheets.
The downturn is especially severe in Tier 2 and Tier 3
cities, where private property developers are mainly
invested and most of the country's housing stock is
located. But property prices in Tier 1 cities, such as
Beijing, Shanghai, and Shenzhen, have done well so far.
Longer-term factors, including a shrinking population,
slowing urbanization, an already high rate of home
ownership, and elevated sector leverage, suggest that
structural issues also underline the property market's
weakness.

**Continued weakness in the property sector would
adversely affect the broader economy given the
market's importance.** The sheer size of the property
sector and its linkages to other sectors indicate that
weaknesses in the market could have significant
spillovers on the rest of the economy. Falling property
prices not only reduce demand for inputs from other
sectors, but can also affect consumption via wealth
and confidence channels. Government finances will
deteriorate from continued weakness in the market,
especially at the subnational level, given its heavy
reliance on revenue from land sales and property- and
land-related taxes.[1] Defaults and debt restructuring by
property developers can also affect the financial system,
given the aforementioned exposure. The entanglement
of property developers, local governments, and the
financial sector heightens the risk of contagion, and this
is already weighing on investor sentiment.

Figure 1.2.2 Property Market Indicators in the People's Republic of China

The weak market has been accompanied by declining property prices.

A. Property Market Indicators

B. Newly Constructed Residential Property Prices

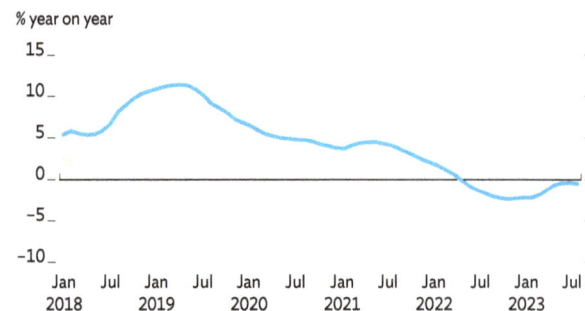

Note: 70-city index (panel B).
Sources: National Bureau of Statistics; Asian Development Bank estimates.

---

[1]   Technically, all land in the PRC belongs to the state and local governments only sell the usufruct rights for up to 70 years of
the land in their jurisdictions.

Input-output (IO) approaches allow an examination of the chain of impacts from a protracted property sector downturn on the broader economy. A comprehensive assessment of the impact of a property sector downturn should account for direct and indirect effects, working via sector and trade linkages. In such a scenario, the direct effects are reflected in decreased production in industries affected by lower spending, most notably real estate and construction. Depressed activity in these industries further reduces demand for the inputs they use, resulting in declining sales for their suppliers in both domestic and overseas markets. These suppliers also reduce their demand for intermediate inputs, and so on down the value chain. The extent of potential losses depends on suppliers' linkages with the industries affected. One of the key attributes of IO models is the ability to account for these secondary effects on upstream sectors. Fixed input-output coefficients are most useful when looking at short-run effects, as prices and behavior will adjust in the longer run. Another important caveat is that the framework does not allow tracking the dynamics of effects.

This analysis uses the Asian Development Bank's Multiregional Input-Output Tables. These capture the entirety of global trade and production flows for 35 sectors in 72 economies—including 29 regional economies in Asia and the Pacific—plus a 73rd economy that captures the rest of the world.[2] The tables provide the widest available coverage of economies in the region and the most up-to-date data for 2022, which are important advantages when doing the analysis.

These tables are combined with supplementary, more granular data on the proportion of real estate construction and shares of private investment by product.

The starting point of the analysis is a possible further decline in real estate investment, which could be accompanied by secondary wealth and confidence effects. The analysis assumes a hypothetical future 10% decline in real estate investment in the PRC. The size of the shock is roughly in line with the typical fall in real estate investment experienced during the downturns of 138 housing cycles in 55 economies during 1970–2010, as documented in Igan and Loungani (2012). As a result of protracted property market weakness, secondary shocks could also materialize. The decline in real estate investment could reduce private consumption via negative wealth effects, and reduce private investment through lower business and investor confidence.[3] The shock assumptions would be consistent with prices falling further. Ahuja and Myrvoda (2012), for example, find that downturns in real estate investment in the PRC tend to lead to a decline in property prices of about 3%. Since real estate accounts for three-fourths of total household wealth in the PRC, a housing price correction could potentially reduce consumption via a decline in wealth, although the empirical evidence on this for the PRC is mixed.[4] Here, the wealth effect is assumed to reduce private consumption by 1.0%. As for business confidence, available evidence of its impact on private investment is scarce, but it points to a small magnitude.

---

[2] For more information on the Asian Development Bank's Multiregional Input-Output Tables, see https://kidb.adb.org/mrio.

[3] An additional channel through which consumption can be affected is consumer confidence. However, the empirical evidence indicates that, netting out the effects of other economic and financial indicators, consumer confidence contributes only modestly to explaining variation in future consumer spending (Ludvigson 2004). One possible explanation for this is that changes in consumer confidence associated with wealth shocks may largely reflect changes in wealth itself, and thus do not provide much additional information once the wealth effect is taken into account.

[4] Dong, Hui, and Jia (2017), documenting heterogeneity in the effect of house prices on consumption across 35 major cities in the PRC, find that the wealth effect on consumption is conditioned on the health of local markets and the degree of financial development. Comparing the PRC with international evidence, Li and Zhang (2021) find that household consumption positively responds to changes in housing wealth, also finding that the link depends on varying levels of government spending and financial development. Sun et al. (2022) find that "the impact of house prices on consumption is asymmetric, with consumption moving in the opposite direction when house prices rise but not when house prices fall." Due to the mixed evidence, the knock-on wealth effects assumed in the Special Topic's analysis are calibrated to be small relative to the shock to real estate investment.

For instance, using data from several economies, Janada and Teodoru (2020) find that a one standard deviation shock to business confidence leads to a 0.4%–2.5% change in private investment. The assumption of a 1.0% fall in private investment used in this analysis is in the middle of this range.[5]

Two policy scenarios are then compared. The shocks just described, if they materialize, would be a significant drag on economic activity in the PRC, and elicit a policy response. This analysis evaluates how different policy responses can attenuate the effects of a downturn in the property market. The following looks at moderate and stronger policy response scenarios in the PRC:

- **Moderate policy response.** In this scenario, policymakers respond to a further weakening in the property sector using a variety of policies. First, policy measures are taken to counteract downward pressure on the property market (e.g., easing borrowing costs or regulations for mortgages, similar to what was implemented in August). This limits the contraction in real estate investment to only 5% relative to the baseline. Second, two types of fiscal stimulus measures are put in place to support domestic demand and activity. Broad government expenditure is raised by 0.25% of GDP, and non–real estate infrastructure investment increases by 0.25% of GDP.[6] And third, monetary policy is eased further.[7] The combined impact of these measures reduces the wealth effect, while business confidence picks up somewhat. As a result, private consumption and private investment each decline by 0.5% relative to the baseline, rather than 1.0%.

- **Stronger policy response.** The same type of policy mix applies to the stronger policy scenario, but the size of the intervention is scaled up. With additional measures to support the property sector, the contraction in real estate investment

eases to only 2.5% relative to the baseline, compared to 5% under the moderate scenario. In addition, fiscal stimulus is assumed to be larger, as government expenditure increases by 0.5% of GDP and infrastructure spending also increases by 0.5% of GDP. Private consumption and investment each decline by just 0.25% relative to the baseline as monetary policy support is greater, the wealth effect is smaller, and confidence is less subdued.

The size of policy interventions considered in the moderate and stronger policy response scenarios is well within the PRC's available policy space. The total stimulus under both scenarios would be a fraction of the size of the stimulus the PRC undertook in 2009 and 2010 in response to the global financial crisis, and is also much smaller than the stimulus enacted in response to the pandemic. Low inflation also means there is further room to ease monetary policy.

In the case of a moderate policy response to a further weakening in the property market, GDP in the PRC would be 0.59 percent lower than in the baseline (Figure 1.2.3). If the shock were to occur over the course of a calendar year, the simulation results could also be interpreted as implying that GDP growth in that year would be roughly 0.59 percentage points lower compared to the baseline forecast. About 78% of the negative impact on the PRC is from the initial decline in real estate investment, 16% is from the wealth effect on private consumption, and the rest from the decline in private investment.

Spillovers to the rest of the region and the rest of the world are relatively limited. World GDP would be 0.13% lower than in the baseline, but most of the loss in global GDP is explained by the impact in the PRC itself. In the rest of the world, the overall loss would be only 0.02% of GDP. Developing Asia excluding the PRC would experience a negligible GDP decline of about 0.04%.

---

[5]   Due to the linearity of the model, assuming larger or smaller shocks results in, respectively, proportionally larger or smaller effects on GDP. In this respect, the assumption of "unit" 1% changes in private consumption and private investment is convenient, as the effects can be easily scaled up or down to assume a different magnitude of secondary shocks.

[6]   The first type of measure can accommodate targeted support for certain sectors such as electric vehicles; the second is the more traditional fiscal stimulus used in the past.

[7]   Under the circumstances of weak overall demand and very low inflation, some easing of monetary policy would be an additional policy lever available to the authorities, and thus could be part of the policy mix. However, there is less certainty on the strength of monetary policy effects, which also have significant lags.

Figure 1.2.3 GDP Impact of Further Property Sector Weaknesses Under Moderate and Strong Policy Responses

Further weakness slows growth in the PRC, but the effect could be offset by policy action.

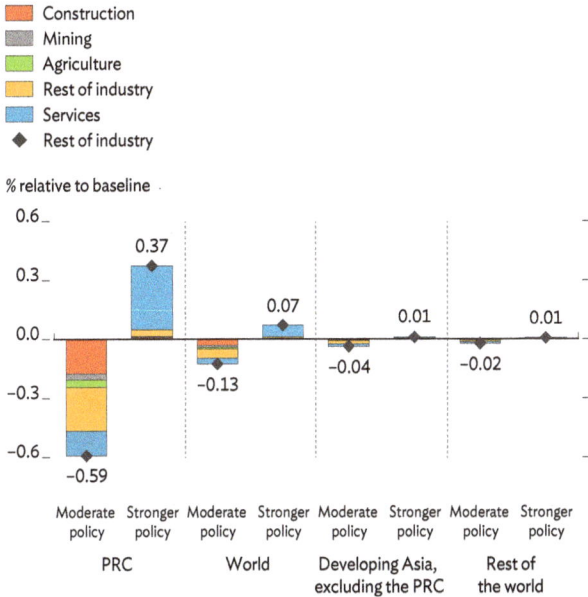

- Construction
- Mining
- Agriculture
- Rest of industry
- Services
- ◆ Rest of industry

% relative to baseline

```
0.6_
                    0.37
0.3_                 ┃
                           0.07
0.0_                        ◆            0.01            0.01
                    ◆             ◆       ◆       ◆       ◆
           ◆       -0.13         -0.04          -0.02
-0.3_
           -0.13
-0.6_
  ◆
-0.59
```

| Moderate policy | Stronger policy | Moderate policy | Stronger policy | Moderate policy | Stronger policy | Moderate policy | Stronger policy |
| PRC | | World | | Developing Asia, excluding the PRC | | Rest of the world | |

GDP = gross domestic product, PRC = People's Republic of China.

Note: In this figure, developing Asia covers Armenia; Bangladesh; Bhutan; Brunei Darussalam; Cambodia; Fiji; Georgia; Hong Kong, China; India; Indonesia; Kazakhstan; the Kyrgyz Republic; the Republic of Korea, the Lao People's Democratic Republic; Malaysia; Maldives; Mongolia; Nepal; Pakistan; the Philippines; Singapore; Sri Lanka; Taipei,China; Thailand; and Viet Nam.

Source: Asian Development Bank estimates.

Stronger intervention could more than offset the negative effects of a property sector correction (Figure 1.2.3). Similar effects ensuing from a moderate policy response drive the simulation results in the stronger policy response scenario. Growth in the PRC would be 0.37 percentage points higher than the baseline. Both here and in the moderate policy response scenario the impact on growth in developing Asia excluding the PRC, as well as the rest of the world, are marginal.

By sector, impacts under the moderate response scenario largely stem from linkages with construction (Figure 1.2.4). Construction is not surprisingly the hardest hit sector in the PRC, declining by 2.5% relative to the baseline under the moderate policy response scenario. After construction, mining declines by 1.0%, and the rest of industry by 0.7%. The services sector declines by only 0.2% relative to the baseline. For developing Asia, the hardest hit sector is mining, which declines by 0.2% due to supply linkages with the PRC's construction sector. Similarly for the rest of the world, which excludes the PRC and developing Asia, mining is the hardest hit sector, especially in Australia and the Russian Federation.

Figure 1.2.4 Sector Impact of Further Property Sector Weakness in the People's Republic of China Under a Moderate Policy Response Scenario

Construction would be the hardest hit sector in the PRC, followed by mining.

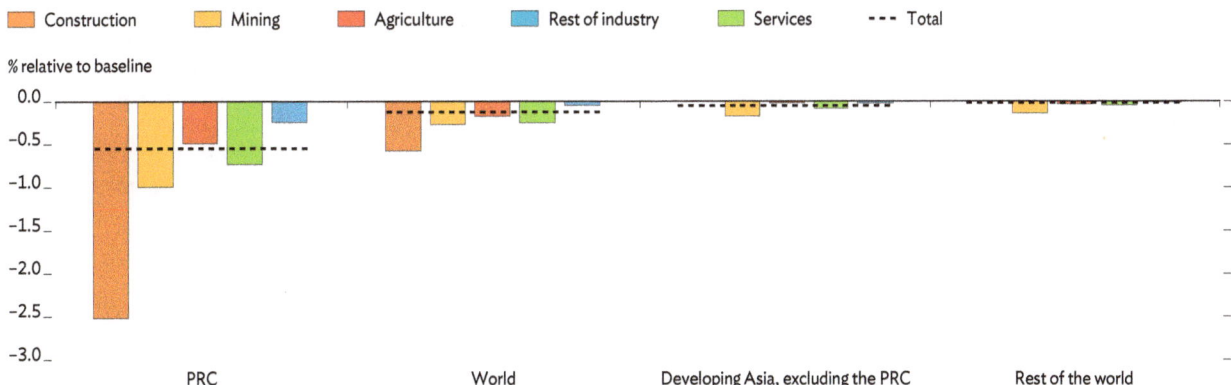

- Construction
- Mining
- Agriculture
- Rest of industry
- Services
- --- Total

% relative to baseline

```
0.0_
-0.5_
-1.0_
-1.5_
-2.0_
-2.5_
-3.0_
        PRC              World       Developing Asia, excluding the PRC    Rest of the world
```

PRC = People's Republic of China.

Note: In this figure, developing Asia covers Armenia; Bangladesh; Bhutan; Brunei Darussalam; Cambodia; Fiji; Georgia; Hong Kong, China; India; Indonesia; Kazakhstan; the Kyrgyz Republic; the Republic of Korea; the Lao People's Democratic Republic; Malaysia; Maldives; Mongolia; Nepal; Pakistan; the Philippines; Singapore; Sri Lanka; Taipei,China; Thailand; and Viet Nam.

Source: Asian Development Bank estimates.

The IO analysis allows for the decomposition of various sector contributions to the overall impact. Here, the contribution of an affected sector depends on the degree of shock, its relative importance to the overall economy, and the size and type of the policy response. In the PRC, the overall impact is largely driven by potential declines in the aggregate manufacturing sector, with key input suppliers like steel and cement industries having the biggest impact (Figure 1.2.5). Construction, while hit the most, accounts for slightly less than a third of the overall decline. Impact contributions by the services sector are softened by a moderate increase in government spending, but still account for over one-fifth of the total decline. Mining and agriculture add little to the potential fallout from a property downturn, partly due to their smaller shares to GDP.

A handful of the PRC's close trading partners would be affected. Under the moderate policy response scenario, Mongolia would be the most affected economy in the region outside of the PRC on a GDP decline of about 0.35% relative to the baseline, equivalent to lower growth of 0.35 percentage points if the shock occurred in a calendar year (Figure 1.2.5). This impact arises primarily from Mongolia's substantial exports of coal, iron ore, and other mining products to the PRC. Taipei,China would also be affected through its exports of electrical components to the PRC, as would Malaysia for its energy and metals exports to the PRC. Other exporters of raw materials and inputs to the PRC's construction sector—such as the Lao People's Democratic Republic, Australia, Kazakhstan, and Brunei Darussalam—would also face GDP losses of about a tenth of a percent. Singapore and Hong Kong, China, would primarily be affected through falling exports of support and transport services to the PRC.

Policy responses could soften or even fully offset the negative impact of a further weakening of the property market on growth in the PRC. The analysis shows that a property market downturn would slow the economy, but policy action could soften or even erase the impact on growth, albeit with some reallocation across sectors. Spillovers to other developing Asian economies and to the rest of the world would be limited, with the exception of a few trading partners tightly linked to the PRC.

Figure 1.2.5 GDP Impact on Selected Economies of Further Property Sector Weakness in the People's Republic of China Under a Moderate Policy Response Scenario

Limited spillovers to other developing Asian economies, with the exception of a few trading partners tightly linked to the PRC.

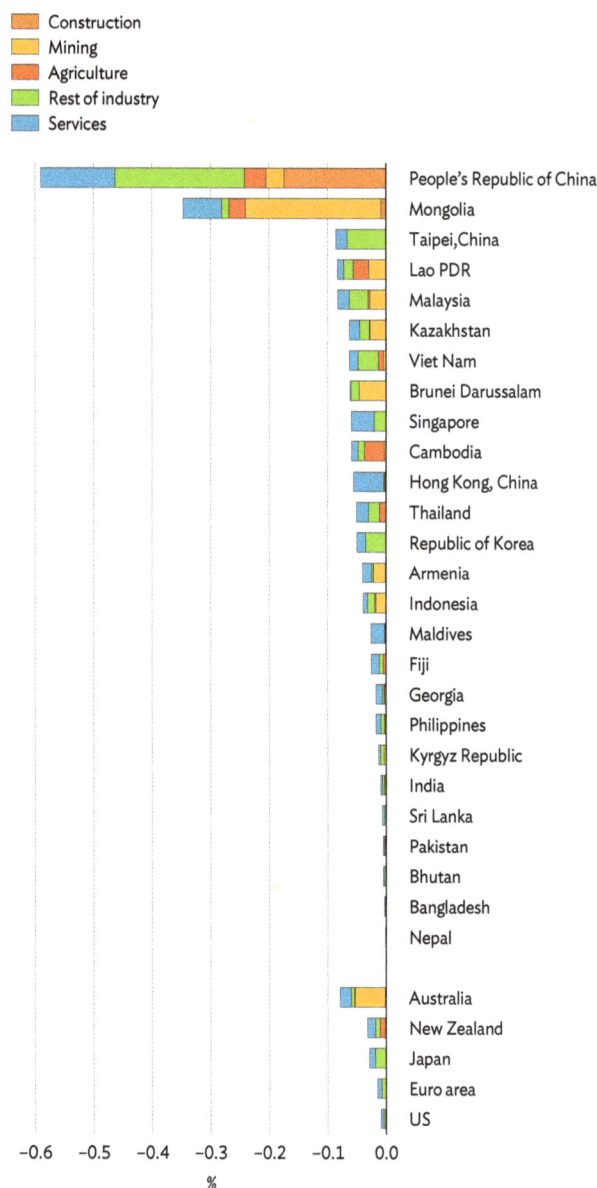

GDP = gross domestic product, Lao PDR = Lao People's Democratic Republic, PRC = People's Republic of China, US = United States.

Note: The moderate policy response scenario assumes a 5% negative shock to real estate-related construction in the PRC, a 0.5% shock to private consumption, a 0.5% shock to private investment, an increase in government expenditure of 0.25% of GDP, and an increase in non-real estate construction (infrastructure) spending of 0.25% of GDP.

Source: Asian Development Bank. Multiregional Input-Output Tables.

The current correction is partly an intended result of policy measures aimed at tackling vulnerabilities in the property sector. If a more severe downturn in the property market materializes, policy responses should not lose sight of the longer-term objective of reducing financial vulnerabilities stemming from over-leveraged developers. Policymakers should aim to engineer a soft landing, providing a floor to the market adjustment to avoid a more significant contraction in the short term, while continuing to pursue the longer-term goal of a more structurally balanced property sector. The stronger policy response scenario in this analysis suggests that a policy mix that includes broad macro policy measures combined with carefully calibrated targeted support to the property sector would be in line with these short- and longer-term objectives.

While IO linkages suggest a limited impact of a property sector downturn on the rest of the world, economies should remain vigilant to guard against spillovers working through other channels. The analysis in this Special Topic suggests that the global and regional impact would be small, but these findings are subject to caveats. Some of these relate to the limitations of the IO analysis itself. Another is that the analysis does not incorporate some other channels through which spillovers could occur. A sharper slowdown in the PRC's growth could, for example, result in a rise in global risk aversion and a flight to safety—and capital outflows, depreciations, and tighter financial conditions in many developing economies could adversely affect their growth.

References

ADB (Asian Development Bank). 2022. Economic Insights from Input–Output Tables for Asia and the Pacific. Section 6.5 and Appendix 6.2.

Ahuja, A., and A. Myrvoda. 2012. The Spillover Effects of a Downturn in China's Real Estate Investment. *IMF Working Paper* No. 12/266. International Monetary Fund.

Dong, Z., E. C. M. Hui, and S. Jia. 2017. How Does Housing Price Affect Consumption in China: Wealth Effect or Substitution Effect? *Cities* 64.

Huang, T. 2023. Why China's Housing Policies Have Failed. *Working Paper* No. 23-5. Peterson Institute for International Economics.

Igan, D., and P. Loungani. 2012. Global Housing Cycles. *IMF Working Paper* No. 12/217. International Monetary Fund.

Janada, C., and I. R. Teodoru. 2020. Confidence as a Driver of Private Investment in Selected Countries of Central America. *IMF Working Paper* No. 20/270. International Monetary Fund.

Li, C., and Y. Zhang. 2021. How Does Housing Wealth Affect Household Consumption? Evidence from Macro-Data with Special Implications for China. *China Economic Review* 69.

Ludvigson, S. C. 2004. Consumer Confidence and Consumer Spending. *Journal of Economic Perspectives* 18(2).

Rogoff, K., and Y. Yang. 2021. Has China's Housing Production Peaked? *China and the World Economy* 29(1).

Sun, X., et al. 2022. The Impact of House Price on Urban Household Consumption: Micro Evidence from China. *Sustainability* 14(12592).

Tilton, A., et al. 2021. How Big Is the China Property Sector. Goldman Sachs China Data Insights.

Xie, Y., and Y. Jin. 2015. Household Wealth in China. *China Sociological Review* 47(3).

Slower Growth in Advanced Economies, But No Recession

The aggregate growth forecast in the major advanced economies is revised up for 2023, but revised down for 2024. The United States (US) is expected to grow by 1.9% this year after a stronger-than-expected first-half performance. In both the US and the euro area, the lagged effects of policy rate hikes will temper economic activity next year. The global slowdown will be a drag on Japan's goods exports in the second half of this year and next. Overall, the major advanced economies are projected to grow by 1.4% in 2023 and 0.9% in 2024 (Table A.1). With inflation decelerating in these economies, risks to the outlook are balanced.

Table A.1 Baseline Assumptions on the International Economy

Stronger-than-expected growth in H1 propped up the 2023 forecasts in the advanced economies, but the lagged effects of higher interest rates tone down expectations for next year.

	2022	2023		2024	
		April	September	April	September
GDP growth, %					
Major advanced economies[a]	2.5	0.7	1.4	1.3	0.9
United States	2.1	0.9	1.9	1.3	0.8
Euro area	3.5	0.5	0.7	1.4	1.1
Japan	1.0	0.8	1.7	0.8	0.5
Prices and inflation					
Brent crude spot prices, average, $/barrel	100	88	83	90	86
Consumer price index inflation, major advanced economies' average, %	7.5	4.4	4.5	2.4	2.3
Interest rates					
United States federal funds rate, average, %	1.7	4.8	5.2	4.7	5.2
European Central Bank refinancing rate, average, %	0.8	3.8	4.0	3.3	3.9
Bank of Japan overnight call rate, average, %	0.0	0.0	0.0	0.0	0.0
$ Libor, %[b]	2.1	4.8	5.2	4.7	5.2

ADO = Asian Development Outlook, GDP = gross domestic product, H = half.
[a] Average growth rates are weighted by GDP purchasing power parity.
[b] Average London Interbank Offered Rate quotations on 1-month loans.
Sources: Bloomberg; CEIC Data Company; Haver Analytics; International Monetary Fund. World Economic Outlook; Asian Development Bank estimates.

This annex was written by Jaqueson Galimberti, Jules Hugot, Matteo Lanzafame, Nedelyn Magtibay-Ramos, Yuho Myoda, Pilipinas Quising, Arief Ramayandi, and Dennis Sorino of the Economic Research and Development Impact Department (ERDI), ADB, Manila, and Michael Timbang and Jesson Pagaduan, ERDI consultants.

Recent Developments in the Major Advanced Economies

United States

The economy continued to expand in the first half of 2023. After the upward surprise in the first quarter (Q1), the economy turned in a stronger-than-expected Q2. In the quarter, gross domestic product (GDP) grew by 2.1%—all growth numbers in the Annex are at a seasonally adjusted annualized rate—surpassing Q1's 2.0% growth (Figure A.1). Net exports, however, were muted, but all elements of domestic demand contributed positively to Q2 growth (Figure A.1).

Figure A.1 Demand-Side Contributions to Growth, United States

All components of domestic demand expanded in Q2.

- Net exports
- Government expenditure & investment
- Private investment
- Private expenditure
- Gross domestic product

Percentage points, seasonally adjusted annualized rate, qoq

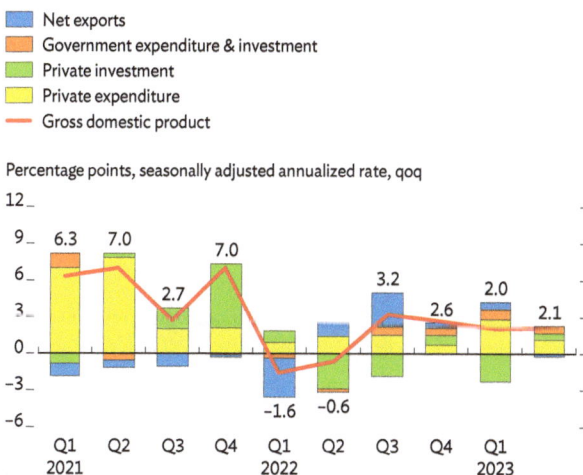

Q = quarter, qoq = quarter on quarter.
Sources: Department of Commerce. Bureau of Economic Analysis; Haver Analytics.

Higher interest rates continue to bite. The growth in private consumption (1.7%) and government spending (3.3%) in Q2 softened significantly relative to Q1 (growing at 4.2% and 5.0%, respectively) primarily because of slower goods consumption and lower government nondefense spending. Although not to a level that offsets the decline in Q1, a rebound in investment in Q2—3.3% versus –11.9% in the previous quarter—compensated for weaker contributions from private and government consumption.

The continuing fall in residential investment dragged the rebound in nonresidential investment, which was driven mainly by investments in transport equipment in response to stronger demand for travel and logistics.

Signals from recent data remain mixed. Investment, particularly in manufacturing, is likely to remain weak, as suggested by the continued contraction in the manufacturing purchasing managers' index (PMI). The manufacturing PMI improved to 47.6 in August after hitting 46.0 in June (Figure A.2)—its weakest since June 2020. The improvement was driven mainly by manufacturing production being steady relative to July. However, other components of the manufacturing PMI continued to decline, suggesting slower manufacturing activity going forward. Industrial production remained weak, suggesting struggles in some parts of the economy. However, services continued to strengthen in August. The nonmanufacturing PMI suggests this is due mainly to expanding orders, business activity, and employment.

Figure A.2 Business Activity, United States

Signals from recent data remained mixed.

- Consumer confidence
- Retail sales
- Manufacturing purchasing managers' index
- Services purchasing manager's index

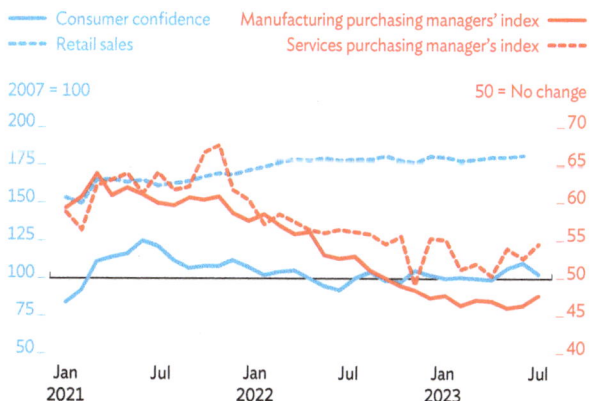

Note: A purchasing manager's index reading <50 signals deterioration, >50 improvement.
Source: Haver Analytics.

Consumption is holding up despite rising interest rates. Retail sales have remained relatively steady since the beginning of the year and earlier signs of weakening consumer confidence were reversed in June. The resilience of consumption is partly supported by pent-up demand as households drew down excess savings built up during the first years of the pandemic.

Nevertheless, slower consumption growth in Q2 suggests that consumption patterns may have started to normalize as the savings buffer depletes.

Inflation is softening despite wage growth. Headline inflation slowed to 3.2% in July, mostly on lower fuel prices (Figure A.3). Core inflation also softened in July, but was still high at 4.7%. Used vehicle prices and airfares continued to fall, but higher rents held up the nonvolatile part of inflation. A softer rise in nonfarm payrolls since June indicates easing labor market conditions. However, the unemployment rate remained low at 3.8% and wages rose further, as indicated by the 0.2% monthly increase in average hourly earnings. The Federal Reserve resumed raising its policy rate with a 25 basis points (bps) increase in July, and it is likely to increase by another 25 bps to lower inflation toward its 2% target.

Figure A.3 Inflation, Federal Funds Rate, and Unemployment Rate, United States

The Fed funds rate increased further as inflation declined to still-high levels.

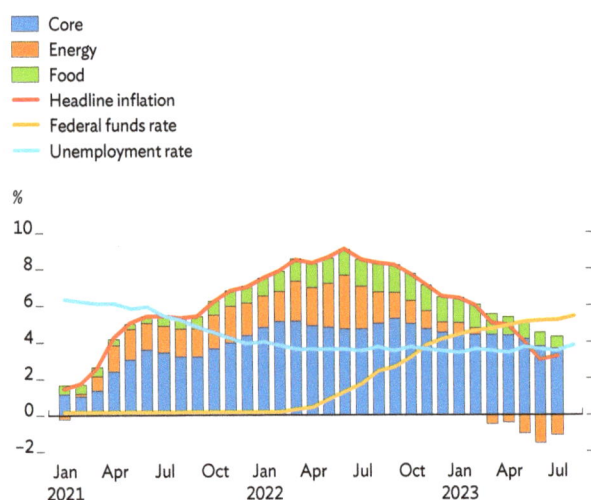

Source: Haver Analytics.

The growth forecast is revised up to 1.9% for 2023 and lowered to 0.8% in 2024. The upward revision reflects unexpectedly stronger growth in the first half. Decelerating inflation will prompt the Fed to tighten perhaps just once more this year. The Fed's "dot plot"—a survey of the projections of Fed officials for the outlook for interest rates—suggests the policy rate will be at 5.50%–5.75% by the end of 2023.

GDP growth is forecast to slow to 0.8% in 2024 as the lagged effects of interest rate hikes kick in. The inflation rate will decline gradually and is forecast at 4.0% this year and 2.4% in 2024. The Fed could start cutting its policy rate next year as inflation returns to normal. With financial turmoil receding after the disruption in Q1, risks to the outlook are more balanced and will depend mostly on how inflationary pressures evolve in the economy.

Euro Area

Growth in the euro area recovered slightly to 0.2% in Q1 2023, following a 0.2% contraction in Q4 2022. Eurostat data revisions in July show the region avoided a technical recession, as defined by two consecutive quarters of negative growth. Rather than contracting by 0.1% as initially estimated, GDP rose by 0.2% in Q1 as net exports contributed 2.6 percentage points (pps) to growth. High inflation and interest rates, however, continued to restrain domestic demand. Total investment fell by 8.5% and subtracted 1.9 pps from growth, while private consumption almost stagnated to 0.1%. Economic activity was also dragged by falling government consumption, subtracting 0.5 pps. In the major economies, France slightly grew by 0.1%, as activity benefited from stronger industrial production and exports. Growth in Italy rebounded to 2.5%, led by household consumption and net trade after a 0.6% contraction in Q4 2022. Spain picked up further, from 1.7% to 2.1%, as tourist arrivals helped private spending. Germany's downturn eased, with output declining by 0.4% in Q1 after contracting 1.6% in the previous quarter.

Economic activity picked up slightly to 0.5% in Q2, driven by a rebound in total investment. Following an 8.5% contraction in Q1, gross capital formation expanded by 8.7% in Q2, and contributed 1.8 pps to growth (Figure A.4). Private consumption expenditure growth remained unchanged at 0.1% amid softening domestic conditions, while government spending increased by 1.0%. Reflecting a worsening external environment, exports declined by 2.7% and, as a result, net exports subtracted 1.6 pps from growth. Across the major economies, GDP in France rose by 2.1% in Q2 on recovering exports and investment more than offsetting the fall in private consumption.

Figure A.4 Demand-side Contributions to Growth, Euro Area

Economic activity picked up in Q2, lifted by growth in total investment.

Private consumption   Net exports
Government consumption Statistical discrepancy
Total investment   Gross domestic product

Percentage points, seasonally adjusted annualized rate, qoq

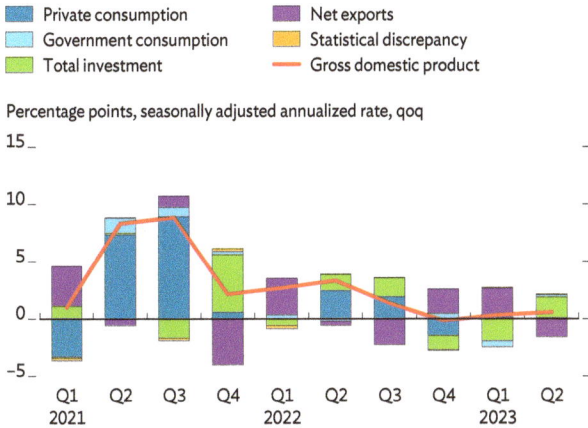

Q = quarter, qoq = quarter on quarter.
Source: Haver Analytics.

Germany, after going into a technical recession in Q1, grew by 0.1% in Q2 on stronger private and government spending. Growth in Spain weakened to 1.7% on falling net exports, while GDP in Italy contracted by 1.6%, dragged by muted domestic demand.

Leading indicators suggest that lingering economic weakness in Q2 persisted in early Q3. Demand conditions soured the composite PMI, which fell to 48.6 in July, below the 50-threshold separating expansion from contraction, and further to 46.7 in August, the lowest in 33 months (Figure A.5).

Figure A.5 Economic Sentiment and Purchasing Managers' Indexes, Euro Area

Leading indicators remained weak in early Q3 on declining economic sentiment.

Composite PMI   Economic sentiment

Index   Long-term average = 100, seasonally adjusted

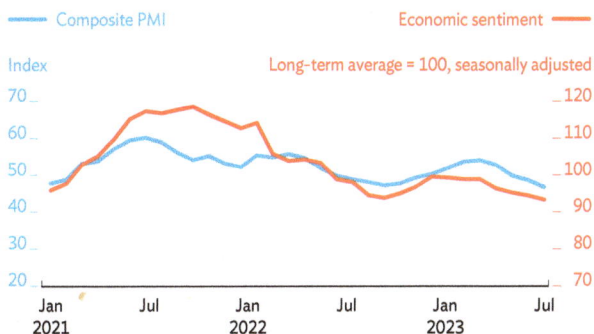

PMI = purchasing managers' index.
Sources: CEIC Data Company; Haver Analytics.

The services PMI contracted for the first time this year and declined to 47.9 in August, the lowest since February 2021, driven by falling exports and volume for new business. Meanwhile, the manufacturing output PMI remained contractionary at 43.4 in August, reflecting steady declines in consumer, investment, and intermediate goods output. The economic sentiment indicator for August stayed below its long-term average of 100, decreasing to 93.3 from 94.5 in July on lower confidence in services, consumer and retail trade, and in construction.

This update raises April's growth forecast to 0.7% for 2023 and trims it to 1.1% for 2024. Although the better-than-expected Q2 performance underpins the slight upward revision for 2023, the euro area is expected to expand only moderately in the second half, despite softer energy prices and improving external conditions. High inflation and tight liquidity will weigh on consumer and capital spending, and residual tailwinds from post-pandemic reopenings will fade. Household consumption expenditure will remain soft, depressed by subdued real income growth. Investment should weaken, dented by monetary policy tightening. Fiscal policy will become gradually less supportive, as governments switch to fiscal consolidation in response to higher bond yields. Economic activity next year will pick up more gradually than assumed earlier, as external headwinds persist and the lagged effects of the European Central Bank's policy rate hikes are felt. Risks to the outlook remain mainly associated with a possible escalation of the Russian invasion of Ukraine and inflation dynamics.

The inflation forecast is retained at 5.7% for this year and 2.5% next year. Headline inflation eased from 6.1% in May to 5.3% in July on falling energy prices. Core inflation, however, remains elevated, at 5.5% in June and July (Figure A.6). Because of this, the European Central Bank raised interest rates by 25 basis points in July, following hikes at the same level in May and June, bringing the main refinancing rate to 4.25%. Headline inflation averaged 6.8% in the first 7 months, but should continue falling over the rest of 2023 on higher interest rates and subdued domestic demand.

Figure A.6 Headline and Core Inflation, Euro Area

Headline inflation cooled on falling energy prices, but core inflation remains elevated.

Legend:
- Headline inflation
- Core inflation

%

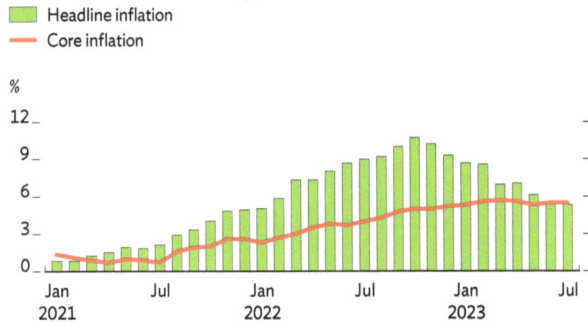

Sources: CEIC Data Company; Haver Analytics.

Japan

The economy grew a robust 6.0% quarter on quarter in Q2 2023, well above market expectations, but domestic demand contracted.
Growth in Q1 was revised up, from 2.7% to 3.7% in the latest GDP estimate. Growth was entirely led by external demand in Q2, both in terms of recovering exports and a continued contraction in imports (Figure A.7). Automobile exports normalized as the semiconductor shortage eased and consumption by inbound tourists, supported by the weaker yen, recovered to pre-pandemic levels. The continued decline in imports, especially pharmaceuticals and fossil fuels, boosted net exports. Domestic demand fell slightly quarter on quarter because of weaker private consumption. Despite the official lifting of pandemic-related regulations in May, leisure consumption, such as eating out, remained below the pre-pandemic trend in the quarter.

Growth is revised up from April's forecast to 1.7% for 2023, but revised down to 0.5% for 2024.
The upward revision for this year is primarily on a better-than-expected first-half performance. Net exports will be this year's growth driver, due to fairly resilient external demand, especially from the US, and the expected recovery of inbound tourism from the People's Republic of China (PRC) in the second half (Figure A.8). However, with the slowdown in key exports, such as machinery to Asia, the boost from net exports is likely to diminish in the second half as base effects fade.

Figure A.7 Demand-Side Contributions to Growth, Japan

Growth accelerated in Q2 2023 due to a recovery in exports and imports continuing to decline.

Legend:
- Public demand
- Private consumption
- Private investment
- Change in inventories
- Exports
- Imports
- Gross domestic product

Percentage point, seasonally adjusted annualized rate, qoq

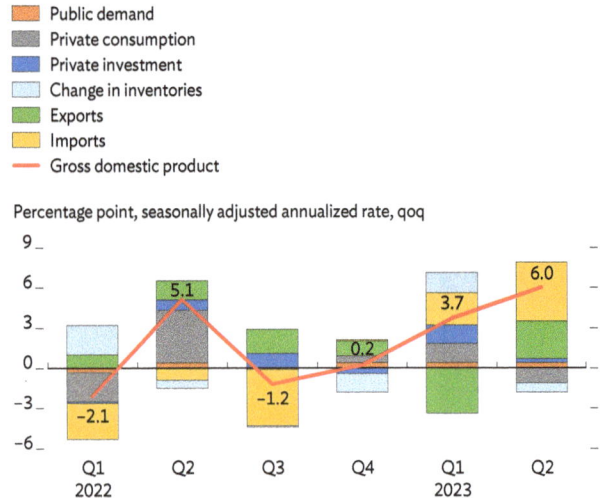

Q = quarter, qoq = quarter on quarter.
Source: Cabinet Office.

Figure A.8 International Tourists Arrivals and Spending, Japan

Inbound tourism expenditure recovered to 2019's level in Q1 2023, but arrivals, especially from the PRC, have not yet rebounded.

Legend:
- Visitors' spending by origin (Q1 2019 = 100)
- Number of arrivals (Q1 2019 = 100)
- Visitors' spending by origin, ¥

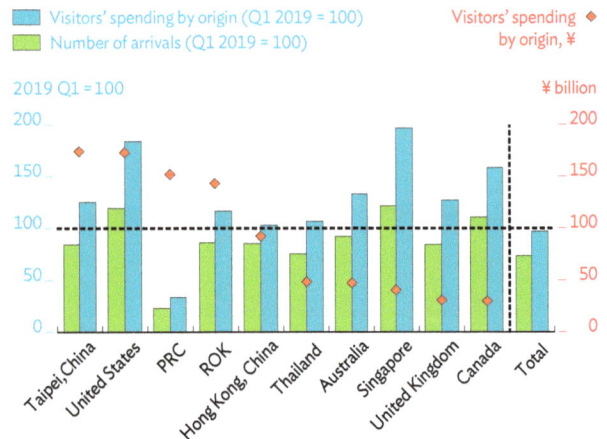

PRC = People's Republic of China, Q = quarter, ROK = Republic of Korea.
Source: Ministry of Land, Infrastructure, Transport and Tourism.

Thus, a recovery in manufacturing investment is likely to be delayed until 2024 or even beyond. Consumption will grow only moderately. Although consumption will be supported by excess savings from the pandemic, elevated consumer prices have been reducing the real disposable income of households. A larger negative carry over will lower growth in 2024.

The forecast for consumer prices is revised up to 2.9% in 2023 and revised down to 1.5% next year. Input prices for the food industry remain high, causing food inflation to accelerate in the first half of this year. Given the thin margins and limited pricing power of food manufacturers, food inflation will stay elevated over the second half. But both core and headline inflation have probably peaked, as the energy component of consumer prices has turned negative on a year-on-year basis since March (Figure A.9). Services inflation remains in check despite the tight labor market, and overall inflation is expected to soften toward the end of the forecast horizon.

Figure A.9 Consumer Price Index Decomposition, Japan

Inflation is slowing in 2023 on lower energy prices.

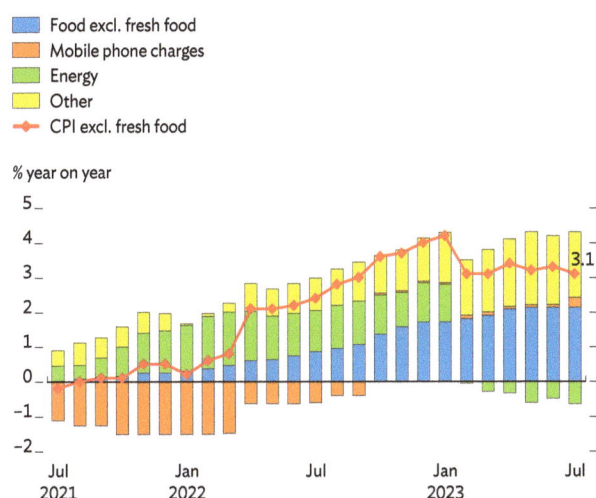

CPI = consumer price index.
Sources: CEIC Data Company; Statistics Bureau.

The Bank of Japan is expected to maintain its accommodative monetary policy, but fiscal policy will be gradually tightened. The fiscal balance is expected to improve as nominal economic growth continues and one-time pandemic-related expenditures fade. However, the improvement in the fiscal balance is expected to be slower than planned due to the increase in spending on security this year and next. The expected slowdown in global economic growth later this year and rate cuts by the Fed in 2024 will likely allow the Bank of Japan to maintain its accommodative policy stance.

Risks to the inflation outlook are tilted to the upside; risks to the growth outlook are balanced. The timing for phasing out subsidies could alter the inflation trajectory. The yen's depreciation and higher oil prices may again increase import and input prices, which could prompt firms to raise prices. The extended inflation may reduce disposable income further and dampen consumer sentiment, leading to lower private consumption. The restructuring of supply chains in key industries because of rising geopolitical tensions will probably reduce goods exports, but it could also lead to the expansion of domestic capital investment in affected industries.

Recent Developments and Outlook in Nearby Economies

Australia

Economic growth will moderate in 2023 as higher interest rates and uncertainty weaken consumption spending. GDP growth decelerated in Q1 to 0.9% from 2.3% in Q4 2022. Consumption growth continued to slow on less household discretionary spending. Retail sales growth declined to 3.0% in June, the lowest in 21 months. While investment is showing early signs of bouncing back from last year's meager growth, it has not been sufficient to counterbalance a larger decline in net exports. Unemployment marginally increased to 3.7% (seasonally adjusted) in July, although firms report that labor shortages have lessened. Inflation appears to have peaked, easing to 6.0% in Q2 from 7.0% in Q1. The Reserve Bank Board retained the cash rate target at 4.1% in August so that it could evaluate the effects of the recent hiking cycle and the economic outlook. Despite the pause, the board signaled that further tightening may be needed.

A prolonged economic slowdown in Australia could hit economies in the Pacific. Import growth slowed in the first 6 months of 2023 after exceeding pre-pandemic levels in 2022 (Figure A.10). More than half of these imports come from East Asia and Southeast Asia. In 2018 and 2019, Australia imported 18% of the exports of Pacific countries, and it is an important source of tourists and remittances to the subregion.

Figure A.10 Imports Customs Value, Australia

Imports flatlined in 2023 after strong growth following the post-pandemic reopening.

■ East Asia
■ Southeast Asia
■ Remaining developing Asia
■ Rest of the world

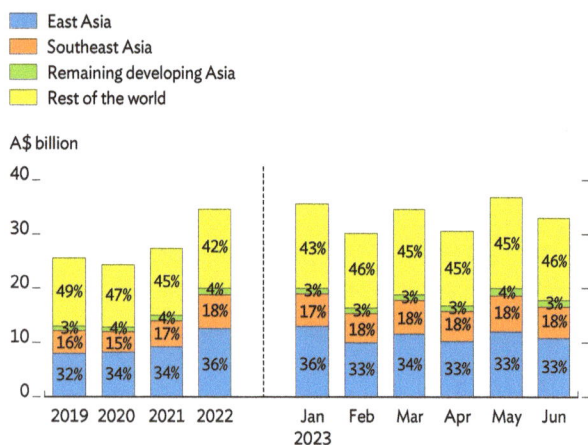

Note: For 2019 to 2022, average of monthly imports; data labels are shares to total.
Source: CEIC Data Company.

Economic growth is expected to decelerate this year and next. Elevated inflation, high interest rates, and declining savings will curtail private consumption. But a strong labor market and global demand for commodities will support the economy. Economic developments in the PRC are key to this outlook. Consensus Forecasts, as of 21 August, had GDP growing by 1.5% in 2023 and 1.3% in 2024.

New Zealand

With the economy entering a technical recession, the central bank has signaled that interest rates may have peaked. GDP contracted again in Q1 2023, albeit at a lower rate of −0.7 pps compared to −3.7 pps in the previous quarter. Consumption and fixed investment recovered on inventory drawdowns. Exports shrank faster than imports. Retail sales continued to grow in Q2, although at a slower pace than in the previous quarter. Consumer and business confidence indices improved in Q2, but were still below the threshold indicating pessimism. On the plus side, short-term visitor arrivals continued to increase and at a fast rate, shoring up demand for services. The inflation rate declined to 6.0% in Q2 from 6.7% in Q1, the steepest decline since the 2022's peak. The Monetary Policy Committee, at its 16 August meeting, kept the official cash rate at 5.5%.

This was the second hold decision since the start of the hiking cycle in 2021, and the record of the meeting states that interest rates must stay at a restrictive level for the near future.

A welcome return of migrants and tourists will smooth New Zealand's recovery and spill over to other Pacific economies. The increase in inward migration, which is now above pre-pandemic levels, is helping to relieve labor shortages (Figure A.11). The increase in migrants from developing Asia could boost remittances to the region. This will be particularly important for Pacific island small states, where remittances accounted for 10.2% of GDP in 2021. The economy is expected to expand at a slower rate in 2023. High interest rates and a weak real estate market will continue dampening domestic demand. However, positive developments in tourism will sustain the economy. A continued softening of global demand and lower economic growth in the PRC are downside risks to the outlook. Consensus Forecasts, as of 21 August, had GDP growing by 0.6 % in 2023 and 1.3% in 2024.

Figure A.11 Migrant Population, New Zealand

Strong return of inward migration since border reopening.

■ South Asia
■ Southeast Asia
■ East Asia
■ The Pacific
■ Rest of the world

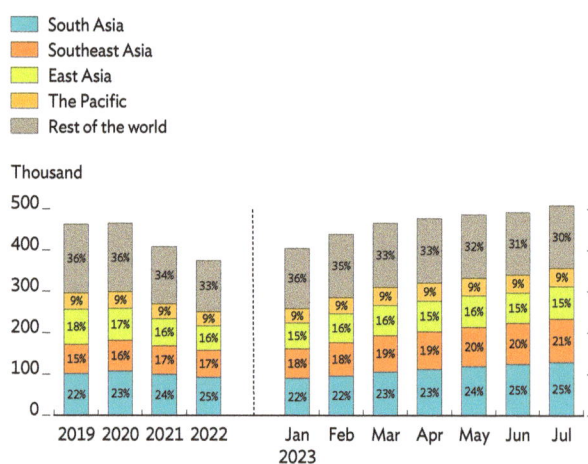

Notes: 2019 to 2022 are average of monthly population. Data labels are shares to total.
Source: Ministry of Business, Innovation & Employment.

Russian Federation

The economy showed more resilience than expected from the repercussions of the invasion of Ukraine. GDP likely rebounded in Q2, as suggested by high-frequency data, after contracting by 1.8% in Q1. Monthly GDP expanded by 4.4% on average in April and May. Supportive fiscal and monetary policies boosted domestic demand through expanded arms procurement, improved import substitution, and stronger credit growth. Private spending also likely strengthened in Q2 on buoyant retail sales, positive wage growth, and record-low unemployment.

Inflation is rising and medium-term inflation risks loom. Headline inflation in June accelerated to 3.3% from 2.5% in May on higher food and nonfood prices. Services inflation remains double-digit. The Central Bank of the Russian Federation, at an unscheduled meeting on 15 August, hiked its key policy rate by 350 bps to 12%. This follows a 100 bps increase at its 21 July meeting. This hawkish monetary policy stance reflects high inflationary pressures due to a weakening ruble, import restrictions imposed by third countries, deteriorating public finances, resilient consumer demand, and a tight labor market. As a result, inflation expectations remained elevated at the start of Q3.

Redirected oil exports from the European Union (EU) to Asia, coupled with resilient domestic demand, brighten the economic outlook. The economy is expected to grow modestly in 2023 despite international sanctions and sustained political and economic isolation. The government announced in February that it will cut oil output by 500,000 barrels per day from March in response to the EU's embargo and the EU and G7 oil price cap. With official data on oil production and exports no longer published, there is no clarity on compliance with these actions, and estimates by the International Energy Agency indicate the cuts have so far fallen short of the target. Bloomberg data show that exports of crude and refined oil have remained robust, driven by effective redirection from the EU to India and the PRC (Figure A.12). Overall, the sharp drop in oil exports, which had been expected to hurt growth this year, is unlikely to happen. As of 14 August, just before the emergency meeting of the central bank, Consensus Forecasts had GDP growing by 1.0% in 2023 and expanding by 1.2% in 2024.

Figure A.12 Monthly Deliveries of Russian Oil by Region

The Russian Federation redirected its crude and oil products exports from the EU to India and the PRC.

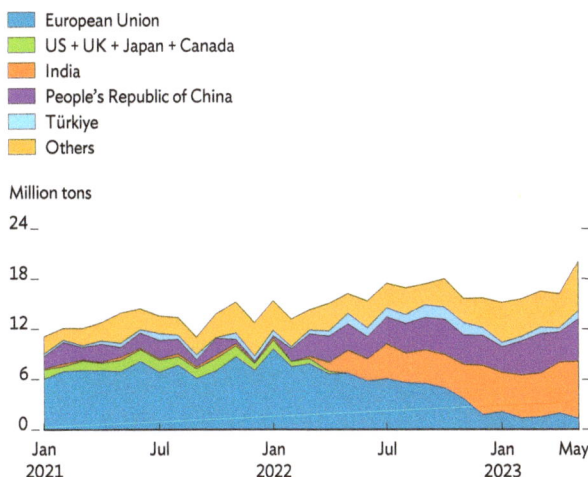

EU = European Union, PRC = People's Republic of China, UK = United Kingdom, US = United States.
Source: Bruegel. Russian Crude Oil Tracker.

Key risks include macroeconomic instability from currency fall and higher inflation and interest rates, further tightening of international sanctions, and domestic political instability.

Oil Prices

Brent crude oil prices increased in August, averaging $86.16 per barrel, a 7.6% increase over the previous month's average. Crude oil prices rose following the start of Saudi Arabia's voluntary cut of 1 million barrels per day in July and its announcement of the cuts continuing until August (Figure A.13). Prices were also supported by the Russian Federation reducing its oil exports by 500,000 barrels per day starting August. The weaker US dollar is also supporting crude oil prices, which is boosting oil demand. Brent crude prices at $88.42 on 9 August were the highest since 1 December 2022. However, persistent fears of a global economic slowdown kept these price rises in check. Brent crude prices hovered around $86 per barrel in August, about $12 less than in the same month last year.

Figure A.13 Brent Crude Spot Price

Brent crude oil prices rise on tightening supplies.

$/barrel

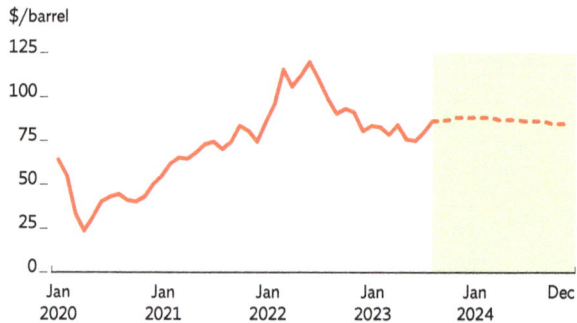

Source: Bloomberg.

Global oil demand growth will be lower than expected earlier, but supply will increase despite production curbs by the Organization of the Petroleum Exporting Countries Plus (OPEC+). The International Energy Agency in July cut its forecast for growth in 2023's global oil consumption to 2.2 million barrels a day (mb/d) from an earlier projection of 2.4 mb/d due to "persistent macroeconomic headwinds, apparent in a deepening manufacturing slump."

For 2024, the International Energy Agency forecasts growth declining to 1 mb/d as the global recovery slows and as the increased electrification of vehicle fleets and greater energy efficiency take hold. The agency forecasts global output rising by 1.5 mb/d to 101.5 mb/d in 2023 as non-OPEC+ output rises by 1.9 mb/d. For 2024, output is forecast rising by 1.3 mb/d to a new high of 102.9 mb/d, with non-OPEC+ accounting for the entire increase.

Oil price indicators signal high prices for the rest of the year and into 2024. Brent crude averaged $80.56 for the first 8 months of 2023. By 24 July, spot prices had surpassed their 200-day moving average, signaling an uptrend, while another indicator, the crack spread, reached a 4-month high, encouraging refiners to buy more oil and refine it into gasoline and distillates. Although crude oil's price increase faltered in the second half of August due to the worsening economic outlook for the PRC, persisting concerns about further monetary tightening in the US, and the strengthening of the dollar, Brent is forecast to remain above $80/barrel for the rest of the year and into 2024, based on expectations of continued tightness in global oil markets.

2

ECONOMIC TRENDS AND PROSPECTS IN DEVELOPING ASIA

CAUCASUS AND CENTRAL ASIA

Economic activity remained strong in the first half (H1) of 2023, driven by domestic demand, though growth slowed in every country except Kazakhstan and Tajikistan, compared to H1 2022. Inflation accelerated in Kazakhstan but slowed in the other seven countries as import prices stabilized, allowing some easing of monetary policy. The outlook remains dependent on external factors, including growth in key trade partners, oil prices, the pace of remittances and private transfers, and inflows of tourists and migrants from the Russian Federation.

Subregional Assessment and Prospects

Subregional growth is projected to fall from 5.1% in 2022 to 4.6% in 2023 and then inch up to 4.7% in 2024. Compared with projections in *Asian Development Outlook April 2023 (ADO April 2023)*, the forecast for average annual growth has been upgraded by 0.2 percentage points for 2023 and by 0.1 percentage points for 2024, reflecting a better outlook in several economies than earlier expected (Figure 2.1.1). The upward revision accommodates domestic demand that beat expectations in Armenia, Georgia, Kazakhstan, Tajikistan, and Uzbekistan. It reflects robust tourism and migrant flows from the Russian Federation, which continue to fuel consumption in Armenia and Georgia; fiscal stimulus in Kazakhstan and Uzbekistan; monetary policy easing in Armenia, Georgia, and Tajikistan; and higher inward money transfers in Georgia and Tajikistan. Growth forecasts have been trimmed for Azerbaijan, where lower oil production weighs on the outlook, the Kyrgyz Republic amid a slowdown in gold production, and for Turkmenistan.

Kazakhstan, the largest economy in the subregion, remained resilient in H1 2023. Economic growth was driven by expansionary fiscal policy, higher oil production, and a robust economy outside of the

Figure 2.1.1 GDP Growth in the Caucasus and Central Asia

Strong growth during the first half of 2023 in a majority of countries prompt an upward revision in growth forecasts.

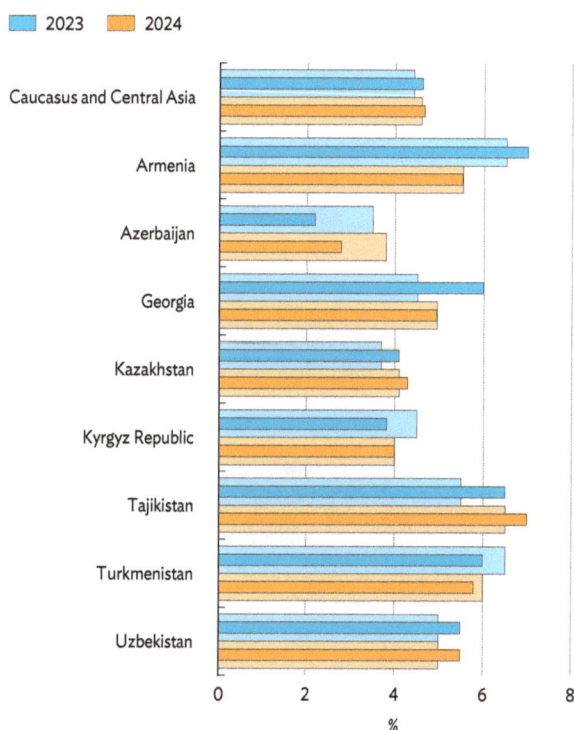

GDP = gross domestic product.
Note: Lighter colored bars are *Asian Development Outlook April 2023* forecasts.
Source: *Asian Development Outlook* database.

The subregional assessment and prospects were written by Lilia Aleksanyan. Kazakhstan was written by Genadiy Rau, and the other economies by Muhammadi Boboev, Begzod Djalilov, Grigor Gyurjyan, Jennet Hojanazarova, Gulnur Kerimkulova, George Luarsabishvili, and Nail Valiyev; and Shuhrat Mirzoev, consultant. All authors are in the Central and West Asia Department.

large petroleum industry. Oil production expanded but still remained below Kazakhstan's voluntary quota agreed with the Organization of the Petroleum Exporting Countries (OPEC). Beyond oil, construction grew by double digits in H1 2023, driven by programs to modernize state infrastructure and support housing, while services accelerated in line with increased private and public consumption. Elsewhere, in Azerbaijan, a steady decline in oil production in H1 2023 trimmed the growth outlook despite robust gas exports. In Armenia, growth led in 2022 by expansion in construction and services continued at a slightly reduced pace in H1 2023. Tourism, consumption, and investment remained strong drivers of growth despite declining net inflow of money transfers from the Russian Federation. Georgia's economy also continued to perform well in H1 2023, helped by expansion in construction and services, steady tourism revenue, trade, and continuing financial inflows from Russian migrants, which have strengthened the Georgian lari. In the Kyrgyz Republic, a drop in gold production in H1 2023 trimmed growth, while in Tajikistan a surge in remittances from a rising number of migrant workers helped sustain unexpectedly strong growth. In Uzbekistan, growth in H1 2023 was higher than anticipated because of continued fiscal support, resilient trade, strong expansion in industry including mining, and robust investment. Consumption, meanwhile, was slowed by persistent double-digit inflation. In Turkmenistan, elevated inflation in H1 2023 continued to hold down real incomes and private consumption, prompting slightly lower growth forecasts.

Subregional inflation is expected to decelerate from 12.9% in 2022 to 10.6% in 2023 and further to 8.0% in 2024. This is a slight upward revision of 0.3 percentage points for the 2023 forecast and 0.5 points for 2024 (Figure 2.1.2). It reflects higher inflation forecasts in Azerbaijan and Kazakhstan for both 2023 and 2024. In Kazakhstan, inflation accelerated—despite some appreciation of the Kazakhstan tenge and the central bank's maintenance of a high policy interest rate—to reach an average of 17.2% year on year in the first 7 months of 2023. With an expected rise in domestic fuel and utility tariffs, more robust economic activity, and higher government spending under a revised budget, average annual inflation is expected to slow to 12.7% in 2023, not 11.8% as forecast in *ADO April 2023*,

Figure 2.1.2 Inflation in the Caucasus and Central Asia

Higher inflation in Azerbaijan and Kazakhstan prompt higher average projected inflation for the subregion.

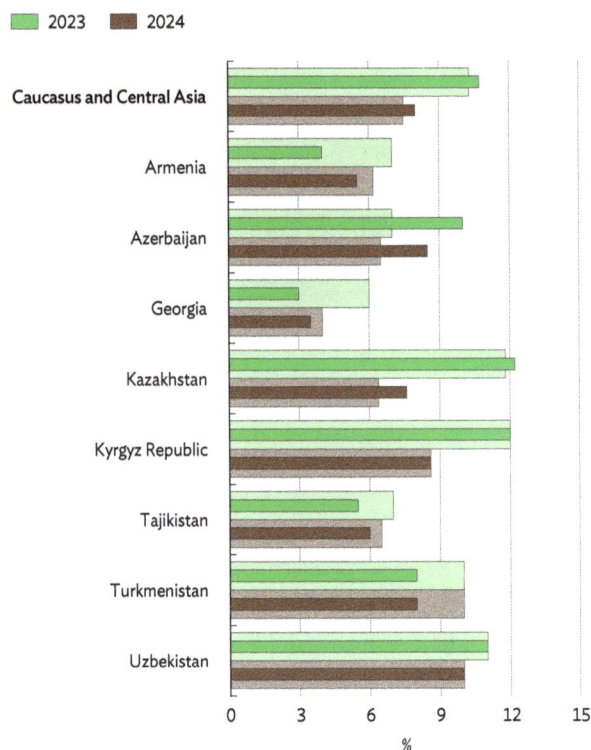

Note: Lighter colored bars are *Asian Development Outlook April 2023* forecasts.
Source: *Asian Development Outlook* database.

and to 7.6% in 2024, not 6.4% as forecast in *ADO April 2023*. In Armenia, Georgia, and Tajikistan, inflationary pressures eased faster than expected in the first 7 months of 2023, prompting downward revisions to inflation forecasts for 2023 and 2024. In Armenia, average annual inflation slowed from 8.3% to 3.6% in line with lower global commodity prices and tight monetary policy. In Georgia, average annual inflation slowed from 12.9% to 4.0%, reflecting a high base, lower commodity prices, and a stronger lari. In Tajikistan, inflation decelerated considerably, from 7.0% in H1 2022 to 3.0% a year later. In response to weaker inflation, the central banks of all three countries recently cut policy rates, with Armenia and Georgia relaxing tight monetary policy for the first time since 2020. In Turkmenistan, a slowdown in price inflation for imports, continued restrictive monetary policy, and price controls are expected to ease inflation more quickly than foreseen in April.

In the Kyrgyz Republic and Uzbekistan, inflation forecasts remained unchanged. In Uzbekistan, inflation accelerated from 10.6% in H1 2022 to 11.0% in H1 2023 on higher wages and pensions and will remain elevated throughout the year with expected hikes in energy tariffs. In the Kyrgyz Republic, inflation decelerated slightly from 13.0% in the first 7 months of 2022 to 12.4% a year later, but an electricity tariff hike and expansionary fiscal policy kept it above the central bank target.

External account developments in the region have been dominated by oil production and prices, exports, and money transfers. Despite moderately rising oil production, lower oil prices will further weaken the current account balance in Kazakhstan, which is likely to revert to deficit at the end of the year, but not in Azerbaijan, where oil prices, though declining, are still high enough to keep the current account in surplus. As Armenia and Georgia see money transfers and trade in services normalize, their current account deficits will likely widen, as in Uzbekistan with declining remittances. In Tajikistan, by contrast, continued strong remittances will help narrow the current account deficit. Despite the Kyrgyz Republic's resumption of gold exports, the current account will remain in substantial deficit as imports surge.

Risks to the outlook remain largely on the downside. Uncertainty and risks to the subregional outlook remain high, notably spillover from a slowdown in Russian economic growth and a further decline in oil prices. Any economic contraction in the Russian Federation in 2023 or 2024 would significantly affect the outlook across the Caucasus and Central Asia, but particularly for countries that depend heavily on migrant remittances. Oil market developments, including price changes and OPEC-mediated production curbs, will weigh on economic activity in oil exporters, with spillover effects on the rest of the region. Disruption to core Caspian Pipeline Consortium infrastructure could affect exports and growth in Kazakhstan.

Kazakhstan

Economic growth accelerated in the first half (H1) of 2023, supported by expansionary fiscal policy and strong global demand for commodities. Because higher spending on infrastructure modernization and social programs lifted consumption and investment more than anticipated, this update revises growth forecasts in both 2023 and 2024. Meanwhile, government-approved petroleum and utility price increases indicate more persistent inflation than projected in *ADO April 2023*.

Updated Assessment

Procyclical fiscal policy supported economic expansion. GDP growth accelerated from 3.6% year on year in H1 2022 to 5.1% a year later (Figure 2.1.3), reflecting higher mineral extraction and increased outlays for infrastructure and social protection financed by export revenue and higher transfers from the National Fund for the Republic of Kazakhstan (NFRK), the sovereign wealth fund. Growth in services rose from 2.6% to 4.9%, driven primarily by increases of 10.4% in wholesale and retail trade, 8.8% in communication, and 7.4% in transport, these gains reflecting low bases as curfews and lockdowns kept activity low in H1 2022. Mining growth similarly rose from 1.9% to 3.7%, with output increasing by 5.6% for oil, 2.5% for gas, and 17.4% for other minerals.

Figure 2.1.3 Supply-Side Contributions to Growth

Growth in the first half of 2023 was higher than a year earlier.

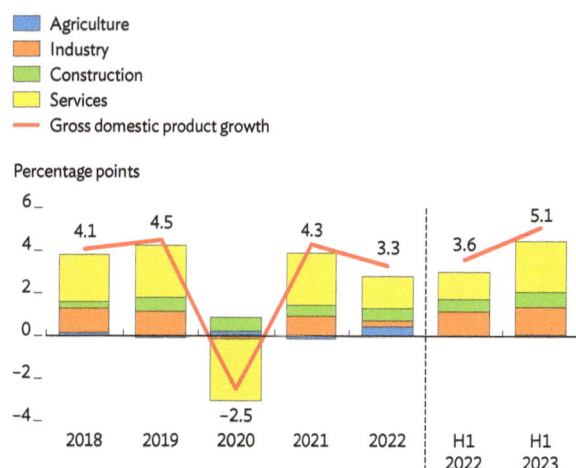

Source: Republic of Kazakhstan. Agency for Strategic Planning and Reforms. Bureau of National Statistics.

Oil production cuts voluntarily agreed with the Organization of the Petroleum Exporting Countries (OPEC) in April did not affect Kazakhstan, which has been increasing oil production since March 2022 while remaining below its quota. Expansion in manufacturing still benefited from firms relocating from the Russian Federation but slowed from 5.8% year on year in H1 2022 to 3.5%. Growth in construction accelerated from 9.2% to 12.3%, strongly supported by state programs to modernize infrastructure and support housing. In March 2023, the government allocated a further $320 million to modernize the country's aging heating supply infrastructure before next winter. Agriculture expanded moderately, as expected, with growth up from 1.4% year on year in H1 2022 to 3.2%.

Higher consumption and investment offset a decline in net exports. Demand-side data, available only for the first quarter of 2023, show consumption reversing 1.9% contraction year on year in the first quarter to grow by 9.5% as private consumption grew by 9.8% and public consumption by 8.4%. Strong infrastructure and housing support boosted overall investment by 29.8%. However, net exports declined as growth in imports of goods and services rose by 31.9% and exports by only 4.0%.

High inflation prompted the National Bank of Kazakhstan, the central bank, to revise its inflation target. Average inflation accelerated from 12.3% in the first 7 months of 2022 to 17.2% a year later, reflecting price increases of 19.0% for food, 17.8% for other goods, and 13.9% for services (Figure 2.1.4). The government approved increases in state-regulated prices of 7.0% for regular gasoline and 15.6% for utilities. A July 2023 survey commissioned by the central bank found respondents expecting, on average, annual inflation to reach 16.9%. The central bank reset its inflation target to 5% in the medium term, phasing out its earlier inflation corridor of 4%–5% for 2023–2024. At the same time, it forecast inflation at 11%–14% in 2023 and 9%–11% in 2024, eventually falling to the targeted 5% after 2025.

Monetary policy remained tight and the exchange rate stable. After raising the key policy rate several times in 2022, the central bank kept it unchanged at 16.75% in H1 2023. The Kazakhstan tenge fluctuated mildly and gradually appreciated by 1.8% against the US dollar in the period (Figure 2.1.5), with no central bank interventions reported since May 2022.

Figure 2.1.4 Average Inflation

Inflation accelerated sharply in the first half of 2023.

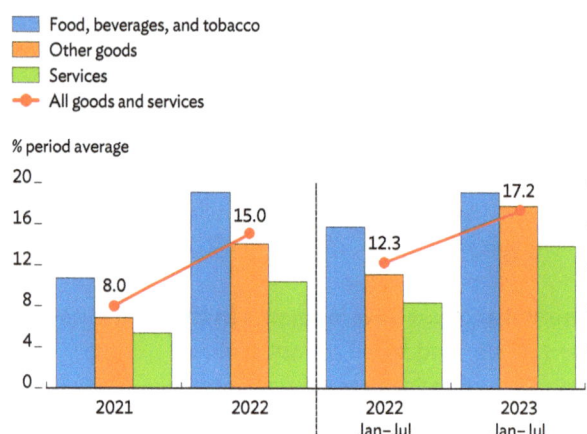

Source: Republic of Kazakhstan. Agency for Strategic Planning and Reforms. Bureau of National Statistics.

Figure 2.1.5 Exchange Rate

The Kazakhstan tenge has been far more stable against the US dollar this year, gradually appreciating to July 2023.

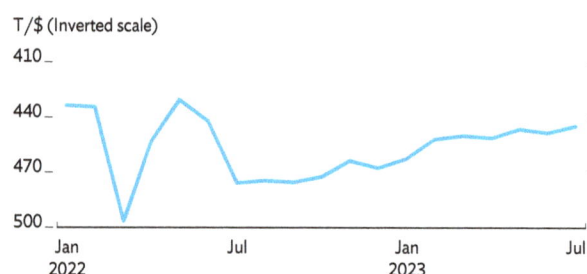

US = United States.

Source: Republic of Kazakhstan. Agency for Strategic Planning and Reforms. Bureau of National Statistics.

During H1 2023, the central bank converted $3.5 billion of NFRK foreign exchange receipts to tenge before transferring them to the state budget. In July 2023, the government reduced the mandatory sale of foreign exchange earnings from 50% of state enterprise earnings to 30%. Following a 13.9% surge in broad money supply over the full year 2022, it expanded by only 1.2% in H1 2023. In the period, deposits grew by 2.8%, and credit by 5.9%, with lending increases of 2.2% to firms, 5.7% for mortgages, and 10.1% for other consumer credit. Foreign currency deposits declined by 13.1% to account for 25.6% of all deposits, while deposits in tenge rose by 9.7%. The share of nonperforming loans increased slightly, from 3.4% at the end of 2022 to 3.6% in June 2023.

State budget dependence on transfers and borrowing persisted. In H1 2023, state budget expenditure was 26.7% higher than in the same period of 2022 (Figure 2.1.6). Government spending rose by 25.8% for education, 28.1% for social services, and 15.2% for health care, such that social expenditure constituted more than half of the budget outlays, even as expenditure on construction and energy infrastructure almost doubled from a low base. In the first 6 months of 2023, tax revenue grew by 25.5% on increases of 41.8% from value-added tax, 27.2% from personal income tax, and 21.0% from corporate tax. Yet the budget remained vulnerable to volatile extractive industry revenue and took a hit as oil export duty receipts declined in H1 2023 by 14.4% because of lower average oil prices on the global market. The higher expenditures are financed by an additional $1.7 billion in NFRK transfers approved in March 2023 and a 68.6% rise in borrowing for the year.

However, NFRK assets increased to an estimated $59.8 billion as budget transfers were 11.0% lower than in the same period last year. By the end of March 2023, nominal external debt had risen to $161.4 billion, equal to 69.4% of GDP. Intercompany debt, primarily for oil and gas projects, had declined to $92.8 billion, or 39.9% of GDP (Figure 2.1.8), with $16.6 billion coming due in 2023. Public sector external debt declined to $30.7 billion, or 13.2% of GDP, with $3.6 billion due this year.

Figure 2.1.6 Fiscal Indicators

Both revenue and expenditure increased in the first half of 2023.

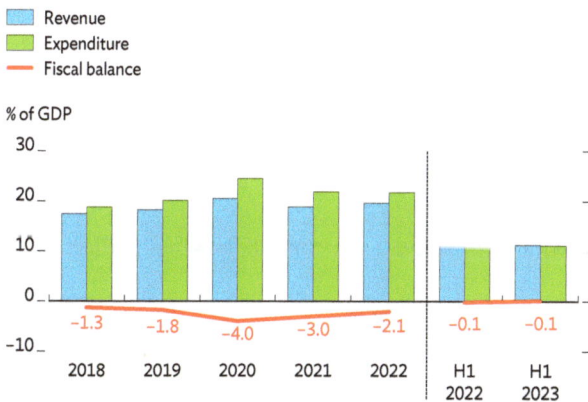

GDP = gross domestic product, H1 = first half.
Source: Republic of Kazakhstan. Agency for Strategic Planning and Reforms. Bureau of National Statistics.

External debt as a share of GDP fell to a decade low. Gross foreign exchange reserves declined by 1.8% to $34.4 billion in June 2023 (Figure 2.1.7), of which 55.7% were in monetary gold. Reserves provided cover for 6.2 months of imports of goods and services. In H1 2023, receipts to the NFRK declined by 28.1% from the same period in 2022 as tax payments from oil companies slid in line with lower oil prices.

Figure 2.1.7 Foreign Currency Reserves and Sovereign Wealth Fund Assets

Gross reserves declined from January to July 2023, while sovereign wealth fund assets increased.

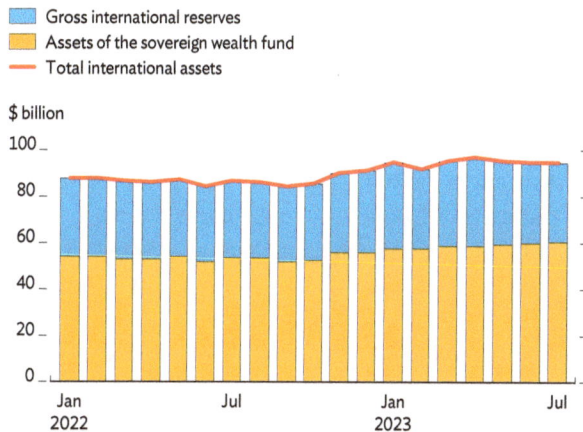

Source: National Bank of the Republic of Kazakhstan.

Figure 2.1.8 External Debt and Intercompany Debt

External and intercompany debt declined in tandem.

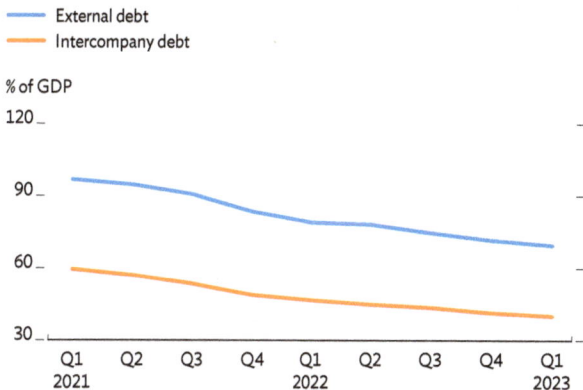

GDP = gross domestic product, Q = quarter.
Source: National Bank of the Republic of Kazakhstan.

The current account reverted to a deficit.
Preliminary estimates for H1 2023 indicate a
current account deficit of $3.6 billion, equal to 1.4%
of GDP, as the trade surplus in goods fell by half.
Despite moderately rising oil production, merchandise
exports declined by 10.6% to $38.5 billion, reflecting
a 25% decline in Brent oil prices. Merchandise imports
grew by 32.1% to $28.7 billion on higher imports of
footwear, textiles, and leather goods. Lower export
earnings reduced foreign investors' profits by 6.8% to
$12.0 billion.

Prospects

Rising incomes will boost consumption. On the
demand side, consumption is now projected to expand
by 3.9% in 2023, revised up from 1.6% in *ADO April
2023*, and by 3.6% in 2024. This trend reflects nominal
household income rising by 17.1% year on year in
the second quarter of 2023 and higher government
expenditure. Increased government investment in
infrastructure modernization will boost gross capital
formation by 9.1% in 2023. Lower prices for major
export commodities and rising imports will drive down
net exports.

**Services and industry will lead broad-based growth
on the supply side.** The forecast for growth in services
this year is revised up from 3.3% in *ADO April 2023*
to 4.2% on anticipated expansion in trade, transport,
and communications. Government efforts to attract
foreign direct investment in mining and manufacturing
are expected to increase local production, while the
government's continuing programs to support housing
and modernize infrastructure will boost construction.
However, escalating trade and investment sanctions
on the Russian Federation, a main trade partner,
pose downside risks to the outlook (Table 2.1.1 and
Figure 2.1.9).

**Inflation will diminish gradually but remain above
the central bank target.** Government-approved hikes
in petroleum prices and utility tariffs have raised the
cost of producing and transporting goods. In addition,
procyclical fiscal policy has adding to inflationary
pressure despite continued tight monetary policy.
This update therefore raises inflation projections
for both 2023 and 2024, but still on an easing trend
(Figure 2.1.10).

**Table 2.1.1 Selected Economic Indicators
in Kazakhstan, %**

*Procyclical fiscal policy supports higher forecasts for growth, and
higher utility and petroleum prices indicate more persistent inflation.*

	2022	2023		2024	
		Apr	Sep	Apr	Sep
GDP growth	3.2	3.7	4.1	4.1	4.3
Inflation	15.0	11.8	12.7	6.4	7.6

GDP = gross domestic product.
Source: Asian Development Bank estimates.

Figure 2.1.9 GDP Growth

Procyclical fiscal policy supports higher forecasts for growth.

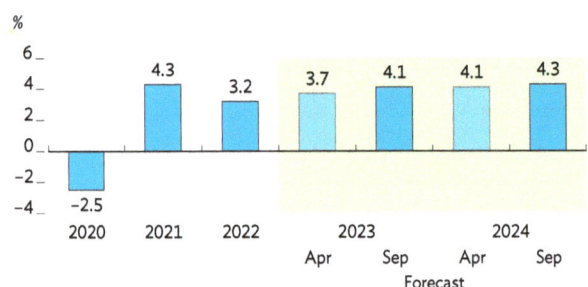

GDP = gross domestic product.
Source: *Asian Development Outlook* database.

Figure 2.1.10 Inflation

Higher utility and petroleum prices indicate more persistent inflation.

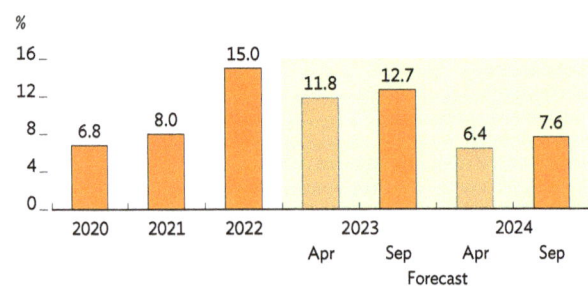

Source: *Asian Development Outlook* database.

**Higher expenditure will outpace growth in tax
revenue.** March 2023 amendments to the state budget
increased state budget expenditure from 21.3% of GDP
this year, as projected in *ADO April 2023*, to 23.0%.
The revenue forecast is also raised, from 18.7% of GDP
to 20.0%, reflecting higher projected tax revenue and a
decision to boost transfers from the NFRK by a quarter.

The 2023 budget deficit will remain equal to 3.0% of GDP as the non-oil deficit rises from 7.2% of GDP to 7.8%. Government and government-guaranteed debt will remain at about 25% of GDP in the forecast period.

The current account will return to deficit. The merchandise trade surplus will fall by a third in 2023 in tandem with lower commodity prices before rebounding in 2024. The service deficit will gradually deepen despite higher earnings from cargo transit, while the primary income deficit will fluctuate along with petroleum earnings.

Strong export earnings will facilitate debt repayment and increase reserves. Despite higher transfers to the budget, NFRK assets at the end of 2023 will exceed the $58.0 billion forecast in *ADO April 2023* to reach $59.0 billion, equal to 26.3% of GDP. Similarly, higher oil prices and production are projected to push assets by the end of 2024 past the earlier forecast of $60.0 billion to $62.0 billion. Projections for gross international reserves are revised down to $34.5 billion at the end of 2023, providing cover for 6.2 months of imports of goods and services, and $36.4 billion at the end of 2024. Assuming continued exchange rate stability, and that oil and mining companies use windfall profits to repay intercompany debt, external debt including intercompany debt is now forecast lower, falling from the equivalent of 69% of GDP at the end of 2023 to 67% a year later, both projections 5 percentage points lower than forecast in April.

Other Economies

Armenia

Growth moderated slightly but remained in double digits. It slowed from 11.1% in the first half (H1) of 2022 to 10.5% in H1 2023, buoyed by still-robust domestic demand. On the supply side, growth in services moderated from 14.9% to 14.2% as rapid gains in a few components—notably information technology at 63.1%, trade at 22.8%, and real estate at 10.4%—were offset by slower growth or declines in other services. Industry excluding construction grew by a mere 0.3% as gains in manufacturing and utilities marginally outweighed a 3.0% decline in mining and quarrying. Construction grew by 19.2% on higher private construction and public investment for roads and social infrastructure. Agriculture contracted by 0.2% as lower livestock output offset gains in crop production. On the demand side, growth in private consumption slowed from 10.3% to 6.7% as net money transfer inflow decreased, and despite lower inflation. Public consumption reversed a 2.6% decline in H1 2022 to grow by 16.1% on public salary increases in January 2023 and higher social spending. Gross fixed capital formation improved on 17.7% growth in H1 2022 with 20.1% a year later, reflecting higher public and private investment. With still-robust expansion in H1 2023 and continued higher spending and investment, both public and private, this update raises the growth forecast for 2023 (Table 2.1.2). It maintains the forecast for 2024, assuming some moderation in domestic and external demand.

Table 2.1.2 Selected Economic Indicators in Armenia, %

Robust growth in the first half of 2023 and heavy investment spending prompt a higher growth projection for 2023, while sharply slower inflation supports lower inflation forecasts for 2023 and 2024.

	2022	2023		2024	
		Apr	Sep	Apr	Sep
GDP growth	12.6	6.5	7.0	5.5	5.5
Inflation	8.6	7.0	4.0	6.2	5.5

GDP = gross domestic product.
Sources: Asian Development Bank estimates.

Inflation fell sharply despite strong aggregate demand. Average annual inflation slowed from 8.3% in the first 7 months of 2022 to 3.6% a year later, in line with waning impact from exogenous shocks last year. Prices rose by 2.6% for food and 2.8% for other goods, offsetting a 5.4% increase for services. Despite buoyant aggregate demand, falling prices for goods—in particular lower import prices with a relatively stable exchange rate—brought deflation at 0.1% month on month in July 2023. With annualized inflation below the 2.5%–5.5% target based on month-to-month data, the Central Bank of Armenia lowered its refinancing rate by a cumulative 50 basis points in two steps in June and August 2023 to 10.25%, the first decreases since the third quarter of 2020. As inflation slowed more than expected in H1 2023, this update reduces inflation forecasts for 2023 and 2024.

Fiscal policy continued to support domestic demand. Budget revenue grew by 18.1%, reflecting solid growth and higher tax collection. Current expenditure rose by 12.1%, primarily on higher social spending and salaries. Capital outlay grew by 18.0% but fell below the semiannual budget target by 46.7%. With the budget surplus in H1 2023 at about $350 million, equal to 2.9% of GDP, the fiscal deficit this year is now projected to be less than the planned equivalent of 3.1% of GDP.

The current account deficit widened from 6.0% of GDP in the first quarter of 2022 to 7.7% a year later. The causes were a larger trade deficit and a deeper deficit in the balance of private transfers, which more than offset a surplus in services. As a percentage of GDP, the trade deficit widened from 12.9% to 14.9% because imports grew more than exports in absolute amounts, although exports, which have been smaller than imports, grew at a slightly faster rate (98.2% versus 89.7%). Imports and exports are expected to moderate somewhat in the rest of this year, narrowing the trade deficit and the current account deficit, as higher transfers and gains from tourism, transportation, and information and communication technology offset part of the larger deficit in goods.

Azerbaijan

A continued decline in oil production cut growth. Weaker performance in hydrocarbons slashed growth from 6.2% in the first 7 months of 2022 to 0.7% a year later. Mining reversed 0.8% growth to contract by 3.4% as oil output fell by 7.7%, and despite a 3.3% rise in gas production. Manufacturing grew by 11.2%, reflecting gains in petrochemicals and food processing. Higher investment boosted growth in construction from 8.7% in the first 7 months of 2022 to 13.2%. Expansion in agriculture, driven mainly by livestock production, was unchanged at 3.3%. Growth in services slowed substantially, from 10.6% to 1.6%, as a 10.5% decline in transportation offset much of a 28.4% gain in hospitality from higher tourist inflows.

Domestic demand remained robust, supported by private and public consumption. Higher household income boosted private consumption by 5.1% in the first half of 2023, though continued double-digit inflation may curb real incomes and consumption later in the year. Public consumption accelerated on higher spending for social services and will remain robust to

the end of 2023. Investment rose by 10.4%, led by projects outside of the large hydrocarbon industry. Net exports contracted as imports outgrew exports in the first 5 months of 2023. In light of slower growth in hydrocarbons and tight monetary policy, this update forecasts a deeper slowdown in 2023 and 2024 (Table 2.1.3).

Table 2.1.3 Selected Economic Indicators in Azerbaijan, %

Continued decline in oil production prompts a projection for a deeper growth slowdown in 2023 and 2024, while unexpectedly high inflation in the first part of 2023 supports a forecast for more persistent inflation.

	2022	2023		2024	
		Apr	Sep	Apr	Sep
GDP growth	4.6	3.5	2.2	3.8	2.6
Inflation	13.9	7.0	10.0	6.5	8.5

GDP = gross domestic product.
Sources: Asian Development Bank estimates.

Inflationary pressures persist despite monetary tightening. Inflation declined from 13.0% year on year in the first 7 months of 2022 to 12.2% a year later with some moderation in food price inflation, from 18.7% to 14.3%, in line with diminishing global food prices. Inflation for other goods rose, however, from 7.0% to 11.0% and for services from 10.1% to 10.4%. With these developments, this update raises inflation projections for 2023 and 2024. To address inflation, the central bank raised the policy interest rate from 8.25% to 9.0% in three steps from January to May, and the government established a working group to monitor prices and recommend ways to curb inflation and achieve price stability.

The fiscal outlook has improved but remains dependent on oil prices. Elevated oil prices and tax collections early in 2023 boosted revenue more than expected. This prompted the government in June 2023 to raise planned 2023 expenditure by 9.2% through increased public investment and social spending. This should help sustain demand. Credit to the economy grew by 8.8% in the first 7 months of 2023, but broad money declined by 2.2% as a 28.5% drop in foreign currency deposits more than offset higher domestic currency deposits. The share of deposits in local currency rose to 64.4%.

High oil prices drove the current account to a surplus equal to 10.0% of GDP in the first quarter of 2023. However, the merchandise trade surplus declined from $5.4 billion in the first quarter of 2022 to $4.7 billion a year later as imports picked up by 40.5% and oil exports declined by 10.4%, with export volumes remaining below Azerbaijan's quota agreed with the Organization of the Petroleum Exporting Countries and other exporters (OPEC+). The current account is forecast to remain in surplus, reflecting a decision by OPEC+ to raise oil prices by tightening supply. Assets of the State Oil Fund of the Republic of Azerbaijan, the sovereign wealth fund, rose by 12.0% from the end of 2022 to $54.9 billion, while the central bank's reserves reached $9.2 billion, bringing total strategic reserves to $64.1 billion, or about twice GDP.

Georgia

Growth has moderated but remains robust, supported by tourism and financial inflows.
Growth moderated from 10.6% in the first half of 2022 to 7.6% a year later as industry contracted by 0.7% and agriculture by 2.3%, and despite strong growth in construction at 15.1% and services at 10.2%. Expansion in services reflected increases of 14.0% in wholesale and retail trade, 15.7% in accommodation and food services, 44.2% in information and communication, and 17.2% in arts, entertainment, and recreation, much of this reflecting a recovery in tourism. On the demand side, growth came from strong domestic demand, reflecting high consumer spending on goods and services, particularly by Russian migrants, and continued revival in investment and tourism. Foreign direct investment remained high at nearly $500 million in the first quarter of 2023, and the unemployment rate declined by more than 3 percentage points to 17.3%. Such encouraging figures prompt this update to raise the growth forecast for 2023 but not for 2024, in light of an expected return to growth potential and possible fallout from slowing global expansion (Table 2.1.4).

Inflation has fallen below target, helped by a relatively stable Georgian lari and prudent macroeconomic policies. With inflation year on year continuing to decline to 0.3% in July 2023, average annual inflation slowed from double digits throughout 2022 to 4.0% in 2023 to July despite increases of

Table 2.1.4 Selected Economic Indicators in Georgia, %

Strong growth and lower inflation in the first half of 2023 prompt a higher growth projection for 2023 and lower forecasts for inflation in 2023 and 2024.

	2022	2023		2024	
		Apr	Sep	Apr	Sep
GDP growth	10.1	4.5	6.0	5.0	5.0
Inflation	11.9	6.0	3.0	4.0	3.5

GDP = gross domestic product.
Source: Asian Development Bank estimates.

7.3% for food, 24.9% for rental housing, and 12.1% for hospitality. Apart from a high base in 2022, slower inflation reflected lower import prices and transport costs with increased transit volume, strong foreign currency inflow that supported the lari, continued fiscal consolidation, and tight monetary policy that kept the policy rate high at 10.25% despite a 0.25% cut in August. Core inflation—which excludes food, nonalcoholic beverages, energy, regulated tariffs, and certain transport charges—slowed from 6.9% in December 2022 to 3.2% in July 2023. The National Bank of Georgia, the central bank, increased reserves to more than $5.0 billion, which the International Monetary Fund declared adequate. With inflation decelerating, this update cuts inflation forecasts for 2023 and 2024.

A small budget surplus in the first half of 2023 reflected strong revenue and ongoing fiscal consolidation. Revenue increased by 18.4% over the first half of 2022, outpacing 15.2% growth in public expenditure that saw substantial social spending and capital outlays for priority public infrastructure. Public sector debt remained low, equal to 39.8% of GDP, as strong economic growth and a relatively stable lari boosted GDP. While three-quarters of this debt is in foreign currency, much of external debt is on concessional terms or at fixed interest rates.

The current account deficit narrowed sharply from the equivalent of 13.3% of GDP in the first quarter of 2022 to 3.2% a year later. This reflected soaring money transfers and higher service surpluses from travel and from information and communication technology. Money transfer inflows, following a record high in 2022, increased in the first 7 months of 2023 at an annual rate of 27.5% to $2.7 billion, nearly half of it coming from the Russian Federation. In the same period, merchandise exports increased by 15.7% on strong vehicle reexports, and imports rose by 19.0% on high domestic demand and a relatively stable lari against the US dollar. In the first half of 2023, revenue from tourism increased by 57.9% year on year to reach $1.8 billion. Downside risks to the current account include, aside from domestic political polarization and geopolitical risks, a possible weakening of external demand, rising global interest rates that could constrain capital inflow, and a widening investment–savings gap.

Kyrgyz Republic

A slowdown in gold production cut growth during the first 7 months of 2023. GDP growth decelerated to an estimated 2.9% during the first 7 months of 2023 from 6.4% during the same period last year as industry contracted by 2.0%. Industry contraction reflected a decline in manufacturing as the production of metals, mainly gold, reversed a 46.7% increase to fall by 11.7%, as well as smaller gains in mining and quarrying. Growth in services accelerated to 4.6%, led by strong performance in wholesale and retail trade and in food and accommodation. Expansion in construction remained robust at 11.2%, reflecting higher domestic investment. Due to unfavorable weather, agriculture contracted by 1.7%, reversing 6.4% growth during the same period last year. On the demand side, with data available from only the first quarter, growth came from higher public consumption and gross fixed capital formation. Net money transfers from abroad including remittances fell by 28.5% year on year in the first half of 2023, likely moderating private consumption. With lower-than-expected growth in the first 7 months of 2023, this update reduces projected growth for 2023 but maintains the *ADO April 2023* forecast for 2024 amid the lagged effect of expansionary fiscal policy (Table 2.1.5). Risks remain on the downside. Growth could slow with any net reversal of capital inflows, lower than projected economic growth in the Russian Federation, lower remittances, or secondary sanctions. Alternatively, the outlook could improve on continued growth in trade and demand from an influx of expatriate Russians.

Table 2.1.5 Selected Economic Indicators in the Kyrgyz Republic, %

Growth was lower than expected in the first 7 months of 2023, prompting a downward revision for 2023 projections, while forecasts of inflation remain unchanged from ADO April 2023.

	2022	2023		2024	
		Apr	Sep	Apr	Sep
GDP growth	6.3	4.5	3.8	4.0	4.0
Inflation	13.9	12.0	12.0	8.6	8.6

GDP = gross domestic product.

Note: GDP statistics were revised by the National Statistics Committee in June 2023 in line with the international standard of the System of National Accounts 2008.

Sources: National Statistics Committee of the Kyrgyz Republic; Asian Development Bank estimates.

Inflation subsided in the first 7 months of 2023 as global food and energy prices began to decline. Average annual inflation slowed from 13.0% in January–July 2022 to 12.4% a year later, decreasing from 15.2% to 11.1% for food but rising from 10.8% to 13.0% for other goods and from 8.8% to 10.5% for services. Average annual core inflation was 13.1% in January–July 2023. Factors contributing to continued inflation included expansionary fiscal policy and higher electricity tariffs and other administered prices. Inflation year on year declined from 15.3% in January 2023 to 10.3% in July 2023 but remained well above the 5%–7% target range of the National Bank of the Kyrgyz Republic, the central bank. Considering persistent uncertainty and elevated inflationary expectations, the central bank has kept its policy rate unchanged at 13.0% since the end of November 2022. To smooth volatility and avoid excessive swings in the exchange rate, the central bank sold $500.2 million in foreign exchange in January–July 2023, more than double sales in the same period of 2022. With slower growth in domestic demand expected, further depreciation of the Kyrgyz som likely, a poor harvest, and elevated core inflation, this update retains earlier forecasts for slowing but still high inflation in 2023 and 2024.

Continued strong tax collection offset the impact of slower growth and higher wage expenditure on the budget. The preliminary general government fiscal balance showed an estimated surplus equal to 1.2% of GDP in the first half of 2023, unchanged from the same period in 2022 and buoyed by energetic tax enforcement and higher value-added tax receipts from increased imports. Fiscal policy is expected to be more expansionary in the rest of this year, reflecting persistent demand for higher public expenditure alongside rising debt servicing cost, in line with expectations in *ADO April 2023*.

Data from the first quarter of 2023 show a massive current account deficit. Already large in 2022, the deficit widened to equal 45.0% of GDP as imports rose by 26.5% under supply chain restructuring in the subregion. At the same time, resumed shipments of gold concentrates boosted exports by 14.2%.

Tajikistan

Growth remains robust, only minimally disrupted by the Russian invasion of Ukraine. Economic expansion accelerated from 7.4% year on year in the first half (H1) of 2022 to 8.3% in H1 2023 as industry and services rebounded, and on sizable remittances from migrant workers in high demand in the Russian Federation. Industry surged by 24.4% on gains in electrical supply and manufacturing, in particular food processing, textiles, and clothing. Expansion in agriculture increased from 6.0% to 7.9% after good weather allowed spring crops to be sown early. Growth in services slowed from 12.8% year on year in H1 2022 to 5.5% a year later with lower growth in transportation, communication, and financial services, and despite large gains in wholesale and retail trade and hospitality services.

Growth has been supported by higher public and private investment. The average inflation-adjusted salary increase accelerated from 2.8% year on year in H1 2022 to 11.8% in H1 2023. Moreover, in March 2023 the government boosted salaries by 20%–25% for military and law enforcement personnel, followed by a 20% rise in July of base pensions and other social benefits—all of which lifted private consumption. Gross investment grew by 27.1% year on year during the first 6 months of 2023. With strong growth reported in H1 2023, this update raises growth projections for 2023 and 2024 (Table 2.1.6).

Inflation has decreased considerably. Inflation dropped sharply from 8.3% year on year in June 2022 to 2.4% in June 2023 as average inflation year on year fell from 7.0% in H1 2022 to 3.0%.

Table 2.1.6 Selected Economic Indicators in Tajikistan, %

Rapid growth in the first half of 2023 prompts upward revisions to projected growth in 2023 and 2024, while falling inflation supports lower inflation projections for both years, with both indicators still deteriorating somewhat from 2022.

	2022	2023		2024	
		Apr	Sep	Apr	Sep
GDP growth	8.0	5.5	6.5	6.5	7.0
Inflation	4.2	7.0	5.5	6.5	6.0

GDP = gross domestic product.
Source: Asian Development Bank estimates.

Food price inflation rose slightly from 2.3% to 2.9% as prices for other goods rose by 2.3%. For services, 1.1% inflation reversed to 0.4% deflation, with planned utility tariff increases postponed to H2 2023. Inflation subdued, the National Bank of Tajikistan, the central bank, lowered its policy rate from 13.0% to 11.0% in February 2023 and to 10.0% in May, partly to boost investment and domestic spending. The Tajik somoni depreciated by 7.0% against the US dollar in H1 2023 but appreciated by 11.4% against the Russian ruble. In view of these developments, and despite upcoming utility tariff increases, this update reduces inflation projections for 2023 and 2024.

Higher revenue and a tight fiscal stance have improved the fiscal outlook. Following a small deficit last year, the government kept the deficit below the equivalent of 0.5% of GDP in H1 2023. Though a new tax code initially reduced revenue in 2022, tax revenue in H1 2023 exceeded original projections by 7.3% to reach 22.5% of GDP. Collection of many major taxes outpaced original projections, with corporate income up by 12.3% from H1 2022, value added by 6.5%, property by 9%, and excise by 32.6%. Expenditure was $1.7 billion in H1 2023, 10.1% shy of the original budget allocation and reflecting a tight fiscal stance. Public debt was $3.6 billion at the end of June 2023, having fallen from the equivalent of 34.8% of GDP at the end of 2022 to 31.1%.

Strong remittances narrowed the current account deficit. The merchandise trade deficit in H1 2023 nearly doubled year on year as exports declined by 44.2% to $0.7 billion while imports rose by 19.1% to $2.7 billion. However, remittances were strong enough to narrow the current account deficit by 28.7%, from 12.4% of GDP in H1 2022 to 7.8% in H1 2023. Gross international reserves rose from $2.5 billion to $3.8 billion, providing cover for 9 months of imports of goods and services.

Turkmenistan

The government reported growth at 6.2% in the first half of 2023, slightly above 6.0% reported a year earlier. On the supply side, growth came from all sectors. Expansion in the large hydrocarbon economy came mainly from reportedly higher production and exports of natural gas, while the economy excluding gas and oil benefited from growth in construction, wholesale and retail trade, transport, and catering. As reported by the government, industry performance aside from hydrocarbons and construction reflected stable output in electricity, chemicals, textiles, food processing, and other agro-industrial products. Private firms engaged in import-substitution programs continued to receive substantial government support. According to half-year reports, strategic crops of cotton and wheat, as well as a large variety of horticultural produce, have been sown with the aim of meeting annual production targets. On the demand side, the government reported higher net exports and public investment in industrial and social infrastructure. At the same time, elevated inflation and constraints on employment continued to hold down real incomes and private consumption. With limited availability of official statistics and continued uncertainty about growth data, the update revises the growth projection for 2023 to align with the official forecast and maintains the projection for 2024 (Table 2.1.7).

Table 2.1.7 Selected Economic Indicators in Turkmenistan, %

The growth forecast for 2023 is revised down to align with government projections, and inflation is now forecast to be slower than in 2022.

	2022	2023		2024	
		Apr	Sep	Apr	Sep
GDP growth	6.2	6.5	6.2	6.0	6.0
Inflation	10.0	10.0	8.0	10.0	8.0

GDP = gross domestic product.
Source: Asian Development Bank estimates.

Import price inflation appears to have stabilized. Observed prices for imported goods and for locally produced goods with imported components appear to have stabilized as of mid-2023. They remain high, however, and could rise further. Monetary policy remains focused on controlling inflation by sustaining the official exchange rate and price controls for certain goods and services. Access to foreign currency remains limited to priority firms in import substitution and export promotion, and a substantial difference persists between official and parallel market exchange rates. In view of these developments, this update slightly reduces inflation forecasts for 2023 and 2024.

The fiscal outlook remains dependent on revenue from hydrocarbon exports. The government aims to keep the state budget balanced in 2023 and 2024, benefiting from the positive outlook for energy exports. However, any assessment of the overall fiscal position is complicated by a lack of data and rising capital expenditure on government construction projects using extra-budgetary funds.

Growth in gas exports to the People's Republic of China in the first half of 2023 is estimated to have been stable. More generally, higher demand for gas exports to the People's Republic of China and other countries in the region may raise total exports in both 2023 and 2024, though no export data are yet available. Imports are projected to rise only slowly, held down by government import-substitution programs and capital controls. With exports currently increasing faster than imports, this update projects a higher current account surplus in 2023 but a lower surplus in 2024.

Uzbekistan

Strong expansion in manufacturing and mining boosted growth beyond expectations in the first half (H1) of 2023. The government reported growth edging up from 5.4% year on year in H1 2022 to 5.6% in the same period of 2023. Growth was higher than anticipated because of strong expansion in industry and robust investment. Expansion in industry accelerated from 4.6% to 5.6%, with modest gains in manufacturing and in mining and quarrying. Growth in agriculture accelerated from 2.6% to 3.8% with healthy gains in crop and livestock production but edged down in services from 7.9% to 6.4% with slower expansion in trade, transport, and storage. Growth in construction slowed from 5.1% to 4.8% with smaller gains in housing, infrastructure, and repairs.

Higher investment was the main driver of growth, while consumption slowed because of high inflation. On the demand side, growth in gross capital formation accelerated from 6.6% year on year in H1 2022 to 7.9% on higher infrastructure spending and upgrades to machinery and equipment. Consumption growth slowed from 9.4% to an estimated 5.6% as persistently high inflation trimmed real household income and demand despite rising wages and pensions. The deficit in net exports widened by 4.4%, with the trade deficit expanding by 18.4% for goods, primarily from higher imports of petrochemicals and of machinery and transport equipment, while expanding tourism boosted the small surplus in services by nearly half.

In H2 2023, persistently high prices for food and energy and sluggish remittances will likely continue to trim real household income and consumption. However, industry, agriculture, and capital investment will likely maintain steadily higher growth in the rest of 2023 and in 2024. With these projections, this update raises growth forecasts for 2023 and 2024 (Table 2.1.8).

Producer prices and wages rose with persisting inflation. Higher costs for imported food and capital goods, along with increased wages and pensions, edged up inflation from 10.6% in H1 2022 to 11.0% a year later. Exemptions from tax and customs duties for essential foodstuffs, set to continue until the end of 2023, helped slow food inflation from 14.2% to 13.8%. However, inflation for other goods accelerated from 9.0% to 9.5%, and for services from 6.6% to 8.3%. Despite persistent inflationary pressure, the monetary authorities retained the policy rate at 14.0% in July 2023. This update thus retains earlier inflation projections for 2023 and 2024.

The current account deficit widened sharply from the equivalent of 2.3% of GDP in H1 2022 to 6.3% a year later. Notable causes were cooling inward money transfers and a larger trade deficit. As the number of Uzbek seasonal migrant workers in the Russian Federation declined, smaller inward money transfers contracted the income surplus, as expected, by 12.3% from H1 2022. Imports rose by 26.0% on larger shipments of machinery and equipment, ferrous metals, and petrochemicals, far outstripping 16.0% higher exports of goods, with notable growth in gold, textiles, foodstuffs, copper, and petrochemicals. Service exports, by contrast, grew by 16.0% as demand for transport and tourism services surged, while service imports rose by only 4.0% on higher demand for shipping, business services, and information and communication services.

Table 2.1.8 Selected Economic Indicators in Uzbekistan, %

Growth forecasts for 2023 and 2024 are raised after growth in the first half of 2023 outpaced expectations.

	2022	2023		2024	
		Apr	Sep	Apr	Sep
GDP growth	5.7	5.0	5.5	5.0	5.5
Inflation	11.4	11.0	11.0	10.0	10.0

GDP = gross domestic product.
Source: Asian Development Bank estimates.

EAST ASIA

Subregional GDP grew at a good pace in the first half of 2023, spurred by the lifting of COVID-19 restrictions in the People's Republic of China. Nevertheless, the growth projection in this update for aggregate GDP in 2023 is revised down slightly from *ADO April 2023*. The 2024 growth projection is unchanged. Inflation has slowed more than expected overall, prompting a significantly lower inflation projection for the subregion this year. The inflation forecast for next year is adjusted marginally up.

Subregional Assessment and Prospects

Real GDP in the subregion expanded in the first half (H1) of 2023 at a rate near what was forecast in *ADO April 2023*. In the People's Republic of China (PRC), growth accelerated following the lifting of COVID-19 restrictions, which boosted consumption. Growth rose from 2.5% year on year in H1 2022 to 5.5% in H1 2023. However, as the year proceeded, growth showed signs of slowing, with merchandise exports hampered by slowing global demand. The economy of Hong Kong, China mirrored that of the PRC following the lifting of pandemic restrictions. Real GDP reversed 2.6% contraction in H1 2022 to expand by 2.2% a year later. Domestic demand recovered robustly, buoyed by a strong pickup in inbound tourism and improved economic prospects, but weak external demand remained a drag on growth. Economic expansion in the Republic of Korea (ROK) moderated from 2.3% year on year in H2 2022 to 0.9% in H1 2023 as manufacturing contracted in line with lower exports of semiconductors and petroleum products. Mongolia's economic recovery continued through H1 2023, expanding by 6.4% year over year, driven by robust external demand following the reopening in the PRC and consequently revived domestic demand. In contrast with growth in other subregional economies, real GDP in Taipei,China contracted by 0.7% in H1 2023, in the wake of a sharp fall early in the year. The most notable negative growth factor was investment, which was adversely affected by contraction in exports to the PRC and the United States (US).

Subregional inflation slowed in H1 2023 but was still higher than targeted. In the PRC, consumer price inflation moderated from 1.8% year on year in the first 7 months of 2022 to 0.5% this year. Though food prices rose by 1.9%, nonfood prices increased by only 0.2% as easing fuel prices provided ballast. In the same period, producer prices in the PRC reversed a 7.3% average increase to drop by 3.2%, brought down by declining prices for energy and raw materials. Inflation in the ROK continued to abate as transport, food, and energy price pressures waned. It averaged 3.7% year on year in the first 7 months of 2023 and eased to 2.3% in July. Robust consumption and employment trends kept core inflation high at an average of 3.8%. Inflation in Taipei,China has been slowing gradually and averaged 2.3% in H1 2023. Coming in below 2.0% for the first time since July 2021, it fell to 1.7% in June, the brakes applied by more moderate increases in food and fuel prices. Core inflation remained at 2.6% in June, bolstered by booming domestic demand.

The section on the PRC was written by Akiko Terada-Hagiwara, Yothin Jinjarak, Wen Qi, and Wenyu Liu, consultant. The part on other economies by David De Padua, Yothin Jinjarak, Matteo Lanzafame, Pilipinas Quising, Irfan Qureshi, Bold Sandagdorj, and Michael Timbang, consultant. All authors are in the East Asia and Economic Research and Development Impact departments of ADB. Subregional assessment and prospects was written by Eric Clifton, consultant, Economic Research and Development Impact Department of ADB.

Headline inflation in Hong Kong, China averaged 2.0% in H1 2023. In Mongolia, annual inflation has been above target for about the past two years, but the 12-month average inflation moderated from 15.2% year on year in December 2022 to 12.5% in July 2023.

Subregional GDP growth is forecast to rise from 2.8% in 2022 to 4.4% in 2023 and then subside to 4.2% in 2024 (Figure 2.2.1). Growth in the PRC is expected to moderate year on year in H2 2023 as quarterly momentum stalls and favorable base effects fade. The growth forecast is revised down by 0.1 percentage points to 4.9% in 2023, still within the government's target of around 5.0% this year, and kept at 4.5% in 2024, as projected in *ADO April 2023*. The growth forecast for the ROK is marked down slightly for 2023 from *ADO April 2023* to 1.3% in light of weaker demand for ROK exports, while the forecast for 2024 is unchanged from April at 2.2%. Taking into account unexpectedly rapid growth early this year in Hong Kong, China, the 2023 growth projection is revised up from 3.6% to 4.3%. Recovery should continue next year, but, primarily because of base effects, the 2024 forecast is lowered from 3.7% to 3.3%. For Taipei,China, given slow export growth from still-weak global demand, this update downgrades the growth forecast for 2023 to 1.2%. It upgrades the 2024 forecast marginally on the expectation that consumption continues to expand and exports gradually recover. For Mongolia, GDP is expected to climb this year by 5.7%, slightly more than forecast in *ADO April 2023*, but marginally less in 2024 at 5.9%. Growth this year will be supported by a substantial recovery in exports and continued fiscal expansion but tempered by persistently high inflation, contractionary monetary policy, and tight domestic financing conditions.

Inflation in East Asia is now forecast at 1.0% in 2023, significantly lower than the *ADO April 2023* projection. The 2024 forecast is raised marginally to 2.1% (Figure 2.2.2). Consumer price inflation in the PRC should stay moderate. Upward pressure from rising service prices should be modest in H2 2023 as recovery in consumption moderates. The forecast for consumer price inflation is revised down to 0.7% in 2023 but unchanged at 2.0% in 2024. In light of developments in the ROK so far this year, inflation forecasts are revised up from April projections to 3.3% in 2023 and 2.2% in 2024.

Figure 2.2.1 GDP Growth in East Asia

The subregion's growth forecast for 2023 is marginally lower.

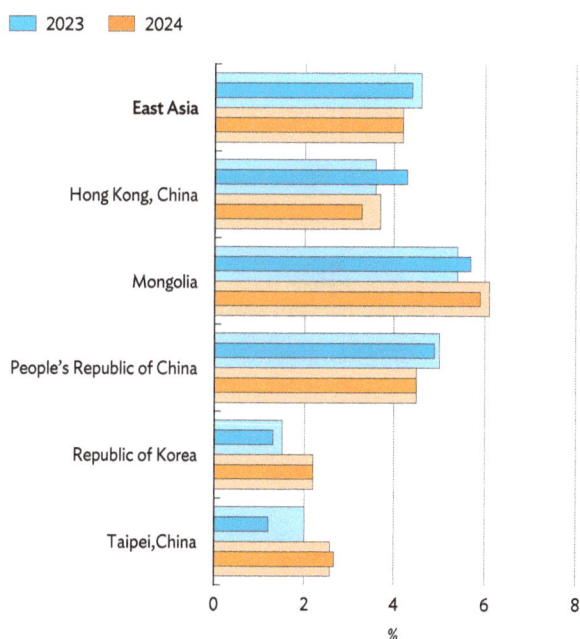

GDP = gross domestic product.
Note: Lighter colored bars are *Asian Development Outlook April 2023* forecasts.
Source: *Asian Development Outlook* database.

Figure 2.2.2 Inflation in East Asia

The 2023 forecast for inflation in the subregion is significantly lower.

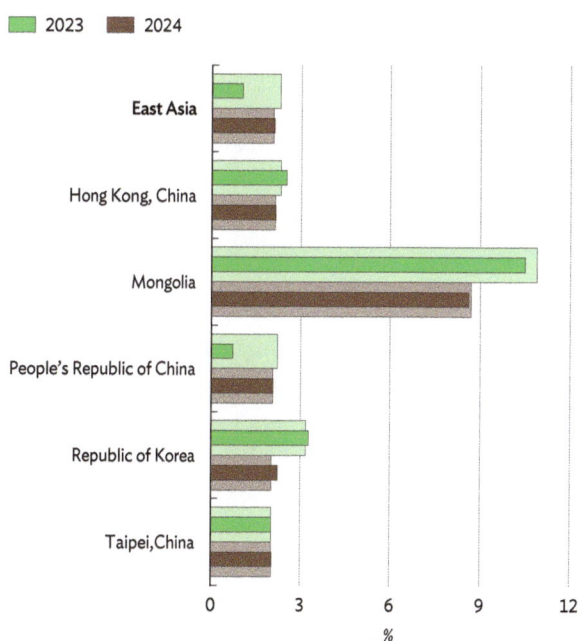

Note: Lighter colored bars are *Asian Development Outlook April 2023* forecasts.
Source: *Asian Development Outlook* database.

The inflation forecast for Hong Kong, China, is revised up for 2023 from 2.3% projected in April to 2.5%, based on the H1 outcome, and maintained for next year at 2.1%. With oil and food prices expected to trend down in the rest of this year, inflation in Taipei,China is expected to slow to 2.0% this year and next, as forecast in April. Given the recent moderation in Mongolian inflation, the forecast is slightly lowered from the April projection to 10.5% in 2023 and 8.6% in 2024.

The outlook for East Asia is subject to significant risks. A forecast El Niño in H2 2023 is one notable cause of uncertainty over the short term from extreme weather and climate change. Moreover, little can be foreseen with certainty about the course of the Russian invasion of Ukraine and consequent energy and food security challenges. Lastly, the possibility looms of further fragmentation of the global economy because of geopolitical factors.

People's Republic of China

The economy rebounded as expected in the first half (H1) of this year, benefiting from the lifting of COVID-19 restrictions and from base effects. Growth slowed quarter on quarter in the second quarter (Q2), though, so the GDP growth projection for 2023 is lowered marginally from 5.0% in *ADO April 2023* to 4.9%. Inflation is now projected to slow more than forecast earlier, in line with weaker than expected domestic demand and softer global commodity prices. The current account is forecast to moderate with softer external demand but stay in surplus.

Updated Assessment

Economic growth in the People's Republic of China (PRC) accelerated following the lifting of COVID-19 restrictions. Growth rose from 2.5% year on year in H1 2022 to 5.5% in H1 2023, accelerating year on year from 4.5% in Q1 2023 to 6.3% in Q2 (Figure 2.2.3). However, quarter on quarter, growth moderated from 2.2% in Q1 to 0.8% in Q2, indicating diminished growth momentum.

Figure 2.2.3 Economic Growth

Economic growth accelerated in the first half of 2023 after COVID-19 restrictions were lifted late in 2022.

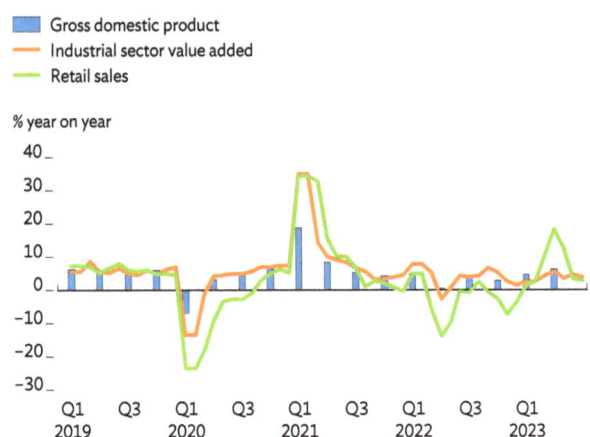

Q = quarter.
Sources: CEIC Data Company; Asian Development Bank estimates.

On the demand side, recovery in consumption drove growth. Consumption contributed 4.2 percentage points to growth in H1 2023, a sharp increase from 0.8 points in H1 2022 (Figure 2.2.4). Growth in real household income nearly doubled from 3.0% in H1 2022 to 5.8% a year later, while growth in real household consumption soared nearly tenfold from 0.8% to 7.6% (Figure 2.2.5). Retail sales reversed 0.2% contraction in the first 7 months of 2022 to grow by 7.3% a year later.

Figure 2.2.4 Demand-Side Contributions to Growth

Consumption was the main driver of growth in H1 2023, while net exports dragged on growth.

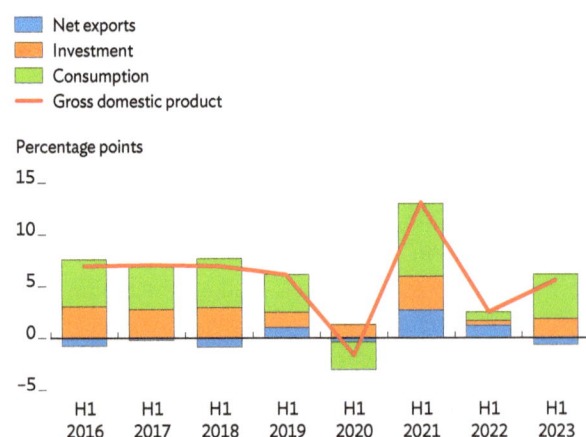

H = half.
Source: CEIC Data Company.

Figure 2.2.5 Growth in Income and Consumption Expenditure per Capita

Consumption and income growth rebounded in H1 2023.

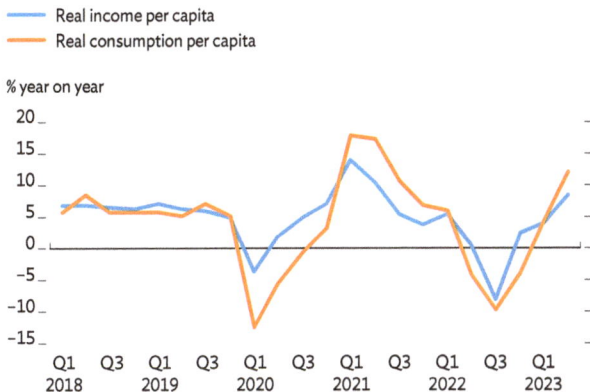

H1 = first half, Q = quarter.
Sources: CEIC Data Company; Asian Development Bank estimates.

Investment remained supportive of growth.
Investment contributed 1.8 percentage points to growth in H1 2023, or 1.3 points more than a year earlier. In the first 7 months of 2023, nominal growth in fixed asset investment slowed from 5.7% year on year a year earlier to 3.4%, dragged down by contraction in real estate investment (Figure 2.2.6). Manufacturing investment grew by 5.7% and infrastructure investment by 6.8%. Real estate investment contracted by 8.5%. Meanwhile, public investment by state-owned enterprises grew by 7.6% in the first 7 months of 2023, while private investment declined by 0.5%.

Figure 2.2.6 Growth in Fixed Asset Investment

Infrastructure investment remained broadly stable in the first half of 2023, though real estate investment contracted.

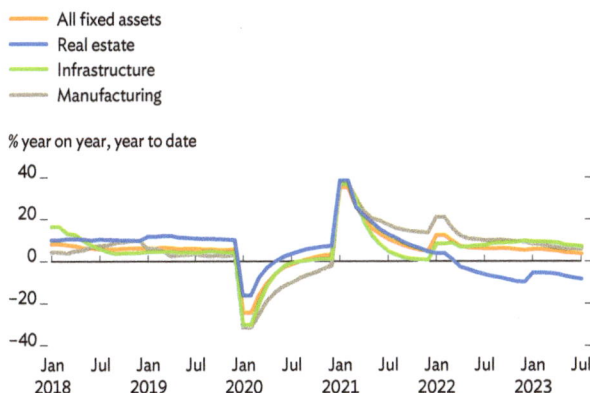

Source: CEIC Data Company.

Net exports dragged on growth. Net exports reversed a 1.2 percentage point contribution to growth in H1 2022 to drag growth down by 0.6 points a year later as merchandise exports declined in line with slowing global demand.

On the supply side, economic recovery was driven by strong services. Services became the main contributor to GDP growth as expansion in the sector accelerated from 1.8% year on year in H1 2022 to 6.4% in H1 2023, thanks to the removal of COVID-19 restrictions (Figure 2.2.7). Broad improvement was most pronounced in accommodation and catering, information, transportation, and wholesale. Growth stayed muted only in real estate services. In H1 2023, travel spending surged, particularly it doubled with urban residents from a year earlier, though total spending on tourism in the first half was still less than in H1 2019, before the pandemic.

Figure 2.2.7 Supply-Side Contributions to Growth

Growth in services outpaced that of industry in H1 2023.

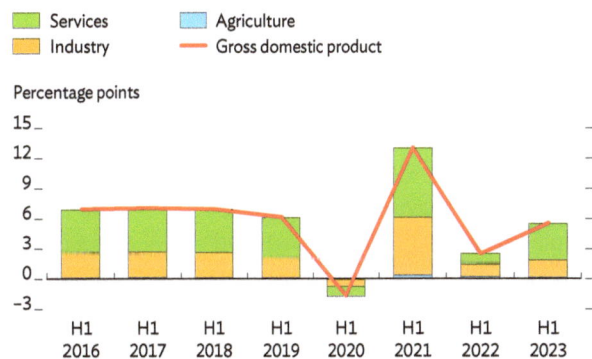

H1 = first half.
Source: CEIC Data Company.

Growth in industry fell behind services. The contribution to GDP growth from industry rose from 1.2 percentage points in H1 2022 to 1.7 points in H1 2023, but it was outshone by a contribution from services rising from 1.0 point to 3.6 points. Growth in the secondary sector increased from 3.2% year on year in H1 2022 to 4.3% a year later. Industry growth increased from 3.3% in H1 2022 to 3.7% in H1 2023, while construction accelerated from 2.8% to 7.7% on solid public infrastructure investment. Growth in agriculture moderated from 5.0% in H1 2022 to 3.7% a year later, contributing 0.2 percentage points to growth.

The labor market improved. The surveyed urban unemployment rate improved from 5.5% in January to 5.3% in July. The economy added 6.78 million new urban jobs in H1 2023, or 240,000 more than in the same period last year. Moreover, the number of rural migrants working in urban areas was 5.8 million higher a year later, reaching 187.1 million at the end of June 2023, which exceeded 182.5 million in June 2019, before the COVID-19 crisis. However, the surveyed unemployment rate for workers aged 16–24 rose from 17.3% in January 2023 to 21.3% in June—a historic high for this age group.

Consumer and producer price inflation trended down. Consumer price inflation moderated from 1.8% in the first 7 months of 2022 to 0.5% a year later (Figure 2.2.8). Though food prices rose by 1.9%, nonfood prices increased only marginally by 0.2% as fuel prices eased. In the same period, producer prices reversed a 7.3% increase on average to contract by 3.2%, brought down by declining prices for energy and raw materials.

Monetary policy gradually eased in H1 2023. After a 0.25 percentage point cut in the reserve requirement ratio for almost all banks in March 2023, the People's Bank of China, the central bank, followed up in June and August by cutting key policy rates—including the 1-year medium-term lending facility rate, 7-day reverse repo rate, and standing lending facility rate—to support credit growth and economic activity (Figure 2.2.9). It also reduced the 1-year loan prime rate twice from 3.65% to 3.45% and trimmed the 5-year loan prime rate, used to price mortgages, by 10 basis points to 4.2%, to support an ailing real estate industry.

Despite some easing of monetary policy, credit growth softened in H1 2023. Growth in total social financing—an aggregate that includes bank loans, shadow bank financing, government and corporate bonds, and equity financing—fell from 10.7% at the end of July 2022 to 9.2% a year later, reflecting weak credit demand (Figure 2.2.10). Growth in loans outstanding rose by 11.1% year on year in the same period, while that of government bonds outstanding slowed from 19.4% at the end of July 2022 to 10.1%, the decline partly reflecting a high base caused by fiscal frontloading in 2022. Shadow bank financing increased marginally by 1.7% at the end of July 2023.

Figure 2.2.8 Monthly Inflation

Consumer and producer price inflation trended down in H1 2023.

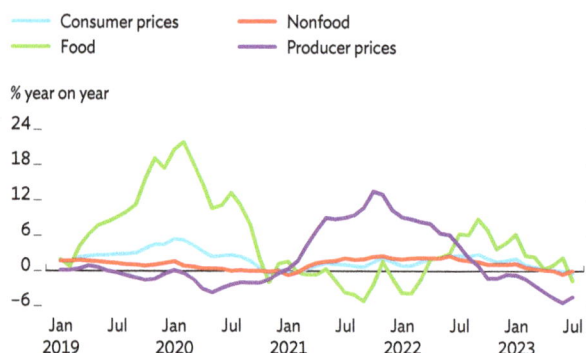

Source: CEIC Data Company.

Figure 2.2.9 Banking Lending and Policy Rates

The central bank cut key policy rates in the first half of 2023.

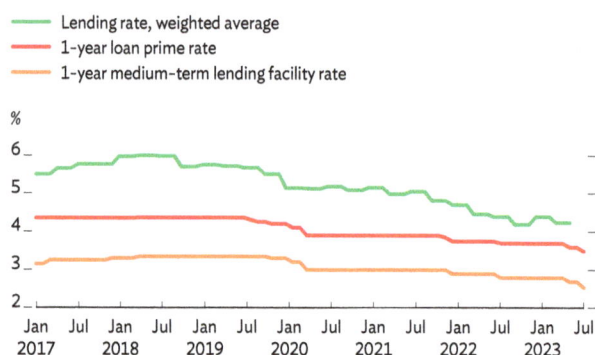

Source: CEIC Data Company.

Figure 2.2.10 Growth in Broad Money, Credit Outstanding, and Government Bonds Outstanding

Despite some easing of monetary policy, credit growth softened in the first half of 2023.

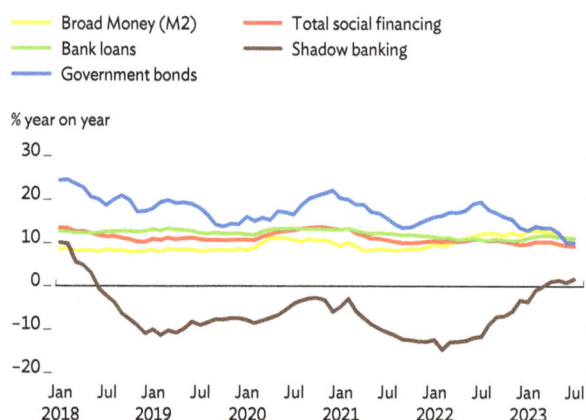

Note: Shadow banking comprises entrust loans, trust loans, and banks' acceptance bills.

Sources: CEIC Data Company; Asian Development Bank estimates.

Growth in broad money (M2) year on year moderated from 12.0% at the end of July 2022 to 10.7% a year later.

On the fiscal side, the budget deficit narrowed as fiscal revenue recovered. The budget deficit fell from the equivalent of 4.2% of GDP in H1 2022 to 2.5% in H1 2023 (Figure 2.2.11). The reduction reflected a 13.3% increase in general government fiscal revenue in H1 2023 that reversed 10.2% contraction a year earlier caused by refunds of value-added tax. Meanwhile, growth in fiscal expenditure slowed from 5.9% in H1 2022 to 3.9% a year later. New issues of local government special bonds—not included in the general budget—amounted to CNY2.5 trillion in the first 7 months of 2023, or 65.7% of the annual quota of CNY3.8 trillion.

The current account surplus stayed broadly stable. The current account surplus equaled 1.7% of GDP in H1 2023, slightly lower than 1.8% in H1 2022. The merchandise trade surplus narrowed from 3.6% of GDP in H1 2022 to 3.4% in H1 2023, while the service deficit widened from 0.4% to 1.2% as outbound travel continued to normalize (Figure 2.2.12). Following high 14.5% growth year on year in the first 7 months of 2022 in US dollar terms, merchandise exports declined by 5.0% a year later as external demand cooled. Geographically, exports to major trade partners fell: to Southeast Asia by 1.6%, to the US by 17.8%, to Japan by 6.9%, and to the European Union by 8.8%. Meanwhile, imports reversed 5.0% growth year on year in US dollar terms in the first 7 months of 2022 to fall by 7.6%, primarily reflecting lower commodity prices.

Net foreign direct investment switched from inflow to outflow. It reversed from net inflow equal to 0.8% of GDP in H1 2022 to net outflow of 0.7% a year later as foreign direct investment inflow plunged by 81.8% in H1 2023. This decline partly reflected weak foreign investor sentiment as the global growth outlook soured and geopolitical concerns intensified. Net portfolio investment outflow, meanwhile, slowed from $79.6 billion in Q1 2022 to $56.4 billion a year later, driven down mainly by net equity inflow thanks to economic reopening. Reserve assets reached $3.4 trillion at the end of July 2023, or $125.2 billion more than a year earlier.

Figure 2.2.11 General Government Fiscal Revenue and Expenditure

As fiscal revenue recovered from a low base, the budget deficit narrowed.

GDP = gross domestic product, Q = quarter.
Note: Public finance budget only.
Sources: CEIC Data Company; Asian Development Bank estimates.

Figure 2.2.12 Current Account Balance and Merchandise Trade

The merchandise trade surplus narrowed on account of weak global demand, while the service deficit widened as outbound travel resumed.

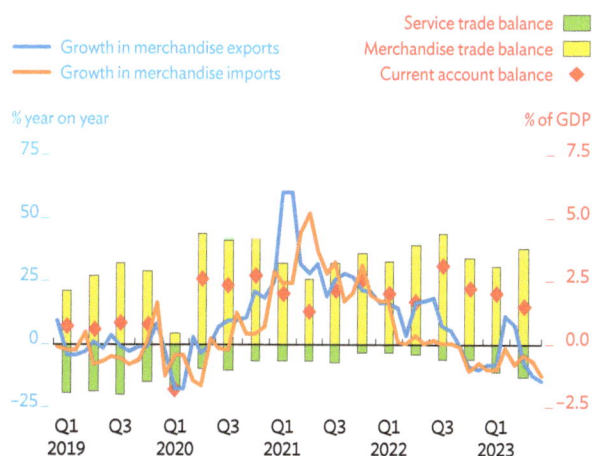

GDP = gross domestic product, Q = quarter.
Note: January and February data are combined to exclude the Lunar New Year effect.
Sources: CEIC Data Company; Asian Development Bank estimates.

The renminbi depreciated against the US dollar in H1 2023. With a boost from reopening, the renminbi appreciated slightly against the US dollar in Q1 2023 before depreciating in Q2 as growth momentum weakened. Overall, the currency depreciated by 2.4% in nominal terms against the US dollar in the first 7 months of 2023 to CNY7.13 (Figure 2.2.13).

In the first 7 months of 2023, the currency depreciated by 3.3% in nominal effective terms, against a trade-weighted basket of currencies, and by 6.5% in real effective terms.

Prospects

Growth is expected to moderate in H2 2023 as momentum slows and favorable base effects fade. Services should continue to pick up in line with recovering household demand, which will prop up a frail private sector and offset some softening of external demand for PRC exports. Meanwhile, steady public infrastructure growth will support investment. Manufacturing investment is likely to slow as external demand cools, and real estate investment should continue to fall as stress persists in the property market. In the rest of this year, both monetary and fiscal policy will be accommodative, aiming in particular to boost domestic demand and private sector activity. Given softer external demand and continued weakness in the property market weighing on recovery, the GDP growth forecast is revised down by 0.1 percentage points to 4.9% in 2023, still within the government's target of around 5.0% this year, and kept at 4.5% in 2024, as projected in *ADO April 2023* (Table 2.2.1).

Domestic demand should continue to improve in H2 2023 but at a slower pace. Growth in manufacturing investment is expected to moderate in line with tepid private sector activity and softening external demand for exports, while infrastructure investment is likely to remain solid thanks to supportive government policy. The property market showed signs of stabilizing in Q1 after the government stepped up support for it in late 2022, but it remains shaky overall as property market indicators—including property sales, prices for newly constructed homes, and floor space in new housing starts—remained weak. With soft market sentiment and ongoing debt restructuring in property developers, real estate investment is expected to continue to fall in H2 and pull down overall investment. As external trade languishes, net exports will remain a drag on growth. Consumption, meanwhile, should continue to recover.

On the supply side, services are likely to outpace industry in H2 2023 as household demand continues to recover. Growth in contact-intensive services such as hospitality, recreation, transportation,

Figure 2.2.13 Renminbi Exchange Rates

The renminbi appreciated slightly in the first quarter of 2023, then depreciated in the second quarter.

Sources: CEIC Data Company; Asian Development Bank estimates.

Table 2.2.1 Selected Economic Indicators in the People's Republic of China, %

The 2023 growth forecast is revised down marginally but still consistent with the government's target of around 5%. The 2023 inflation forecast is revised down in line with softening energy and food prices.

	2022	2023		2024	
		Apr	Sep	Apr	Sep
GDP growth	3.0	5.0	4.9	4.5	4.5
Inflation	2.0	2.2	0.7	2.0	2.0

GDP = gross domestic product.
Sources: CEIC Data Company; Asian Development Bank estimates.

and tourism in particular should continue to chalk up gains from a low base set under COVID-19 restrictions last year. Industry will face headwinds from moderating exports. The weak housing market will likely weigh on construction, but steady infrastructure investment will provide some lift. Given the dim outlook for external demand in general, manufacturing could suffer moderating exports, but external demand is expected to remain strong in some areas, notably new energy vehicles, lithium batteries, and solar cells. Agriculture, meanwhile, should expand steadily in H2 2023.

The labor market, particularly in services, should benefit from economic reopening and higher household consumption. Loosening regulations in the technology industry and easing restrictions in the property market will boost demand for labor.

However, challenges remain in the labor market, especially for young job seekers. The youth unemployment rate has been propelled by multiple demand- and supply-side factors, notably slow recovery in manufacturing and the private sector, as well as mismatches between the skills provided by college education and those needed by employers.

Consumer price inflation should stay moderate. Average consumer price inflation was muted in the first 7 months of 2023 by weak domestic and external demand and softer global commodity prices. Upward pressure from rising service prices should be modest in H2 2023 as recovery in consumption moderates. The forecast for consumer price inflation is revised down to 0.7% in 2023 but unchanged at 2.0% in 2024.

Fiscal policy is expected to remain supportive in H2 2023. To facilitate economic recovery, the government may mobilize additional off-budget spending by increasing the amount of credit offered by policy banks and using central bank lending facilities. As noted above, by the end of July 2023, only 65.7% of the annual quota for new local government special bonds had been used. This compared with 95.0% in July 2022 and 78.4% before COVID-19 in July 2019, indicating room to accelerate local government special bond issues in H2 2023.

Fiscal policy measures should aim to deleverage once economic recovery takes hold. General government debt reached a historic high in 2022 equal to 50.4% of GDP (Figure 2.2.14). If not contained, rising debt threatens to dent the government's ability to support growth through fiscal expansion. Meanwhile, with the property market under stress, land sales have suffered, inhibiting the ability of local governments to raise revenue for increased spending. To ease fiscal pressure on them, higher transfers from the central government may be necessary.

Monetary policy is expected to continue to support recovery. Enabled by modest domestic inflation, a reduction in the required reserve ratio for commercial banks is expected to spur credit growth in H2 2023. However, the effects of monetary policy easing on the renminbi and capital flows should be closely monitored, considering that 10-year US Treasury note yield has surpassed PRC government bond yield since May 2022,

Figure 2.2.14 Debt Structure

General government debt increased to a new high in 2022.

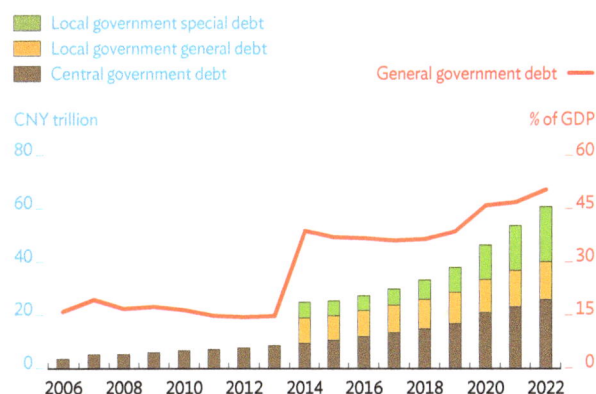

GDP = gross domestic product.
Sources: CEIC Data Company; Asian Development Bank estimates.

and a negative interest rate spread has continued to widen. In July, the authorities rolled out supporting measures that, notably, extended existing loans for property developers to ease liquidity pressure on them in the near term. More supportive measures are expected in H2 2023.

External trade should continue to moderate in H2 2023. PRC exports weakened again in Q2 after a surge in March and April that occurred as suppliers filled order backlogs following COVID-19 and supply chain disruption. The lagged effects of aggressive policy tightening last year in the US and Europe will continue to weigh on economic activity in the advanced economies, which will likely restrain PRC exports. At the same time, the service trade deficit should widen as outbound travel normalizes following the easing of travel restrictions early this year. Overall, the current account surplus is expected to narrow to below the equivalent of 2% of GDP in 2023 and gradually ease further in 2024.

Risks to the outlook are both domestic and external. Domestic risks center on the possibility that policy effects fall short, which could further undermine already fragile consumer and investor sentiment. Further deterioration in the housing market could undermine financial stability and threaten the growth outlook. Notable external risks are renewed energy and food security challenges brought about by the Russian invasion of Ukraine, fragmentation in the global economy, and changing weather patterns, including a forecast El Niño in H2 2023.

Other Economies

Hong Kong, China

Having contracted by 2.6% year on year in the first half (H1) of 2022, the economy expanded by 2.2% in H1 2023. With COVID-19 restrictions lifted, GDP grew by an unexpectedly robust 2.9% year on year in the first quarter (Q1) and then, on solid growth in consumer spending and trade in services, by 1.5% in Q2. Domestic demand was buoyed by improved economic prospects as accelerating visitor arrivals drove up exports of services by 19.6% in H1. Private consumption surged by 10.5% and added 6.9 percentage points (pps) to growth, as consumer sentiment revived with recovery in contact-intensive activities and the disbursement of consumption vouchers. Despite tightened financial conditions, gross fixed capital formation increased by 3.2% and contributed 0.5 pps on upbeat business sentiment. Meanwhile, government consumption declined by 4.0%, and external demand for goods further weakened, weighed down by a challenging global environment. As goods exports plummeted by 17.1%, goods imports also fell sharply, by 11.7%, while services imports grew by 24.7%. In sum, net exports subtracted 2.5 pps from growth.

On the supply side, output in most sectors saw growth rebound in Q1. Services reversed 4.2% decline year on year in Q4 2022 to expand by 3.1%. Accommodation and food services registered double-digit growth in the quarter, as did transportation, storage, postal, and courier services. Growth in manufacturing also rose to 3.8%, on improved business prospects. However, import and export services and wholesale and retail trade dropped by 7.4% as a weak external environment continued to drag down imports and exports alike. Following an 8.0% increase in Q4 last year, construction shrank by 1.7%.

Private consumption and services will drive growth this year and next. Leading indicators signal slowing momentum at the beginning of Q3. The headline composite purchasing managers' index declined for the first time in 7 months, from 50.3 in June to 49.4 in July, while the latest business surveys showed less optimism by enterprises. However, the same tailwinds encountered in H1 should continue to shape the economy in the rest of 2023.

Despite considerable recovery in tourism in the first 6 months of 2023, arrivals returned to only 37% of the number in the same period in 2019. Inbound tourism is projected to continue growing vigorously this year as residual pandemic disruption to transportation and handling capacity fade. A solid labor market should further boost consumption, domestic demand, and services, despite tight financial conditions. On the negative side, goods exports will remain weak with slower growth in the advanced economies, even as recovery in the People's Republic of China provides some lift. On balance, and taking into account the unexpectedly fast growth in Q1, the 2023 growth projection is revised up (Table 2.2.2). Normalizing external and domestic conditions will underpin continued recovery next year, but the 2024 growth forecast is revised down primarily to accommodate a base effect.

Table 2.2.2 Selected Economic Indicators in Hong Kong, China, %

Growth will be higher in 2023 than projected in April as private consumption and services continue to recover, but inflation will remain moderate.

	2022	2023		2024	
		Apr	Sep	Apr	Sep
GDP growth	−3.5	3.6	4.3	3.7	3.3
Inflation	1.9	2.3	2.5	2.1	2.1

GDP = gross domestic product.
Source: Asian Development Bank estimates.

The April inflation forecast is revised up for this year but maintained for next year. Headline inflation fell marginally from 2.0% year on year in May to 1.9% in June, with smaller price increases for food, electricity, gas, and water utilities, and averaged 2.0% in H1 2023. The underlying inflation rate also declined slightly, from 1.8% to 1.7%. External price pressures are expected to moderate somewhat with favorable base effects, but inflation is still forecast higher in H2 2023 in tandem with local economic recovery—easing, as previously forecast, in 2024.

Mongolia

Economic recovery continued through the first half (H1) of 2023. GDP expanded by 6.4% year over year, driven by robust external demand following reopening in the People's Republic of China (PRC), and consequently revived domestic demand. With PRC demand strong for coking coal and base metals, mining and merchandise exports in H1 2023 outperformed expectations in *ADO April 2023*. Net exports contributed 16.7 percentage points to growth, and consumption added 5.5 points, but investment shrank by 29.1% year on year, mainly in line with a significant decline in inventories, dragging growth down by 15.8 points. On the supply side, recovery was uneven in terms of sector contributions. Mining contributed 4.6 percentage points to growth, and services added 3.7 points. Recovery in industry other than mining was slow, contributing only 0.2 points to growth, with growth rates in construction and manufacturing below 1%. Agriculture contracted by 10.5% with livestock and crop production battered by severe weather, subtracting 2.1 points from growth.

The rebound improved current account and fiscal balances and boosted foreign exchange reserves. Government revenue increased on higher corporate and personal income tax receipts, social insurance premiums, and value-added tax, while mineral revenue benefited from comparatively high commodity prices and a threefold increase in coal export volume year on year as of July 2023. On the expectation that fiscal revenue would outperform the 2023 budget projection by 11.4%, the budget was amended to increase planned expenditure, which will now grow by 23.2% over 2022, to finance higher pensions and civil servant wages, continued social welfare transfers, and measures implemented to ease traffic congestion in the capital city. These measures will turn a budget surplus in 2022 equal to 0.8% of GDP into a 0.9% deficit in 2023, while bolstering household consumption and capital expenditure in the rest of the year.

GDP will climb this year slightly more than forecast in *ADO April 2023* but marginally less in 2024 (Table 2.2.3). Growth this year will be supported by substantial recovery in exports and continued fiscal expansion, but tempered by persistently high inflation, contractionary monetary policy, and tight domestic financing conditions. In 2024, GDP growth will accelerate further but remain below the April forecast. It will be driven by private sector lending, mining growth, and positive spillover into transport and other services, but constrained by lower growth in agriculture because of severe weather and a lower contribution from net exports owing to a sharp increase in imports.

Table 2.2.3 Selected Economic Indicators in Mongolia, %

Growth will rise above the April forecast in 2023, and inflation will moderate more than forecast in both years.

	2022	2023		2024	
		Apr	Sep	Apr	Sep
GDP growth	5.0	5.4	5.7	6.1	5.9
Inflation	15.2	10.9	10.5	8.7	8.6

GDP = gross domestic product.
Sources: National Statistics Office of Mongolia. 2023. Statistical Information Services; Asian Development Bank estimates.

Average inflation remained high in H1 2023, but forecasts for both years are revised down slightly from *ADO April 2023*. Annual inflation has been above the target set by the Central Bank of Mongolia for the past 27 consecutive months, but 12-month average inflation moderated from 15.2% year on year in December 2022 to 12.5% in July 2023 and is likely to trend downward in H2. Owing to unexpectedly robust exports, foreign exchange reserves have stabilized at $3.7 billion–$3.9 billion since April 2023, or cover for 3.5 months of imports of goods and services. This has eased pressure on the exchange rate, which should temper price increases in 2024. The current account improved significantly in H1 2023 to record a surplus equal to 3.2% of GDP. The current account deficit will be smaller than forecast in *ADO April 2023* for this year and next, mainly because of higher exports.

Several external factors pose downside risks to the outlook. They include any decrease in PRC demand for bulk commodities, a fall in coal or copper prices, new trade restrictions, disruption caused by exacerbated geopolitical tensions, negative spillover from tighter financing conditions, global uncertainty and slowdown, or capital flow reversal.

Republic of Korea

Growth moderated to 0.9% year on year in the first half (H1) of 2023. This was down from 2.3% in H2 2022 and 3.0% in H1 2022. Government consumption rose by 2.6% on increased social security benefits, household transfers, and capital expenditure. As unemployment improved from 2.9% in January to 2.6% in June, private consumption rose by 3.0% with rising service expenditure on recreation, culture, restaurants and accommodation, and travel. Investment growth accelerated to 4.7% as building construction recovered from last year's downturn and investment in facilities and intellectual property products expanded. On the supply side, manufacturing contracted in line with lower exports of semiconductors and petroleum products, but services sector growth was maintained.

Inflation continued to abate as transport, food, and energy price pressures waned. It averaged 3.7% year on year in the first 7 months of 2023 and eased to 2.3% in July. Strong consumption and employment trends kept core inflation, which excludes energy and agricultural products, high at an average of 3.8%— higher, in the past 4 months, than headline inflation. According to the Bank of Korea, the central bank, core inflation has eased at a slower pace because of cost pressures accumulated during pandemic supply disruption and from strong demand for services. The central bank has kept its policy rate unchanged at 3.5% since January 2023, after having raised it seven times in 2022 by a total of 225 basis points and by a further 25 basis points in January 2023. The Republic of Korea won depreciated by an average of 2.8% against the US dollar in the first 7 months of 2023 because of a deteriorating trade balance and monetary tightening in the US.

Both exports and imports declined in H1 2023. Merchandise exports fell by 12.5% in nominal US dollar terms as external demand weakened. Imports declined by 5.9%, reflecting both tepid domestic demand and lower global prices for oil and other commodities. The merchandise trade surplus thus slipped into deficit of $3.5 billion. Trade in services was likewise in deficit, at $11.9 billion, but the primary income account recorded a surplus of $19.5 billion.

Overall, the current account surplus plunged by almost a factor of 10 from $24.9 billion in H1 2022 to $2.4 billion a year later, equal to 0.3% of GDP.

Economic growth this year is now projected to be slower than forecast in April (Table 2.2.4). Growth picked up quarter on quarter from 0.3% in the first quarter to 0.6% in the second, but improvement reflected a significant positive contribution from net exports that is unlikely to be repeated. Further, semiconductor exports have been declining since August 2022, albeit at a slowing rate in recent months. Nevertheless, domestic chipmakers are well placed to benefit more than others from artificial intelligence developments such as High Bandwidth Memory, given their competitive advantage at producing the most advanced chips. Exports are therefore expected to improve in H2 2023 as the information technology industry recovers. Private consumption and investment will be constrained by high interest rates and a sluggish housing market but are still expected to contribute to growth.

Table 2.2.4 Selected Economic Indicators in the Republic of Korea, %

Growth projections are revised down for this year and retained for 2024, with inflation somewhat higher than earlier forecast.

	2022	2023 Apr	2023 Sep	2024 Apr	2024 Sep
GDP growth	2.6	1.5	1.3	2.2	2.2
Inflation	5.1	3.2	3.3	2.0	2.2

GDP = gross domestic product.
Source: Asian Development Bank estimates.

Inflation forecasts are revised up from the April projections. In the year to date, inflation, though easing has remained strong and may not abate significantly anytime soon. Indeed, the central bank expects inflation to hover at about 3% in H2 2023, staying above its 2% target for some time to come.

Taipei,China

GDP shrank in the first half (H1) of 2023 despite a rebound in the second quarter (Q2). Contraction by 1.0% year on year in H1 reflected sharp 3.3% contraction in Q1 and a return to growth, at 1.4%, in Q2. Led mainly by spending on dining out, accommodation, recreation, and transportation, private consumption rose by 9.4% in H1 2023, contributing 4.2 percentage points to growth. Government consumption, which included a tax rebate, grew by 2.7% and contributed 0.3 points. Investment declined by 9.3% and dragged down growth by 2.5 percentage points as investment in construction and in machinery and equipment declined in line with falling exports. Reflecting broad weakness in global demand and ongoing inventory adjustment, exports fell by 9.0% as those to the People's Republic of China (PRC), a key trade partner, contracted by a whopping 29% and those to the US contracted by 15%. With imports declining by only 6.1%, net exports pulled down growth by 3.0 percentage points.

On the supply side, the services sector was the main driver of growth in H1 2023. Services grew by 3.4% year on year, driven by transportation and storage, while robust consumption saw food, accommodation, and entertainment and recreation bolster services. Agriculture grew by 1.3%, but the sector accounts for a small portion of the economy. Meanwhile, industry contracted by 10.3%, led by an 11.2% decline in manufacturing as demand weakened for semiconductors, chemicals, metals, and machinery and equipment.

Growth will slow in 2023 more than projected in April before rebounding next year. Industrial production has declined steadily this year, contracting by 17.2% year on year in June, in line with weak exports. The manufacturing purchasing managers' index fell to a pessimistic 44.8 in the same month, which bodes ill for industry and export prospects well into H2 2023. On the bright side, retail trade grew by 13.3% year on year in June, reflecting robust private consumption, which is expected to bolster the economy through the rest of the year. Consumer confidence for the coming 6-month time frame, having hit a low of 59.1 in December 2022, climbed to 68.4 in July.

On balance, given slow export growth from still-weak global demand, this update downgrades the *ADO April 2023* growth forecast for 2023 (Table 2.2.5). However, it upgrades the forecast for 2024 marginally on the expectation that consumption will continue to expand and exports recover gradually as global demand improves.

Table 2.2.5 Selected Economic Indicators in Taipei,China, %

The growth forecast is revised down for 2023 but raised for 2024, and the April inflation forecast is maintained for both years.

	2022	2023		2024	
		Apr	Sep	Apr	Sep
GDP growth	2.4	2.0	1.2	2.6	2.7
Inflation	2.9	2.0	2.0	2.0	2.0

GDP = gross domestic product.
Source: Asian Development Bank estimates.

Inflation slowed gradually to average 2.3% in H1 2023. It fell to 1.7% year on year in June as food and fuel price increases moderated. Core inflation declined at a slower pace, from 3.0% in January to 2.6% in June, sustained by booming domestic demand, particularly for dining, rental property, and entertainment services. With oil and food prices expected to trend down in the rest of the year, inflation is projected to slow further in 2023 and 2024 to meet the April forecast.

The main risk to the outlook is persistently weak global demand continuing to weigh on exports. While private consumption has bolstered growth, the positive effects of loosened COVID-19 restrictions will wane, and this export-oriented economy will need to find new drivers of growth. Meanwhile, exports to the PRC have not picked up in recent months despite continuing growth there, and any reconfiguration of supply chains could further dampen Taipei,China exports. A risk to the inflation forecast would be elevated price pressures from global commodities rising above expectations.

SOUTH ASIA

Subregional economic growth is forecast to slow in 2023 slightly more than projected in *ADO April 2023*. It will likely reaccelerate in 2024 as previously forecast. Current growth outlooks for individual economies in the subregion largely confirm earlier projections, except for Nepal, where growth will be significantly lower in 2023. Inflation will be higher than forecast in April, especially in 2024, as domestic demand recovers.

Subregional Assessment and Prospects

Economic developments in the first half (H1) of 2023 were broadly similar to those expected in April. India's economy grew by 7.8% year on year in the first quarter of fiscal year 2023 (FY2023, ending 31 March 2024), reflecting strong growth in services and rising investment fueled by public investment and bank credit to the private sector. The Afghan economy showed some signs of recovery in H1 2023, following 3 successive years of recession. Growth in Bangladesh, though higher than forecast earlier, decelerated in FY2023 (ended 30 June 2023) as industry growth moderated because of high input prices and energy shortages, agriculture suffered from floods and cyclones, and domestic and external demand faltered on account of rising prices, a slowdown in the US and Europe, and import restrictions. Growth in Maldives was kept robust by strong tourism and public investment. In Pakistan, growth is estimated to have slowed to 0.3% in FY2023 (ended 30 June 2023), halting gains made in post-pandemic recovery. Massive floods at the outset of FY2023 damaged cotton and rice crops, cutting expansion in agriculture to one-third of sector growth in FY2022. The other economies of the subregion did not do well either.

Sri Lanka's economy contracted in the first quarter of 2023 as both industry and services contracted, though economic conditions have since stabilized with food and fuel becoming more readily available. In Nepal, contractionary monetary and fiscal policies and import restrictions pushed growth markedly lower in FY2023 (ended mid-July 2023) than was forecast in April, though agricultural output rose thanks to normal weather patterns. In Bhutan, services showed steady recovery as tourist arrivals picked up, but erratic monsoon rains undermined crop production and a shortfall in hydropower production hurt industrial output.

Aggregate subregional GDP is forecast to expand by 5.4% in 2023 and 6.1% in 2024, much as projected in April (Figure 2.3.1). The outlook excludes Afghanistan because meaningful forecasts are precluded by the unsettled situation there and lack of credible data. The subregional growth shadows the pattern of growth in India, which accounts for 80% of the subregional economy. Indian growth in the rest of this fiscal year and next will be propelled by robust domestic consumption as consumer confidence improves, and by investment, including large increases in government capital expenditure.

The section on Bangladesh was written by Soon Chan Hong, Barun K. Dey, and Mahbub Rabbani; India by Chinmaya Goyal and Kriti Jain; Pakistan by Khadija Ali and Farzana Noshab. The sections on other economies were written by Dinuk de Silva, Lakshini Fernando, Elisabetta Gentile, Abdul Hares Halimi, Manbar Singh Khadka, Sonam Lhendup, Ahmad K. Miraj, and Neelina Nakarmi, Milan Thomas, and consultants Abdulla Ali and Macrina Mallari. The subregional assessment and prospects was written by Reza Vaez-Zadeh and Trisha Chandra, consultants. ADB placed on hold its regular assistance in Afghanistan effective 15 August 2021.

Figure 2.3.1 GDP Growth in South Asia

South Asia will grow at a brisk pace in 2023 and see growth accelerate in 2024.

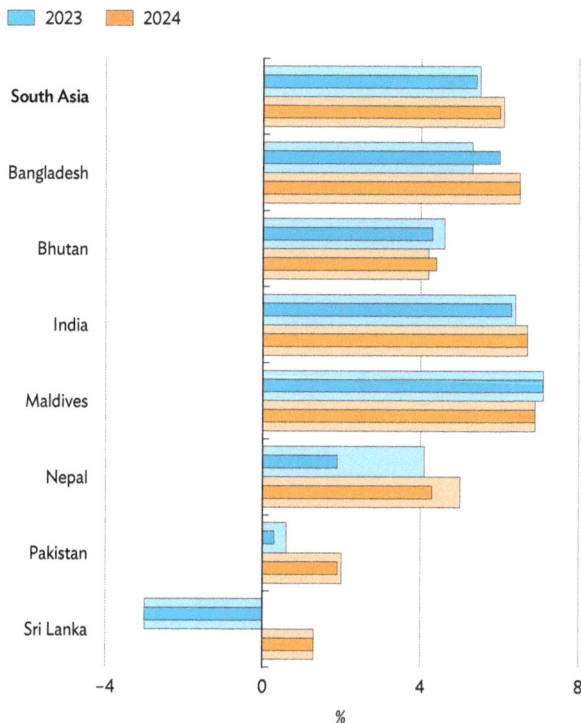

Note: Lighter colored bars are *Asian Development Outlook April 2023* forecasts.
Source: *Asian Development Outlook* database.

However, as slowing exports could foment headwinds for the economy, and erratic rainfall patterns are likely to undermine agricultural output, the growth forecast for FY2023 is revised down marginally to 6.3%. The forecast is retained at 6.7% for FY2024, when rising private investment and industrial output are expected to drive growth.

Growth prospects in the rest of South Asia are mixed. In Afghanistan, economic expansion will be constrained by governance issues, policy uncertainties, ongoing drought, and the exclusion of women from the labor force. However, If humanitarian assistance to the country continues at the 2022 level, modest growth can be expected there this year and next. In Pakistan, growth is forecast at 1.9% in FY2024, slightly below the April projection, assuming continued implementation of reforms and supportive macroeconomic policies, recovery from flood-induced supply shocks, and improving external conditions.

Political stability following general elections later this year, if achieved, will boost business confidence, as will a new standby arrangement agreed with the International Monetary Fund to support economic stabilization and rebuild fiscal buffers. Sri Lanka's economy will remain in recession again in 2023, as forecast in April. However, indications are still for modest recovery in 2024, as supply conditions have improved, official international reserves have risen, and consumer and investor confidence are expected to rise with the implementation of a program agreed with the International Monetary Fund. In Nepal, continued restrictive macroeconomic policies, lower external demand, and delayed monsoon rains will moderate growth in FY2024 below the previous projection. Bangladesh's growth forecast for FY2024 remains unchanged from April. Growth will be sustained there by rising exports, higher consumption as remittances grow, and higher government investment. The growth forecast for Bhutan is revised down for 2023 from April projections, owing to disappointing growth in agriculture and industry. The forecast for 2024 is revised up slightly, however, as energy output is expected to expand with the opening of new hydropower plants next year. In Maldives, April growth forecasts are retained for both this year and next.

Forecasts for subregional inflation are revised up from April to 8.6% in 2023 and 6.6% in 2024 (Figure 2.3.2). The revision for this year mainly reflects higher expected inflation in Pakistan and India. Average inflation in Pakistan will soar from 12.2% in FY2022 to 29.2% on higher food prices caused by supply shortages, continued currency depreciation, import restrictions, and fiscal stimulus for post-pandemic recovery. Normalized food supplies and lower inflation expectations, albeit tempered by higher power and gas tariffs and likely currency depreciation, could ease inflation somewhat in FY2024, but Pakistan's inflation rate is now expected to remain at 25.0% in FY2024, substantially higher than forecast in April. Headline inflation in India will moderate from 6.7% in 2022 to 5.5% in 2023. The forecast is higher than the *ADO April 2023* forecast because of unexpectedly high food prices. Inflation is expected to moderate to 4.2% in FY2024, slightly lower than previously forecast, due to core inflation becoming more subdued.

Figure 2.3.2 Inflation in South Asia

Soaring prices in Pakistan will push South Asia's inflation higher.

■ 2023   ■ 2024

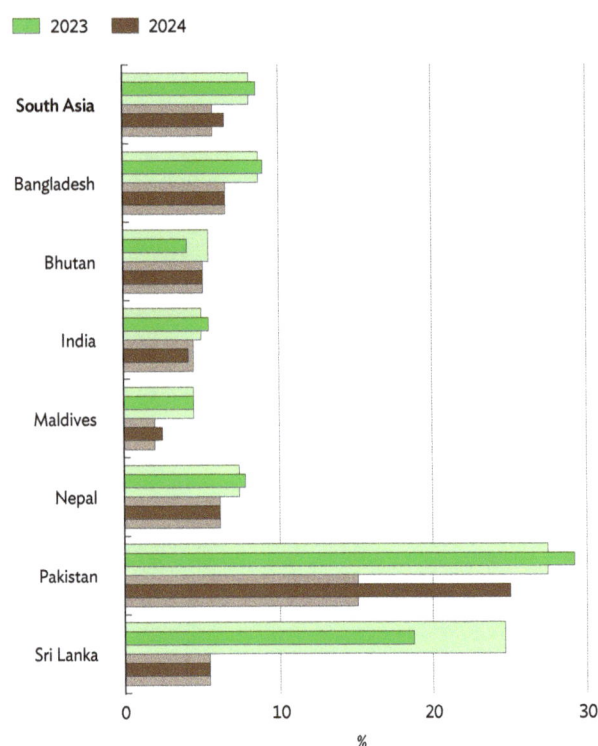

Note: Lighter colored bars are *Asian Development Outlook April 2023* forecasts.

Source: *Asian Development Outlook* database.

Inflation forecasts for the rest of the subregion are broadly unchanged from April projections.
Inflation in Sri Lanka moderated more than expected in H1 2023 on subdued demand. The downward trend is expected to continue, with inflation sharply lower in 2023 than previously forecast and in single digits in 2024. In Bangladesh, inflation exceeded the April forecast in FY2023 on rising energy and food prices, but it will ease in FY2024 to the rate projected in April as global nonfuel commodity prices fall, monetary policy gradually tightens and crop production improves. The inflation forecast for Bhutan is revised down for this year from April owing to a midyear drop in fuel prices and low food inflation. The April forecast for 2024 is retained. Inflation in Nepal was slightly higher in FY2023 than the April projection, reflecting a broad-based increase in prices, but the forecast is retained for FY2024 in anticipation of subdued increases for oil and moderating inflation in India, Nepal's dominant source of imports.

Inflation in Maldives is likely to be lower in 2023 than forecast in April as the hike in goods and services tax is now expected to have a more moderate impact on prices. In 2024, inflation will rise slightly higher than forecast in April owing to a base effect.

The economic outlook for South Asia is subject to significant risks. They include extreme weather conditions under climate change that may bring erratic rainfall, energy and food security challenges posed by the Russian invasion of Ukraine that could intensify inflationary pressures, and slippage in needed policy reform implementation that could dampen consumer and investor confidence.

Bangladesh

Growth, though higher than expected, moderated in fiscal year 2023 (FY2023, ended 30 June 2023).
This was in the face of the sharp decline in growth in major advanced counties that provide the external demand propelling the country's export-oriented economy. Inflation intensified on high commodity prices and shortfalls in meeting fuel and energy demands. Exports continued to grow, and a marked fall in imports sharply reduced the current account deficit. Growth in FY2024 is expected to edge up and inflation to ease.

Updated Assessment

GDP growth is estimated at 6.0% in FY2023.
Growth outperformed the projection of 5.3% in *ADO April 2023* but moderated from actual growth of 7.1% in FY2022 (Figure 2.3.3). On the supply side, the decline was mainly due to lower industrial activities. Industry sector growth declined to 8.2% in FY2023 from 9.9% in FY2022, mainly reflecting reduced export demand from advanced countries and domestic power and energy shortages. Large-scale manufacturing production growth fell from 15.7% to only 8.5% in FY2023. Growth in agriculture declined to 2.6% from 3.1% a year earlier as a result of inclement weather including floods, cyclones, and droughts. Services growth also declined to 5.8% from 6.3% following the trend in agriculture and industry, as domestic demand weakened due to erosion in incomes.

Figure 2.3.3 Supply-Side Contributions to Growth

Growth slowed on weak external demand in 2023, but will turn higher in 2024.

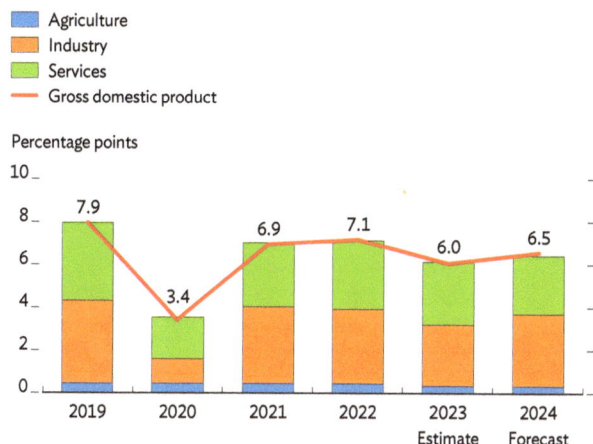

- Agriculture
- Industry
- Services
- Gross domestic product

Percentage points

Note: Years are fiscal years ending on 30 June of that year.
Sources: Bangladesh Bureau of Statistics; Asian Development Bank estimates.

On the demand-side, lower growth in private consumption and investment contributed to the dip in GDP growth. Decline in consumer purchasing power with rising inflation significantly affected private consumption, while public consumption expanded on higher recurrent expenditure. Private investment was constrained by higher input costs and restrictions on the issuance of import letters of credit to ration foreign exchange. Growth in public investment also decreased as only 84.2% of the annual development program was implemented in FY2023, compared to 92.7% in FY2022. With a sharp decline in imports, net exports added to growth.

Inflation surged to an average of 9.0% in FY2023 from 6.2% in FY2022 (Figure 2.3.4). Food inflation increased to 8.7% in FY2023 from 6.1% in FY2022 and nonfood inflation to 9.4% from 6.3%. Weaker agricultural production, some upward adjustments in administered domestic fuel and energy prices, although subsidies prevented a full pass-through of energy price increases, and the marked depreciation of the taka against the US dollar were the main causes of the sharp updraft in inflation and its stickiness through the end of the fiscal year.

Figure 2.3.4 Monthly Inflation

Price pressures intensified in 2023.

- Food
- Nonfood
- Overall

% year on year

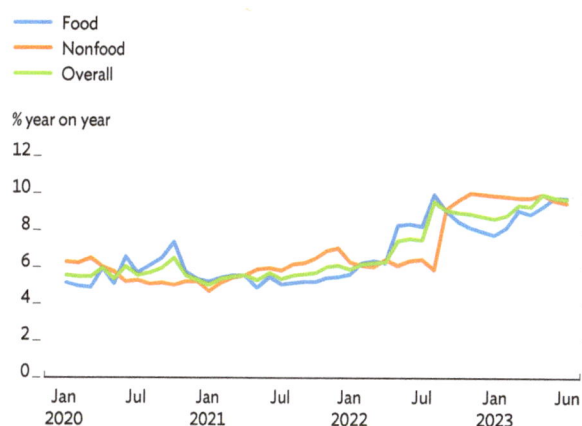

Source: Bangladesh Bank. 2023. *Monthly Economic Trends.* August.

Broad money growth increased to 10.5% in FY2023 from 9.4% in FY2022. Growth in credit to the public sector rose to 35.0% with a sharp increase in credit utilization by the government and other public sector organizations amid a decrease in the issuance of national savings certificates (Figure 2.3.5). Private sector credit in the same period grew by 10.6%, down from 13.7%, on lower investment amid import restrictions. To restrict credit growth and contain inflationary pressure, Bangladesh Bank, the central bank, raised its policy rate, the repo rate, by 1 percentage point to 6.0% in FY2023.

Figure 2.3.5 Growth of Monetary Indicators

Government borrowing from the banking system soared.

- Broad money
- Net credit to the government
- Credit to other public enterprises
- Credit to the private sector

%

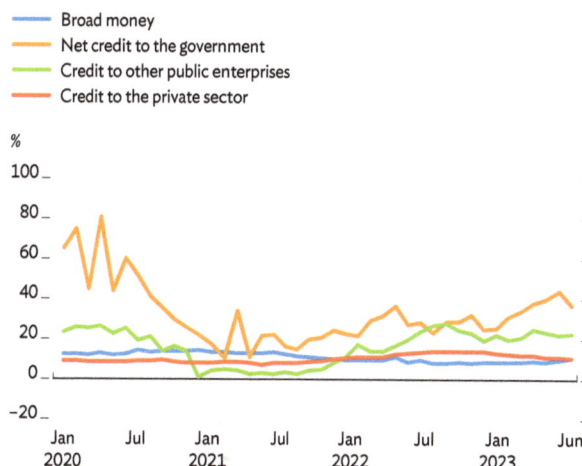

Source: Bangladesh Bank. 2023. *Major Economic Indicators: Monthly Update.* July.

The government's revised budget targets for FY2023 remained ambitious. The FY2023 revised budget targeted revenue collection and spending to grow by 29.4% and 27.5% over that in FY2022, equivalent to 9.8% of GDP and 14.9% of GDP, respectively. However, actual revenue collection by the National Board of Revenue expanded by only 10.2% in FY2023, while public spending rose by only 16.7% in the first 9 months. On balance these shortfalls are expected to be largely offsetting, and the FY2023 fiscal deficit is expected to widen to 5.1% of GDP, in line with the revised budget target and up from 4.6% in FY2022.

Exports grew by only 6.3% in FY2023, decelerating sharply from 33.4% expansion in FY2022. Export growth was entirely due to expansion in garment exports, which grew by 10.3%, as other exports fell sharply by 9.5%. The marked economic slowdown in the European Union and the US was mainly responsible for the sharp deceleration of export growth. Continued domestic energy and electricity shortages in factories also played a role.

Imports contracted by 15.8% to $69.5 billion in FY2023 from the marked 36.0% expansion in FY2022. Imports of intermediate goods decreased sharply by 19.8%, driven by decline in both garment-related intermediates and other intermediate goods for manufacturing. Capital goods imports decreased by 17.4%. Petroleum-related goods imports also declined. However, fertilizer and rice imports increased, driven by the government efforts to ensure food security. Import restriction measures taken by the central bank to limit a marked decline in its foreign exchange reserves played a significant role in the contraction along with slower growth.

The trade deficit narrowed to $17.2 billion in FY2023 as imports were sharply reduced while exports expanded moderately (Figure 2.3.6). Remittances increased to $21.6 billion, helped by a sharply depreciated Bangladesh taka, government cash incentives, and increased ease of transfer through mobile financial services. Because of the lower trade deficit and higher remittances, the current account deficit narrowed sharply to $3.3 billion or 0.7% of GDP in FY2023, from $18.6 billion or 4.1% of GDP in FY2022 (Figure 2.3.7).

Figure 2.3.6 Monthly Exports and Imports

The trade deficit narrowed on a decline in imports.

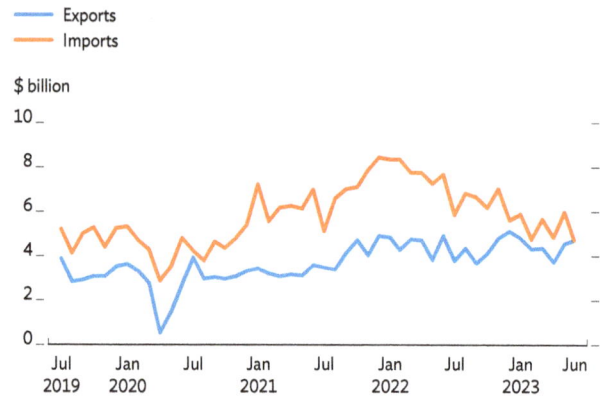

Source: Bangladesh Bank. 2023. *Major Economic Indicators: Monthly Update.* July.

Figure 2.3.7 Current Account Components

The current account deficit sharply narrowed on a fall in the trade deficit and growth in remittances in 2023.

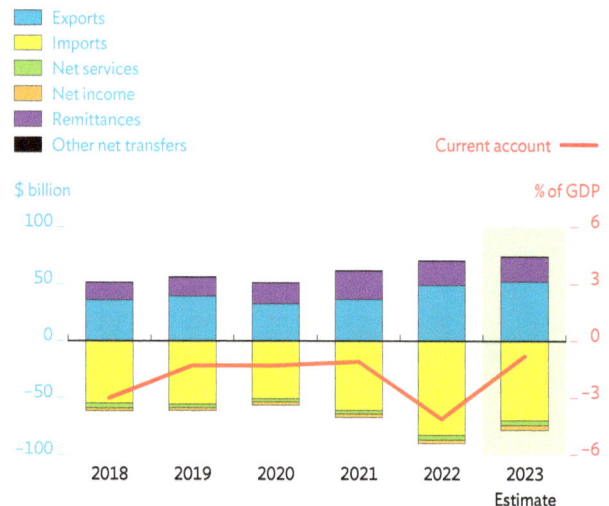

GDP = gross domestic product.
Note: Years are fiscal years ending on 30 June of that year.
Source: Bangladesh Bank.

Even with a significantly reduced current account, sharply reduced financial inflows including a decline in medium- and long-term loans and other short-term loans of the private sector led to gross foreign exchange reserves falling by $10.6 billion, about 25%, to $31.2 billion. This level provided cover for over 4 months of imports of goods and services (Figure 2.3.8).

Figure 2.3.8 Gross Foreign Exchange Reserves

Foreign exchange reserves have declined markedly since January 2022.

Source: Bangladesh Bank.

Figure 2.3.9 Exchange Rates

The taka depreciated sharply against the US dollar and in real effective terms.

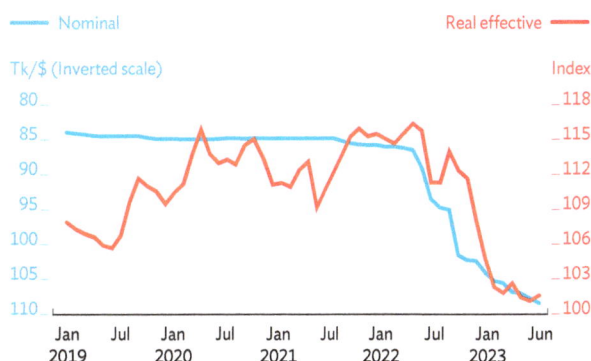

Source: Bangladesh Bank. 2023. *Monthly Economic Trends*. August.

The taka depreciated by 13.8% against the US dollar at the end of June in FY2023 from a year earlier (Figure 2.3.9). Bangladesh Bank followed a path of gradual adjustment of US dollar exchange rate toward a market-driven rate as it sold net $13.4 billion during the year to commercial banks to curb excessive exchange rate volatility. The taka depreciated in real effective terms by 8.6% in June 2023 from a year earlier.

Prospects

The economy is expected to grow slightly faster in FY2024 with easing inflation and some improvement in export growth. GDP growth projection in FY2024 is retained at 6.5%, higher than 6.0% in FY2023, due to continued export growth supported by economic recovery in the euro area (Table 2.3.1). Import growth is expected to return to positive territory due to an increase in demand for export-related intermediates and government imports. Moderate inflation and an increase in remittances will contribute to reviving private consumption, while completion of a number of major government infrastructure projects will increase investment (Figure 2.3.10). Private investment, however, may be dampened by the initial higher interest rates resulting from a revision in the country's monetary policy framework.

Table 2.3.1 Selected Economic Indicators in Bangladesh, %

Growth slowed somewhat less than expected on weak global demand but will meet the ADO April 2023 forecast in 2024.

	2022	2023		2024	
		Apr	Sep	Apr	Sep
GDP growth	7.1	5.3	6.0	6.5	6.5
Inflation	6.2	8.7	9.0	6.6	6.6

GDP = gross domestic product.
Note: Years are fiscal years ending on 30 June of that year.
Sources: Bangladesh Bureau of Statistics; Asian Development Bank estimates.

Figure 2.3.10 Demand-Side Contributions to Growth

Subdued consumption and investment pulls down growth in 2023.

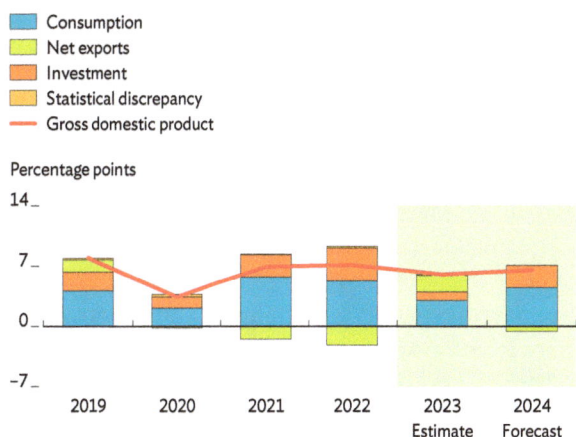

Note: Years are fiscal years ending on 30 June of that year.
Sources: Bangladesh Bureau of Statistics; Asian Development Bank estimates.

On the supply side, industry is expected to contribute most to growth. Agriculture sector growth is projected to increase to 2.9% in FY2024 assuming normal weather and government policy support including distribution of quality seed, fertilizers, and training to farmers. Growth in the industry sector is expected to rise to 9.3% in FY2024, driven by improvement in power supply and better access to imports. However, growth in the services sector is expected to be slower at 5.5%, with expected lower growth in real estate and human health and social work activities.

Inflation is projected to decline to 6.6% in FY2024. Though high inflation may persist in the first months of the fiscal year, it is expected that it will come down with some fall in global nonfuel commodity prices, expected higher agricultural production, and the initial tightening of monetary policy under the new framework.

Monetary policy is expected to be tightened in FY2024. It will feature a transition from a monetary aggregate targeting framework to an interest rate-targeting framework. Bangladesh Bank has increased the policy interest rate from 6.0% to 6.5% accompanied by a symmetric corridor of 200 basis points for the standing loan and deposit facilities. Bangladesh Bank also replaced the cap lending rate with a market-driven lending rate for bank loans based on a reference lending rate called SMART (6-month moving average rate of treasury bills). In FY2024, applicable lending rates will be SMART plus a margin of up to 3% for banks, and SMART plus a margin of up to 5% for nonbank financial institutions. Loans to cottage, micro, small, and medium-sized enterprises, and consumers could be charged an additional fee of up to 1 percentage point on top of above margin to cover supervision costs. Bangladesh Bank is also adopting a single market-driven exchange rate and calculating gross foreign exchange reserves in accordance with the sixth edition of the International Monetary Fund's Balance of Payments and International Investment Position Manual.

The government's FY2024 budget is ambitious. It aims to achieve a ratio of revenue to GDP at 10.0% and of expenditure to GDP at 15.2% with a resulting fiscal deficit of 5.2% of GDP, marginally higher than FY2023 revised budget target of 5.1%.

The policy is directed at slimming current expenditure and expanding capital expenditure. It is expected that 60.0% of the deficit will be financed domestically: 85.2% from banks and the remaining 14.8% from nonbank sources, mostly the sale of national saving certificates.

As part of the government's ongoing structural reform program, the Income Tax Act, 2023 was passed in Parliament. The new law includes changes to accounting methods, depreciation and amortization rules, provisions related to capital gains, income from intangible assets, transfer pricing, and alternative dispute resolution provisions. To facilitate business and investment, instead of filing 29 returns and statements related to tax deduction at source in the existing law, only 12 are required in the new law. The new tax law will help enhance domestic resource mobilization by ensuring tax compliance, greater tax return filing under self-assessment, better return process and audit provisions, and international standardization.

Export growth is projected to slightly accelerate to 9.0% in FY2024. Improved electricity and energy supply and a fully market-oriented exchange rate are expected to support higher growth, especially for non-garment exports, which sharply declined in FY2023. Imports are expected to rebound and grow at 7.0% with an increase in import demand for intermediates and capital goods.

The trade deficit is forecast to slightly widen to $17.3 billion in FY2024 as the increase in imports surpasses that of exports in nominal terms. Remittances growth will accelerate to 8.4% as a market-driven exchange rate and cash incentives are expected to encourage increased transfer through official channels. With increased remittances, the current account deficit is forecast to narrow slightly to 0.5% of GDP in FY2024.

However, there are some downside risks to growth. These include the effects of any adverse weather events and further deterioration in the balance of payments situation if global demand is weaker than expected.

India

Despite global uncertainties, the economy showed robust growth in the first quarter (Q1) of fiscal year 2023 (FY2023, ending 31 March 2024), driven by strong government and private investment and private consumption. The growth forecast for FY2023 is modestly lowered from the projection in *ADO April 2023* due to lower-than-expected agricultural output but retained for FY2024 as corporate profitability and strong bank credit buoy private investment. Inflation has moderated broadly, but the forecast for FY2023 is raised owing to a spike in food prices, and the forecast for FY2024 is marginally lowered as core inflation moderates.

Updated Assessment

Robust domestic demand pushed GDP growth to 7.8% year on year in Q1 FY2023. Investment growth was above 8% for the past 5 quarters on rising government infrastructure and private investment outlays. Private consumption growth rose to 6% in Q1 FY2023 after tepid growth in the previous 2 quarters. The recovery was expected, given improving consumer sentiment and labor market conditions, but was dampened by subdued rural demand. Public consumption remained weak as the government's focus has been on raising capital expenditure. The contribution of net exports to growth was negative as exports fell by 7.7% in real terms on weak external demand (Figure 2.3.11).

On the supply side, the services sector was the main contributor to GDP growth, rising by 10.3%. Financial, real estate, and business services grew by 12.2% year on year in Q1 FY2023, and trade and hotel and communication services by 9.2%. The manufacturing and electricity sectors grew moderately by 4.7% and 2.9%, respectively, and the agriculture sector by 3.5% (Figure 2.3.12).

Inflationary pressures broadly moderated, but food prices spiked. Consumer inflation averaged 5.3% during April–July FY2023, much lower than 7.1% in the corresponding period of FY2022. The broad moderation in inflation was led by cooling global energy prices, particularly for crude oil and coal, which has helped lower fuel inflation and input costs. Core inflation, which was sticky at around 5.8% in July 2022, was down to 4.9% year on year in July 2023 (Figure 2.3.13).

Figure 2.3.11 Demand-Side Contributions to Growth

Investment and private consumption drove growth in Q1 2023.

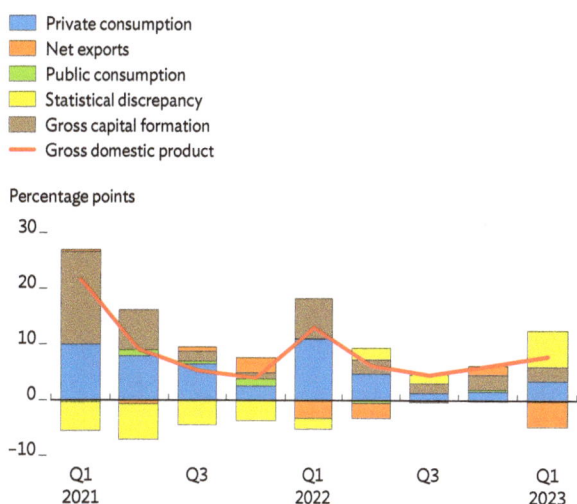

Q = quarter.
Note: Years are fiscal years ending on 31 March of the next year.
Source: Ministry of Statistics and Programme Implementation.

Figure 2.3.12 Supply-Side Contributions to Growth

The services sector was the main contributor to growth in Q1 FY2023.

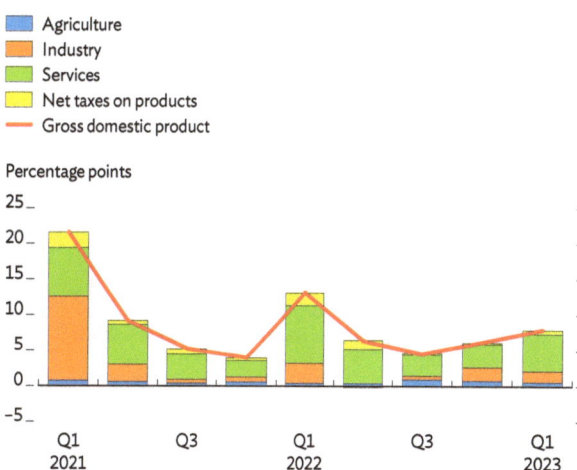

FY = fiscal year, Q = quarter.
Note: Years are fiscal years ending on 31 March of the next year.
Source: Ministry of Statistics and Programme Implementation.

However, food prices have risen sharply, led by high inflation in cereals, pulses, and vegetables. While vegetable price inflation is likely short term, resulting from supply volatility, the erratic rainfall patterns across regions could result in lower crop production in the summer (*kharif*) cropping season, putting further pressure on food prices (Figure 2.3.14).

Figure 2.3.13 Consumer Inflation

Inflation rose in July 2023 on a spike in food prices.

- Headline
- Core
- Food and beverages
- Fuel and light

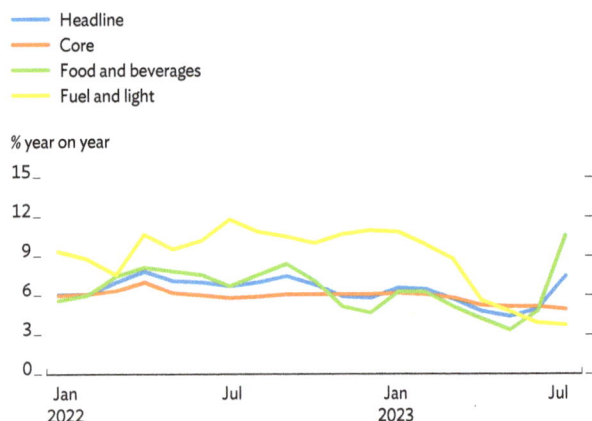

Source: Reserve Bank of India.

Figure 2.3.15 Interest Rates

Lending rates have edged up but less than the policy rate.

- Lending rate
- Policy rate
- Government securities yield (10 years)

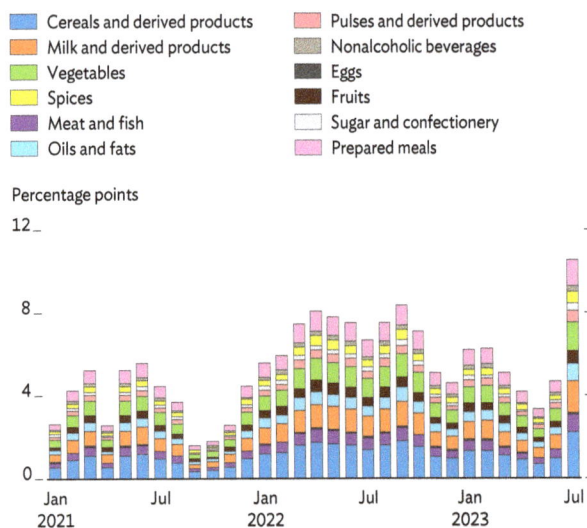

Source: Reserve Bank of India.

Figure 2.3.14 Contributions to Food Price Inflation

Food prices spiked from higher prices for many categories.

- Cereals and derived products
- Milk and derived products
- Vegetables
- Spices
- Meat and fish
- Oils and fats
- Pulses and derived products
- Nonalcoholic beverages
- Eggs
- Fruits
- Sugar and confectionery
- Prepared meals

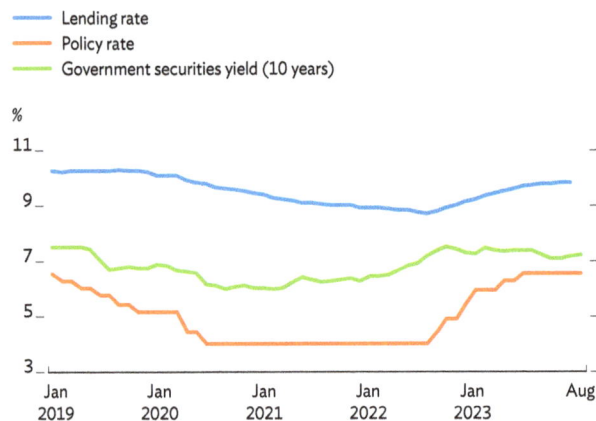

Source: Reserve Bank of India.

The monetary policy rate has remained stable since February 2023 as inflation moderated.
To combat inflation, the Reserve Bank of India, the central bank, raised its policy (repo) rate from 4.0% to 6.5% from April 2022 to February 2023. Since then, the policy rate has been unchanged. However, broader monetary policy remains focused on bringing consumer inflation closer to the medium-term target of 4%, while supporting economic growth.

It is important to note that, while the policy rate has risen by 250 basis points since April 2022, the average bank lending rate has increased by only 106 basis points, indicating incomplete monetary policy transmission (Figure 2.3.15).

Bank credit growth remains robust and nonperforming loans remain low. Nonfood bank credit (excluding working capital loans for public food purchases) grew by 19.8% year on year in July 2023, compared to 13.8% in July 2022, faster than nominal GDP growth (Figure 2.3.16). The services sector and personal loans were major contributors to faster growth, while credit flow to large industrial firms was muted. High personal loan growth is driven by housing and vehicle purchases and consumer durables loans. India's banking sector has been relatively insulated from the global financial turmoil, helped by low nonperforming loans, an improved capital base, and a stronger regulatory regime to deal with delinquencies. At the end of March 2023, gross nonperforming assets in the banking sector were at their lowest point in the past 10 years, amounting to 3.9% of total loans compared to 5.0% in September 2022. Financial sector stress in India has sometimes emerged from the vulnerabilities of the nonbanking financial corporations. However, reflecting greater regulatory oversight by the central bank, the gross nonperforming assets of nonbanking financial corporations have remained low, falling to 3.8% of their loans in March 2023 from 5.8% in March 2022.

Figure 2.3.16 Growth in Nonfood Bank Credit

Nonfood bank credit has grown steadily.

- Agriculture
- Industry
- Services
- Personal loans
- Other nonfood credit
- Nominal GDP

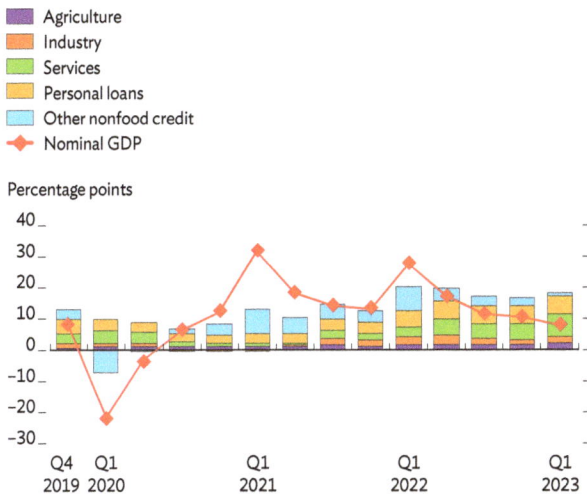

GDP = gross domestic product, Q = quarter.
Source: Haver Analytics.

Government investment is growing at a fast rate, but revenue collections have been slow. In the first 4 months of FY2023, central government revenues (net of states' share) grew by 0.7%, affected by dampened collections from corporate tax and taxes on petroleum sales, despite income tax and goods and services tax collections growing by 6.4% and 11.4% respectively. The gap in revenue collection has been partly mitigated by the flow of central bank dividend payments to the central government, which increased to ₹874 billion from ₹303 billion in Q1 FY2022. Central government capital expenditure increased by 52% year on year during April–July FY2023, putting the government on track to meet its budget target of a 35% increase in capital spending in FY2023. Current expenditure also increased by 15.9% in the first 4 months of FY2023, leading to total expenditure increasing by 22.5%. As a consequence of larger capital expenditure and low revenue growth, the central government's fiscal deficit reached 35% of the annual target by July 2023, in comparison to 21% in the previous year. The state governments have also ramped up their capital expenditure in Q1 FY2023, with data for 23 states showing an increase in capital expenditure by 74%.(Figure 2.3.17).

The trade deficit shrank during the first 4 months of FY2023 as both imports and exports contracted. Goods imports declined by 14% year on year during April to July 2023. Low crude oil prices lowered petroleum imports. Most major categories of nonpetroleum imports also saw contraction, including gold, fertilizers, pearls and precious stones, coal, coke and briquettes, and vegetable oil. Goods exports contracted by 14.5% year on year during April–July 2023 due to muted demand in advanced nations and lower commodity prices, although electronic goods continued to show double-digit growth. During Q1 FY2023, service exports and imports growth also slowed year on year to 7.6% and 0.2%, respectively (Figure 2.3.18).

Figure 2.3.17 Central Government Revenue and Expenditure

Total government spending has fallen as its capital expenditure has risen.

- Revenue receipts
- Revenue expenditure
- Capital expenditure
- Total expenditure

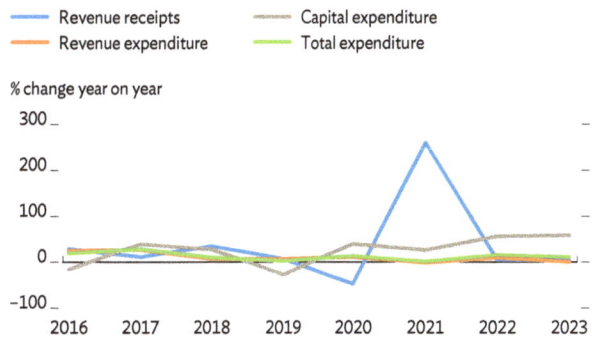

Note: Data show growth in the April–July period over the corresponding period of the previous year.
Source: Comptroller General of Accounts.

Figure 2.3.18 Trade Balance

The trade deficit shrank as balances for both services and goods improved.

- Goods balance
- Service balance
- Trade balance

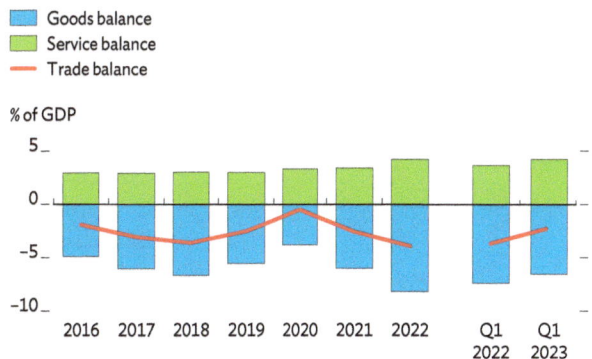

GDP = gross domestic product, Q = quarter.
Note: Years are fiscal years ending on 31 March of the next year.
Source: CEIC Data Company.

Foreign direct investment declined during the first 2 months of FY2023, but foreign portfolio investment flows were strong. Net foreign direct investment declined to $5 billion in Q1 FY2023 from $13.4 billion in Q1 FY2022. This was balanced by a strong increase in net portfolio investment despite tighter monetary policy globally, from net outflows of $14.0 billion in Q1 FY2022 to net inflows of $15 billion. Due to a lower trade deficit and high growth in personal remittances, the current account deficit decreased from 2.0% of GDP in Q3 FY2022 to 0.2% of GDP in Q4 FY2022. Foreign exchange reserves remained robust and covered 11 months of imports at the end of July 2023. The rupee–dollar exchange rate was relatively stable in the first 4 months of FY2023 at an average value of ₹82.19 per dollar, almost unchanged from the end of FY2022.

Prospects

The growth trajectory is broadly consistent with expectations in *ADO April 2023* (Table 2.3.2). An exception is lower growth of the agriculture sector. Since *ADO April 2023*, monsoon rainfall under the influence of a developing El Niño has led to erratic weather patterns, including flooding in certain regions and deficient rains, particularly in August. The erratic rainfall patterns have resulted in damage to the rice crop in particular and lower sowing in 2023 for pulses in the *kharif* season. The *ADO April 2023* forecast of robust growth of the sector in FY2023 had assumed no extreme weather shocks. However, given the current rain patterns, agriculture growth projection is revised down by almost a percentage point for FY2023, with FY2024 growth remaining the same under the assumption of normal rainfall next year.

Table 2.3.2 Selected Economic Indicators in India, %

The growth forecast is lowered marginally for FY2023 and retained for FY2024, while forecast inflation is raised for this fiscal year and lowered for next year.

	2022	2023		2024	
		Apr	Sep	Apr	Sep
GDP growth	7.2	6.4	6.3	6.7	6.7
Inflation	6.7	5.0	5.5	4.5	4.2

GDP = gross domestic product.

Note: Years are fiscal years ending on 31 March of the next year.

Sources: Ministry of Statistics and Programme Implementation, Government of India; Reserve Bank of India; Asian Development Bank estimates.

Growth in services is forecast higher, while the industry outlook remains the same. The services sector will continue to grow strongly in FY2023 and FY2024, supported by a high-performing banking sector, as well as professional services and real estate. Purchasing managers' indexes for manufacturing and services remain high (Figure 2.3.19), as does the industrial business outlook (Figure 2.3.20). Manufacturing sector growth will be slower than services in FY2023 but will improve in FY2024 on the back of a more optimistic industrial outlook and the government's policy efforts to boost manufacturing output.

Figure 2.3.19 Purchasing Managers' Indexes

Purchasing managers' indexes remain high.

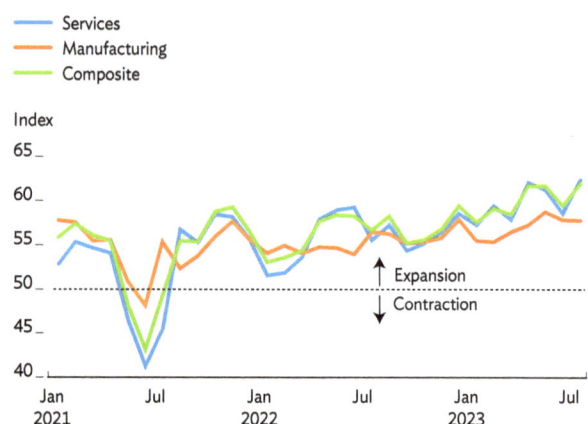

Source: CEIC Data Company.

Figure 2.3.20 Industrial Business Outlook

The business outlook remains healthy.

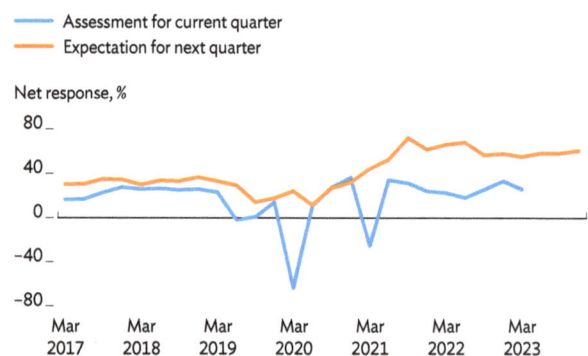

Notes: Net response is the difference between the percentage of respondents reporting optimism and those reporting pessimism. A value >0 indicates optimism for expansion, <0 pessimism about contraction.

Source: Reserve Bank of India.

Consumption will be robust in FY2023 with an improving labor market, especially formal sector employment. The gradual lowering of consumer price inflation will further fuel consumption growth. Consumer confidence is improving, as expected, with the index increasing from 84.8 in January 2023 to 88.1 in July 2023 (Figure 2.3.21). Consumer sentiment is expected to further improve in 2024. Nevertheless, consumption growth in 2023 would be lower than expected in *ADO April 2023* due to expected weakness in rural consumption. As the agriculture sector contributes majorly to the rural economy, erratic rainfall patterns affecting *kharif* crop output will likely lower agricultural income, thus affecting consumption. Export restrictions on certain varieties of rice and onions and other measures to contain prices may also impact farmer incomes.

Prospects for investment are getting better steadily despite the rise in interest rates. Both central and state government capital expenditure growth is expected to continue to be strong in FY2023 and FY2024. Further, there is a continued uptick in the new investment project announcements, including by the private sector (Figure 2.3.22). Infrastructure sectors like roads and energy projects account for the majority of the increase in new projects, due to policy emphasis in these sectors. Private sector investment growth is driven by improving business outlook owing to rising corporate profitability, as input price increases have cooled off, and bank credit flows have been strong. This is expected to continue in 2024 as well, along with a pickup in large manufacturing investments, driven by the implementation of private sector projects announced under the government production-linked incentives scheme. Household investment in real estate will also continue to grow strongly, fueled by improvement in housing affordability and improving urban incomes.

External demand is muted, and lower commodity prices will lower imports. The contraction in goods exports and slowing of services exports will continue in the remaining part of FY2023 due to weak demand in global markets, as expected in *ADO April 2023*. However, falling prices for imported energy relative to 2022 will help improve economic growth in FY2023. Both exports and imports are expected to improve in FY2024. On balance, net exports' contribution to growth will be negligible in FY2023 and FY2024.

Figure 2.3.21 Consumer Confidence Survey

Consumer confidence is rising.

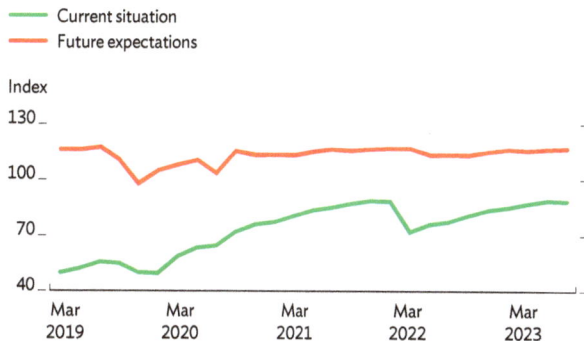

Notes: The consumer confidence index is based on the responses of respondents on the economic situation, income, spending, employment, and prices. A value >100 indicates net optimism, <100 net pessimism.
Source: Reserve Bank of India.

Figure 2.3.22 New Investment Projects Announced

Rising project announcements point to robust investment growth.

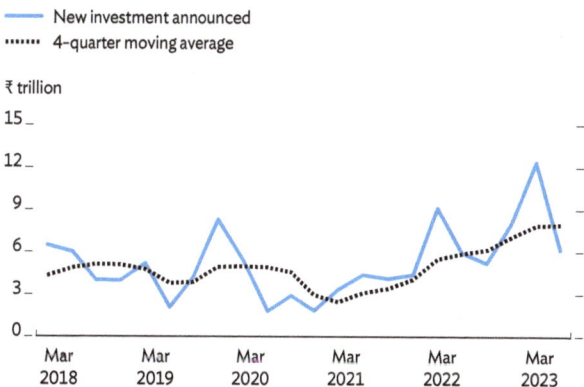

Source: Centre for Monitoring of Indian Economy.

Monetary and fiscal policies are expected to broadly support economic growth. Risks to growth from further monetary policy tightening are diminishing as core inflation and inflationary expectations have started to moderate, as indicated by central bank surveys. Given the current inflation outlook, the central bank is not expected to raise its policy rate in FY2023 and may lower it in FY2024. Fiscal policy is expected to be supportive of growth, by maintaining high government investment levels, and also with further fiscal consolidation, greater financial space will be available for the private sector borrowings to fund investment.

GDP growth forecast is revised down from the ADO April 2023 projection to 6.3% in FY2023 and maintained at 6.7% for FY2024. On balance, India's economic growth will be resilient and strong. The lower FY2023 growth forecast takes into account the impact of extreme rainfall spatial patterns on *kharif* output, while the forecast for FY2024 assumes that rising private investments and industrial expansion will propel growth.

Inflation is expected to moderate to 5.5% in FY2023 and 4.2% in FY2024. The forecast for FY2023 is higher than that in *ADO April 2023* on account of expectations of higher food prices. This forecast takes into account the effect of various government policy actions to reduce inflation, including export prohibition on non-basmati varieties of rice, export duties on other rice varieties, the maintenance of buffer stocks of pulses and onions, the removal of import duties on pulse imports, and a new fuel subsidy for cooking gas. On the other hand, core inflation is moderating at a faster-than-expected rate, which will dampen overall consumer inflation in FY2024 to 4.2%, lower than projected in *ADO April 2023*.

The current account deficit is forecast at the equivalent of 1.8% of GDP in FY2023, lower than projected in *ADO April 2023*. A shrinking trade deficit, robust growth in service exports and improving remittances are key factors for improving external balances. The current account deficit is expected to be equivalent to 1.7% of GDP in FY2024. While foreign direct investment is expected to continue to be tepid, portfolio inflows can be expected to improve further, leading to stronger balance of payment position for India going forward.

The outlook is subject to both upside and downside risks. The downside risks arise from global geopolitical tensions, which may further create economic uncertainty and/or lead to a rapid rise in the global food prices. Further weather-related shocks either at the time of harvesting of *kharif* season (July–October) or during the October–April rabi season may further affect agriculture growth. On the upside, economic growth could be higher in FY2024 than expected if foreign direct investment inflows are larger, particularly in the manufacturing sector, as a result of multinational corporations diversifying their supply chains by including India as a production location.

Pakistan

In fiscal year 2023 (FY2023, ended 30 June 2023), the economy was buffeted by severe floods, global price shocks, and political instability. Expansionary fiscal and monetary policy hit their limits. Growth fell, inflation jumped, the Pakistan rupee weakened, and international reserves shrank. In response, fiscal and monetary policy have been tightened. Adherence to an economic adjustment program through April 2024 will be critical for restoring stability and the gradual recovery of growth, which is projected to reach a moderate 1.9% in FY2024, with price pressures remaining elevated. Downside risks to the outlook remain exceptionally high.

Updated Assessment

Before FY2023, Pakistan had 2 years of strong growth but with rising imbalances. In FY2021 and FY2022, growth averaged 6.0%. Domestic demand was robust, stoked by fiscal deficits averaging 7.0% of GDP, negative real policy rates, and concessionary lending schemes. The current account deficit swelled from 0.8% of GDP in FY2021 to 4.7% in FY2022, driven by large trade deficits. Average inflation rose from 8.9% to 12.2% in FY2022.

Severe shocks and policy slippage raised economic volatility in FY2023. Massive floods hurt farm output and food stocks, jacking up food prices. Political unrest reduced investor confidence and consumer spending. High global prices for food and fuel cut purchasing power and raised import costs. Slower global growth curbed exports, and global monetary tightening reduced financing flows. Nevertheless, expansionary policies were continued, including large fuel and electricity subsidies. Due to missed targets under an International Monetary Fund (IMF) extended fund facility, IMF financing ceased, and flows from bilateral and multilateral sources also slowed. Tight foreign exchange controls reduced imports, which curtailed production due to the scarcity of critical inputs.

Consequently, real GDP stagnated, and inflation jumped. Growth is provisionally estimated to have reached only 0.3% in FY2023 after 6.1% in FY2022 (Figure 2.3.23).

Figure 2.3.23 Supply-Side Contributions to Growth

Growth slowed significantly in 2023 across all productive sectors.

- Agriculture
- Industry
- Services
- Gross domestic product

Percentage points

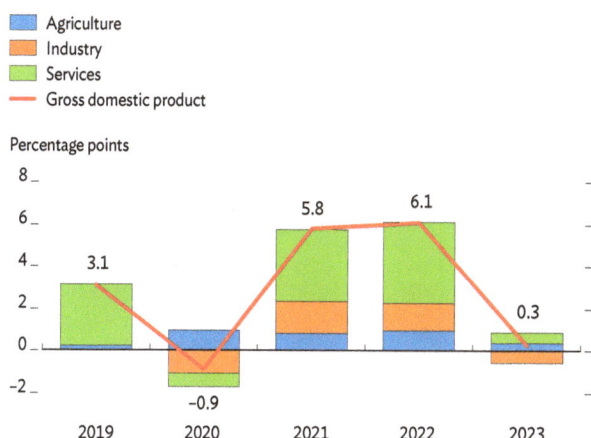

Notes: Years are fiscal years ending on 30 June of that year. GDP at basic prices excludes indirect taxes less subsidies.
Source: Pakistan Bureau of Statistics, *National Accounts Tables Base FY2016.*

Figure 2.3.24 Inflation

Inflation jumped to a 5-decade high due to high food and fuel prices.

- Food, contribution to inflation
- Nonfood, contribution to inflation
- Headline
- Core, urban
- Core, rural

% year on year

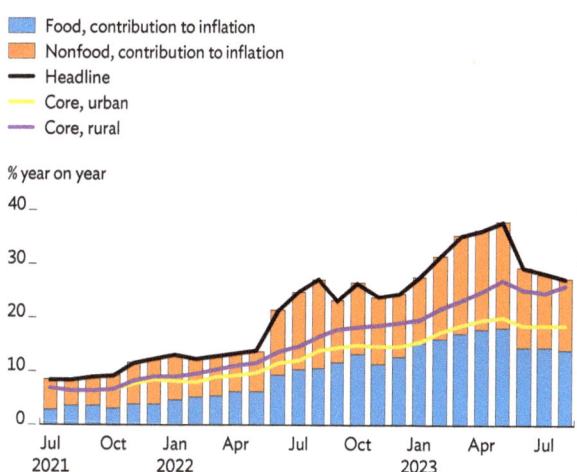

Source: Pakistan Bureau of Statistics, *Monthly Review on Price Indices, July 2023.*

Headline inflation averaged 29.2% in FY2023, a 5-decade high, largely reflecting higher food prices. But core inflation, which excludes food and energy prices, was also high, at 16.1% for urban areas and 20.5% for rural (Figure 2.3.24).

The slowdown spanned the main productive sectors. Agricultural output grew by only 1.6%, compared to 4.3% the previous year. Cotton and rice production fell, offsetting higher output of sugarcane, wheat, and livestock. Industrial production declined by 2.9%, against growth of 6.8% in FY2022. Manufacturing output shrank by 3.9%, with especially large declines in textiles (18.7%), autos (50.0%), and pharmaceuticals (28.8%) (Figure 2.3.25). Construction decreased by 5.5%. Service output grew by only 0.9%, compared to 6.6% in FY2022. Strong increases in education and in information and communication services barely overcame contraction in trade, finance and insurance services, and general government services.

The slowdown was similarly broad across demand categories. Private consumption, which represents 88% of GDP, grew by 1.6%, compared to 6.8% in FY2022. Gross fixed capital formation fell by 17.8%, reflecting declines both in private and public sector investment. Exports shrank to 9.2% of GDP from 10.2% in FY2022 in national income account terms due to the supply shock from floods and ad hoc import controls.

Figure 2.3.25 Large-Scale Manufacturing

Manufacturing output shrank in key sectors from high global fuel prices and import controls.

- Quantum Index of LSM
- Growth

LSM = large-scale manufacturing.
Note: Years are fiscal years ending on 30 June of that year.
Source: Pakistan Bureau of Statistics. *Quantum Index Numbers of Large-Scale Manufacturing Industries.* June 2023.

But because imports fell much more than exports, net exports contributed 3.4 percentage points to GDP growth (Figure 2.3.26).

Lending stagnated on reduced activity, lower confidence, and higher interest rates. Loans to the private sector in FY2023 barely grew, compared to a rise of 21.1% in the previous year. While lending for fixed investment expanded by 6.6%, lending for working capital and consumer financing declined by 3.6%, reversing a 20.9% increase in FY2022.

Figure 2.3.26 Components of Demand Growth

Private consumption stagnated, while investment fell sharply.

- Final consumption
- Net exports
- Gross capital formation
- Total demand

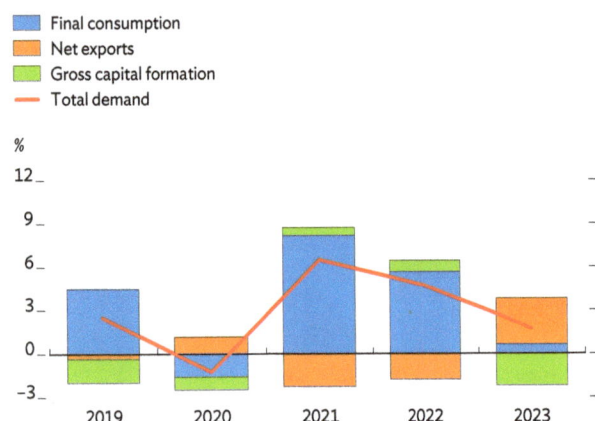

Notes: Years are fiscal years ending on 30 June of that year. Total demand is gross domestic product at market prices, which includes indirect taxes less subsidies.
Source: Pakistan Bureau of Statistics, *National Accounts Tables Base FY2016.*

Figure 2.3.27 Bank Lending

Lending to the private sector stagnated, on low confidence and high interest rates.

- Lending to government
- Lending to private sector
- M2

PRs billion   % of GDP

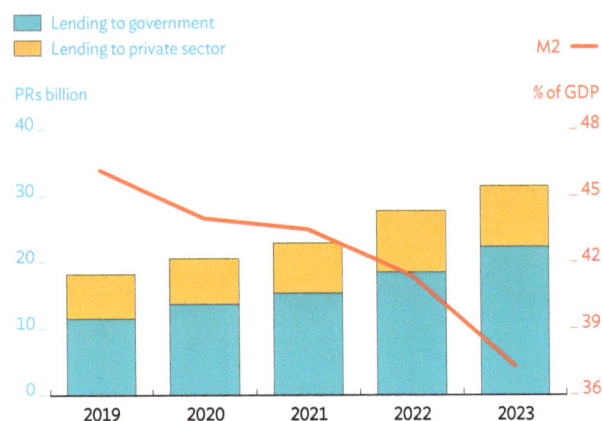

Notes: Years are fiscal years ending on 30 June of that year. Lending to government is net government borrowing for budgetary support.
Source: State Bank of Pakistan. Monetary Policy Compendium. July 2023.

However, strong capital and liquidity buffers kept the banking sector stable in FY2023. At the end of June 2023, banks' capital adequacy and liquidity coverage ratios stood at 17.8% and 107.9%, respectively, well above the statutory requirements. Gross nonperforming loans as a percentage of all loans fell from 7.8% in March 2023 to 7.4% in June 2023. However, provisioning against nonperforming loans continued its rise since December 2022, reaching 94.4% at the end of June 2023 (Figure 2.3.27).

Ad hoc import controls cut the current account deficit but at some cost. The current account deficit shrank by 85% in FY2023 to $2.6 billion (or 0.7% of GDP) from $17.5 billion (or 4.7% of GDP) in FY2022 (Figure 2.3.28). Imports of goods and services fell by 29.0% in FY2023 to $60.0 billion. Imports of key merchandise, including petroleum, machinery, and metals, declined, although food imports rose because of higher edible oil prices and imports of wheat to rebuild stocks. Import controls raised production costs, made critical inputs scarce, and thus hurt exports, with textiles and agriculture most affected. Exports of goods and services slipped by 11.1% to $35.2 billion (Figure 2.3.29). Administrative efforts to control the exchange rate led to the emergence of a parallel foreign exchange market with a substantial premium over the official exchange rate (Figure 2.3.30).

Figure 2.3.28 Current Account Balance

The current account deficit shrank after strict import controls were imposed.

- Trade balance
- Income
- Services balance
- Current transfers, including remittances
- Current account balance

$ billion

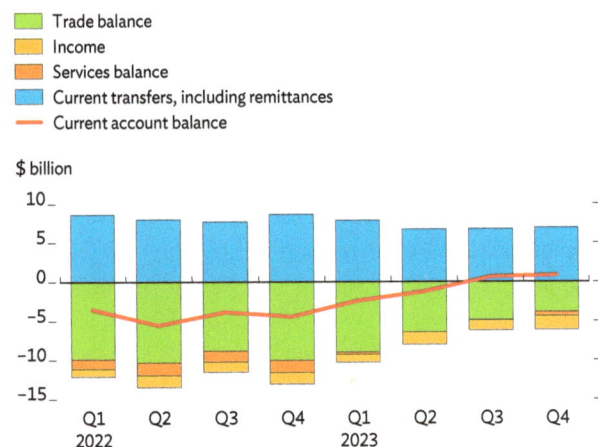

Q = quarter.
Note: Years are fiscal years ending on 30 June of that year.
Source: State Bank of Pakistan. *Economic Data: External Sector.* Summary Balance of Payments as per BPM6—August 2023.

This, in turn, led to a further tightening of foreign currency liquidity in the interbank market by encouraging the use of the parallel market for inward remittances and proceeds from service exports. Consequently, recorded workers' remittances fell by $4.3 billion to $27.0 billion in FY2023.

Figure 2.3.29 Balance of Trade

The trade deficit narrowed, though cuts in imports also reduced exports.

- Merchandise exports
- Merchandise imports
- Merchandise trade balance

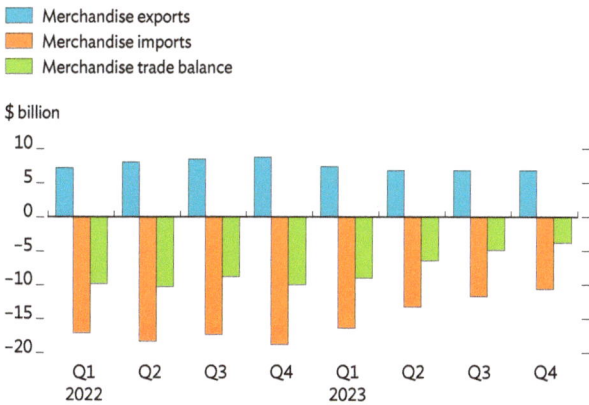

Q = quarter.

Note: Years are fiscal years ending on 30 June of that year.

Source: State Bank of Pakistan. *Economic Data: External Sector.* Summary Balance of Payments as per BPM6—August 2023.

Figure 2.3.30 Interbank and Open Market Foreign Exchange Rates

Exchange rate controls led to a substantial difference between the official interbank and open market rates.

- Interbank
- Open market
- % difference

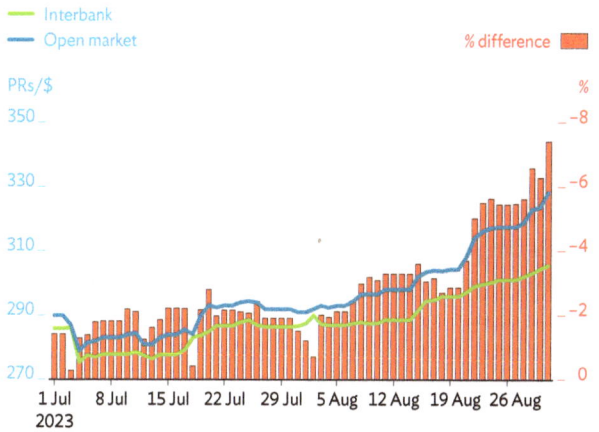

Source: State Bank of Pakistan. *Economic Data.*

Despite a sharply narrowed current account deficit, international reserves plunged. Net international reserves fell by more than half during FY2023, to $4.5 billion from $9.8 billion at the end of FY2022, reflecting a 40% larger outflow for external debt repayments (Figure 2.3.31). Official inflows declined by 12% from FY2022 as multilateral and bilateral flows diminished with the suspension of the previous IMF program. Pakistan could not issue bonds in international capital markets, while inflows of foreign direct investment declined by 33% to $1.5 billion in FY2023, less than in each of the previous 3 years, reflecting low confidence from economic volatility and political uncertainty. Portfolio investment saw a net outflow of $1.0 billion, as the Sukuk (Islamic) dollar bond came due for repayment in December 2022. In July 2023, after Pakistan reached agreement with the IMF, the IMF disbursed $1.2 billion while Saudi Arabia and the United Arab Emirates lent a total of $3.0 billion, raising foreign reserves to $8.2 billion.

The fiscal deficit remained high, on weak tax collection and higher interest outlays. The target FY2023 budget deficit was raised from 4.5% of GDP to 6.9% of GDP, to allow for flood relief and rehabilitation. The actual deficit was higher, 7.7% of GDP, little changed from 7.9% in FY2022 (Figure 2.3.32). The primary balance registered a deficit of 0.8% of GDP, also above the revised target, although less than the 3.1% deficit in FY2022. Although tax revenues grew

Figure 2.3.31 Gross Official Reserves and Exchange Rate

Foreign reserves plunged with the suspension of the previous International Monetary Fund program.

- Gross official reserves
- PRs/$ Exchange rate

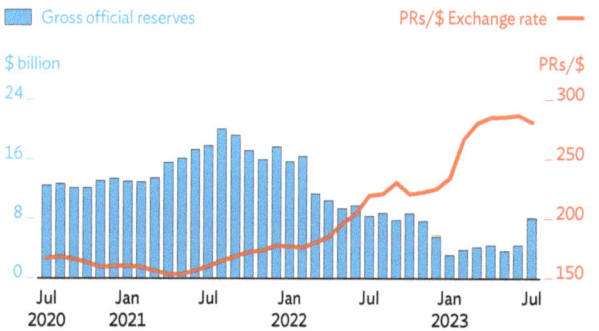

Source: State Bank of Pakistan. *Economic Data.*

by 15.7%, they fell to 9.2% of GDP in FY2023 from 10.1% of GDP in FY2022, reflecting poor collections of sales taxes and customs duties from the economic slowdown and contraction in imports and industrial output. The decline would have been even larger if direct taxes had not risen by 0.4% of GDP, thanks to tax policy measures enacted through a mini budget revision in February 2023. Nontax revenues increased to 2.1% of GDP from 1.9% a year earlier, helped by an increase in the petroleum development levy to the statutory upper limit. Interest payments equaled 6.9% of GDP, 0.6 percentage points above the revised estimate and absorbing three-fourths of all tax revenues.

To contain the deficit, the government cut development and noninterest current spending, restricting total expenditures to the revised estimate of 19.1% of GDP.

Debt vulnerabilities rose significantly. Because of the large fiscal deficit, the weaker rupee, and slow growth, public debt rose to 74.3% of GDP in FY2023, above the 73.9% of GDP in FY2022. External debt, despite a decline in dollar terms due to scarce external finance, increased to about 32.1% of GDP from 30.5% of GDP in FY2022, reflecting the large exchange rate depreciation (Figure 2.3.33). Credit rating agencies downgraded the country's sovereign ratings to just above the default threshold. Nevertheless, the IMF's latest assessment concluded that public debt remains sustainable, assuming steadfast implementation of the adjustment program.

Prospects

The economy's near-term prospects will heavily rely on progress under the economic adjustment program. The program aims to stabilize the economy and rebuild buffers for domestic and external balance, thereby providing a foundation for a possible successor program under the new government expected to be elected in the first quarter of calendar year 2024. The program involves fiscal consolidation, monetary tightening, and a return to a market-determined exchange rate, as well as structural reforms in energy, state-owned enterprises, banking, and climate resilience.

The economy is projected to recover modestly in FY2024 with base effects from the post-flood recovery. Uncertainty will linger, though, and stabilization measures will limit the growth of demand. Growth in FY2024 is projected to be 1.9%, slightly lower than the *ADO April 2023* forecast (Table 2.3.3). The revised projection assumes a modest rebound in demand, with private consumption and private investment growing by about 3% and 5%, respectively. Fiscal and monetary tightening will crimp demand, as will inflation staying in double digits. On the other hand, implementation of the economic adjustment program and a likely smooth general election should boost confidence, while the easing of import controls should support investment as fiscal tightening restrains public consumption.

Figure 2.3.32 Fiscal Indicators

The fiscal deficit persisted on weak tax collection and high interest payments.

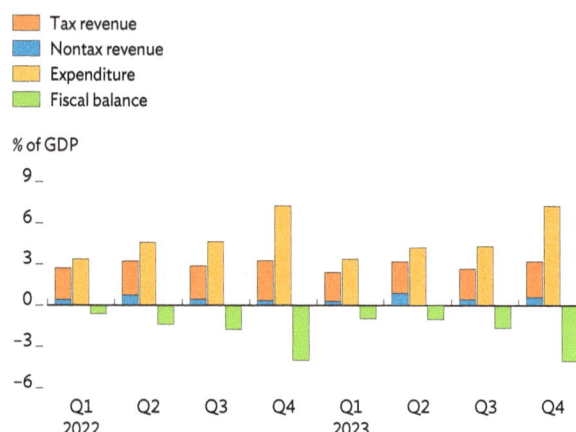

GDP = gross domestic product, Q = quarter.
Note: Years are fiscal years ending on 30 June of that year.
Source: Ministry of Finance, Pakistan Summary of Consolidated Federal & Provincial Fiscal Operations, July–June FY2023.

Figure 2.3.33 Government Domestic and External Debt

External debt remained high in 2023.

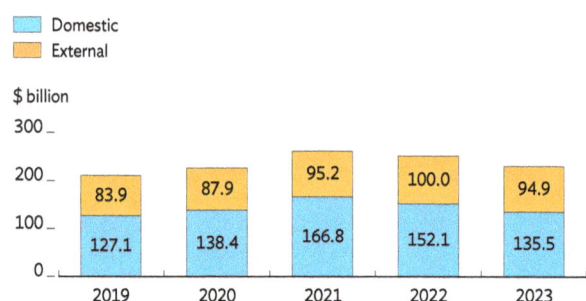

Notes: Years are fiscal years ending on 30 June of that year. External debt includes government and other external liabilities and public corporations.
Source: State Bank of Pakistan, *Economic Data.*

Table 2.3.3 Selected Economic Indicators in Pakistan, %

Growth in FY2023 proved lower, and inflation higher, than in ADO April 2023, while the forecast inflation for FY2024 has been raised in light of the high inflation in FY2023.

	2022	2023		2024	
		Apr	Sep	Apr	Sep
GDP growth	6.1	0.6	0.3	2.0	1.9
Inflation	12.2	27.5	29.2	15.0	25.0

FY = fiscal year, GDP = gross domestic product.
Note: Years are fiscal years ending on 30 June of that year.
Sources: Pakistan Bureau of Statistics; Asian Development Bank estimates.

On the output side, better weather conditions will enable an increase in the area under cultivation and in yields, supporting recovery in agriculture. The government's relief package of free seeds, subsidized credit, and fertilizer will also help. In turn, the recovery of farm output will feed through to industry, which will also benefit from the increased availability of critical imported inputs. The recovery of output will enable exports to pick up, although imports will grow much faster, due to pent-up demand. However, the downside risks are significant, including from global price shocks and slower global growth.

Fiscal tightening will come from raising revenues and containing spending. The FY2024 budget targets a primary surplus of 0.4% of GDP and an overall deficit of 7.5% of GDP, gradually declining over the medium term. Tax revenues are programmed to hit 10.3% of GDP in FY2024. Provincial spending will be cut by 0.4% of GDP and spending on defense and energy subsidies will be limited, while protecting priority social and development outlays. The government has committed to granting no further tax amnesties or issuing new tax preferences or exemptions.

Despite continued monetary tightening, disinflation faces headwinds. Inflation is expected to ease in FY2024, as base-year effects set in, food supply normalizes, and inflation expectations moderate. In addition, the central bank will likely raise the policy rate from the 22% it set in July 2023 to gradually reduce inflation to its medium-term target of 5%–7% (Figure 2.3.34). The central bank has agreed to achieve positive real interest rates, refrain from introducing new refinancing schemes, and contain refinancing credits. However, significant inflationary pressures remain. Sharp increases in petroleum, electricity, and gas tariffs are envisaged under the program. As import and exchange rate controls are eased, the rupee could further weaken, raising the cost of imported goods. (Figure 2.3.35). El Niño and the continuing Russian invasion of Ukraine could disrupt supplies and raise prices of wheat, rice, and other basic foodstuffs. Hence, inflation will likely remain high at about 25% in FY2024, significantly higher than projected earlier in *ADO April 2023*.

Figure 2.3.34 Interest Rates

The central bank raised interest rates, but rates remained negative in real terms.

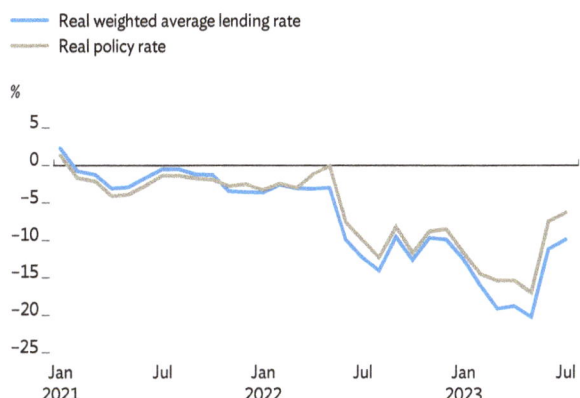

Note: Years are fiscal years ending on 30 June of that year.
Source: State Bank of Pakistan, *Economic Data*.

Figure 2.3.35 Exchange Rates

The rupee weakened through FY2023.

Note: Years are fiscal years ending on 30 June of that year.
Source: State Bank of Pakistan, *Economic Data*.

Easing import and exchange rate controls will have competing effects on the current account balance and reserves. Imports should increase as economic activity recovers and as businesses find it easier to import inputs. But exports should also recover, despite slower global growth, on greater availability of inputs, improved farm output, and a more competitive rupee. On balance, the current account deficit is projected to increase to about 1.5% of GDP in FY2024. Despite the larger deficit, international reserves should grow. The new program with the IMF has improved the prospects for multilateral and bilateral financing, while a more market-determined exchange rate is expected to stabilize the currency market and encourage remittance inflows through official channels.

Downside risks to the outlook remain exceptionally high. On the external front, tighter global financial conditions and potential supply chain disruptions from any escalation of the Russian invasion of Ukraine will weigh on the economy. Amid the upcoming election season, persistent political instability will remain a key risk to implementing reform toward growth stabilization, the restoration of confidence, and sustainable debt. Disbursement from multilateral and bilateral partners would remain crucial for reserve accumulation, exchange rate stability, and improved market sentiment.

Other Economies

Afghanistan

In the first half (H1) of 2023, the economy showed some signs of recovery following 3 successive years of recession. Exports and revenue collection rose, banks became slightly more liquid, the afghani exchange rate and inflation stabilized, and work availability for both skilled and unskilled labor improved following a seasonal slump from November 2022 to February 2023. These developments were mainly due to continued international humanitarian and basic needs support, lower global food and oil prices, and better security. However, recovery remains fragile, particularly with tightening restrictions on women's education and their employment in nongovernment organizations and United Nations agencies, and exclusion of women from other economic activities such as closure of beauty salons. Officially excluding women from the workforce has complicated the delivery of humanitarian assistance, degraded women's skills, and negated their economic potential. Less directly, it has intensified instability, outward migration, and the consequent loss of trained professionals and other experts.

While mining showed some improvement in H1 2023, industry, services, and agriculture remained subdued. Business confidence was weak because of governance issues, policy uncertainty, and the risk of macroeconomic instability. Agriculture, already suffering from drought, could weaken further under a threatened locust outbreak in H2 2023, with potential wheat losses forecast at 0.7–1.2 million tons.

Moreover, the successful suppression of opium—without, so far, any announcement of an official effort to supply alternative livelihoods—could eliminate more than $1 billion in rural earnings annually, hitting trade, transport, exports, and construction.

Inflation has turned around this year. After global oil and food price shocks caused sharp spikes in the first 3 quarters of 2022, with average inflation reaching 15.0% year on year in January–April 2022, inflation braked to 2.0% in the same period of 2023, with 1.0% deflation year on year in April, the deepest in 5 years, as food prices declined by 3.3% and prices for other goods by 1.8%. The main reasons for lower inflation were falling import prices and afghani appreciation against the Pakistan rupee, the Iranian rial, and major international currencies, including the US dollar.

Afghanistan's trade deficit widened to $2.4 billion in the period from January to May 2023. Imports soared by 36% over the same 5-month period in 2022 to $3.1 billion, while exports grew by only 9% to $0.73 billion, reflecting mainly increases in textiles, coal, and vegetables. With the formal banking system crippled, informal money service providers have thrived and facilitated import financing and remittances.

Revenue collection reached AF63 billion in the first 4 months of fiscal year 2023 (FY2023, ending on 20 March 2024). This was a 16% increase over the same period of FY2022. Growth came mainly from the surge in imports, which increased revenue collection at the border by 23%. Inland revenue collection rose by 7% on higher mining royalties.

Afghanistan's economic outlook is challenging. Humanitarian assistance is critical to the economy, which lacks other drivers for a rebound. If humanitarian assistance continues at the 2022 level, modest growth is expected in FY2023, with annual average inflation in the middle single digits in calendar year 2023. Inflation relief could bolster real household income and possibly improve food security. However, further economic contraction and high inflation could come from any decline in humanitarian assistance or as spillover from economic and political difficulties in neighboring countries.

Bhutan

Adverse weather has diminished Bhutan's growth prospects in 2023, hitting both agriculture and industry. Summer monsoon rains have been erratic this year, undermining crop production in every part of the country. The growth forecast for agriculture is thus revised down from 3.2% in *ADO April 2023* to 2.8%. Projected growth in industry is similarly revised down from 3.2% to 2.8% in response to a 7.4% fall in hydropower output year on year in the first 5 months of 2023. After adjusting for a low base because the Tala hydropower plant was shut down in January–February 2022, the shortfall in hydropower output approaches 19%, caused by subpar hydrological flows. In addition, projected growth in construction is revised down by 2.0 percentage points following the suspension in June of credit for building commercial housing projects and hotels. The suspension aimed to address concerns about nonperforming loans and conserve foreign exchange reserves. With developments in manufacturing and mining unfolding as expected, manufacturing is still projected to grow by 3.3% and mining to contract by 1.5%. Growth in services is now forecast 0.3 percentage points higher, with improvement in tourist arrivals expected to continue under a new government incentive from 1 September that cut the prevailing daily sustainable development fee of $200 by half. Tourist arrivals picked up from 22% of the pre-pandemic number in the first quarter of 2023 to 46% in April.

The growth forecast is downgraded for 2023 but upgraded for 2024 (Table 2.3.4). The 2023 downgrade follows adverse developments affecting hydropower and construction, which together provided 26.0% of GDP in 2022. The 2024 growth forecast is revised marginally higher because of the lower base now projected for 2023. Major factors behind 2024 projections made in April are unchanged, notably the opening of the Nikachhu hydropower plant by the end of 2023 and the Punatsangchhu II plant by the end of 2024.

Risks to growth derive mainly from energy, especially the schedule for commissioning new hydropower plants. Further delays affecting Nikachhu and Punatsangchhu II would derail growth prospects, but none are expected as both projects are close to completion.

Table 2.3.4 Selected Economic Indicators in Bhutan, %

Projections now see slightly slower growth and significantly slower inflation in 2023, with forecast growth improvement in 2024 mostly from a base effect.

	2022	2023		2024	
		Apr	Sep	Apr	Sep
GDP growth	4.7	4.6	4.3	4.2	4.4
Inflation	5.6	5.5	4.1	5.1	5.1

GDP = gross domestic product.
Sources: Royal Government of Bhutan, Ministry of Finance; Royal Monetary Authority, Bhutan; Asian Development Bank estimates.

Another domestic risk to growth is continued deterioration in Bhutan's foreign reserve position, which declined from $766.6 million in December 2022 to $549.1 million in May 2023 as the nominal value of imports, as reported by Bhutan Trade Statistics, grew by 30% quarter on quarter in the first quarter of 2023 while exports held steady. This continues a steady decline in reserves from $1.5 billion in March 2021. In addition to high commodity prices in 2022, a contributing factor has been the import of over $200 million in information technology equipment since mid-2021, a significant part of which is likely to support digital asset mining, mostly Bitcoin. Other risks to growth include constrained fiscal space and skilled workers' steady emigration to advanced economies.

Headline inflation in the first 5 months of 2023 averaged 3.7% year on year. This was much lower than expected, thanks to a midyear drop in fuel prices and low food inflation at only 1.8%. Inflation in the second half of the year is projected to rise to 4.5% as food price pressure results from the impact of the erratic monsoon on domestic agriculture, export restrictions imposed by neighboring countries on food commodities, and expected increases in global prices. The 2024 inflation forecast is maintained.

Maldives

Robust tourism was sustained in the first half (H1) of 2023 as arrivals grew by an impressive 14.3% year on year. Expansion mainly reflected restored tourism from the People's Republic of China (PRC) beginning in the first quarter and recovery in the Russian market from a weakened 2022.

With the resumption in flights from the PRC, arrivals from the country surged in H1 2023, accounting for 51.3% of the growth in arrivals and 6.8% of total arrivals. In the same period, arrivals from the Russian Federation rebounded by 33.0% year on year, to provide 23.2% of growth in arrivals. Despite arrivals growing by only 6.1%, Europe continued to be the dominant regional tourist market with a 58.6% share. And, though arrivals declined by 8.5% year on year, India remained the largest single country tourist market, accounting for 11.9% of tourist arrivals. Bed-nights sold, a proxy for tourism income, grew by 9.8%. Growth in construction and investment was also strong, as evidenced by a 16.8% increase year on year in imports of construction materials in H1 2023, largely reflecting higher public investment.

Projections for 2023 and 2024 are for continued strong growth, though falling short of sizable expansion in 2022. High growth that year reflected continued recovery from an enormous 33.5% GDP contraction in 2020 because of COVID-19. With 929,607 tourists arriving in H1 2023, the *ADO April 2023* projection of 1.8 million tourists in the whole year is attainable, especially as the fourth quarter is the peak tourism season. Strong travel demand is likely to carry over into 2024 as more airlines recommence direct flights with the PRC. Construction is also poised to remain expansive, thanks to substantial public investment scheduled for H2 2023 and 2024. On balance, *ADO April 2023* forecasts for GDP growth in 2023 and 2024 are retained (Table 2.3.5).

Table 2.3.5 Selected Economic Indicators in Maldives, %

ADO April 2023 *growth projections are retained, while the inflation forecast for 2023 is trimmed and that for 2024 is raised.*

	2022	2023		2024	
		Apr	Sep	Apr	Sep
GDP growth	13.9	7.1	7.1	6.9	6.9
Inflation	2.3	4.5	3.5	2.0	2.5

GDP = gross domestic product.
Sources: Maldives Monetary Authority. Monthly Statistics. July 2023; Asian Development Bank estimates.

The main downside risk to the outlook would be a major shortfall from forecast global growth, disrupting tourism. In addition, global interest rates substantially higher than expected would further deteriorate fiscal and debt sustainability in Maldives, considering the country's scant foreign exchange reserves.

Inflation will remain low, though with adjustments to forecasts in 2023 and 2024. Average inflation in H1 2023 climbed to 3.5% year on year, reflecting a hike in goods and services taxes from 1 January that exerted upward pressure on local prices. Inflation in H2 2023 appears likely to average 3.5% as well, with the impact of the tax hike less than expected in *ADO April 2023*. In 2024, inflation will rise slightly higher than forecast in April due to the lower base now projected for 2023. In view of the foregoing, the 2023 inflation forecast is lowered, while that for 2024 is revised slightly higher.

The merchandise trade deficit improved from $1.5 billion in H1 2022 to $1.3 billion a year later as exports grew and imports contracted. The services balance weakened in January–April 2023, however, because advance travel sales for 2023 were booked in the fourth quarter of 2022 to avoid the hike in goods and services taxes. Developments to date are within expectations in *ADO April 2023*, which projected trade and current deficits narrowing in 2023 on moderating prices for oil and other commodities and improved travel receipts, then widening marginally in 2024 as global oil prices pick up.

Nepal

Following 2 years of strong expansion since the pandemic shock, growth fell more than expected in fiscal year 2023 (FY2023 ending mid-July 2023). This update lowers the growth projection for FY2023 to align with the preliminary estimate (Table 2.3.6). Significant growth moderation reflects tight monetary policy and fiscal consolidation used by the authorities to address rising inflation and pressure on foreign exchange reserves. The overnight repo policy rate was raised from 5.5% to 7.0% in August 2022. Affected by higher interest rates, import restrictions in the first 5 months of FY2023, and sharply lower growth in external demand, industry grew by only 0.6% as manufacturing and construction contracted.

Table 2.3.6 Selected Economic Indicators in Nepal, %

Growth will accelerate from a low base in fiscal 2024 as the authorities revise macroeconomic policies.

	2022	2023		2024	
		Apr	Sep	Apr	Sep
GDP growth	5.6	4.1	1.9	5.0	4.3
Inflation	6.3	7.4	7.7	6.2	6.2

GDP = gross domestic product.

Note: Years are fiscal years ending in mid-July of that year.

Source: Asian Development Bank estimates.

Growth in services fell by half to 2.3% as wholesale and retail trade contracted. Agriculture, however, expanded by 2.7% as a normal monsoon boosted rice yields. On the demand side, 4.1% expansion in private consumption underpinned growth as fixed investment contracted by 10.9%—with private investment down by 7.6% and public investment by 20.2%—subtracting 3.9 percentage points from GDP growth. Moreover, a steep drop in stocks reduced overall capital formation by 13.0%. Net exports were the major contributor to growth in FY2023 as imports contracted by 17.2%.

The growth forecast for FY2024 is revised down from the *ADO April 2023* projection. This reflects weaker projected growth in the major advanced economies than in April baseline forecasts and the need to continue guarded macroeconomic policies and strengthen structural reform. While notable progress in restoring external balance has been made, fiscal challenges persist. On balance, economic activity in FY2024 will be curtailed by low domestic and external demand, continued weakness in investor confidence, high interest rates, and deficient rainfall in June that will likely suppress agricultural output. Considering these developments, Nepal Rastra Bank, the central bank, adjusted its monetary stance by lowering the policy rate by 50 basis points to 6.5% and by relaxing provisions on working capital loans to revive investor confidence, while the government has prioritized capital budget execution with the issuance of guidelines for its effective implementation. Fixed investment will provide the main impetus to growth in FY2024, reversing the drag it exerted in FY2023. With foreign exchange reserves rebuilt, there is little risk to external balance.

Inflation in FY2023 averaged 7.7%, a bit higher than *ADO April 2023* projected. Annual food inflation averaged 6.6% as prices rose for cereal grains, spices, dairy products, and eggs. Nonfood inflation averaged 8.6%, despite a sizable decline in global fuel charges, as prices rose for transportation, health, education, and housing and utilities. The inflation forecast for FY2024 is retained in anticipation of a subdued increase for oil and lower inflation in India, Nepal's main source of imports.

The current account deficit in FY2023 narrowed by a massive 89.2% to $557.1 million, equal to 1.4% of estimated GDP. This reflected a 22.2% decline in the trade deficit and a 12.1% increase in remittance inflow, the traditional offset to the trade deficit, which brought foreign exchange reserves to $11.7 billion in FY2023, providing import cover for 10.0 months. This was a marked improvement from $9.5 billion in FY2022, which covered only 6.9 months. The current account deficit is expected to widen to 1.8% of GDP in FY2024 as growth revives, albeit less than projected in *ADO April 2023*.

Sri Lanka

Economic conditions have gradually stabilized. Increased food and fuel availability signals better supply conditions since *ADO April 2023*. Official reserves, which include a People's Bank of China swap, have strengthened but still languish below 3 months of import cover. Better foreign currency liquidity has allowed most import controls to be lifted. The government has made progress on reforms envisaged under the International Monetary Fund program, having enacted an anticorruption bill and legislation that enhances the independence of the Central Bank of Sri Lanka and its powers to manage financial crises.

In the first quarter of 2023, the economy contracted by 11.5% year on year. Industry shrank by 23.4%, constrained by higher production costs, higher taxes, and lackluster demand. Services contracted by 5.0%, mostly from declining financial and insurance services and real estate, but agriculture grew by 0.8%. Constrained economic conditions and fiscal austerity lowered both private and government consumption, and gross capital formation continued to decline.

Net exports contributed positively to GDP as imports remained constrained.

Leading indicators remain muted. The manufacturing purchasing managers' index remained below 50 in July, indicating contraction for a fourth consecutive month, and the index of industrial production contracted by 10.9% in the first half of 2023. However, the services purchasing managers' index surpassed 50 in April and every month since. With developments since April in line with expectations, growth forecasts for 2023 and 2024 are unchanged (Table 2.3.7).

Table 2.3.7 Selected Economic Indicators in Sri Lanka, %

Growth forecasts remain unchanged, but lower inflation is now projected for 2023.

	2022	2023		2024	
		Apr	Sep	Apr	Sep
GDP growth	−7.8	−3.0	−3.0	1.3	1.3
Inflation	46.4	24.6	18.7	5.5	5.5

GDP = gross domestic product.
Sources: Central Bank of Sri Lanka; Asian Development Bank estimates.

Inflation has decelerated more than expected. Subdued demand and better supply conditions drove down inflation, as measured by the Colombo consumer price index, from 69.8% year on year in September 2022 to 6.3% in July 2023. The central bank reduced its policy rate by 2.5 percentage points in June and a further 2.0 points in July, and cut the statutory reserve ratio by 2.0 percentage points in August amid muted demand for private sector credit. Market interest rates have declined but remain in double digits. Given these developments, the inflation forecast for this year is revised down from the April projection.

Weak global demand and higher production costs lowered export earnings, but imports also declined. In the first half of 2023, export earnings fell by 10.0% year on year, but imports plunged by 18.6%, shrinking the trade deficit from $3.5 billion a year earlier to $2.3 billion. With gradual relaxation of import restrictions and continued weak exports, the trade deficit is expected to widen in 2023. Remittances in January–July 2023 soared by 78.0% year on year, and tourist arrivals improved by 67.4%. The current account flipped from $1.3 billion deficit in the first quarter of 2022 to $644 million surplus a year later.

Official reserves doubled to $3.8 billion in the 7 months to the end of July. The rebuilding of reserves reflected support from international financial institutions, inflow into government securities, and central bank net dollar purchases of $1.5 billion in the period, during which the local currency appreciated by 10.2% against the US dollar.

Parliament approved in July a framework to optimize domestic debt. This allows the reprofiling of Treasury bills held by the central bank and bonds held by superannuation funds through step-down coupons and maturity extensions, the conversion of provisional advances to the government into Treasury bonds, and the restructuring of dollar-denominated local debt. However, to minimize impact on the financial system, these provisions exclude government securities owned by banks. Government bond yields have dropped as uncertainty has eased.

Economic conditions have improved, but risks remain. Sri Lanka needs to implement structural benchmarks and meet quantitative performance criteria under the International Monetary Fund program and ensure the timely completion of debt restructuring. Adverse weather could have a prolonged impact on agriculture. Also, outward labor migration, particularly by highly skilled workers, may constrain recovery.

SOUTHEAST ASIA

Growth slowed down for most economies in Southeast Asia. Deceleration reflected the cumulative effects of rising inflation, monetary tightening, and weaker global demand for manufactured goods from key trading partners. However, robust domestic demand and continued recovery of the services sector—particularly tourism—have contributed to better job and income prospects, keeping growth close to its long-run average. Growth in agriculture is also affected by the early onset of El Niño.

Subregional Assessment and Prospects

Economic performance has been mostly weaker across the region, with growth prospects for seven economies revised down. The main reasons are slowing global growth, high commodity prices, and tightened global financial conditions. Cambodia, the Lao People's Democratic Republic (Lao PDR), Malaysia, the Philippines, Singapore, Timor-Leste, and Viet Nam are expected to post lower growth this year compared to the *ADO April 2023* forecast (Figure 2.4.1). Weaker external conditions and demand for the region's manufactured and commodity exports are the main reasons behind the slower growth, along with lower agricultural output from adverse weather. Meanwhile, growth forecasts are maintained for Myanmar and raised for Brunei Darussalam, Indonesia, and Thailand on brighter domestic demand prospects. Growth forecasts for 2023 and 2024 are downgraded from 4.7% in *ADO April 2023* to 4.6% and from 5.0% to 4.8%, respectively.

Contractions of manufactured export growth have hurt the major exporting economies in the subregion. Accelerated rate hikes in major economies created a credit crunch that dragged down demand. As a result, Cambodia, highly dependent on garments, footwear, and travel goods, saw an 18.6% decline in shipments to its key trading partners in the first half of 2023. Viet Nam's manufacturing output also shrank, by 0.4%, resulting in closures of businesses in the first 8 months of 2023. Lower demand for commodities, meanwhile, reduced exports from Indonesia and Malaysia while the trade slump in Singapore continued for the 10th straight month in July. Weak manufacturing will likely drag down growth in 2023 and 2024 as evident from the manufacturing purchasing managers' index in August 2023 remaining under 50 for Malaysia and falling below 50 for the Philippines and Thailand, signaling contraction in the sector. Weaker-than-expected demand from the People's Republic of China and Southeast Asian neighbors, and a delay in the recovery of the semiconductor industry cycle, are also seen to drag exports lower.

The subregional assessment and prospects was written by James Villafuerte and Dulce Zara. The section on Indonesia was written by Priasto Aji and Henry Ma; Malaysia by James Villafuerte, Mae Hyacinth C. Kiocho, and Joyce Marie P. Lagac, consultants; the Philippines by Cristina Lozano and Teresa Mendoza; Thailand by Chitchanok Annonjarn; Viet Nam by Nguyen Ba Hung, Nguyen Luu Thuc Phuong, and Chu Hong Minh. The other economies, by Emma Allen, Poullang Doung, Kavita Iyengar, Yothin Jinjarak, Soulinthone Leuangkhamsing, Eve Cherry Lynn, Nedelyn Magtibay-Ramos, Joel Mangahas, Duong Nguyen, Arief Ramayandi, Shu Tian, Mai Lin Villaruel, and Anthony Baluga, consultant. The authors are in the Southeast Asia and Economic Research and Development Impact departments, ADB. Effective 1 February 2021, ADB placed a temporary hold on sovereign project disbursements and new contracts in Myanmar.

Figure 2.4.1 GDP Growth in Southeast Asia

Weaker global demand for exports from the region limited growth prospects in 2023.

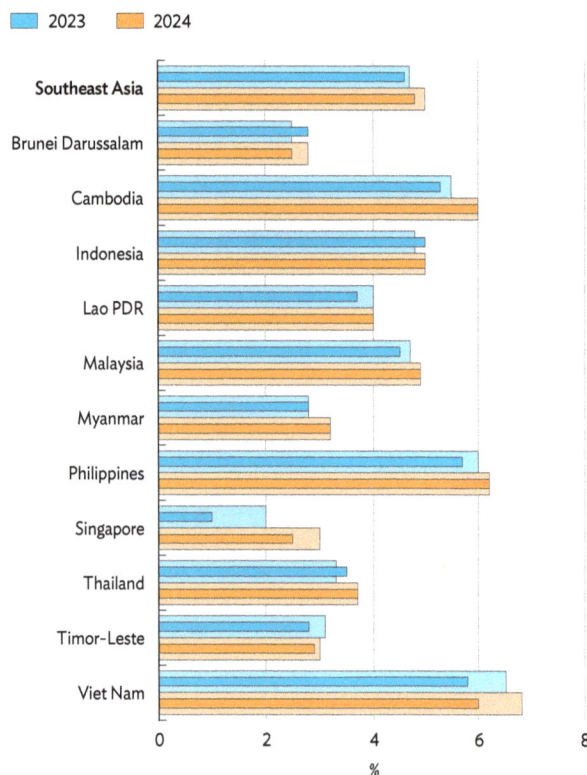

GDP = gross domestic product, Lao PDR = Lao People's Democratic Republic.
Note: Lighter colored bars are *Asian Development Outlook April 2023* forecasts.
Source: *Asian Development Outlook* database.

Services, particularly tourism, have strongly contributed to growth in most economies.
Economies in the region are getting a lift from higher tourist receipts given the strong rebound in tourist arrivals since last year. Likewise, accommodations, food services, transportation, and storage recorded strong growth. Cambodia has benefited from hosting the 2023 Southeast Asian Games in May. Growth in international arrivals has accelerated for most economies in January to July this year, approaching pre-pandemic monthly averages in the case of Cambodia, Indonesia, and Singapore. Efforts to contain rising inflation and stimulate the economy have also benefited domestic tourism in Viet Nam. Meanwhile, the government's domestic travel stimulus package aided domestic tourism recovery in Thailand.

Private consumption remained the biggest contributor to growth in the first half of 2023.
Buoyed by improved labor market conditions and income, consumption has benefited from the large regional market, and the recovery in tourism and other associated services. However, tightened financial conditions are holding back further spending particularly for households in Malaysia and Thailand. Credit and investment demand from businesses also faltered due to higher costs of borrowing throughout the region. However, most central banks in the subregion moderated their pace of rate hikes in the first half of 2023. This contrasts with the quick tightening observed from 1 August to 31 December 2022. The State Bank of Vietnam was the first central bank that reversed its monetary policy in 2023 by lowering the key policy rate by 50 basis points in April, May, and June to stimulate economic growth. And some could begin to follow especially if growth continues to weaken further.

Higher interest rates, inflation concerns, global uncertainty, and fiscal constraints have also slowed down investment. Private investment activity remained muted in Thailand. The delay in approving the fiscal 2024 budget bill may lead to postponing approvals of new construction projects from the last quarter of 2023 to next year. In Viet Nam regulatory constraints have impeded accelerated public investment disbursements. Foreign investment will be hampered by the global economic slowdown. Limited fiscal headroom and increasing debt levels are expected to constrain private and public investments. Fiscal policies will likely become tighter going forward as fiscal consolidation measures are introduced to rein in higher fiscal deficit and debt. Public debt rose to 97% of GDP at the end of 2022 from 76% a year earlier in the Lao PDR. Meanwhile, debt-to-GDP ratios increased significantly compared to pre-pandemic levels for Malaysia, the Philippines, and Thailand.

Inflation has slowed but remains elevated in some countries due to currency depreciation and climate impacts on food production. Generally, easing oil and commodity prices have decelerated price increases for most economies in the subregion. In particular, inflation has eased for Brunei Darussalam, Indonesia, Malaysia, Thailand, and Viet Nam in the first 7 months of the year. However, inflation remained elevated (above 5%) in the case of the Lao PDR, Myanmar, the Philippines, and Timor-Leste.

Food inflation is also particularly high for the smaller Southeast Asian economies, which have been affected by depreciating local currencies and lower agricultural production due to unpredictable weather conditions. El Niño weather disturbances and the adverse impacts of Cyclone Mocha have affected agricultural production in Myanmar. India's recent ban on rice exports is seen to affect rice importers such as Indonesia, Malaysia, the Philippines, and Singapore as international rice prices have already gone up by 18.9% year on year in the first 7 months of 2023. The inflation forecast for 2023 for Southeast Asia is slightly down to 4.2% from 4.4% in April but maintained at 3.3% in 2024 (Figure 2.4.2).

Local currencies have depreciated substantially against the US dollar. This has added to inflation pressure and elevated the domestic cost of foreign debt repayments. The Lao PDR is the most affected since local currency depreciation is estimated to account for two-thirds of inflation in January to August this year. Its external public debt servicing requirements are sizable and are expected to average $1.3 billion annually over the next 5 years, equivalent to 7% of GDP. Meanwhile, with Malaysia's foreign currency-denominated debt accounting for 66.6% of total external debt, the depreciation of the ringgit along with increased debt holdings of nonresident investors led to a less improved external debt position. Malaysia's external debt rose from 64.5% of GDP in the first quarter of 2023 to 67.1% in the second.

The main risks to the outlook are weak global growth, still elevated oil and commodity prices, and persistent inflation. These factors coupled with the continuing Russian invasion of Ukraine have impacted food prices in the region. High interest rates also contribute to a wait-and-see attitude for private investments that could further undermine growth in the subregion. Weaker-than-expected recovery in the People's Republic of China could also dampen the spillover effect to the region and delay the improvement of external demand for Southeast Asian manufactured goods exports. The subregion is also vulnerable to major climate change risks and challenges. For this year, the effect of El Niño is expected to lead to unstable weather conditions, which could lower agriculture harvests and productivity.

Figure 2.4.2 Inflation in Southeast Asia

Inflationary pressures eased in most economies but limited by currency depreciation and elevated food prices for some economies.

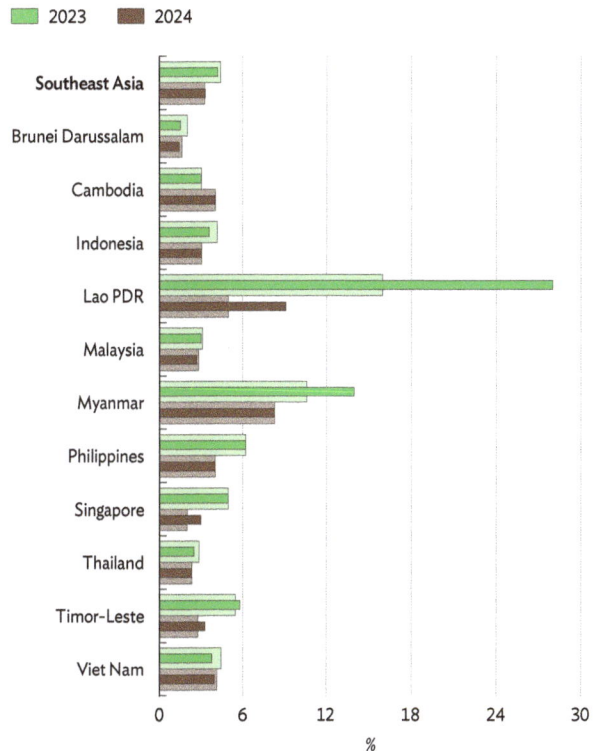

Lao PDR = Lao People's Democratic Republic.
Note: Lighter colored bars are *Asian Development Outlook April 2023* forecasts.
Source: *Asian Development Outlook* database.

Indonesia

Domestic demand is taking over from commodity exports as the driver of growth. Compared with the forecasts in *ADO April 2023*, growth is now expected to be higher and inflation lower. Fiscal and monetary policy are appropriate for the economy's stage in the economic cycle. The financial sector is stable, and the external position is sound. While the current account is shrinking, international reserves and the national currency are expected to be broadly stable.

Updated Assessment

Healthy growth continued in the first half of 2023, with signs of acceleration, while inflation kept easing faster than expected. GDP growth was 5.0% in Q1 2023 and rose to 5.2% in the next quarter.

Inflation slowed from 5.3% year on year in January to 3.1% in July. The outlook through December is sanguine.

Domestic demand is driving growth somewhat more than expected. The contribution to growth of domestic demand rose from 3.0% in Q1 to 5.2% in Q2, returning to its pre-pandemic share. The bunching in Q2 of religious holidays and wage bonuses spurred spending. Consumers then turned mainly to low-priced goods and services. But because such spending is generally not import-intensive, import demand was contained. Gross fixed capital formation grew by 4.6%, double the rate in Q1. Construction in Q2 rebounded from its year-long slump and contributed about half of fixed investment growth (Figures 2.4.3–2.4.5).

The export boom has started to wane. For the first time since Q1 2021, exports of goods fell in Q2 2023, by 5.6% in national account terms and by 18% in nominal terms in the balance of payments. Prices for Indonesia's goods exports started falling year on year in January 2023, and volumes started falling in April—both developments partly from base effects. But even on a month on month basis, exports have been slowing since Q3 2022.

Figure 2.4.3 Demand-Side Contributions to Growth

Domestic demand is taking over as the driver of growth.

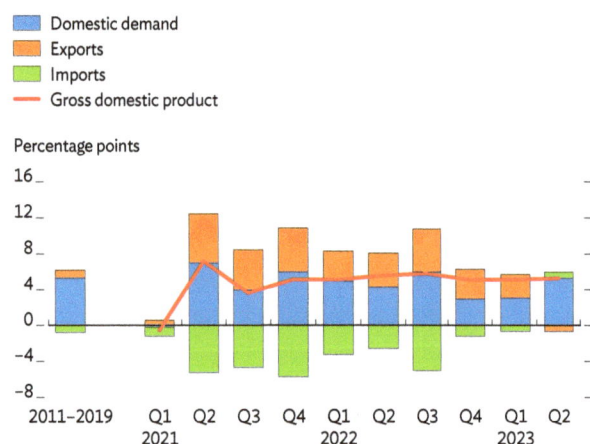

GDP = gross domestic product, Q = quarter.
Notes: The statistical discrepancy is distributed proportionately to the components of GDP. Domestic demand is the sum of private consumption, government consumption, and gross capital formation.
Source: Statistics Indonesia.

Figure 2.4.4 Contributions to Private Consumption Growth

Consumers, while not revenge spending, are "rebound spending."

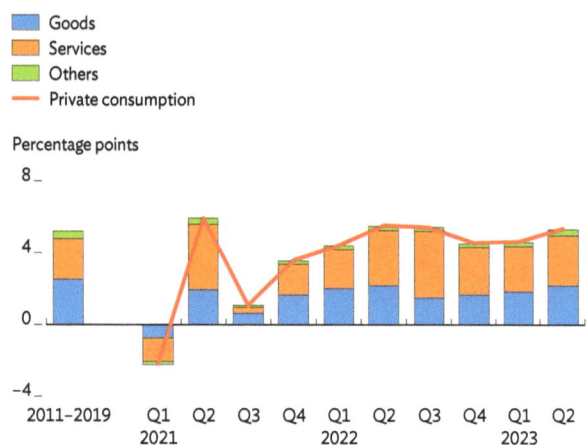

Q = quarter.
Source: Statistics Indonesia.

Figure 2.4.5 Contributions to Investment Growth

Businesses are shrugging off a wait-and-see attitude.

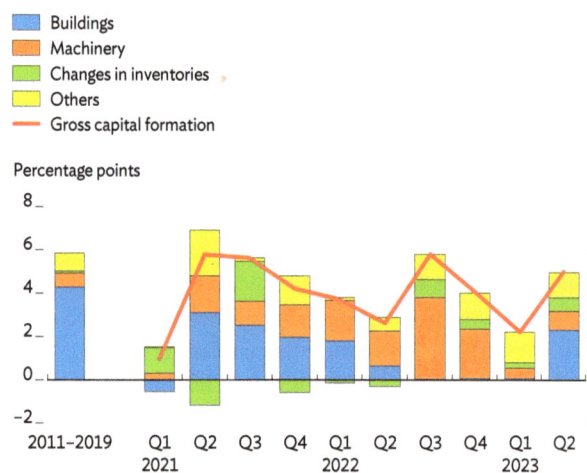

Q = quarter.
Source: Statistics Indonesia.

Exports of services were robust with the recovery of foreign tourism, albeit from a low base. In Q2, service exports grew by 43% in national account terms. Meanwhile, total imports fell in real terms by 3.1%. But these two offsets to slowing merchandise exports were not large enough, and the contribution of net exports to overall growth shrank from 2 percentage points in Q1 to zero in Q2 (Figure 2.4.6).

Figure 2.4.6 Merchandise Trade

A. Commodity Prices

Prices of key commodities have fallen sharply this year...

Index, 100 = 2019 Average

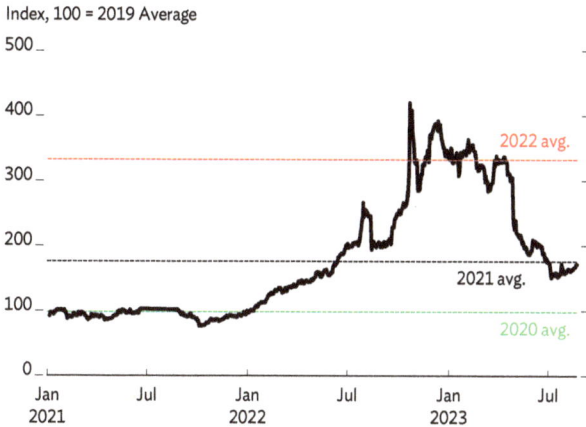

B. Contributions to Growth of Merchandise Exports

... but so have export volumes...

- Palm oil
- Mineral products
- Others
- Growth of value
- Export volume

Percentage points / % change year on year

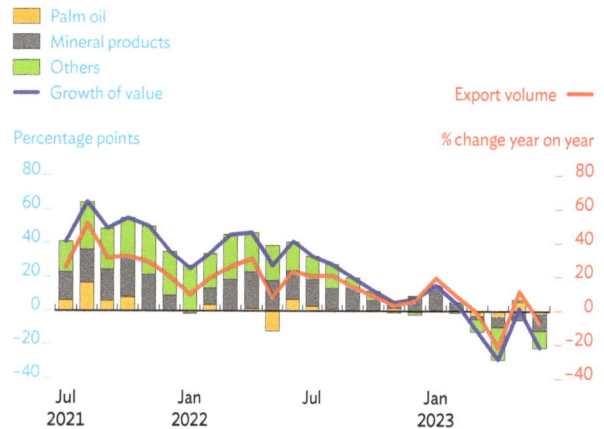

C. Merchandise Exports, by Destination

... and the slowdown is evident in all major trading partners.

- United States
- European Union
- Japan
- People's Republic of China

% change year on year, 3-month moving sum

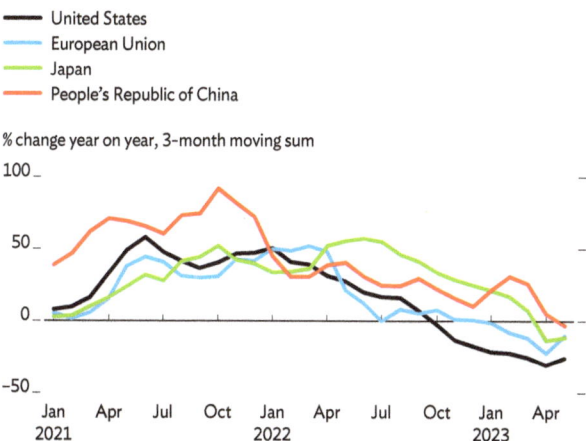

D. Contributions to Growth of Merchandise Imports

Commodity exports can be import-dependent; as these exports slowed, so did their imports.

- Consumption goods
- Raw materials
- Capital goods
- Growth of value
- Import volume

Percentage points / % change year on year

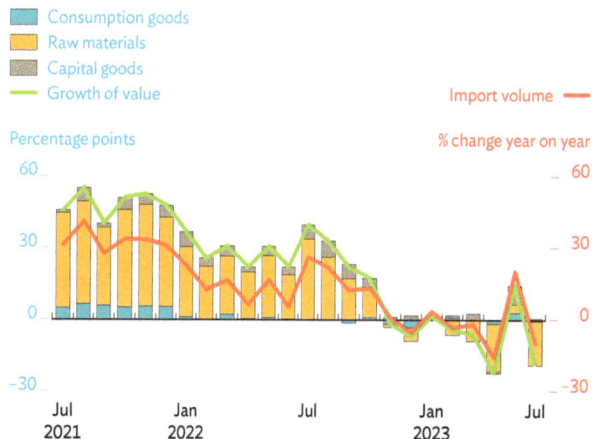

Notes: Prospera Commodity Price Index comprising crude palm oil, coal, nickel, rubber, and copper weighted by their export shares in 2019.
The prices are the Malaysian CPO Spot Price, Newcastle Coal Price, CMX Copper Price, LME Nickel Spot Price, and the Singapore TSR20 Rubber Price.
Sources: Prospera; Statistics Indonesia.

Slowing exports and external debt repayments dented international reserves, but the external position remains sustainable. Because imports slowed at about the same pace as exports, the trade balance remained in surplus in July for a 41st consecutive month. The usual deficits in service trade and external incomes, however, led to a current account deficit in Q2 equal to 0.5% of Q2 GDP, the first deficit since early 2021. The financial account was also negative in Q2 as the government and the national oil company made large payments on maturing external debt. International reserves, which had risen by $8 billion in Q1 on increased foreign buying of government bonds, fell back by the same amount in Q2, ending at $137 billion. This is cover for 6 months of imports and external debt service, or twice the stock of short-term external debt by residual maturity. The exchange rate has been about Rp15,000 to the dollar since January (Figure 2.4.7).

Inflation has been brought down to the target band. Inflation jumped to almost 6% in September 2022, after fuel prices were increased to contain subsidies, and averaged 5.4% in the second half of 2023.

Figure 2.4.7 External Balances

A. Current Account

Smaller trade surpluses and the usual deficits in services and incomes produced a current account deficit.

- Balance of trade in goods
- Balance of trade in services
- Balance of primary and secondary income
- Current account balance

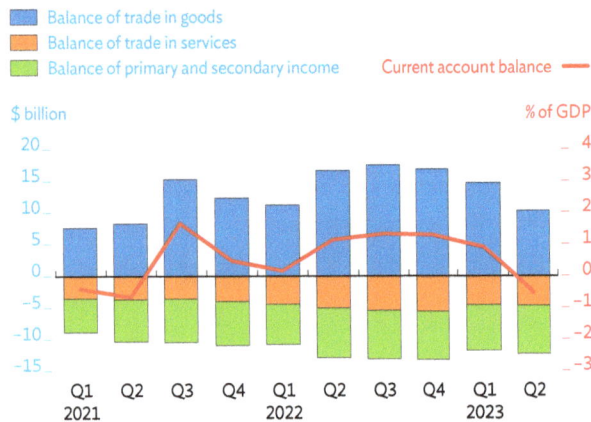

B. Balance of Payments

External debt was paid down, reducing the financial account...

- Current account
- Financial and capital accounts
- International reserves

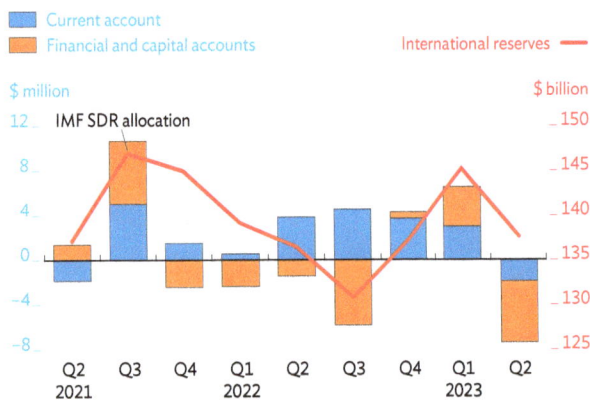

C. External Debt Indicators

... but also reducing external vulnerabilities.

- Public debt
- Private debt
- International reserves/ Short-term external debt

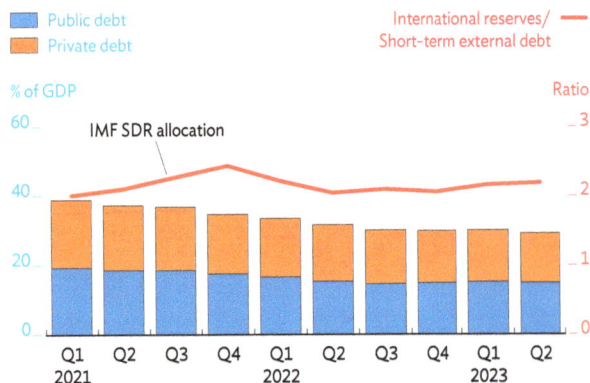

GDP = gross domestic product, IMF SDR = International Monetary Fund special drawing rights, Q = quarter.
Note: Net errors and omissions are included in the financial and capital accounts.
Source: Bank Indonesia.

All throughout, core inflation remained below 3.5%, indicating that inflation expectations were well-anchored. As commodity price shocks in 2022 wore off, headline inflation fell steadily and has been comfortably in the 2%–4% target band since May. The consensus forecast for average inflation in 2023 fell from 4.1% in April to 3.7% (Figure 2.4.8).

Figure 2.4.8 Inflation and Exchange Rates

A. Contributions to Inflation and Inflation Trends

Disinflation has been successful...

- Services contribution
- Goods contribution
- Headline inflation
- Core inflation
- Headline inflation forecast 1 year ahead

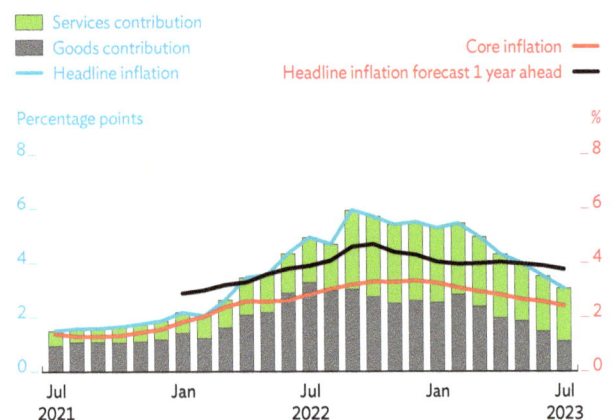

B. Exchange Rates

... helping to make the Indonesian rupiah more competitive in real terms.

- Nominal
- Real effective

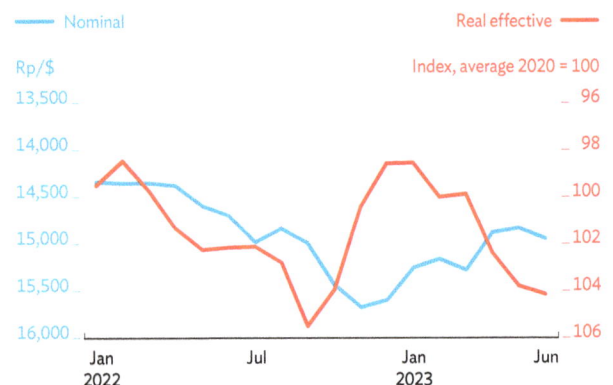

Sources: Haver Analytics; Bank for International Settlements; Statistics Indonesia.

The fiscal deficit is on track to remain below the ceiling this year and next. In 2022, a year ahead of the scheduled return to the 3% ceiling, the deficit was 2.3% of GDP. In 2023 to July, the government had a surplus of Rp154 trillion, equal to 0.7% of GDP and up from Rp106 trillion, or 0.5% of GDP, a year earlier.

Slowing exports cut revenue growth from about 50% in January–July 2022 to 4% a year later. However, increased spending on subsidies has so far not been needed this year, and lower inflation has enabled reduced spending on goods and services and a modest increase in wage outlays. Consequently, the government revised its projection of the fiscal deficit for 2023 from 2.85% of GDP to 2.30% and slowed its auctions of public debt. Public spending, particularly for construction, is usually bunched in Q4, which this year will also see election spending. But the size of the surplus so far this year makes it likely that despite higher spending in Q4, the deficit will be below 2.3% of GDP. Meanwhile, the recently published 2024 budget envisages a deficit equal to 2.29% of GDP (Figure 2.4.9).

Monetary policy, having tamed inflation, remains appropriate. The central bank has kept the policy rate at 5.75% since December. The lagged effect of the monetary tightening has pushed down inflation, as have lower global prices. As inflation expectations fell, the real policy rate edged up. Consequently, the central bank is not expected to raise the policy rate further unless there are downward pressures on the rupiah (Figure 2.4.10).

Domestic financial indicators are stable, but loan growth tepid (Figure 2.4.11). Nonperforming loans remained below 3% of all loans in August 2023, and the average capital adequacy ratio was about 25%. Lending has continued to grow, albeit at a slowing rate. Higher interest rates have induced businesses to self-finance rather than borrow. In any case, banks are attracted to higher rates on government bonds. To spur lending, banks that lend to priority sectors will be granted a small reduction in the minimum reserve requirement. One priority sector is micro, small, and medium-sized enterprises, which the government envisages obtaining 30% of all loans by 2024. To that end, the authorities are considering a plan for restructuring the nonperforming loans of smaller enterprises to help jump-start lending.

Measures were recently initiated related to sustainable finance and export proceeds. In May, Indonesia sold ¥20.7 billion worth of samurai blue bonds, the first issue by a sovereign borrower. It aligns with Indonesia's commitment to promote sustainable finance, diversify funding sources, and widen its investor base.

Figure 2.4.9 Fiscal Indicators

Two more years of a successful return to the fiscal deficit ceiling.

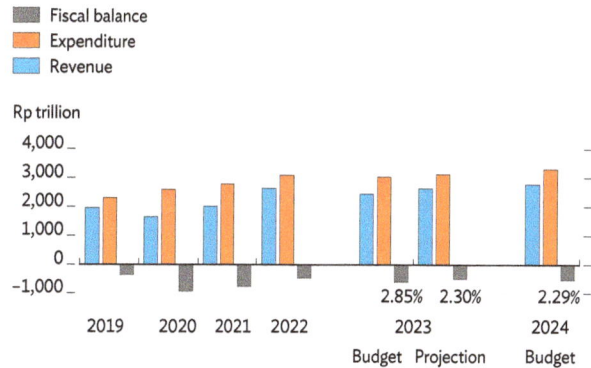

Note: Percentages are of gross domestic product.
Source: Ministry of Finance.

Figure 2.4.10 Bank Indonesia Policy Rate

With inflation tamed, monetary policy is broadly appropriate.

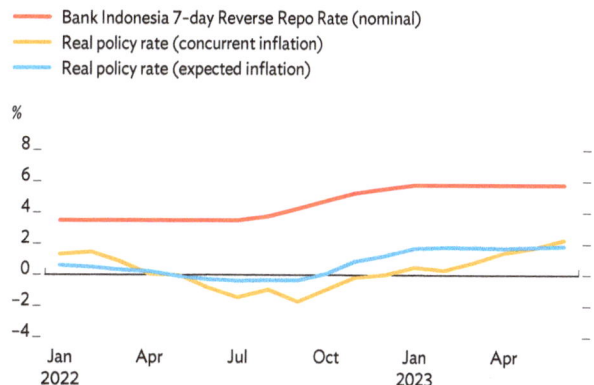

Sources: Bank Indonesia; Asian Development Bank estimates.

Figure 2.4.11 Monetary and Financial Indicators

Financial intermediation is surprisingly slow.

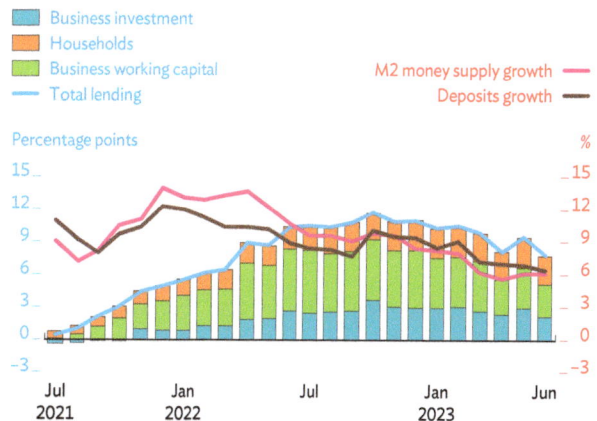

Source: Haver Analytics.

Starting in August, commodity exporters must deposit 30% of their proceeds in excess of $250,000 for at least 3 months in domestic banks. The regulation is meant to increase domestic dollar availability. At current rates, the deposits would earn 4.7%–5.0% at the central bank's term facility, or 3.2%–3.4% deposited in commercial banks. This compares with 5.0% in Singapore.

Policy initiatives continue to address trade and industrialization. In March, the government began to subsidize purchases of electric scooters, but uptake has been slow, motivating the government to expand buyer eligibility. To speed up the domestic processing of nickel, the government plans to acquire a majority stake in the country's largest nickel miner. To spur the completion of copper smelting facilities, it has imposed a new tax on exports of copper ore. To ensure that sufficient palm oil is domestically available, it imposes export taxes at progressive rates.

Social indicators continued to improve. Indonesia regained the status of upper-middle-income economy, based on the World Bank estimate of nominal gross national income per capita in 2022. From September 2022 to March 2023, the poverty rate fell from 9.6% to 9.4%, and the unemployment rate from 5.9% to 5.5%. However, the Gini coefficient of inequality worsened from 0.381 to 0.388, indicating greater inequality.

Prospects

This update projects a more sanguine scenario for 2023 than *ADO April 2023*. The forecast for growth in 2023 is raised from 4.8% in *ADO April 2023* to 5.0%, and the projection for 2024 is kept at 5.0% (Table 2.4.1). The projection for inflation in 2023 is revised down from 4.2% to 3.6% and for 2024 is kept at 3.0%.

Table 2.4.1 Selected Economic Indicators in Indonesia, %

Prospects have improved for 2023 and remain unchanged for 2024.

	2022	2023 Apr	2023 Sep	2024 Apr	2024 Sep
GDP growth	5.3	4.8	5.0	5.0	5.0
Inflation	4.2	4.2	3.6	3.0	3.0

GDP = gross domestic product.

Source: Asian Development Bank estimates.

Domestic demand is expected to more than offset slowing goods exports. In the rest of 2023, full normalization of mobility and higher purchasing power with lower inflation will stoke "rebound spending," though higher interest rates may somewhat crimp demand. Meanwhile, general expectations that the forthcoming election and political handover will be smooth will spur business investment (Figure 2.4.12). International tourism is recovering very strongly and will pick up some of the slack from weakening exports of goods. The current account surplus is projected to shrink but remain in surplus, and foreign direct investment inflow to remain healthy. These developments will offset scheduled repayment of maturing external debt in the remainder of 2023. International reserves are thus expected to remain stable and adequate.

Downside risks to the 2023 forecasts are mainly external. Interest rates in the US could stay higher and longer than expected. Demand from the People's Republic of China, Indonesia's largest trade partner, could fall further if that economy weakens. El Niño and the continuing Russian invasion of Ukraine could trigger price shocks.

The economy, however, has enough margin for growth. A large domestic economy provides a cushion for external demand shocks. Support for growth, if needed, can be readily provided using ample fiscal space or the monetary policy margin enabled by lower inflation. The stable financial sector and healthy foreign reserves should guard against external financial shocks.

Beyond 2023, it will be a challenge to achieve growth above 6%. For Indonesia to become a high-income economy by 2045, the Ministry of Planning estimates that GDP would need to grow by at least 6.0% annually, well above the pre-pandemic average of 5.3%. Notable challenges to this goal are potential labor scarring and learning losses from the pandemic; barriers to Indonesian exports arising from trade partners' regulations on deforestation, carbon border adjustment levies, and geopolitical reshoring; and long-standing inadequacies in domestic infrastructure, skills, and business regulations. On the other hand, potential growth could be enhanced by ongoing structural reforms to promote investment and job creation, improve the business environment, and foster financial deepening and efficiency.

Figure 2.4.12 Leading Indicators

A. Consumer Confidence

Consumer demand indicators are broadly at their pre-pandemic levels, ...

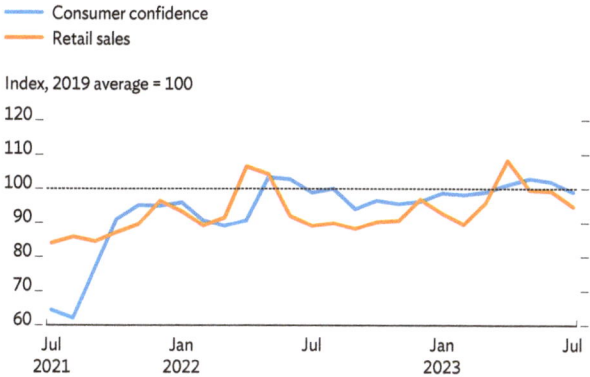

B. Business Activity

... forward-looking indicators of business activity are healthy, ...

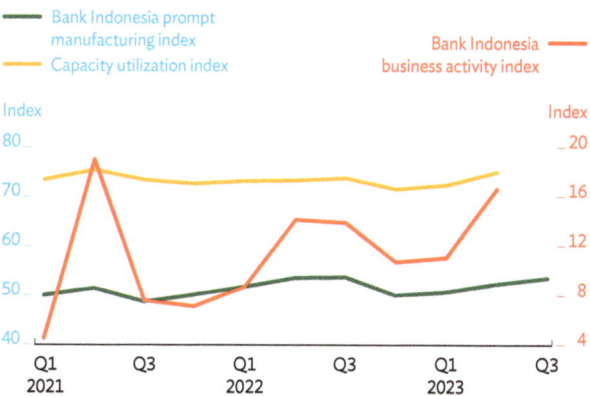

C. Tourism

... and a robust recovery in tourism will partly make up for slowing exports of goods.

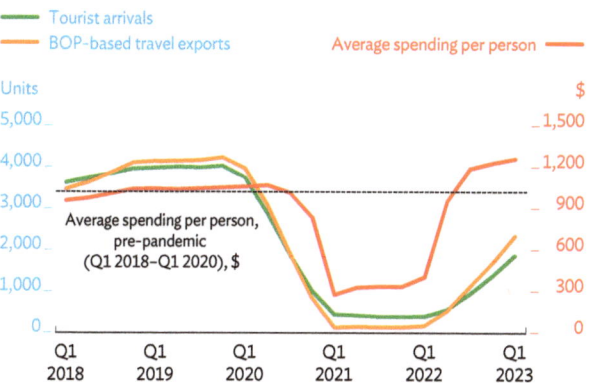

BI = Bank Indonesia, BOP = balance of payments, Q = quarter.
Notes: In the BI prompt manufacturing index, a value greater than 50 indicates expansion. All data are in 3-month moving averages. Tourist arrivals are in thousand persons, BOP-based travel exports are in $ million.
Sources: Bank Indonesia; Statistics Indonesia; Asian Development Bank estimates.

Further, the global energy transition could spur a boom in the near term for primary resources such as nickel, lithium, and renewable energy. In any case, the economy is expected to continue its path in 2024 and grow by about 5.0%. This projection assumes a return to the pre-pandemic pattern. Inflation is projected to be 3.0%, assuming no global price shocks and the central bank sustaining its current monetary policy framework.

Lao People's Democratic Republic

This update revises down the 2023 growth forecast and raises inflation projections for this year and next. Growth prospects in the Lao People's Democratic Republic (Lao PDR) are dimmed by slower growth in the People's Republic of China, a late monsoon, and macroeconomic pressures arising from high public debt and a weak Lao kip. Sharp depreciation of the kip will translate into much more persistent inflation this year and next than earlier forecast.

Updated Assessment

Public debt rose as a share of GDP from 76% at the end of 2021 to 97% a year later. Even with a decline in nominal terms from $12.4 billion in 2021 to $12.0 billion in 2022, sharp kip depreciation rendered public debt unsustainable, undermining growth prospects (Figure 2.4.13).

Figure 2.4.13 Public Debt

Public debt has changed little in nominal terms but is sharply higher as a share of GDP.

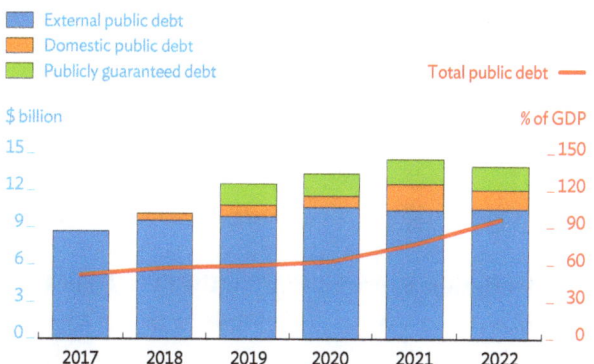

GDP = gross domestic product.
Source: Ministry of Finance.

The government has responded by tightening its borrowing and financing policies, pursuing debt deferrals, and rolling over maturing bonds to improve liquidity and lighten debt service pressures. However, risk aversion in the Thai bond market meant a weak reception for baht-denominated bonds offered in August by the government and its state-owned electricity generator, EDL-Generation Public Company. Domestic banks have stepped in with short-term loans to cover maturities. The government expects that available sources of foreign currency funding will adequately cover all its obligations in the rest of this year.

Rainfall has been hit by the late onset of the monsoon. The World Meteorological Organization expects El Niño weather disturbances in 2023. Previous El Niño events have reduced rainfall by as much as 30% and worsened flood and drought risk. This has implications for hydropower as well as agriculture. EDL-Generation estimates that water flowing into its basins for hydropower this year will be 81.2% of the 2022 flow. This shortfall can be offset to some extent, however, by new generating capacity that has or will commence commercial operations in 2023, generation by independent power producers in the central part of the country, and reservoir storage serving three-quarters of hydropower capacity.

Currency depreciation and consequent high inflation tempered household spending in the first half of the year. After falling by half against the US dollar and by 44% against the Thai baht in the year to the end of 2022, the kip depreciated from January to August 2023 by a further 13.6% against the dollar and 14.8% against the baht (Figure 2.4.14). Consumer price inflation remains elevated, having peaked at 41.3% year on year in February before gradually declining to 25.9% in August. Average inflation in the first 8 months was 35.4%, with currency depreciation estimated to account for two-thirds of it (Figure 2.4.15). In response, Prime Minister Order No. 10 on 14 July facilitated improved oversight of foreign exchange management.

Food inflation averaged 45.6% in the first 8 months of 2023. It rose from 12.3% in the same period a year earlier on pass-through from imported food and higher production costs from imported agricultural inputs. Falling household purchasing power has forced

Figure 2.4.14 Exchange Rate

Pressure on the Lao kip continues.

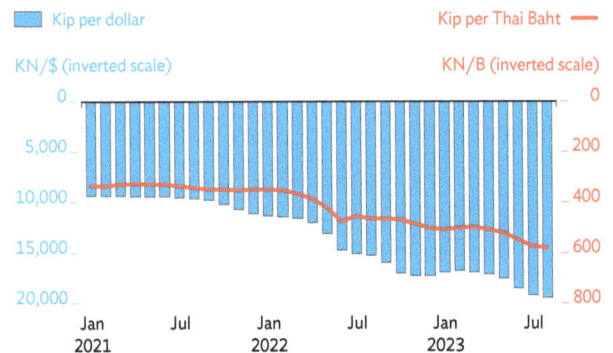

Source: Bank of the Lao PDR.

Figure 2.4.15 Monthly Inflation

Local currency depreciation and rising food prices have kept inflation in double digits in 2023.

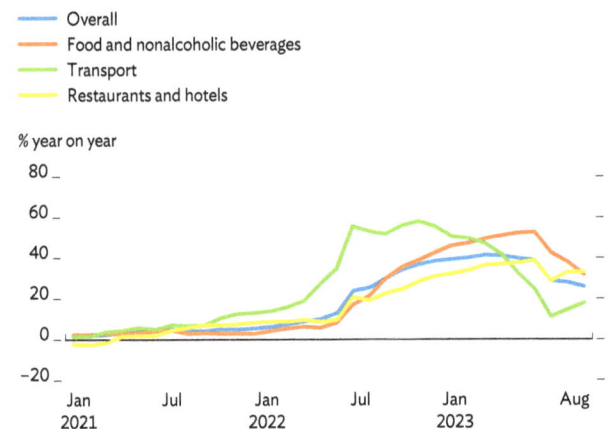

Source: Lao Statistics Bureau.

many families to cope by eating less frequently and adopting less diverse diets, which may depress health and development outcomes over the longer term. The government has raised the minimum wage and civil servant allowances to compensate somewhat for lost purchasing power.

Macroeconomic pressures have slowed private sector recovery, and a weak labor market has created few jobs. An estimated 39% of youth aged 15–24 years are neither employed nor in school or training. Labor force participation among those aged 15 years and over is only 47%, with most participants engaged in the informal economy.

The weak labor market motivates many to travel to neighboring countries for employment, such that more than half of households in the country depend on remittances, which equaled 1.3% of GDP in 2022, to bolster their incomes and mitigate their vulnerability.

Prospects

This update lowers the *ADO April 2023* forecast for GDP growth in 2023 from 4.0% to 3.7%. It maintains the 4.0% projection for 2024 (Table 2.4.2). Macroeconomic instability linked to unsustainable public debt and high inflation has eroded household spending and tapered commitments for new public and private investment. Prospects for growth in agriculture and hydropower have moderated with the late onset of the monsoon. These trends, coupled with tightening monetary and fiscal policy and an economic slowdown in the People's Republic of China, have delayed Lao PDR recovery.

Table 2.4.2 Selected Economic Indicators in the Lao People's Democratic Republic, %

Growth in 2023 will be lower than previously projected, but inflation much higher this year and next.

	2022	2023		2024	
		Apr	Sep	Apr	Sep
GDP growth	2.5	4.0	3.7	4.0	4.0
Inflation	23.0	16.0	28.0	5.0	10.0

GDP = gross domestic product.
Source: Asian Development Bank estimates.

International tourist arrivals are projected to reach 2.6 million in 2023, boosting recovery in related services. With upgrades to connectivity infrastructure complete and borders reopened, the outlook for 2024 remains as earlier forecast. Further, the Lao PDR chairing the Association of Southeast Asian Nations (ASEAN) next year promises to bring in more international travelers, which will boost confidence and demand for transport, accommodation, and dining out. To address fiscal and financing difficulties facing the country, Prime Minister Order No. 13 at the end of August further empowered the central bank to manage foreign exchange toward reducing import dependence, especially on fossil fuels, by shifting to e-vehicles and stimulating local industrial production.

A new credit line will provide funds equal to 1.0% of GDP to selected industries, notably in tourism and along the agriculture value chain, to spur the production of domestic goods and services each year over 2023–2025.

Inflation is projected to remain high until year-end, lifting average annual inflation to 28%. With high demand for services in 2024 and price adjustments linked with ongoing kip depreciation, double-digit inflation is expected to persist in 2024 at 10%. Low official reserves and high external debt service payments, averaging $1.3 billion each year in 2023–2027, put continued risk exerting pressure on the kip that will translate into further consumer price inflation. The central bank managed to bolster foreign reserves from $1.1 billion at the end of 2021 to $1.5 billion at the end of June 2023, but reserves still provide only 2 months of import cover.

Liquidity and solvency risks remain critical concerns. Low foreign exchange reserve adequacy and high public debt require urgent attention. Resolving the country's debt distress will take a coordinated and sustained effort across the government and from all creditors to make public financing practices more transparent and sustainable.

Malaysia

Growth decelerated during the first half (H1) of 2023 with subdued external demand, sluggish commodity production and weak trade performance. Inflation declined, tempered by easing commodity prices and the growth slowdown. With deceleration, GDP growth in 2023 is now projected to slow more than forecast in *ADO April 2023*. Inflation in 2023 and 2024 is similarly projected to slow marginally more than earlier forecast.

Updated Assessment

Growth in H1 2023 was 4.2%, well below the 6.8% of H1 2022 due to declining exports and a global slowdown. Growth slowed in the first quarter (Q1) of 2023, though domestic demand and the services sector remained resilient.

The slowdown continued in Q2 even though consumption and investment remained strong and tourism supported services (Figure 2.4.16).

Private consumption remained robust with improvements in the labor market and income. The increase in private consumption was still solid at 5.1% in H1 2023, but lower than the rapid increase in H1 2022 of 11.4%. The expansion in private consumption was supported by improving labor market conditions with greater employment opportunities and higher incomes. The deceleration in private consumption growth came from receding impacts from pent-up spending since the reopening of the economy in April 2022.

Public consumption increased by only 0.8% in H1 2023, well below the 4.6% increase in H1 2022, primarily due to the zeroing out of the COVID-19 fund this year. In 2022, the COVID-19 fund expenditures reached RM31.0 billion with the government spending approximately RM900 per capita for COVID-19. There was also a delay in the passage of the 2023 budget which also contributed to slightly lower budget execution in the first half of the year.

Positive momentum in investment, supported by large infrastructure projects, tempered the decline in growth. Both private and public investment accelerated in Q2 2023 expanding to 4.9% and 6.7%, respectively, in H1 2023, higher than the increases in the same period in 2022 of 3.4% and 0.9%. Higher government fixed assets spending and advances in multiyear infrastructure projects such as the Light Rail Transit 3 and the Pan Borneo Highway in Sabah backed the rise in investment.

Weakening global demand continued to drag down exports. In H1 2023, exports contracted by 6.4%, a downturn relative to the growth of 14.1% in the same period in 2022. Lower commodity prices pulled down the exports of petroleum products. In addition, exports of palm and palm oil-related products contracted in H1 2023 by 29.4%. Although exports decreased overall, major merchandise exports such as of petroleum products and electrical products remained resilient in H1 2023, increasing by 17.8% and 1.4%, respectively, but at a more moderate pace compared to the growth in the same period last year of 59.6% and 32.4%, respectively (Figure 2.4.17).

Figure 2.4.16 Demand-Side Contributions to Growth

Domestic demand boosted growth.

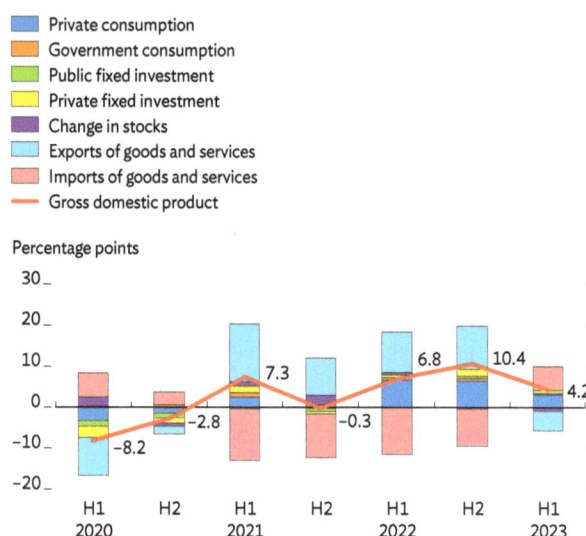

GDP = gross domestic product, H = half.
Source: Haver Analytics.

Figure 2.4.17 Merchandise Exports

The slowdown of global demand continued to weigh down exports.

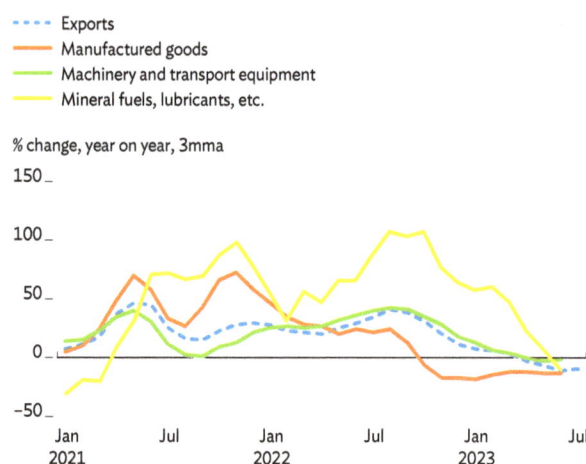

3mma = 3-month moving average.
Source: Haver Analytics.

The deceleration in domestic consumption over H1 2023 negatively impacted imports. H1 2023 saw a decline in imports by 8.1%, a reversal compared to the increase of 18.1% in H1 2022. The decrease in imports was mainly driven by the reduction in the imports of intermediate and consumption goods, which decreased by 13.0% and 1.3%, respectively, in the first 6 months of 2023.

From the supply side, a large expansion was observed in construction, while agriculture and mining struggled (Figure 2.4.18). In H1 2023, construction expanded by 6.8% with ongoing large infrastructure projects. In contrast, H1 2023 saw agriculture decline by 0.1%, while mining posted minimal growth of 0.1%. Hot and dry weather lowered palm oil and fishery production. Meanwhile, there was reduced oil and gas production due to plant maintenance.

Tourist arrivals boosted services. The services sector was second to construction in driving growth, increasing by 6.0% in H1 2023. Relatively good private consumption and a continuous influx of tourist arrivals backed sector expansion. From January to May 2023, tourist arrivals reached 7.5 million, an increase of 544.6% from the number of tourist arrivals in the same period last year (Figure 2.4.19).

Slowing global demand and a downturn in technology continued to diminish expansion in manufacturing. In June 2023, the manufacturing purchasing managers' index, at 47.7, indicated contraction for a 10th consecutive month (Figure 2.4.20). In H1 2023, the sector expanded by 1.7%, substantially lower than the 7.9% growth in the same period in 2022. Most manufacturing industries decelerated and some contracted in H1 2023 relative to a substantial expansion in H1 2022. Growth in all-important electrical and electronic manufacturing was cut significantly, expanding by only 1.8% in H1 2023 compared to 17.8% growth in H1 2022.

Labor market conditions continued to improve. The unemployment rate declined to 3.5% in Q2 2023 from 3.9% in Q2 2022. Steady growth in the country has continued to generate employment, increasing the number of jobs to 8.83 million in the Q2 2023, up by 21,200 jobs from the previous quarter, and up by 208,200 jobs from a year ago. A large increase in employment came in services, accounting for almost half of job addition over the same quarter last year.

Inflation continued to ease, reaching its lowest rate in the year at 2.4% in June 2023 (Figure 2.4.21). A large part of the decrease in inflation was due to easing pressures in prices of transport goods and services, posting zero inflation in June 2023 compared to 4.0% at the start of the year.

Figure 2.4.18 Supply-Side Contributions to Growth

Construction led growth, while services continued to expand.

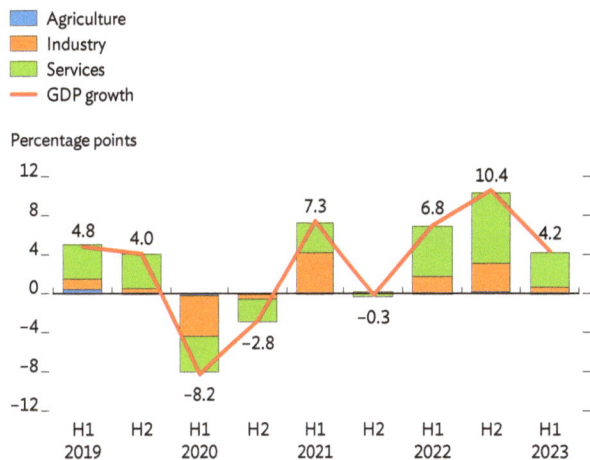

GDP = gross domestic product, H = half.
Source: Haver Analytics.

Figure 2.4.19 Tourist Arrivals

Tourist arrivals from key markets improve.

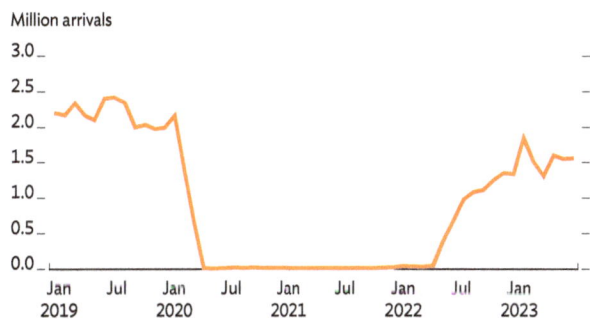

Source: CEIC Data Company.

Figure 2.4.20 Manufacturing Purchasing Managers' Index

Manufacturing was adversely affected by reduced global demand.

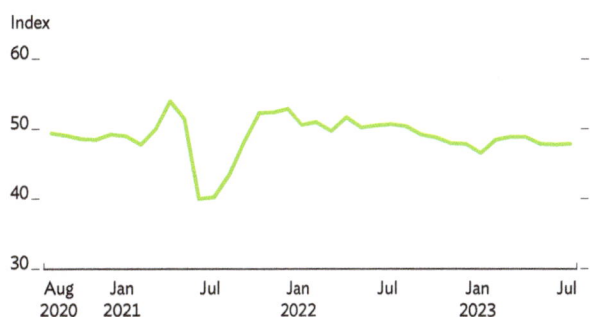

Note: A purchasing managers' index reading <50 signals deterioration, >50 improvement.
Source: CEIC Data Company.

The low inflation in transport goods and services prices was attributed to the declining unleaded petrol prices. The average inflation rate in H1 2023 was 3.2%, within the target of 2.8%–3.8% set by Bank Negara Malaysia, the central bank.

Tight monetary policy was maintained as core inflation and global interest rates remained elevated. In May 2023, the central bank increased monetary policy rates by 25 basis points to 3.0%, the first hike so far this year. Even though inflation trended down, core inflation remained sticky at 3.4% in Q2 2023 on firm demand. Since the increase in May 2023, the Monetary Policy Committee has maintained the policy rate, with inflation expected to be manageable for the rest of the year.

External pressures weakened the Malaysian ringgit. In Q2 2023, the ringgit averaged RM4.58 per US dollar, having depreciated from RM4.38 in the previous quarter (Figure 2.4.22). The ringgit's depreciation relative to the dollar came from increased demand for safe-haven assets, as the US economy performed relatively well in Q2 2023.

The external position remained stable. The current account surplus as a share of GDP increased to 2.1% in Q2 2023 from 1.0% in the previous quarter. The service and primary income deficits shrank, given increasing tourism receipts and larger income from overseas investment. With debt denominated in foreign currency accounting for 66.6% of all external debt, the depreciation of the ringgit and increased debt holdings of nonresident investors pushed external debt as a share of GDP to 67.1% at the end of H1 2023. Import coverage remained steady at 5.1 months in July 2023, though there was a slight decline in international reserves by 2.2% to $112.9 billion in July 2023 from $115.5 billion in March 2023.

Prospects

The economic outlook for the rest of 2023 is somewhat weaker than forecast in *ADO April 2023* (Table 2.4.3 and Figure 2.4.23). Domestic demand will continue to drive growth with positive developments in the labor market and continuing income support from government policy measures. Stronger tourism is evident as tourist arrivals from major tourism markets improve.

Figure 2.4.21 Monthly Inflation

Cheaper transport goods and services eased inflationary pressure.

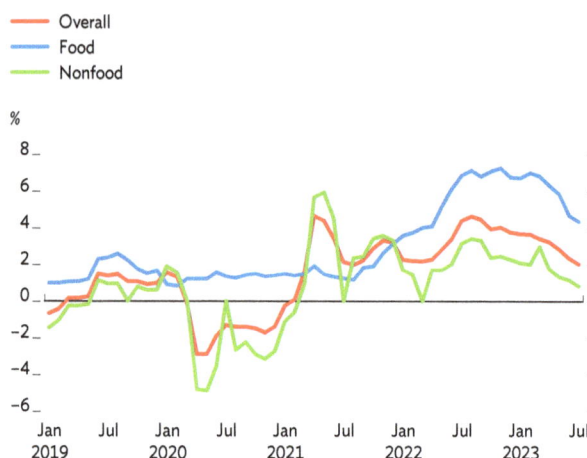

Source: Haver Analytics.

Figure 2.4.22 Exchange Rate

The Malaysian ringgit depreciated on strong demand for the dollar.

RM = Malaysian Ringgit.
Source: CEIC Data Company.

Table 2.4.3 Selected Economic Indicators in Malaysia, %

The growth projection for 2023 is lowered as well as the inflation forecast for both years.

	2022	2023		2024	
		Apr	Sep	Apr	Sep
GDP growth	8.7	4.7	4.5	4.9	4.9
Inflation	3.4	3.1	3.0	2.8	2.7

GDP = gross domestic product.
Source: Asian Development Bank estimates.

Growth in commodities and manufacturing for export remains a key constraint, hampered by weaker external demand for manufactures. This could be partly a lag effect from a weaker external outlook that has since improved. In contrast, fading growth factors are expected to slow growth further with a lower base effect in H2 2023. The GDP growth forecast in 2023 is lowered to 4.5% compared to the 4.7% made in April, while the 2024 GDP growth forecast is maintained at 4.9%.

Private spending will continue to support economic growth. Household spending will be supported by greater employment opportunities, increased incomes, and lower inflationary pressures. The realization of approved investments the previous year may translate to job opportunities this year. An increase in the minimum wage from RM1,200 to RM1,500 in July 2023 is expected to improve household incomes and support further growth of private spending in the latter part of the year.

Reforms to improve the business environment and to develop the digital economy bode well for investment. To attract investment, the government is focusing on simplifying the business procedures, improving the ease of business and turnaround of business approvals, and streamlining the role of investment promotion agencies. Investment opportunities will likely improve through government plans to position the country as a data hub for Asia and by further developing its digital economy. The government has recognized the important role of Malaysia's digital economy, with the contribution of the digital economy to GDP projected to reach 25.5% by 2025 (Figure 2.4.24).

Nevertheless, business optimism and consumer sentiment are on downward trajectories amid global economic uncertainty. The global economic slowdown has affected sales both domestically and abroad. The business conditions index decreased to 82.4 in Q2 2023 from 95.4 during the previous quarter. Similarly, there is growing pessimism among consumers due to inflation and concerns regarding future finances. The consumer sentiment index dropped by 8.4 points from 99.2 in Q1 2023 to 90.8 in Q2 2023 (Figure 2.4.25).

Figure 2.4.23 GDP Growth

Growth is expected to moderate.

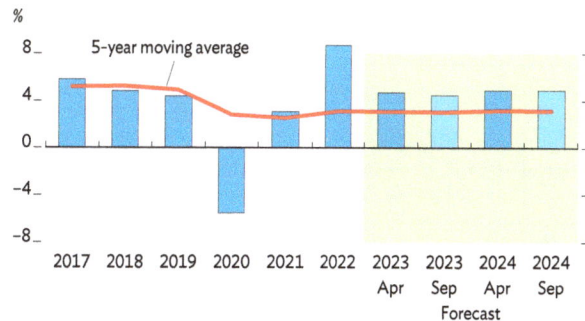

GDP = gross domestic product.
Source: Asian Development Bank estimates.

Figure 2.4.24 Investment

The steady investment growth can continue to support growth and offer greater employment opportunities.

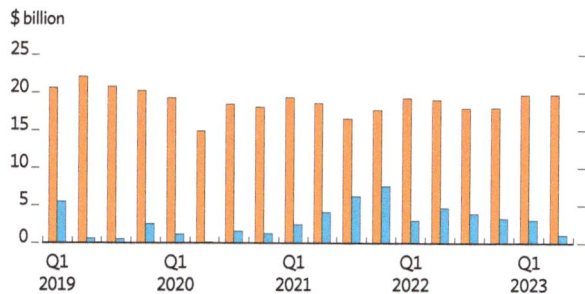

Q = quarter.
Sources: Haver Analytics; CEIC Data Company.

Figure 2.4.25 Consumer and Business Confidence

Consumer and business confidence lessened.

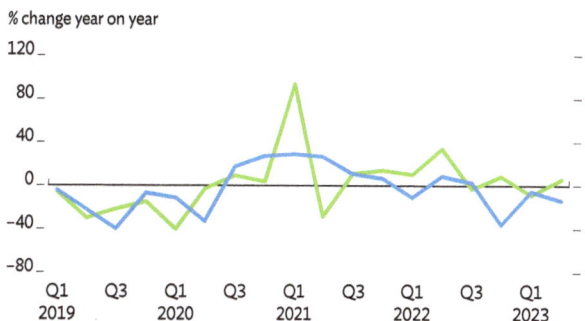

Q = quarter.
Sources: Haver Analytics; CEIC Data Company.

Inflation is forecast to continue its downward path, though upside risk factors could push prices up. Downward pressure will continue to come from weakening global demand, falling commodity prices, and the efforts by the government to reduce the cost of living. Upside risks to inflation include the threat of El Niño, an Indian rice export ban, and changes in price subsidies and controls. The headline inflation rate is forecast at 3.0% in 2023, down from the earlier 3.1% projection. The inflation forecast for 2024 is at 2.7%.

No increase in the short-term monetary policy rate is expected. The central bank maintained its overnight policy rate at 3.0% due to slowing growth and easing inflationary pressures, stating that current monetary policy remained supportive of the economy. The rate is expected to remain unchanged for the rest of this year.

The central bank said it will intervene in the foreign exchange markets if needed to stabilize the ringgit. Although ringgit depreciation can make exports more competitive, it also pushes up foreign debt servicing. In addition, steep ringgit depreciation could undermine investor confidence in the country.

Slowing global demand is expected to weigh on Malaysia's near-term growth prospects. Downside risks stem from weaker-than-expected global demand and a prolonged technology downcycle. Manufacturing exports are likely to contract further if economic recovery is derailed in the People's Republic of China. El Niño weather disturbance threatens to undermine domestic commodity production. The growth outlook could improve with increased tourism and the implementation of new and existing investment projects, such as the 10 flagship catalyst projects under Phase 1 of the National Energy Transition Roadmap.

Malaysia's credit ratings remain stable. Fitch Ratings affirmed in February 2023 Malaysia's long-term foreign-currency issuer default rating of BBB+ with a stable outlook. In June 2023, S&P Global Ratings reaffirmed its A– long-term and A-2 short-term foreign currency sovereign credit ratings.

Philippines

Domestic demand enabled the economy to post 5.3% GDP growth in the first half (H1) of 2023, though softening in the second quarter (Q2) from the brisk pace in the prior year. The growth forecast is revised down to 5.7% this year and maintained at 6.2% in 2024. Domestic demand and public investment are expected to continue to support growth. As in *ADO April 2023*, inflationary pressures are projected to moderate next year and the current account deficit to narrow.

Updated Assessment

Growth slowed to 4.3% in Q2 2023, bringing H1 2023 growth down to 5.3% from 7.8% in H1 2022. Inflationary pressures, monetary tightening, and external headwinds weighed on growth. Domestic demand fueled the economic expansion, though with a broad-based moderation in Q2 as pent-up demand eased. High inflation and interest rates weighed on consumer demand and investment.

Household consumption remained the biggest contributor to GDP growth. Following the rapid 9.3% increase in H1 2022, private consumption rose by 6.0%, in line with its trend growth prior to the pandemic (5.9% on average in 2010–2019). It was the dominant driver of the economic expansion, followed by investment (Figure 2.4.26).

Figure 2.4.26 Demand-Side Contributions to Growth

Domestic demand, led by household consumption, underpinned growth.

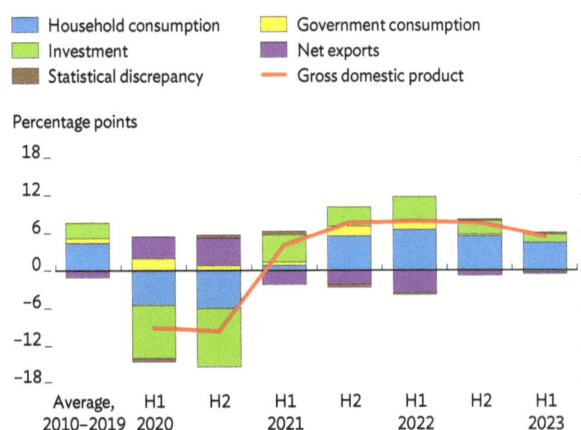

Legend:
- Household consumption
- Government consumption
- Investment
- Net exports
- Statistical discrepancy
- Gross domestic product

Percentage points

H = half.

Sources: Philippine Statistics Authority; CEIC Data Company.

Growth in spending for clothing, household equipment and furnishings declined after a strong rebound last year, while that for transport, recreation, and restaurants and hotels sustained double-digit expansion, reflecting in part vigorous domestic tourism. On the other hand, government expenditures were lower by 1.4% in H1, reversing the 7.6% growth in H1 2022 during the national elections. Procurement-related difficulties were among the factors that led to lower spending.

Rising employment and steady remittance inflows continued to support household spending.
The unemployment rate declined to 4.5% in June 2023 from 6.0% in June 2022 despite a higher labor force participation rate (66.1% from 64.8%) (Figure 2.4.27). About 2.2 million new jobs were created over the year, mostly in services. Remittances from overseas workers rose by 2.9% in H1.

Investment growth slowed to 5.4% in H1 2023 from 17.4% in H1 2022. It was flat in Q2 as inventories fell and fixed investment moderated. Subdued construction tempered fixed capital growth to 6.9% in H1 (from 11.8% in H1 2022), with growth slowing in Q2 (3.9%). Investment in durable equipment, including road transport and machinery, sustained a healthy expansion of 9.3% in H1 2023.

Net exports weighed on GDP growth in H1.
Merchandise exports declined by 8.0% in real terms on weak external demand. Merchandise imports also fell, though to a lesser extent, by 2.4%, partly reflecting the subdued demand for raw materials and components for export-oriented manufacturing, as well as the slowdown in domestic demand. Strong services exports (14.8% higher in H1 2023), driven by tourism and business process outsourcing partly cushioned the merchandise trade deficit.

Services largely fueled the growth in GDP with broad expansion across major subsectors.
Services growth was fairly strong at 7.2% in H1 2023 on top of an 8.8% expansion in H1 2022, contributing 80% of the expansion in GDP (Figure 2.4.28). Transport, accommodations, and restaurants sustained double-digit growth on buoyant tourism. Growth in retail trade, accounting for nearly a fourth of total services, remained buoyant at 6.6% as well as in finance (6.9%) and professional and business services (7.2%).

Figure 2.4.27 Labor Force Participation and Unemployment Rates

The unemployment rate continued to decline to below prepandemic levels.

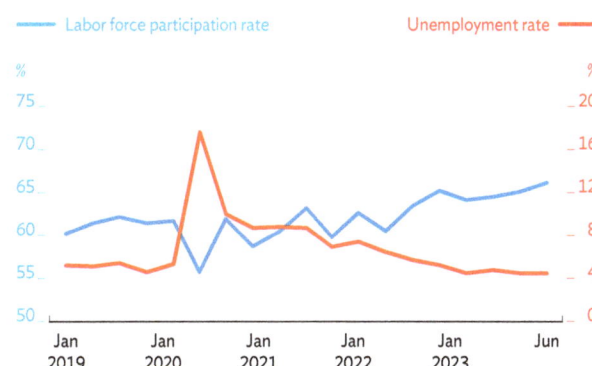

Sources: Philippine Statistics Authority; CEIC Data Company.

Figure 2.4.28 Supply-Side Contributions to Growth

Services largely propelled GDP growth.

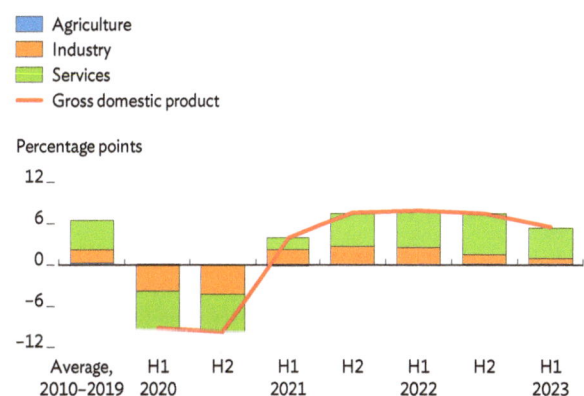

GDP = gross domestic product, H = half.
Sources: Philippine Statistics Authority; CEIC Data Company.

Industry growth was more than halved (3.0% in H1 2023 from 8.0% H1 2022) on smaller gains in manufacturing and construction. Weak external demand dampened manufacturing growth to 1.6% in H1 2023 from 5.9% in H1 2022. The growth in construction slowed (6.4% in H1 2023 from 16.5% in H1 2022) largely from a moderation in public construction. The agriculture sector rose by 1.2%, with higher output in palay (3.5%), livestock (3.3%), and poultry (2.3%), partly offset by a decline in fisheries (−6.8%).

Elevated food and oil prices have stoked inflation.
Headline inflation moderated from February to July this year, though quickened to 5.3% year on year in August to an average of 6.6% in the first 8 months (Figure 2.4.29). Price pressures stemmed from elevated global commodity prices and tight domestic food supply caused in part by bad weather. Food inflation rose to 8.2% in August from 6.3% in July with higher rice and vegetables prices among the key drivers. The government temporarily lowered tariffs on key agricultural commodities and provided targeted cash transfers to mitigate the impact of inflation on poor households. Inflation for nonfood items including transport services also rose in line with higher global oil prices. Fuel subsidy programs have been extended for qualified public utility vehicle drivers and operators, and fuel discounts for farmers and fisherfolk. Core inflation has steadily eased since April this year to 6.1% in August (year-to-date average 7.4%), though remains higher than headline inflation. The central bank's policy interest rate has been maintained since a cumulative 425 basis point hike from May 2022 to March 2023 (Figure 2.4.30). The higher policy rate reined in growth in broad money (M3) from 7.2% year on year in June 2022 to 5.9% a year later. Bank lending to businesses continued to grow by 6.3% year on year in June, though slower than 12.0% a year earlier.

The fiscal deficit narrowed as revenues picked up while expenditures grew modestly. The deficit was 4.8% of GDP in H1 2023 compared to 6.5% in H1 2022. Revenue was up by 7.7% year on year, while spending rose marginally (0.4%). Current expenditure declined while infrastructure spending increased by 7.8% year on year. Government debt rose slightly to 61.0% of GDP as of the end of June 2023 from 60.9% at the end of 2022. Domestic debt comprises 70% of total debt, with long-term debt at three-fourths of the total (Figure 2.4.31). In line with the fiscal program of a narrowing fiscal deficit, the ratio of debt to GDP is programmed to start declining in 2024 and reach below 60% by 2025. The country's investment-grade sovereign credit rating was affirmed in 2023.

The current account deficit slightly widened to 4.3% of GDP in Q1 2022 from 4.2% in the same period last year. The merchandise trade deficit widened to 16.6% of GDP from 16.4% a year earlier.

Figure 2.4.29 Contributions to Inflation, 2018 = 100

Elevated food prices largely drove inflation.

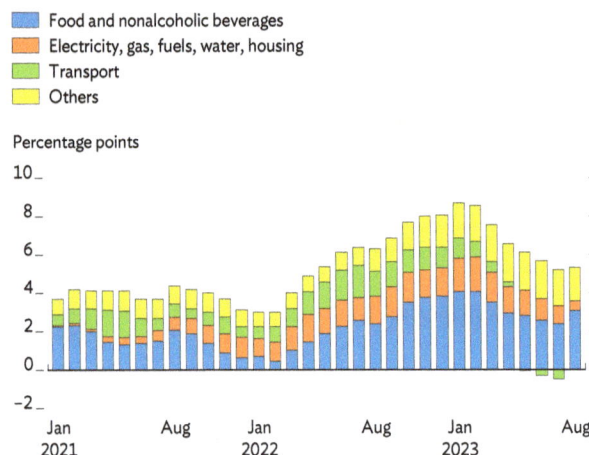

Source: CEIC Data Company.

Figure 2.4.30 Inflation and Policy Interest Rate

The policy rate has been kept steady since a cumulative 425 basis point hike from May 2022 to March 2023.

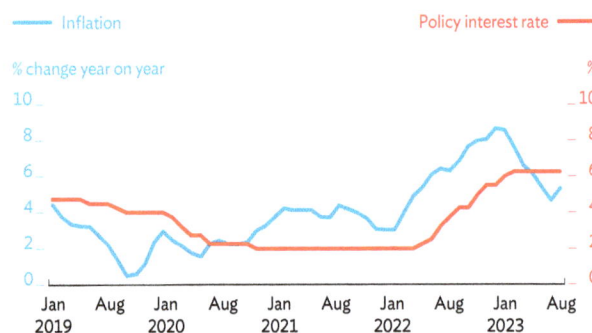

Note: Policy interest rate refers to the overnight reverse repurchase rate.
Sources: Bangko Sentral ng Pilipinas; CEIC Data Company.

Figure 2.4.31 National Government Debt

Debt is largely domestic.

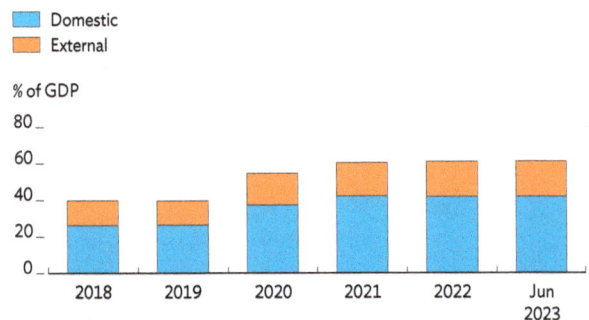

GDP = gross domestic product.
Sources: Bureau of the Treasury; CEIC Data Company.

Robust service exports mitigated the weakness in merchandise exports, and rising remittances also lifted the current account (Figure 2.4.32). The surplus in service exports expanded on gains in business process outsourcing, finance, and tourism. Higher net inflows were registered in the financial account. Portfolio investment reversed the net outflows a year earlier, though this was partly offset by lower net inflows of direct investment. The overall balance of payments registered a higher surplus equivalent to 3.4% of GDP in Q1 2023 from 0.5% in Q1 2022.

Official reserves were $99.8 billion at the end of August 2023. They provided cover for 7.4 months of imports of goods and services and income payments. The ratio of external debt to GDP rose to 29.0% of GDP at the end of March 2023 from 27.5% of GDP at the end of December 2022. The Philippine peso depreciated by 1.6% since the start of the year to the end of August.

Prospects

Growth is expected to remain strong, albeit tempered by inflationary pressures and global headwinds. The growth forecast in 2023 is revised to 5.7% (from 6.0% in April) and maintained at 6.2% in 2024 (Table 2.4.4 and Figure 2.4.33). Private consumption and investment will continue to underpin growth. A moderation in inflationary pressures next year bode well for domestic demand.

Public expenditure is expected to pick up and accelerate next year. Spending, excluding interest payments, recovered with 15.3% growth year on year in July. Expenditure for social services and infrastructure disbursement rose. Measures are being undertaken to improve agencies' budget utilization, including the conduct of early procurement activities, simplified implementing rules and regulations for procurement, and the digitalization of government disbursements and collections. The digitalization of social registries is also underway, along with the adoption of the Philippine Identification System, or the national ID, to improve targeting and public service delivery. The government approved in May 2023 the implementation of an integrated financial management information system across all agencies, streamlining processes and paving the way for the full digitalization of public financial management systems.

Figure 2.4.32 Current Account Components

Services exports and steady remittances support the current account.

GDP = gross domestic product.
Source: CEIC Data Company.

Table 2.4.4 Selected Economic Indicators in the Philippines, %

Growth will moderate in 2023 more than earlier forecast before picking up in 2024, underpinned by domestic demand.

	2022	2023		2024	
		Apr	Sep	Apr	Sep
GDP growth	7.6	6.0	5.7	6.2	6.2
Inflation	5.8	6.2	6.2	4.0	4.0

GDP = gross domestic product.
Source: Asian Development Bank estimates.

Figure 2.4.33 GDP Growth

Growth is expected to remain strong despite a moderation in 2023.

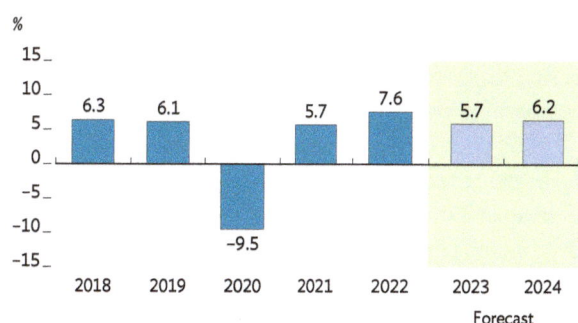

Source: *Asian Development Outlook* database.

Other priority measures are right-sizing the government bureaucracy by streamlining and restructuring to enhance government operations, and reforming the military pension system to make it financially sustainable.

Public infrastructure spending should hold up with several large projects underway. Infrastructure spending in H1 2023 was equal to 5.3% of GDP, within the government's target. Among the government's flagship infrastructure projects, 71 are ongoing, worth about $75 billion as of July 2023, while another 27 have been approved for implementation. Most of the projects aim to improve physical connectivity with railways, bridges, and airports or to strengthen water management through irrigation, water supply, and flood control. Climate change mitigation and adaptation are prioritized, as are projects on digital connectivity, energy, and agriculture. The government has enhanced the guidelines for project formulation, prioritization, and monitoring, and for expediting the issuance of permits and licenses.

The proposed national budget for 2024 is 9.5% higher than the 2023 budget. Larger outlays are planned for social programs and infrastructure. The allocation for infrastructure is 6.6% higher, including road networks and railways, the subway in Metro Manila, school buildings, hospitals, and health centers. Infrastructure spending will be maintained at over 5% of GDP in 2024 and the medium term. The government approved in July 2023 the country's first sovereign development fund to provide additional financing support for its projects.

Social services comprise nearly 40% of the total budget. Items include education subsidies, national health insurance, conditional cash transfers to poor families, and recently launched food vouchers to address the nutrition needs of food-poor Filipinos. These programs support the adoption of the social protection floor approved in April 2023, which sets basic social security guarantees, including health care and social services, that aim to reduce poverty and vulnerability. Poverty alleviation remains central to the government's development plan, especially in light of the adverse impact of the pandemic. Poverty incidence declined from 23.5% of the population in 2015 to 16.7% in 2018. But it rose to 18.1% in 2021 under the impact of the pandemic, equivalent to 20 million poor people, an increase of 2.3 million from 2018.

The government is mobilizing more revenue to support higher investment while keeping within its fiscal consolidation goals. The tax revenue increased to 14.6% of GDP in 2022, the highest in over a decade. Measures such as an increase in excise taxes on petroleum products, cigarettes, and alcohol have lifted tax collections. Revenue is planned to rise by 12.2% next year, with the fiscal deficit narrowing to 5.1% of GDP from this year's 6.1% of GDP deficit ceiling. Proposed additional measures include new taxes on digital service providers and single-use plastics, and higher taxes on sweetened beverages and junk food. The simplification of the taxation of passive income and financial intermediaries is also being pursued while carbon emission taxes are being studied. Digitalization programs are being ramped up to improve tax administration, including electronic filing of returns and invoicing.

Private consumption should remain firm in the near term while easing from last year's rapid growth. A low unemployment rate and continued growth in remittances should support private consumption. Moreover, a reduction in personal income tax rates in 2023 benefits most workers.

Indicators of future economic activity are mixed. The manufacturing purchasing managers' index fell below the 50 threshold in August to 49.7, signaling a contraction, compared to 51.9 in July (Figure 2.4.34). Still, manufacturers expect growth in output in the next 12 months and were keen to build on stocks in anticipation of greater sales. On the other hand, there was sustained strong growth in building permits for privately constructed commercial establishments and sales of motor vehicles (passenger and commercial). Imports of some capital goods, including transport equipment, and consumer goods continued to rise in July.

Figure 2.4.34 Manufacturing Purchasing Managers' Index

The index slipped below the 50 threshold in August, indicating contraction.

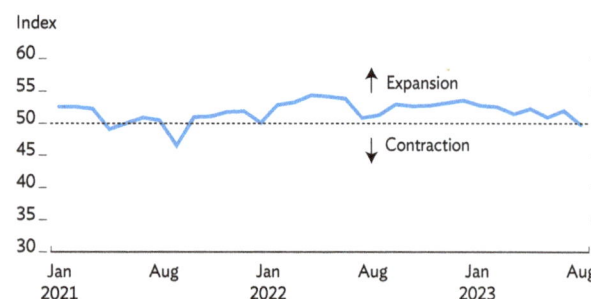

Note: A purchasing managers' index reading <50 signals deterioration, >50 improvement.

Sources: Bangko Sentral ng Pilipinas; CEIC Data Company.

Private investment will benefit from reforms that have made the economy more open to foreign investment and trade. Restrictions on the participation of foreign investors have been eased, opening several sectors, such as renewable energy, airports, telecommunications, railways, and expressways, to full foreign ownership. These reforms complement the Philippines' ratification of the Regional Comprehensive Economic Partnership in February 2023. The Corporate Recovery and Tax Incentives for Enterprises Law reduced the corporate income tax rate from 30% to 25% (20% for micro, small, and medium-sized enterprises).

The regulatory framework for public–private partnerships is being strengthened. The guidelines for joint ventures have been simplified and enhanced to improve the competitive processes by which partners are selected, ensure that projects are technically and financially sound, and facilitate fast and efficient implementation. The guidelines align with recently revised implementing rules and regulations governing build-operate-transfer projects and the bill on public–private partnerships currently pending in Congress.

Growth in services, which provide about 60% of GDP, is expected to remain healthy. Private consumption will underpin retail trade, while growing international tourist arrivals will benefit a range of services, most notably hotels and restaurants, and transport. There were 3.6 million foreign visitor arrivals from January to August, surpassing the 2.65 million recorded in all of 2022.

Inflation forecasts are maintained at 6.2% this year and 4.0% in 2024. Inflation is expected to soften, though the onset of El Niño and elevated global commodity prices may slow the pace of deceleration. Second-round effects from higher transport fares and minimum wage hikes are also factors. The government is considering extending the period for the reduced tariffs for some food items including rice which are due to expire by December 2023, to keep inflation contained. With core inflation easing slowly, the monetary authorities will likely maintain policy rates before considering cutting them next year. The central bank is also looking at reducing banks' reserve requirement ratio.

The current account deficit will narrow from 2022, supported by the strength in service exports and steady remittances. Tourism and business process outsourcing should remain buoyant, while merchandise exports will stay subdued. Weaker economic prospects for major export markets, including the US, Japan, and the People's Republic of China, will temper merchandise exports. The steady growth in remittances from overseas workers will continue to help lift the current account.

Downside risks weigh on the outlook. Risk factors include a sharper-than-expected slowdown in major advanced economies, heightened geopolitical tensions, and global commodity prices above expectations. An intensified and prolonged El Niño, other severe weather disturbances, and a continuation of the Russian invasion of Ukraine could elevate inflationary pressures.

Thailand

The growth forecast published in *ADO April 2023* is upgraded for 2023 but unchanged for 2024. Tourism and private consumption are the main engines of growth, while sluggish merchandise exports subtract from growth amid global economic volatility. Headline inflation is on a declining trend as global oil prices weaken. Risks to the growth outlook remain on the downside, most notably from global economic conditions. A successful transition to a new prime minister in August reduces the biggest domestic risk to the growth outlook.

Updated Assessment

In the first half (H1) of 2023, economic recovery remained on track. Real GDP expanded by 2.2% year on year with tourism and private consumption making strong comebacks. Exports of goods and services grew by 1.4%. The number of international arrivals was 12.9 million, surpassing 11.5 million in the whole of 2022 (Figure 2.4.35). A significant rise in international tourist arrivals was the main driver of service exports, which expanded by 66.1%. In contrast, merchandise exports contracted by 6.0% as global economic uncertainty weighed on demand. While global manufacturing has shown signs of recovery from production chain disruption during and after the pandemic, new export orders did not significantly increase (Figure 2.4.36).

Figure 2.4.35 Monthly International Tourist Arrivals

The number of international tourist arrivals continued to recover year on year—and month on month to December 2022, the traditional peak season.

Million visitors

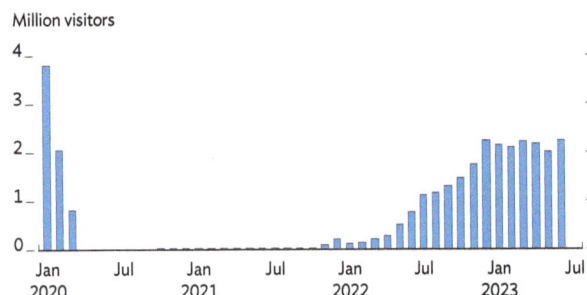

Source: CEIC Data Company.

Figure 2.4.36 Demand-Side Contributions to Growth

Tourism and private consumption were the main growth drivers in H1 2023.

- Private consumption
- Gross fixed capital formation
- Net exports
- Government consumption
- Change in inventories
- Statistical discrepancy
- Gross domestic product

Percentage points

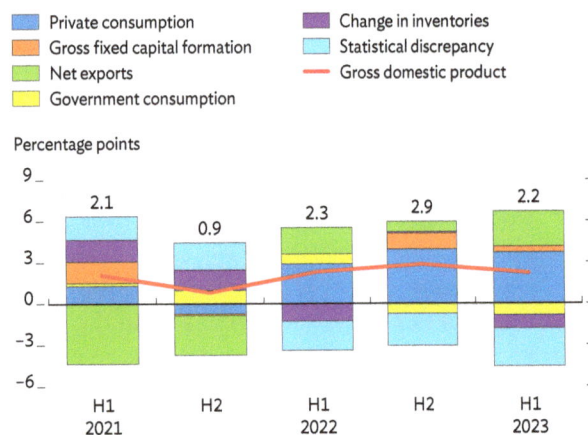

H = half.
Source: Office of the National Economic and Social Development Council.

Private consumption grew by a rapid 6.8% year on year, primarily on purchases of consumer goods in the wake of revived tourism.
Employment and consumer confidence also improved. The unemployment rate hit a 3-year low in H1 2023, declining from 1.3% in H1 2022 to 1.1%. Employment in agriculture expanded by 0.7%. Revived tourism benefited wholesale and retail trade, hotels, and restaurants. However, employment in manufacturing declined slightly from H2 2022 following a slowdown in merchandise exports. In contrast to private consumption, public consumption contracted by 5.3%, reflecting lower social transfers as COVID-19 response wound down.

Growth in private investment decelerated from 2.6% in H1 2022 to 1.8% in H1 2023. This tracked decelerating investment in machinery and equipment and in construction, particularly in export-oriented industries. Public investment increased by 1.9%, mainly on higher road and bridge construction. Meanwhile, the ratio of the public debt to GDP at the end of June 2023 stood at 61.15%, well below the 70% limit set by the State Finance and Financial Discipline Committee (Figure 2.4.37).

Figure 2.4.37 Public Debt

Fiscal stability remained strong.

% of GDP

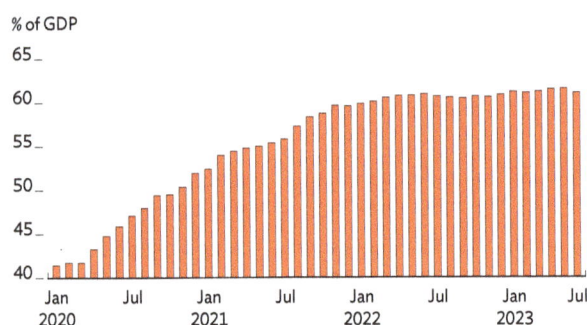

GDP = gross domestic product.
Source: Public Debt Management Office.

Imports declined by 1.7% year on year in H1 2023.
This mainly reflected lower imports of raw materials and intermediate goods such as electronics and computer parts, natural gas, steel, and chemicals in line with weakened export demand. Meanwhile, imports of consumer goods increased significantly on skyrocketing electric vehicle imports, especially from the People's Republic of China (PRC), in line with government policy to promote them. A government incentive package includes a 40% reduction in the import duty for battery-only electric vehicles priced at up to B2 million, a 20% reduction in 2022 and 2023 for those priced at B2 million–B7 million with batteries rated over 30 kilowatt-hours, and an excise tax cut from 8% to 2% for imported electric vehicles.

By sector, agriculture was particularly strong, expanding by 3.4% year on year in H1 2023.
Good weather with sufficient rain in Q1 2023, and favorable selling prices for agricultural products, encouraged more production of off-season rice, sugarcane, and maize. Manufacturing output declined

by 3.2% in the first half as merchandise exports remained sluggish. The production of hard disk drives, textiles and apparel, rubber and plastics, and chemical products continued to decline quarter on quarter from Q4 2022. On the other hand, passenger car production was resilient as a shortage of microchips eased. Services expanded by 4.7% year on year in H1 thanks to the significant rise in international tourist arrivals and upward trend in private consumption. Accommodation, food services, transportation, and storage recorded double-digit growth, supported by rising numbers of foreign tourists and a government package to stimulate domestic travel. Apart from a strong rebound in tourism, expansion in transportation and storage was underpinned by an increase in freight transport, especially of agricultural products, in line with growth in agricultural production (Figure 2.4.38).

Inflation and external accounts improved in H1 2023 from a year earlier. Headline inflation averaged 2.5%, slowing from H1 2022 in tandem with lower food and energy prices. A high base also slowed core inflation to 1.9%. In Q1 2023, the current account balance returned to surplus, equal to 2.7% of GDP, reflecting trade surpluses for both goods and services. A fall in oil import payments was the main driver of the trade surplus in goods, while rising international tourism receipts contributed to the surplus in services. International reserves provided cover for 2.3 times short-term external debt or 8 months of imports. Since April, the Bank of Thailand, the central bank, has raised the policy interest rate from 1.75% to 2.25% as the economy expanded (Figure 2.4.39). In January to July 2023, the Thai baht depreciated against the US dollar by 4%, reflecting policy rate hikes in the advanced economies and domestic political uncertainty.

Prospects

The growth forecast for 2023 is upgraded from 3.3% in April to 3.5%. The growth projection for 2024 is maintained at 3.7% (Table 2.4.5 and Figure 2.4.40). The upward revision for 2023 mainly accommodates growth in private consumption and tourism outpacing expectation. A key factor that has constrained the rate of economic recovery in 2023 is weak merchandise exports. However, the economy is expected to gather momentum in H2 2023 and gradually rise in 2024 in line with global economic recovery.

Figure 2.4.38 Supply-Side Contributions to Growth

Agriculture and services grew robustly, while manufacturing contracted in line with a slowdown in merchandise exports.

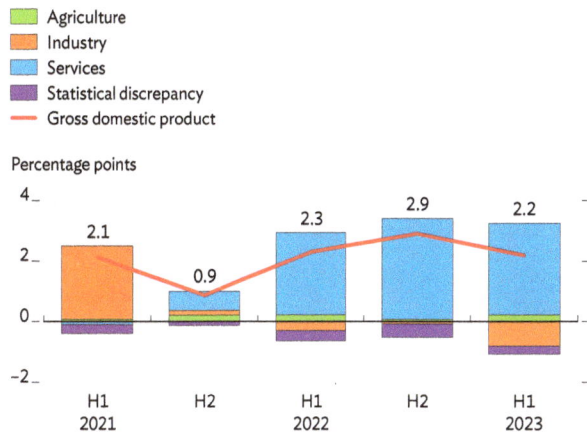

H = half.
Source: Office of the National Economic and Social Development Council.

Figure 2.4.39 Inflation and Policy Interest Rate

Inflation slowed, while the policy interest rate increased by 0.25% in May and again in August.

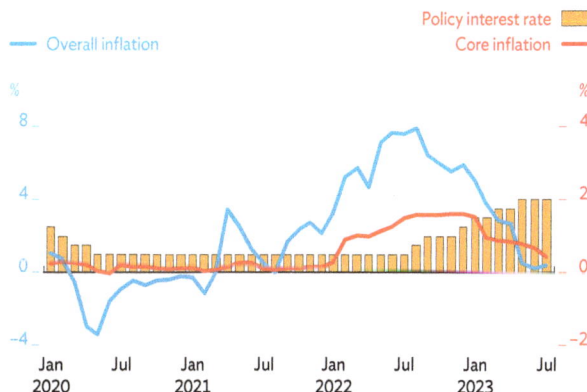

Source: CEIC Data Company.

Table 2.4.5 Selected Economic Indicators in Thailand, %

The economy is projected to continue to recover on rebounding tourism and private consumption.

	2022	2023		2024	
		Apr	Sep	Apr	Sep
GDP growth	2.6	3.3	3.5	3.7	3.7
Inflation	6.1	2.9	2.5	2.3	2.3

GDP = gross domestic product.

Sources: Office of the National Economic and Social Council; Asian Development Bank estimates.

Figure 2.4.40 GDP Growth

The growth forecast for 2023 is upgraded from 3.3% to 3.5%.

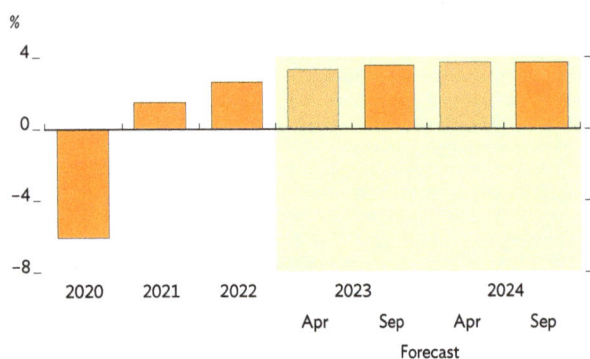

GDP = gross domestic product.
Source: *Asian Development Outlook* database.

Merchandise exports could slow further in H2 2023 if global demand remains soft. Orders for industrial products such as computers and parts, petroleum, and such agricultural products as rubber and tapioca are projected to decline. On the positive side, PRC reopening and easing chip shortages could boost exports of automobiles, parts, and electric appliances. However, Thailand's exports remain fragile given signs of weaker manufacturing in its major trade partners.

Buoyant tourism calls for export forecasts to be revised up. The forecast for growth in exports of goods and services in 2023 is revised up from 6.6% to 7.0% and in 2024 from 6.3% to 6.7%. The number of international tourist arrivals in H1 2023 was slightly above the *ADO April 2023* forecast and is expected to continue to rise in the rest of 2023 and 2024. The projection for international arrivals in 2023 is revised up from 28 million in April to 30 million, and in 2024 from 35 million to 36 million. This promises to support continued recovery in the labor market, especially employment in tourism and related industries.

Growth in imports and private investment is now projected lower than in *ADO April 2023*, in line with weaker merchandise exports. The forecast for private investment growth is thus revised down from 2.5% in April to 1.9%. For 2024, the forecast is revised up from 3.5% to 3.9%. The projection for growth in imports of goods and services is adjusted down from 2.6% to 1.6% in 2023, accelerating to 5.2% in 2024. Slowing imports are in line with weaker merchandise exports and easing global oil prices.

Private consumption should continue to grow on positive prospects for employment. Easing inflation following lower fuel prices is also expected to support private consumption. However, growth could be dragged down by the struggles of vulnerable households with low income and high debt, as well as by farmers who may be affected by drought under El Niño in H2 2023 and in 2024. While the authorities have continued to relax loan classification norms in favor of borrowers, this will do little to stimulate private consumption. In sum, the forecast for growth in private consumption in 2023 is revised up from 3.0% to 4.2%, and the forecast for 2024 is revised down from 3.6% to 3.0%.

The budget bill for fiscal year 2024 (FY2024, ending 30 September 2024) awaits possible revision by the new government. The bill may be further delayed and come into effect only early in calendar 2024. This could hinder budget disbursement. Public consumption in FY2023 is thus projected to contract by 2.7%, not 1.3% as previously forecast. In FY2024, it is still expected to expand slightly by 0.9%, as forecast in April. Projections for growth in public investment are kept at 2.3% in FY2023 and 5.4% in FY2024. New megaprojects with approved bidding and construction, such as the expressway extension and road extension to link with U-Tapao airport, will likely continue under the new government. However, delays affecting the FY2024 budget bill would likely postpone approvals for new construction projects meant to be launched in Q4 2023.

On the production side, the forecast for growth in agriculture in 2023 is maintained at 3.0%. Despite surprisingly high output in H1 2023, growth in agriculture is projected to slow in H2 under El Niño weather disturbances, which could be severe. Impacts from El Niño should be limited this year but are expected to worsen in 2024. The forecast for growth in agriculture in 2024 is thus adjusted down from 3.3% to 2.9%. Industry is projected to grow by 2.1% in 2023, with lower export-oriented manufacturing, before rebounding to 3.4% in 2024. According to the Federation of Thai Industry, manufacturers in 25 industries have begun to reduce work shifts and overtime payments following an export downturn. Their capacity utilization is down because of lower overseas purchase orders.

In the meantime, manufacturing for the domestic market is expected to continue to grow in line with private consumption. The forecast for growth in services in 2023 is revised up from 9.4% to 10.3%, and in 2024 from 9.7% to 10.6%, owing to strong recovery in tourism and private consumption.

Forecasts for inflation and external accounts are now more favorable. Headline inflation in 2023 is adjusted down from 2.9% to 2.5% as energy prices will likely continue to fall for the rest of the year. Decelerating merchandise exports and rising policy interest rates would help contain inflationary pressure (Figure 2.4.41). For next year, the headline inflation forecast is maintained at 2.3%. With a higher growth forecast for exports of goods and services and a downward adjustment for imports, the current account surplus projected for 2023 is now expected to be wider, no longer the equivalent of 2.8% of GDP projected in April, but 3.4%.

Figure 2.4.41 Inflation

Energy prices are projected to continue to decline, easing inflation pressure.

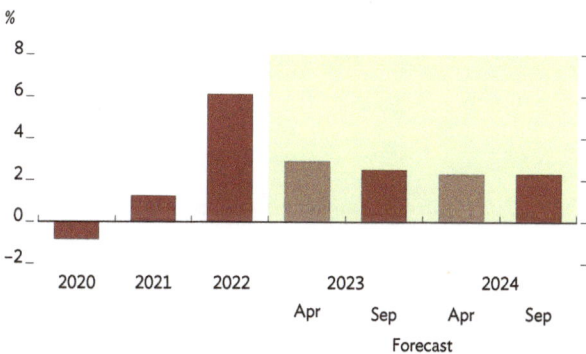

Source: *Asian Development Outlook* database.

Risks to the outlook remain tilted to the downside, mainly from external factors. Global economic recovery that fails to meet expectations could hit exports of goods and services. Risk from political uncertainty has eased since a new coalition government was formed in August, but its economic policies will merit close monitoring in light of its political diversity. Potential policy disagreement could complicate effective policy making. Further, weather issues could push up food inflation, which would dampen consumer purchasing power, especially for low-income households.

Viet Nam

The economy slowed more than expected in the first half (H1) of 2023, impacted by falling external demand. Given the unanticipated slowdown, the growth forecast in *ADO April 2023* is downgraded to 5.8% in 2023 (from 6.5%) and 6.0% in 2024 (from 6.8%). Inflation is now expected to be slightly lower than forecast in April, with stable domestic commodity prices holding consumer price increases to 3.8% in 2023 and 4.0% in 2024.

Updated Assessment

Economic recovery was adversely impacted by declining external demand. Economic growth slowed to 3.7% in H1 2023 compared to 6.5% in the same period in 2022 (Figure 2.4.42). Thanks to strong domestic consumption, the services sector expanded by 6.3% and contributed 2.7 percentage points to the total growth. In the first 8 months of 2023, international visitors to Viet Nam were 7.8 million, 5.4 times higher than a year earlier (but still slightly below 70.0% of pre-pandemic level).

Figure 2.4.42 Supply-Side Contributions to Growth

Economic growth slowed compared to the same period in 2022.

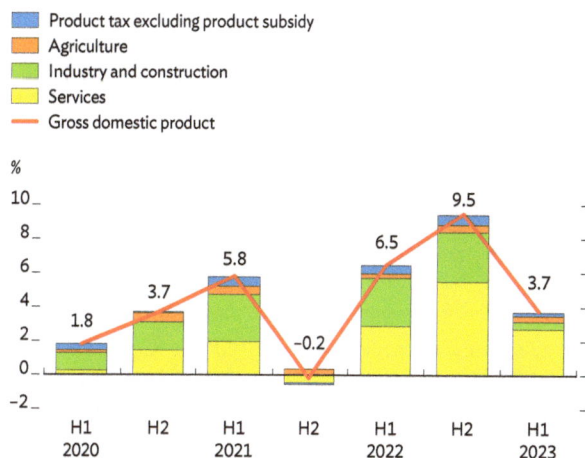

Source: General Statistics Office.

Weak external demand, including from a subdued recovery in the People's Republic of China (PRC), hampered export-led manufacturing. The industrial production index shrank by 0.4% in the first 8 months of 2023, resulting in increased closures of businesses.

On average, 15,600 firms closed monthly, and hundreds of thousands of workers were laid off. The growth of industry and construction in aggregate dropped to 1.1% in H1 2023. Of this, construction growth however increased to 4.7% from last year's 4.2% as mobility restrictions were lifted. Agriculture sustained strong growth at 3.1% following a pickup in commodity prices which encouraged increased farming activities.

On the demand side, the recovery of domestic travel led consumption to grow by 2.7% in H1 2023. Investment, however, remained subdued in H1 2023 as gross capital formation growth declined to 1.2% from 3.8% a year earlier. Foreign direct investment (FDI) disbursements were $10 billion in H1 2023, the same level as the previous year. However, FDI commitments in H1 2023, estimated at $13.4 billion, decreased by 4.3% year on year as a result of geopolitical tensions and tightened global financial conditions. Weak external demand worsened trade, impeding overall growth.

During the first 8 months of the year, inflationary pressure eased slightly with a decrease in oil prices and a stable exchange rate (Figure 2.4.43). Although headline inflation averaged at 3.1% over the same period last year, core inflation (which removes the impact of temporary factors) remained high at 4.6%.

Falling growth and slightly moderating inflation led the government to pursue a more pro-growth monetary policy. In June 2023, the State Bank of Vietnam, the central bank, cut its key policy interest rate by 50 basis points, its fourth policy rate adjustment this year (Figure 2.4.44). The refinance rate was cut to 4.5%, the discount rate to 3.0%, and the average lending interest rates of commercial banks were brought down by 1.0% accordingly. To help distressed clients, on 23 April 2023, the central bank allowed banks to restructure business and consumer loans without downgrading the loan category until 30 June 2024.

Nevertheless, credit demand remained weak, reflecting difficulties in the real economy. Credit growth expanded at an estimated 9.3% year on year in H1 2023 compared to a growth of 16.8% recorded a year earlier. Total liquidity growth slowed to 5.3% in H1 2023 from 9.2% in the same period last year (Figure 2.4.45).

Figure 2.4.43 Monthly Inflation

Inflationary pressure slightly eased.

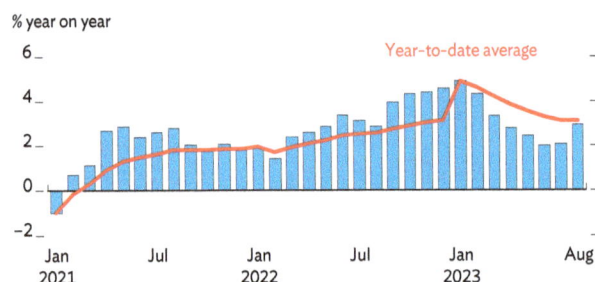

Source: General Statistics Office.

Figure 2.4.44 Policy Interest Rates

The central bank cut its key policy interest rates four times in the first 8 months of 2023.

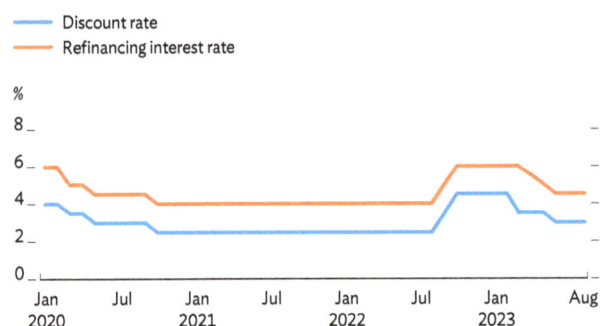

Source: State Bank of Vietnam.

Figure 2.4.45 Credit and Money Supply Growth

Money supply and credit growth slowed.

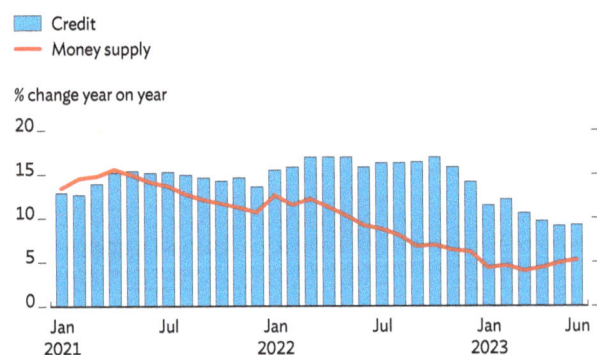

Sources: State Bank of Vietnam; Asian Development Bank estimates.

A flexible monetary policy with accommodative policy interest rate changes and a stable foreign exchange rate helped the economy to recover. The Viet Nam dong depreciated by 1.0% against the US dollar in H1 2023.

The corporate bond market has been shrinking primarily due to turbulence in the real estate sector.
Market sentiment has somewhat stabilized due to timely regulatory revisions and policy forbearances, including bond restructuring. However, corporate bond issuances, especially real estate bond issuances, declined significantly. Problematic bonds outstanding are small relative to total bank credit, but irregularities in the corporate bond and real estate markets may have potential spillover into the banking sector. To help stabilize the corporate bond market, the central bank allowed banks to repurchase unlisted bonds with the highest internal ratings without waiting 1 year after selling. It also instructed banks to implement a preferential credit package of D120 trillion for housing finance.

Slow recovery in the global economy pulled down exports and imports. High interest rates in the US and Europe slowed down recovery and reduced demand from major trade partners. Export receipts in the first 8 months of 2023 were down by 10.0% compared to the same period in 2022. The declining demand was much more substantial in Viet Nam's key markets, with exports to the US down by 20.6%, the European Union by 9.7%, and the Association of Southeast Asian Nations (ASEAN) by 6.8%. Shipments of mobile phones, computers, and electronic products, accounting for 30.0% of total exports, decreased by 15.0%. Meanwhile, export of machinery and equipment, accounting for 12.0% of total exports, fell by 10.0%.

Stagnant manufacturing depressed imports of production inputs. Production inputs account for 93.8% of total imports but dropped significantly by 16.4% to $194.7 billion in the first 8 months of 2023. As imports declined faster than exports, the trade surplus widened, reaching $20.2 billion in the same period. For the first half of 2023, the current account of the balance of payments turned into a surplus estimated at 6.0% of GDP from a deficit of 3.6% a year ago (Figure 2.4.46).

Reduced capital inflows shrank the financial and capital account surplus from 6.4% of GDP in H1 2022 to an estimated 3.2% in H1 2023. Despite this narrowing, the current account surplus turned the overall balance of payments from a deficit of 3.1% of GDP in H1 2022 into an estimated surplus of 1.6% in H1 2023. By the end of June 2023, foreign reserves were estimated to cover 3.7 months of imports, improving from 2.8 months at the end of 2022.

Figure 2.4.46 Balance of Payments Indicators

A current account surplus lifted the overall balance.

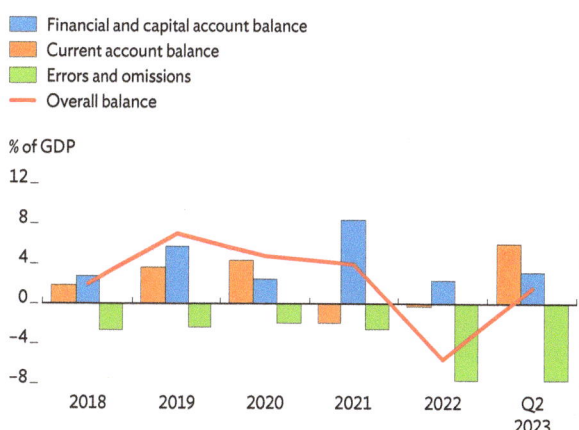

GDP = gross domestic product, Q = quarter.
Sources: State Bank of Vietnam; Asian Development Bank estimates.

Monthly fiscal deficits continued in 2023, narrowing the state budget fiscal surplus.
A decline in receipts from trade activities and shortfalls in domestic revenue collection made government revenue fall by 8.8% year on year in the first 8 months of 2023. Expenditure increased by 13.0%, with capital expenditure up by 40.3%. However, public investment disbursements still lagged behind the annual plan. The budget surplus narrowed to approximately 1.5% of GDP in H1 2023 from around 5.1% in the same period in 2022.

Prospects

Growth and inflation forecasts are revised down in this update from those in *ADO April 2023*.
Economic growth is now expected to slow to 5.8% in 2023 before improving to 6.0% in 2024 (Table 2.4.6).

Table 2.4.6 Selected Economic Indicators in Viet Nam, %

Growth and inflation will moderate more than expected in ADO April 2023.

	2022	2023		2024	
		Apr	Sep	Apr	Sep
GDP growth	8.0	6.5	5.8	6.8	6.0
Inflation	3.2	4.5	3.8	4.2	4.0

GDP = gross domestic product.
Sources: General Statistics Office; Asian Development Bank estimates.

The inflation forecast is also marked down. The main forces impacting the economy have been the global economic slowdown, monetary tightening in some advanced countries, and the continuing impact of the Russian invasion of Ukraine.

Declining global demand hit manufacturing in Viet Nam, leading to cuts in the forecast for related sectors. The manufacturing purchasing managers' index edged above 50 (expansionary) in August 2023 after 5 consecutive months of contracting, indicating recovery of consumption-led manufacturing (Figure 2.4.47). Industry is forecast to grow at 7.0% in 2023. Construction could pick up if major infrastructure projects can be implemented as planned.

Other sectors are forecast to display healthy growth. Services are expected to continue expanding, supported by revived tourism and the recovery of associated services. In August, retail sales improved 7.6% year on year, increasing sales in the first 8 months of 2023 by 10.0% over the same period last year (Figure 2.4.48). Agriculture will benefit from rising food prices, and the sector is now expected to expand by 3.2% in 2023.

On the demand side, domestic consumption will be supported by moderate inflation and maintain growth in the rest of the year. Public investment will be the key driver for economic recovery and growth in 2023. The government is committed to disbursing around $30 billion in the year. In recent months, strong political commitment has resulted in significant improvements in disbursement despite persistent regulatory constraints. In the first 8 months of 2023, almost 50.0% of the annual planned public investment disbursement were made (increased from 33.0% at the end of June 2023). Accelerating government spending could give a welcomed stimulus to demand in the remaining part of the year. Foreign investment showed signs of recovery despite the global economic slowdown, with FDI commitments by August 2023 at $18.2 billion, an 8.2% annual increase, and disbursed FDI slightly increased by 1.3%, at $13.1 billion (Figure 2.4.49).

The fiscal deficit will further increase in H2 2023. The National Assembly passed a 2.0% reduction in the value-added tax effective until the end of 2023, and expansionary fiscal policy is expected to continue.

Figure 2.4.47　Purchasing Managers' Index

The indicator improved in August 2023, indicating recovery.

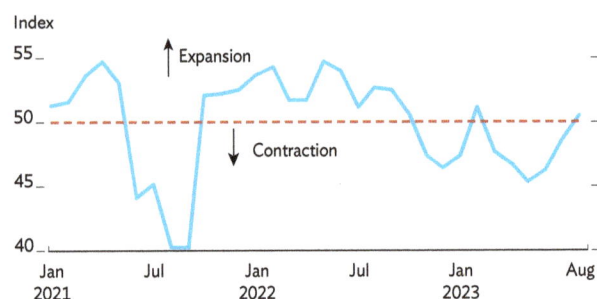

Note: A purchasing managers' index <50 signals deterioration, >50 improvement.
Source: IHS Markit.

Figure 2.4.48　Retail Sales

Retail sales in the first 8 months of 2023 were higher than last year's same period.

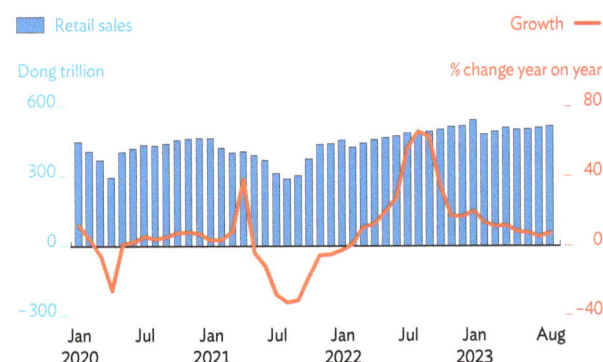

Source: General Statistics Office.

Figure 2.4.49　Foreign Direct Investment

Foreign direct investment started to pick up in H2 2023.

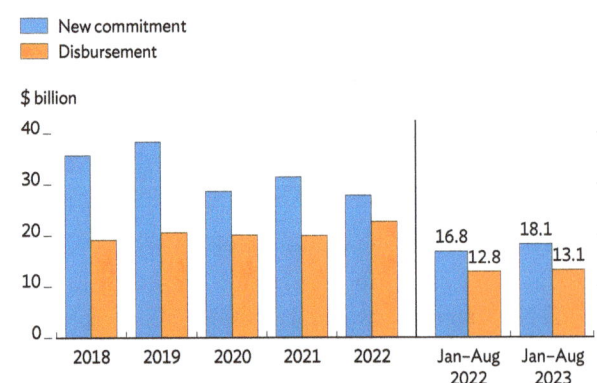

H = half.
Source: General Statistics Office.

Nevertheless, it is critical to swiftly implement this policy as it will spur business activity. Viet Nam should also accelerate the disbursement of public investment projects, as this will directly support industries such as construction and materials, and provide more employment opportunities.

Weak global demand will dampen trade prospects for the rest of 2023 and 2024. However, export in August 2023 showed a recovery signal by increasing 7.7% monthly (Figure 2.4.50). Import and export growth are expected to return to a modest rate of 5.0% this year and next year with the revival of external demand. Robust trade activity will help to maintain the current account balance in surplus this year, estimated at around 3.0% of GDP. As manufacturing activity is restored, pushing up imports for production inputs, the current account balance is projected to narrow to 2.0% of GDP in 2024.

The *ADO April 2023* inflation forecast is lowered to 3.8% for 2023 and 4.0% for 2024. Inflationary pressure in the near term may come from the disruption of global supply chains due to the continued Russian invasion of Ukraine. However, this pressure could be contained by subdued gas and petroleum prices in the year's second half and stable domestic food prices.

Coordinated policy can effectively support economic recovery, considering relative price stability and weak demand. In the near term, monetary policy should be accommodative and fiscal policy expansionary. Slow credit growth indicates that monetary policy loosening must be closely coordinated with fiscal policy implementation to effectively boost economic activities. Banks' credit provision is expected to grow slowly due to rising gross nonperforming loans, estimated at around 5.0% by March 2023, and increased provisioning requirements accordingly.

Risks to Viet Nam's economic outlook remain elevated. Domestically, systemic problems with disbursements of public investment and structural weaknesses in the real economy are the main downside risks to the economy. Externally, a substantial slowdown in global growth and weak recovery in the PRC could adversely affect Viet Nam's exports, manufacturing activity, and employment.

Figure 2.4.50 Trade Growth

Exports showed signs of recovery as 2023 progressed.

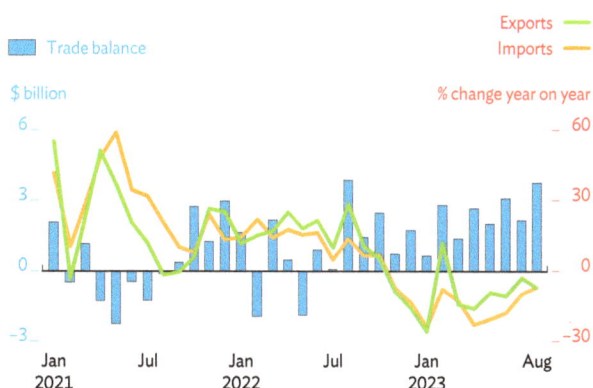

Source: General Statistics Office.

Sustained high interest rates in the US and Europe and a stronger US dollar may cause further problems for the recovery of external demand and lead to weakness in the dong exchange rate.

Other Economies

Brunei Darussalam

This update revises growth and inflation forecasts offered in *ADO April 2023* in light of a downgraded GDP assessment for 2022. With deeper contraction and a lower base GDP realized last year, real growth is now expected to be somewhat higher this year and lower in 2024 (Table 2.4.7). Inflation is expected to moderate more quickly than previously forecast.

Table 2.4.7 Selected Economic Indicators in Brunei Darussalam, %

Inflation is expected to ease as the economy improves.

	2022	2023		2024	
		Apr	Sep	Apr	Sep
GDP growth	–1.6	2.5	2.8	2.8	2.5
Inflation	3.7	2.0	1.5	1.6	1.4

GDP = gross domestic product.
Sources: CEIC Data Company; Asian Development Bank estimates.

The economy contracted more in 2022 than earlier estimated. Actual GDP contraction was much deeper than the April estimate of 0.5%. After recovering in the third quarter (Q3) of 2022 from 7 consecutive quarters of contraction, the economy returned to contraction in Q4, by 1.6% for the quarter and for the whole year. A positive contribution from private consumption of 4.4 percentage points was more than offset by lower net exports, fixed investment, and government expenditure. Full border reopening increased domestic demand, but maintenance on oil and gas plants hampered production enough to induce 4.8% contraction in the large oil and gas industry. Meanwhile, services and other pursuits outside of petroleum posted growth at 2.9%.

Stronger consumption pushed growth to return positive at 0.8% in Q1 2023, despite lower activity elsewhere. The 24% growth of domestic consumption in the quarter—supported primarily by more spending on clothing, food, and travel—compensated for the decline in investment, government spending, and trade. However, net exports still contributed 1.9 ppts to the GDP growth rate as imports decelerated faster than exports. Merchandise exports and imports continued to slow in the first 4 months of the year. Exports declined by 24.5%, mainly reflecting reduced output of petroleum products, particularly mineral fuels, and chemicals. Deceleration in downstream manufacturing caused imports to contract by 25.2%, most notably imports of mineral fuels and manufactured goods. The current account surplus in 2022 equaled 19.6% of GDP but is expected to decline in 2023 and 2024 as prices for liquefied natural gas and crude oil fall in both years.

Lower energy prices softened consumer price inflation. Persistently high inflation over the past 3 years dropped to an average of 0.8% in the first 5 months of 2023. The rate of price increase in April 2023 was 0.2%, the lowest since January 2020, but it revived marginally to 0.8% in May. Transport and communication prices declined, and increases slowed for housing and utilities and for food.

Expansion in investment and trade will boost economic activity. More economic opportunity will derive from the commencement of a direct container ship route connecting Brunei Darussalam with the People's Republic of China, and from the country's accession to the Comprehensive and Progressive Agreement for Trans-Pacific Partnership. Investment is expected to increase with the expansion of oil refineries and petrochemical plants, particularly the Hengyi plant. Muara Port redevelopment will stimulate downstream chemical and fertilizer production, which will spur exports and GDP growth. Imports of goods will also increase to provide inputs for expansion. In parallel, the services sector will continue to be robust following the removal of COVID-19 restrictions. With the government's diversification plan, agriculture and fisheries will expand to moderate the country's reliance on imported food and thus strengthen food security.

Growth forecasts are revised to accommodate data updates. Considering all these factors, in particular a lower GDP base in 2022, the growth forecast is revised up for 2023 but down for 2024. Risks to the outlook are evenly distributed and depend mostly on external factors, particularly developments in the global oil market. Government subsidies and the local currency exchange rate link to the Singapore dollar should contain inflation. With further decreases in commodity prices expected this year, inflation forecasts are revised down for both years.

Cambodia

This update lowers the growth forecast for 2023 from 5.5% in *ADO April 2023* to 5.3%. The downgrade reflects industry and agriculture growing less than expected in the first half (H1). The growth forecast for 2024 is unchanged (Table 2.4.8). Inflation forecasts are maintained for this year and next despite quarterly fluctuation in international fuel prices.

Table 2.4.8 Selected Economic Indicators in Cambodia, %

Growth forecast is lowered for 2023 but maintained for 2024.

	2022	2023		2024	
		Apr	Sep	Apr	Sep
GDP growth	5.2	5.5	5.3	6.0	6.0
Inflation	5.3	3.0	3.0	4.0	4.0

GDP = gross domestic product.
Source: Asian Development Bank estimates.

Industry growth slowed in H1 2023 but is expected to improve in H2. Exports of garments, footwear, and travel goods fell by 18.6% year on year in H1. The decline was partly offset by a 22.9% rise in exports of manufactures other than garments, notably vehicle parts, solar panels, and furniture. Imports of construction materials dropped by 6.3% over the same period, reflecting weak recovery in construction. Better growth prospects in major advanced economies should improve Cambodian exports in H2. The projection for industry output growth in 2023 is cut from 5.8% to 4.8%, but output is expected to expand by 8.0% in 2024.

Agriculture experienced tepid growth this year. Milled rice exports rose by 12.4% in H1 2023 compared with a year earlier. However, rubber exports declined by 9.9%, and banana exports by 10.3%. High production costs, market instability, and unfavorable weather have constrained crop and livestock production. The forecast for agricultural growth in 2023 is revised down from 1.1% to 0.9% and in 2024 from 1.2% to 1.1%.

Services made the most significant contribution to growth. Sector growth beat expectations in H1 2023, mainly as tourism recovered strongly, supported by Cambodia hosting the Southeast Asian Games. Bank credit in the first 5 months to wholesale and retail trade rose by 12.5% year on year, transportation by 9.6%, and hotels and restaurants by 7.4%. The forecast for growth in services in 2023 is revised up from 7.3% to 8.0%, but sector growth is expected to ease to 6.5% in 2024.

Normalized merchandise trade and tourism recovery should gradually narrow the current account deficit. Despite lower garment exports, overall merchandise exports fell only marginally because of a threefold rise in gold exports in H1 2023. Merchandise imports fell by 22.9% year on year, with imports of fabric declining by 17.9%, fuel by 10.0%, and vehicles by 26.9%. With the gradual normalization of merchandise trade to pre-pandemic levels and upward trends in tourism receipts and private transfers, the current account deficit is expected to narrow in 2023 and 2024. Foreign direct investment inflow increased by 41.6% year on year in H1 to $2.3 billion, helping to push gross international reserves from $17.8 billion at the end of 2022 to $18.4 billion at the end of June 2023.

Fiscal consolidation is planned from 2024. The government has budgeted a $1.6 billion deficit in 2023, equal to 5.1% of GDP. Government revenue is budgeted at 22.0% of GDP and expenditure at 27.1%. After years of robust fiscal expansion to stimulate the economy, the government plans to gradually shrink the budget deficit starting in 2024 to rebuild its fiscal buffer, which proved critical to the economy during the pandemic.

Bank regulatory forbearance measures introduced during the pandemic are being withdrawn. The National Bank of Cambodia, the central bank, raised the reserve requirement ratio (RRR) for foreign currencies from 7.0% to 9.0% in January 2023. As part of its strategy to phase out COVID-19 measures, the central bank plans to normalize the RRR for foreign currencies to the pre-pandemic level of 12.5% in 2024 while maintaining the RRR for Cambodia's riel at 7.0%.

Risks to the outlook remain tilted to the downside. They include weakened growth in advanced economies, lower tourist arrivals and foreign direct investment inflow, any prolonged tightening of global financial conditions, rising energy prices, concerns over high private debt and domestic financial stability, and extreme weather worsened by climate change.

Myanmar

Moderate gains in industry and services have driven modest economic recovery. Developments suggest growth this year and next consistent with the *ADO April 2023* forecasts (Table 2.4.9).

Table 2.4.9 Selected Economic Indicators in Myanmar, %

Growth forecasts are unchanged, but inflation is now seen more persistent in 2023 than projected in April.

	2022	2023		2024	
		Apr	Sep	Apr	Sep
GDP growth	2.0	2.8	2.8	3.2	3.2
Inflation	18.4	10.5	14.0	8.2	8.2

GDP = gross domestic product.
Note: Years are fiscal years ending on 30 September of that year.
Sources: Central Statistical Organization; Asian Development Bank estimates.

Political uncertainty and continuing domestic conflict undermine prospects for stronger and more sustainable growth able to alleviate widespread poverty and food insecurity. Inflation is expected to stay higher than in the April forecast in light of lingering effects from sharp depreciation of the Myanmar kyat, supply disruption, and low domestic food production.

Modest improvement in manufacturing and construction supported growth in industry in the first half of fiscal year 2023 (FY2023, ending 30 September 2023). The S&P manufacturing purchasing managers' index improved significantly across industries, riding above a neutral forecast reading of 50 since February 2023. Construction gradually recovered with the resumption of public investment projects and increased demand for real estate development. Recovery in the services sector outpaced expectations, driven by moderate growth across the board. While security concerns remain high, international tourist arrivals were more than 4.5 times higher in the first 8 months of FY2023 than a year earlier. Agriculture will likely contract, as projected in *ADO April 2023*, because of unfavorable weather caused by Cyclone Mocha in May and the effects of El Niño. Also depressing agricultural output were higher transportation and production costs and heightened armed conflict in some rural areas.

This update raises the inflation forecast for FY2023. Inflation accelerated sharply in FY2022 and into FY2023. In the first quarter of FY2023, it reached 31.9% year on year before declining to 24.2% in the second quarter. Despite a huge decline in average food inflation from 41.4% in the first quarter to 27.5% in the second quarter of FY2023, food prices are expected to remain high in the near term given the low agricultural production and high imported inflationary pressure. Following steep depreciation of the kyat in FY2022, the exchange rate stabilized in the first half of FY2023. With lower inflows of foreign direct investment, export earnings, and official development assistance, foreign exchange remains in short supply, which threatens further depreciation of the kyat and intensifying imported inflation in the near term. The forecast for inflation is thus revised significantly higher for this year, with the 2024 forecast for lower inflation unchanged.

External trade has grown moderately this year. Trade grew by 1.9% in the first 10 months of FY2023, driven largely by import growth, which reached 9.5% on strong demand for capital goods. With lower global demand, merchandise exports contracted by 5.4% in US dollar terms in the same period, generating a trade deficit of $1.6 billion. Foreign direct investment remained low, declining in June by 38.3% year on year to $413.1 million. Given recent developments, this update revises up the *ADO April 2023* forecast for the FY2023 current account deficit from the equivalent of 2.0% of GDP to 5.3%.

Downside risks to the forecast are significant. They include continued political tensions, logistic constraints, currency depreciation, international sanctions on the country, trade restrictions, and weaker global demand.

Singapore

Economic growth slowed to 0.4% year on year in the first half (H1) of 2023 as external demand weakened. After a slowdown in the first quarter (Q1) of 2023, the economy grew by 0.5% year on year in Q2. Services rose by 2.3% in H1 as all subsectors posted robust growth except for insurance and banking. Construction grew by 6.8% as both public and private sector construction expanded. However, manufacturing contracted by 6.4% as output declined across all segments except transport engineering. Domestic demand was propped up by higher public consumption as growth in private consumption slowed in response to an increase in the goods and services tax. Weak external demand slowed growth in exports, but imports fell, leaving net exports positive.

Weak external demand and tighter financial conditions will moderate growth in 2023 and 2024. The government's Economic Development Board reported in July 2023 that business sentiment in manufacturing toward the next 6 months remained slightly positive. However, the manufacturing purchasing managers' index languished that month under 50, albeit slightly improved from June, with the electronics index at 49.3, signaling contraction. Weak manufacturing will likely drag on growth, countered by robust services and sustained expansion in construction, given a sizable pipeline of government projects.

Growth in the services sector will be supported by continued improvement in trade services, information and communication, and a robust tourism industry, but tempered by lingering uncertainty regarding monetary tightening in the US that could adversely affect financial services. The boost from border reopening in the region will likely fade in H2 2023. Private consumption is expected to moderate as higher consumer prices restrain spending and higher borrowing costs threaten to dampen investment growth. Any rebound in the People's Republic of China will be driven largely by consumption, which is unlikely to provide major support to Singaporean exports. Forecasts for GDP growth in Singapore this year and the next are thus revised down from projections made in April (Table 2.4.10).

Table 2.4.10 Selected Economic Indicators in Singapore, %

Forecasts for growth are revised down as manufacturing and external demand weaken, while inflation in 2024 will likely rise above that projected in April on elevated international price pressures.

	2022	2023		2024	
		Apr	Sep	Apr	Sep
GDP growth	3.6	2.0	1.0	3.0	2.5
Inflation	6.1	5.0	5.0	2.0	3.0

GDP = gross domestic product.
Sources: Ministry of Trade and Industry. *Economic Survey of Singapore Second Quarter 2023*; Asian Development Bank estimates.

Inflation has eased but remains elevated.
The consumer price index rose by an average of 5.4% in the first 7 months of 2023, and core inflation by 4.8%. From May to July 2023, both core and headline inflation moderated year on year as price increases slowed for all index components except for health care, recreation, and household durables and services. Nevertheless, the Monetary Authority of Singapore has not changed its monetary policy stance since a tightening in October 2022, because price pressures have remained persistent despite some easing. In the first 7 months of 2023, the Singapore dollar appreciated against the US dollar by 0.7%, and by 1.3% in nominal effective terms. Pressure on consumer prices arising from higher business costs will likely reverse in H2 2023 as oil and food prices moderate.

Private transport inflation is expected to moderate in H2 with a higher quota for certificates of entitlement for vehicle ownership, and accommodation cost increases may slow with improved availability of rental units. On balance, the forecast for inflation is unchanged from the April projection for 2023 but revised up for 2024 in line with elevated inflation expected worldwide.

Timor-Leste

This update revises growth and inflation projections in *ADO April 2023* based on recent developments (Table 2.4.11). Growth has been hampered by slow execution of fiscal expenditure. Inflation forecasts are revised up largely because of higher global commodity prices.

Growth projections are downgraded for 2023 and 2024. Real GDP growth in Timor-Leste is driven by government spending, which depends in turn on the Petroleum Fund. Execution rates for both current and capital expenditure have fallen short because of the government transitioning after recent elections and an uncertain global outlook. Lower government expenditure held back private consumption and investment.

Inflation is now forecast as more persistent in both years. Timor-Leste has been exposed to rising global commodity prices, notably for food and energy, since the Russian Invasion of Ukraine in early 2022. Consumer price inflation remained elevated, averaging 8.5% year on year in the first half of 2023.

Table 2.4.11 Selected Economic Indicators in Timor-Leste, %

Projections for growth are revised down and those for inflation revised up.

	2022	2023		2024	
		Apr	Sep	Apr	Sep
GDP growth	3.2	3.1	2.8	3.0	2.9
Inflation	7.0	5.5	5.8	2.8	3.3

GDP = gross domestic product.
Sources: Government estimates for 2022; Asian Development Bank estimates.

In June 2023, headline inflation was 7.0%, driven primarily by price hikes for food and nonalcoholic beverages at 8.0%, with the price increases for rice at 10.3% and for bread and cereals other than rice at 9.2%. While tradable goods were subject to significant increases, prices for non-tradable goods remained stable.

Government spending softened, with budget execution falling from 35.3% in January–July 2022 to 30.0% a year later. After Parliament approved a high 2023 budget ceiling of $2.2 billion, budget execution was muted by political changes and an election that brought in a new government in July. Cumulative government spending was down by 17.1% year on year in January–July 2023, and cumulative spending on transfers was down by 37.5%, threatening to weaken private consumption, especially household spending. Cumulative capital spending was down by 1.0%, posing a risk to private sector sentiment toward investment.

The outlook for the current account deficit is little changed from April. Merchandise imports and exports have trended down, reflecting sluggish government spending. With exports outside of the large off-shore petroleum industry down by 14.1% year on year in January–May 2023, and coffee exports plunging by 27.9%, the current account deficit is expected to deteriorate from the equivalent of 21.9% of GDP in 2022 to 41.0% this year and 50.1% in 2024. This is only slightly better than projected in *ADO April 2023*. Remittance inflow, which has become the largest non-oil contributor to the economy, dropped from $80.3 million in the first quarter of 2022 to only $59.7 million a year later.

Increased annual withdrawals from the Petroleum Fund will undermine its sustainability. The Petroleum Fund had $18.1 billion at the end of June 2023. Though below the 2021 closing value of $19.6 billion, which was the highest ever, it improved on the 2022 closing value of $17.3 billion. As production at the offshore Bayu-Undan oil and gas condensate field started to wind down in 2022, oil and gas output that year fell by 75.4%. With the end of oil production and using current spending rates, the Petroleum Fund is projected to be entirely depleted by 2034.

There are significant risks to the forecast. Timor-Leste depends heavily on crude oil exports and food imports, which expose it to volatile global economic forces. Price volatility caused by supply disruption could further aggravate food insecurity, which may be exacerbated as well by climate and disaster risks that undermine livelihoods, economic performance, and infrastructure. However, recent parliamentary elections brought a single-party majority to power for the first time in 5 years. This is expected to usher in a stable government able to sustain public management reform and thus ensure fiscal sustainability over the long run.

THE PACIFIC

The 2023 and 2024 forecasts for growth in the Pacific economy are revised up from *ADO April 2023*'s projections. A strong recovery in tourism and stimulus-inducing public infrastructure projects have driven faster-than-expected growth, particularly in Fiji, the second-largest economy in the subregion. Capacity constraints exacerbated by the pandemic weigh on the outlook, especially for smaller economies. The inflation forecast is revised down for 2023 and up for 2024. International commodity prices remain elevated and their lagged pass-through to domestic markets is keeping inflation high in many Pacific economies.

Subregional Assessment and Prospects

This update forecasts growth of 3.5% for the Pacific economy in 2023, up from 3.3% projected earlier (Figure 2.5.1). Visitor arrivals to Fiji have been higher than expected, prompting an upward revision in the country's growth projection for the year. Similarly, arrivals have also been stronger than expected in the Cook Islands, Samoa, and Tonga. The Marshall Islands' growth forecast is revised up on higher fisheries output and construction, including development partner–funded projects and preparations for the Micronesian Games in June 2024. Faster growth is expected in Tuvalu as loosened travel restrictions and reduced shipping bottlenecks ease the implementation of infrastructure projects.

Some parts of the subregion will see subdued growth this year. The forecast for Papua New Guinea, the largest economy, is revised down because output in sectors other than mining and liquefied natural gas (LNG) has been lower than initially expected. Other contributing factors include difficulties in sourcing foreign exchange and disruptions in power and water supply. Nauru's growth forecast is adjusted down due to the base effects of higher growth in the previous fiscal year.

Figure 2.5.1 GDP Growth in the Pacific

The growth outlook for the subregion is revised up on robust recoveries in tourism and public construction.

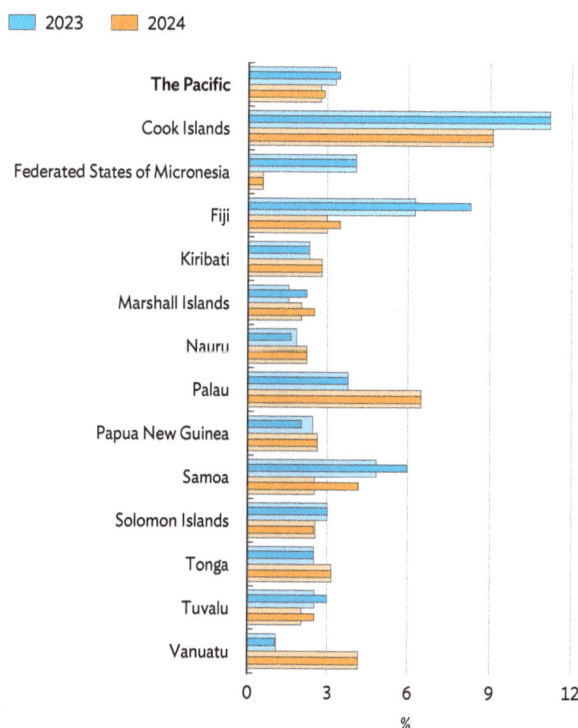

GDP = gross domestic product.
Note: Lighter colored bars are *Asian Development Outlook April 2023* forecasts.
Source: *Asian Development Outlook* database.

The write-up on the Pacific was prepared by Lily-Anne Homasi, Magdelyn Kuari, Katherine Passmore, Marcel Schroder, and Isoa Wainiqolo of ADB's Pacific Department (PARD); Remrick Patagan and Cara Tinio of the Economic Research and Development Impact Department, ADB; James Webb of the Sectors Group, ADB; and Prince Cruz and Noel Del Castillo, PARD consultants.

The 2024 growth forecast for the Pacific is increased to 2.9% from 2.8%. This reflects expectations of faster growth in Fiji on a continued strong recovery in tourism and increased government spending on infrastructure. Growth in Samoa will be driven by tourism and public spending. Construction projects should drive faster growth in the Marshall Islands and Tuvalu than was forecast in April. Growth in the Marshall Islands is projected to get a further lift from hosting the Micronesian Games. However, Tonga's economy is expected to grow more slowly than was earlier forecast as competition from other international tourist destinations and difficulties in local air capacity impede the recovery in visitor arrivals. Slower growth is also forecast for Nauru as the slowdown in Regional Processing Centre operations dampens economic activity.

Capacity constraints that emerged during the pandemic pose significant downside risks to the outlook. The impact of COVID-19 on economic activity in the subregion led many workers to seek employment elsewhere, notably under temporary worker schemes in Australia and New Zealand. Closed borders caused tourism facilities to fall into disrepair and disasters triggered by natural hazards damaged or destroyed properties. Labor constraints are affecting the implementation of infrastructure projects which, coupled with a shortage of tourist facilities, could dim tourism's recovery prospects and make it difficult to attract reinvestment in the sector.

Vulnerability to disasters and climate events continue to have serious implications on growth and inflation in Pacific economies. An expected El Niño will likely depress agriculture and fisheries output and reduce local food supply. This, together with more frequent climate events, could worsen damage and losses, and hinder recovery by weakening food and water security. Climate events also pose a threat to fishing revenue, a major source of income for many governments in Pacific economies.

Inflation is now forecast at 4.9% this year, down from April's 5.0% projection (Figure 2.5.2). Inflation in Fiji will slow on lower fuel prices, and declining utility and transport costs. The downward revision, however, masks upward adjustments to the inflation forecasts of some smaller economies.

Figure 2.5.2 Inflation in the Pacific

The subregional forecast for 2023 is revised slightly down on slowing inflation in Fiji, but higher-than-expected inflation has raised the forecasts for smaller economies.

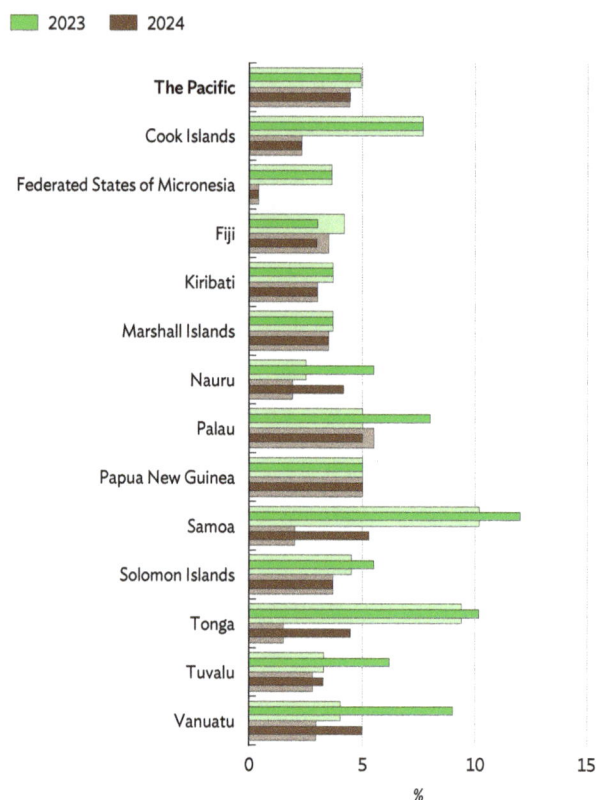

Note: Lighter colored bars are *Asian Development Outlook April 2023* forecasts.
Source: *Asian Development Outlook* database.

In the Cook Islands, Nauru, and Samoa, elevated international food and fuel prices—due in part to the lingering impacts of the Russian invasion of Ukraine—and their lagged pass-through to domestic prices caused higher-than-expected inflation in fiscal year (FY) 2023. These factors, coupled with a reduced petroleum subsidy, are also behind Kiribati's raised inflation forecast.

Domestic developments are contributing to the higher inflation forecasts for 2023 for some economies. Elevated import prices initially lifted inflation in Tonga in FY2023; this was later accelerated by supply constraints and surging costs of locally produced food. Tuvalu's inflation forecast is raised because the impact of the November 2022 drought on food prices has been more severe than expected.

Palau's is raised on the introduction of value-added taxes, which increased food and fuel prices, and higher electricity and wastewater tariffs that affected the cost of household utilities. Inflation accelerated in the first quarter of 2023 in Solomon Islands on higher prices for transportation and food. Although this has eased somewhat, price pressures are expected to return in the fourth quarter, when the country hosts the Pacific Games. Higher inflation—possibly the highest in decades—is expected in Vanuatu because the impact of cyclones in March on crops and local supply chains has been more severe than estimated in *ADO April 2023* and because of price pressures from a 36% increase in the minimum wage implemented in June.

This update revises the forecast for subregional inflation in 2024 to 4.5% from the earlier 4.4% projection. Continued lags in the impact of international commodity price trends on local prices will keep domestic inflation high in Nauru and Samoa. The 2024 inflation forecasts for Tonga, Tuvalu, and Vanuatu are raised on adverse price movements in these economies. Lower inflation, however, is forecast for Fiji next year following recent local price trends. For Palau, the high base estimated for FY2023 will result in softer inflation than was forecast in April.

Fiji

The growth forecasts for Fiji for 2023 and 2024 are revised up. A stronger-than-expected recovery in tourism and a notable increase in government spending, as announced in the budget for fiscal year 2024 (FY2024, ending 31 July 2024), prompted the revisions (Table 2.5.1). *ADO April 2023* assumed that intense competition from other tourist destinations would moderate the recovery in visitor arrivals.

However, the numbers have been greater than expected, with arrivals in the year to date exceeding the same period in 2019. This update expects the rebound in tourism will be sustained, despite monetary policy tightening in Fiji's major tourism source markets. Fiscal spending was earlier projected to fall in FY2024, but the government has allocated higher spending, with notable increases in key infrastructure allocations, such as for road transport and hospitals.

Tourism's stronger-than-expected recovery is being driven by visitor arrivals from Australia and New Zealand, Fiji's traditional source markets. Visitor data as of July 2023 show monthly arrivals have outperformed 2019 levels since September 2022 for Australia, October 2022 for Canada, December 2022 for New Zealand (except July 2023), and July 2023 for the United States. Arrivals from Canada have been boosted by a Vancouver–Nadi direct flight, which started at the end of 2022. Tourist arrivals in the first 7 months of 2023 were up 20% for Australia, 6% for New Zealand, and 60% for Canada compared to the same period in 2019. To cater to the increased demand, Fiji Airways, the national airline, deployed two new wide-body aircraft in August, adding around 30,000 new seats from the fourth quarter of 2023; introduced direct flights to Canberra; and increased the frequency of flights to other destinations, including Hong Kong, China. Other airlines will start new flights out of Fiji in late 2023. Increased competition and moderating demand in major source markets remain downside risks in 2024. Even so, post-pandemic, tourists from these markets are staying longer and spending more.

The performances of other sectors have been mixed. Construction improved despite the higher cost of building materials, exports of non-sugar agricultural products increased in the first 5 months of 2023, and there was a notable increase in the exports of taro and spices. But gold production declined due to low-quality ore, and timber was affected by supply issues, including bad weather and limited accessibility to forests.

Government revenue improved, buoyed by increased tourism. The better-than-expected recovery in tourism translated into higher government revenue and a narrower FY2023 fiscal deficit, equivalent to 6.2% of GDP compared to 7.4% forecast in *ADO April 2023*. Government revenue increased by 22.6% in FY2023, and expenditure was up a modest 0.6%.

Table 2.5.1 Selected Economic Indicators in Fiji, %

Stronger economic growth is being buoyed by a sustained recovery in tourism and moderate inflation.

	2022	2023		2024	
		Apr	Sep	Apr	Sep
GDP growth	20.0	6.3	8.3	3.0	3.7
Inflation	4.3	4.2	3.0	3.5	3.0

GDP = gross domestic product.
Sources: Fiji Bureau of Statistics; Asian Development Bank estimates.

The government is targeting a 37.8% increase in FY2024 revenue to finance a 26.0% increase in budgeted spending. If the target is hit, the fiscal deficit's downward trend should continue, to a forecast 4.8% of GDP in FY2024 and a lower debt-to-GDP ratio of 79.3%, compared to 81.2% in FY2023.

The inflation forecasts are revised down for 2023 and 2024 on lower-than-expected consumer prices, especially since April. Lower fuel prices translated into utility prices declining by 4.6% and transport prices by 9.9% in the 12 months to July 2023. The new value-added tax and import duties rates, effective August, will keep inflation at a forecast 3.0% for 2023 and 2024.

Papua New Guinea

Growth is revised down for 2023 because of a worse-than-expected economic performance so far this year (Table 2.5.2). Sales in various sectors are reported to be down 20%–30% in the first half. Imports plummeted by 61% in the first quarter year on year (yoy) across all product categories, including machinery, which suggests postponed or abandoned private investments. The slowdown is also being caused by the difficulties businesses are having in sourcing foreign exchange. The Bank of Papua New Guinea, the central bank, continues to release only $100 million monthly to the foreign exchange market, falling short of demand. Other reasons for the slowdown are power and water supply disruptions, frequent flight cancellations due to technical problems with Air Niugini's aging fleet, and glitches in the rollout of a new operating system at Bank of South Pacific, the country's largest bank.

Table 2.5.2 Selected Economic Indicators in Papua New Guinea, %

Growth is revised down for 2023 after a tough first half for businesses and consumers.

	2022	2023		2024	
		Apr	Sep	Apr	Sep
GDP growth	3.2	2.4	2.0	2.6	2.6
Inflation	5.3	5.0	5.0	5.0	5.0

GDP = gross domestic product.
Sources: Bank of Papua New Guinea; Asian Development Bank estimates.

The problems related to the rollout have affected businesses and consumers through delayed staff payments, trouble with reconciling financial data, and banking operations failing to function smoothly. Moreover, mining, one of the economy's largest sectors, has weakened its contribution to growth due to decreased gold production in the first half of the year and a less optimistic outlook for copper output.

On the upside, some services are benefiting from resumed international travel and easing global supply chain disruptions. These include accommodation and restaurants, communication, and real estate. Additional government spending will provide some stimulus this year. The outlook for LNG production has also improved following higher-than-expected output in the first quarter, but LNG output over the whole of 2023 will still likely be lower than in 2022. The 2024 growth forecast remains unchanged from *ADO April 2023*, with growth driven by non-resource sector output.

In July, fuel supply issues reemerged, prompting the government to declare a 30-day national emergency. This decision came after the two largest airlines suspended domestic flights when Puma Energy, the country's only aviation fuel supplier, announced its intention to limit the distribution of fuel because of a dispute with the central bank over forex and regulatory issues. The government, however, aims to ensure fuel availability and explore introducing competition in the fuel market.

The government has announced that it will embark on a macroeconomic reform agenda. This will be aided by an International Monetary Fund (IMF) program approved in March 2023, following a request by the government for an SDR684.3 million budget-support loan (equivalent to $918.3 million) tied to governance-related reforms over 38 months. These reforms will focus on (i) strengthening debt sustainability through a multiyear fiscal consolidation program and creating the fiscal space to meet critical social needs, (ii) strengthening the mandate and autonomy of the Bank of Papua New Guinea, (iii) alleviating forex shortages by transitioning to a market-clearing exchange rate, and (iv) operationalizing the Independent Commission Against Corruption.

Headline inflation eased in the first quarter of 2023, and April's projection for full-year inflation is retained. Price increases for clothing and footwear, communication, health, and recreation were below 2.0% yoy. The prices of alcoholic beverages, tobacco, and betel nut declined by 6.3% yoy and education by 22.9%. However, price pressures on some essential consumer items remained elevated, including food and nonalcoholic beverages, up by 8.7% yoy, household equipment (12.2%), and transport (4.9%). The Kina Facility Rate remains unchanged at 3.50%.

The revenue collection performance in the first half of 2023 was mixed. Tax collection was on track for almost half the budget forecast for the year, but nontax revenue was significantly behind. Stronger collection in salaries and wages tax, corporate profit tax from the resources sector, and import excise in the first half of the year resulted in revenue being revised up by K1.6 billion from the 2023 budget forecast. All of this additional revenue will be allocated to recurrent expenditure, leaving the projected overall fiscal deficit unchanged at the equivalent of 4.4% of GDP this year. Expenditure on compensation of employees, comprising mainly the public sector wage bill, was within the budget plan in the first half of the year, although a risk of overruns remains. Public debt is forecast at 52.2% of GDP in 2023. Under the IMF program, Papua New Guinea is required to limit the present value of new external borrowing to $1.405 billion, maintain a fiscal deficit not exceeding K4.985 billion (4.3% of GDP), collect at least K12.558 billion in non-resource taxes, and maintain social expenditure of at least K3.866 billion (3.4% of GDP).

The outlook is subject to several upside risks related to major resource projects. Porgera Gold Mine's reopening is making progress after Barrick Niugini, the operator of the mine, and the government signed the Porgera Project Commencement Agreement, but the issuance of a special mining lease and other requirements, such as a public hearing, are pending. A final investment decision on the Papua LNG project is expected in early 2024. The project getting underway would stimulate economic activity, boost tax revenue, and help alleviate foreign exchange shortages. The main downside risk is disruptions caused by the limited supply of foreign exchange, such as fuel rationing, particularly if the shortage drags on.

Solomon Islands

Growth forecasts are retained for 2023 and 2024 (Table 2.5.3). The recovery in growth, after 3 years of contraction, is still expected to be driven by government spending and investment associated with the Pacific Games this year and elections next year. The games, to be held in Honiara in November, should boost retail trade, accommodation and food services, and logistics and transport. Gains in these sectors are expected to partially compensate for otherwise weaker domestic demand due to higher-than-expected inflation. Additional sources of growth include the pick-up in business activity following the lifting of COVID-19 restrictions, higher exports, and the resumption of development partner–funded projects.

Table 2.5.3 Selected Economic Indicators in Solomon Islands, %

A moderate recovery is expected, but increased global commodity prices are putting upward pressure on inflation.

	2022	2023		2024	
		Apr	Sep	Apr	Sep
GDP growth	−4.2	3.0	3.0	2.5	2.5
Inflation	5.5	4.5	5.5	3.7	3.7

GDP = gross domestic product.
Sources: Central Bank of Solomon Islands; Asian Development Bank estimates.

Increased government spending has widened the fiscal deficit in line with *ADO April 2023*'s expectation. Expenditure was up 27% in the first half of the year from the same period in 2022, with higher outlays for goods and services, salaries and wages, and support to state-owned enterprises. But revenue fell 6% over the same period. A supplementary budget in June raised expenditure by 8% compared to the original budget, mainly for the Pacific Games. The increased deficit is expected to be financed largely by development partners.

Export growth is largely being driven by minerals and higher-than-expected shipments of logs and timber. Exports in the first half of 2023 rose 45% from the same period in 2022, boosted by a 300% increase in mineral exports, largely from the reopened Gold Ridge Mine. Log exports rose 15% in the first half of 2023, following a 6% increase in production.

Fish exports rose by 10%, with the fish catch rising by a similar percentage. The first half of 2023 saw boosted exports of palm oil and cocoa.

The current account deficit in the first half of 2023 was slightly lower than in the first half of 2022, but is still expected to widen for the year as a whole. Exports of goods and services increased by 45%, but imports rose by only 36%, mainly due to a nearly 100% increase in the imports of machinery and transport equipment and a 60% rise in fuel imports. Imports are expected to increase in the second half of the year, particularly machinery and transport equipment, food, fuel, and manufactured goods for the Pacific Games. Construction of 161 telecommunication towers funded by a $65 million concessional loan began in August. Twenty towers are targeted for completion before the start of the games.

Remittances, higher by 55% in the first half of 2023 from the same period last year, are helping to lower the current account deficit. Seasonal workers from Solomon Islands in Australia and New Zealand totaled 6,090 in June, up 56% from June 2022. The government expects this to total 7,000 by the end of the year.

Visitor arrivals are expected to rise on a further recovery in tourism and improved aviation infrastructure. International travel will benefit from the arrival of Solomon Airlines' second long-haul aircraft in August. The first aircraft was grounded several times in the first half of 2023 for maintenance, leading to significant delays and disruptions. The second aircraft is financed by a $3 million loan from the Solomon Islands National Provident Fund. Other aviation developments include the completion of the new Honiara International Airport terminal in March, the construction of a new terminal at Munda International Airport, and the return of the Brisbane–Munda route, planned for October.

This update revises up the inflation forecast for 2023 from April's projection. Inflation accelerated to 9.2% in the first quarter before slowing to 4.9% in the second. Higher overall inflation was mainly due to rapid increases in the indices for transportation (up 18.5%) and food and nonalcoholic beverages (up 14.3%).

After raising the cash reserve ratio from 5% to 6% in March, the Central Bank of Solomon Islands maintained its tight monetary policy stance in September. Inflation is expected to decelerate in the third quarter, but likely to pick up in the fourth due to increased demand from the Pacific Games.

Vanuatu

The forecast for weak growth in 2023, due to extensive damage caused by twin cyclones in March, is retained (Table 2.5.4). The cyclones' impact continued to be felt in the second quarter, particularly through high inflation, which is also being lifted by the lagged effects of increased global commodity prices. The economic pressure on households is expected to be offset by higher government spending in the second half of the year. A strong economic recovery is still expected in 2024.

Table 2.5.4 Selected Economic Indicators in Vanuatu, %

Damage from disasters has constrained growth and is pushing inflation higher than earlier forecast for 2023 and 2024.

	2022	2023		2024	
		Apr	Sep	Apr	Sep
GDP growth	2.0	1.0	1.0	4.2	4.2
Inflation	6.7	4.0	9.0	3.0	5.0

GDP = gross domestic product.
Sources: Vanuatu National Statistics Office; Asian Development Bank estimates.

The cyclones exacerbated technical and institutional challenges to the implementation of projects, as anticipated in *ADO April 2023*. Government expenditure in the first half of 2023 was in line with expectations, with capital expenditure 70% lower than the same period last year, while the use of goods and services was down by 12%. Expenditure on salaries and wages rose by 3%, and expenditure on subsidies, grants, and transfers was up 8%. The implementation of infrastructure projects has still not fully recovered, despite the lifting of pandemic restrictions.

The fiscal deficit is now expected to widen because of substantial post-disaster reconstruction and rehabilitation needs. A supplementary budget in May raised the overall budget by 8%, increasing capital expenditure by 33% and expenditure on goods and services by 7%. With grant revenue projected to rise by 8% and tax and nontax revenues to remain unchanged, the fiscal deficit is now expected to rise from the equivalent of 5.0% of GDP in the original budget to 7.8% in 2023. The government's post-disaster needs assessment estimated damage and loss from the cyclones at $433 million (40% of GDP).

Revenue from honorary citizenship programs continues to fall. Revenue was 5.2% lower in the first half of 2023 compared to the same period in 2022. Although the drop was in line with assumptions in *ADO April 2023*, the situation is expected to worsen in the second half of 2023 and put further pressure on the fiscal situation. In July, the Government of the United Kingdom revoked the visa waiver for Vanuatu passport holders, which is likely to further reduce demand for honorary citizenships. Revenue from the programs, which peaked in 2020, declined by 10% in 2021 and 34% in 2022.

Visitor arrivals remain below pre-pandemic levels. Data on visitors from Australia and New Zealand indicate that arrivals were back to 76% of their pre-pandemic level in the first half of 2023, in line with the projections in *ADO April 2023*. Tourism activity is expected to increase further in the second half as flight disruptions decline and benefits from Vanuatu's first full year of open borders since the pandemic are realized. The resumption in June of direct flights from Brisbane to Vanuatu's second largest city, Luganville, will further boost tourism. In August, the government introduced new visa categories that are mainly intended to allow in more foreign workers, especially for the tourism industry.

Remittances from seasonal workers in Australia and New Zealand continue to support domestic demand. The impact of the cyclones on households would have been worse were it not for the remittances of seasonal workers. Studies show that remittances tend to increase after disasters, mainly for relief and reconstruction. In line with *ADO April 2023*, participation in seasonal worker programs is expected to increase. Visa approvals under the New Zealand

scheme rose by 42% in the year to June 2023 compared to the same period in 2022, and approvals in the Australian schemes are also expected to be significantly higher.

The forecast for inflation in 2023 is revised sharply up from April's projection. Damage to crops and disruptions to supply chains caused by the cyclones were considerably greater than estimated earlier. This, together with a 36% increase in the minimum wage in June, means that inflation in 2023 is now expected to be at its highest level in decades and monetary policy is therefore expected to be tightened in September. The inflation forecast for 2024 is also revised up. Inflation next year is expected to be lower than 2023's rate, but still above the Reserve Bank of Vanuatu's 1%–4% target range.

Central Pacific Economies

Forecasts for the Central Pacific economies are mixed. Kiribati's growth forecasts are unchanged from *ADO April 2023*'s, but inflation for 2023 is revised up due to the rising prices of imports. Nauru's growth forecasts for 2023 and 2024 are revised down due to the reduced activities of the Regional Processing Centre; the inflation estimates for both years are significantly revised up. Higher inflation forecasts for Tuvalu due to external factors and last November's drought are risks to the upward revisions to the growth forecasts for 2023 and 2024.

Kiribati

GDP growth forecasts for 2023 and 2024 are unchanged (Table 2.5.5). This is consistent with expectations that economic activity related to energy, water, and transport projects will continue to support the recovery. Elevated social protection expenditure equivalent to 29.5% of GDP in 2023 is expected to underpin the forecasts. However, ever-present natural hazards could cause delays in project implementation.

***ADO April 2023*'s forecast of a fiscal surplus for 2023 is revised to a deficit.** Government revenue is now forecast to be lower amid sustained higher spending. Although revenue from fishing licenses is expected to be lower as changing weather patterns affect fish catches, this should be more than offset by growth—forecast at 46.2%—in tax revenues from company, excise, and value-added taxes. Total revenue is expected to grow by 4.5% in 2023. Government spending is forecast to increase slightly faster than revenue, driven by social protection spending.

Table 2.5.5 Selected Economic Indicators in Kiribati, %

Inflation is expected to accelerate in 2023 on higher prices for imported goods.

	2022	2023		2024	
		Apr	Sep	Apr	Sep
GDP growth	1.8	2.3	2.3	2.8	2.8
Inflation	5.0	3.7	6.0	3.0	3.0

GDP = gross domestic product.
Source: Asian Development Bank estimates.

The forecast for inflation is revised up for 2023 and unchanged for 2024. Prices are expected to remain elevated, with external factors influencing domestic price movements. The government inflation report for the second quarter of 2023 indicated price increases in imported food products, such as canned goods, frozen goods, and powdered beverages, as well as transport fares. The latest price movements are in line with the increase in petroleum prices in Kiribati after the government reduced the subsidy last year. The inflation forecast for 2024 is unchanged as state-owned Kiribati Oil Company, the sole oil importer, restored oil prices to lower levels, following a higher subsidy for 2023.

Nauru

This update revises down the estimate for GDP growth in fiscal year 2023 (FY2023, ended 30 June 2023) due largely to the reduced operations of the Regional Processing Centre (RPC). These were caused by the RPC's shift in July 2023 to an enduring capability model, whereby the center remains operational regardless of its level of activity. Because the RPC was the second biggest employer after the national government from 2014 to 2021, changes in its operations have a huge impact on the economy. The downward revision to FY2023's growth forecast also reflects a base effect, as FY2022's growth estimate was revised up to 2.8% from *ADO April 2023*'s 1.2% projection (Table 2.5.6).

Government spending rose by a mere 0.9% in FY2023 after increasing 11.4% in FY2022. Although capital expenditure fell by 53.2%, and social spending declined 31.8%, personnel costs, which account for 21% of total expenditure, increased by 18.9%, largely reflecting a 10% cost-of-living adjustment. With revenue and grants decreasing by 3.9%, the fiscal surplus declined to the equivalent of 17% of GDP in FY2023 from 25% of GDP in FY2022.

The growth forecast for FY2024 is revised down. The FY2024 budget projects a 10.0% decrease in revenue and grants, with tax revenue expected to fall by 59.0%. RPC-related revenue is projected to decline by 14.6% due to the loss of visa fees, and reduced hosting fees and related tax revenue. This will be partly offset by a one-off funding provision from the Government of Australia to provide training to RPC employees under the Alternative Pathway program to prepare them for non-RPC employment. The training is expected to be provided by Fiji National University, covering key skills, including construction, nursing, and fisheries. Because of the anticipated decrease in revenue and grants, the government aims to reduce expenditure by 11%, resulting in a slightly reduced surplus for FY2024, forecast at 16% of GDP.

Inflation in FY2023 was higher than forecast earlier. There has been a considerable lag in the impact on domestic prices of higher global commodity prices caused by the Russian invasion of Ukraine. Higher inflation in FY2023 was mainly driven by transportation costs (up 20%) and food and nonalcoholic beverages (up 10%). Updated data indicate that inflation for FY2022 was just 1.0%, lower than *ADO April 2023*'s 2.3%.

Table 2.5.6 Selected Economic Indicators in Nauru, %

The Regional Processing Centre's reduced operations led to lower growth in 2023, while inflation was higher on the lagged impact of global prices.

	2022	2023		2024	
		Apr	Sep	Apr	Sep
GDP growth	2.8	1.8	1.6	2.2	1.6
Inflation	1.0	2.5	5.5	1.9	4.2

GDP = gross domestic product.
Note: Years are fiscal years ending on 30 June of that year.
Source: Asian Development Bank estimates.

High inflation is expected to persist in FY2024, but at a lower rate than FY2023. This is mainly in line with the lag in the impact of global price movements on domestic inflation. But inflation is expected to ease slightly in the second half of FY2024 in line with anticipated global price movements. Subsidies for electricity and freight costs were maintained in the 2024 budget.

Tuvalu

The forecasts for growth in 2023 and 2024 are revised up. The removal of travel restrictions and fewer shipping bottlenecks have improved the economic outlook from the expectations in early 2023 (Table 2.5.7). Infrastructure projects are likely to continue to drive economic growth. The recent opening of the harbor in Nukulaelae, and the completion of harbors in the other outer islands in the next few years, will increase mobility and economic activity. A renewable energy project is underway and is due for completion in 2024. The drought in November 2022 caused the government to declare a state of public emergency. Alongside the increased occurrence of disasters, climate change can threaten Tuvalu's economy through impacts on fishing revenues, food and water security, damage to infrastructure, and loss of human lives.

Table 2.5.7 Selected Economic Indicators in Tuvalu, %

Inflation remains high and may be a drag on growth in 2023 and 2024.

	2022	2023		2024	
		Apr	Sep	Apr	Sep
GDP growth	0.7	2.5	3.0	2.0	2.5
Inflation	12.2	3.3	6.2	2.8	3.3

GDP = gross domestic product.
Source: Asian Development Bank estimates.

The inflation forecast for 2023 is revised significantly up. This reflects higher-than-expected inflation in the first half due to high domestic food prices caused by the drought. Food prices rose by 8% in the second quarter after an average 18% increase in the preceding 3 quarters, with fruit and vegetable prices rising 30% from the second quarter of last year.

The forecast for slightly higher inflation in 2024 than April's projection reflects recent price outcomes and despite a reduction in freight charges, as proxied by the Drewry World Container Index.

Fiscal deficit forecasts are unchanged. The deficit is expected to widen to an equivalent of 9.2% of GDP in 2023 and 11.9% of GDP in 2024. Although tax collection will grow moderately this year, lower fishing revenue will weaken total revenue. Higher infrastructure spending and expectations of a softer revenue performance will also widen the deficit.

North Pacific Economies

Growth forecasts for the Marshall Islands are revised up from *ADO April 2023*'s projections, but unchanged for the Federated States of Micronesia (FSM) and Palau. The inflation forecast for Palau is adjusted to incorporate the impact of tax and tariff measures; inflation forecasts for the FSM and the Marshall Islands are unchanged. Food and fuel prices are at risk from an expected El Niño that could disrupt local agriculture and fisheries production, and the possibility of further international commodity shocks due to the Russian invasion of Ukraine. Likely extensions of Compacts of Free Association with the US bode well for fiscal resources.

Federated States of Micronesia

Growth forecasts are unchanged from *ADO April 2023*'s projections. The economy is on track to recover to its pre-pandemic level in fiscal year 2023 (FY2023, ending 30 September 2023 for all three North Pacific economies), underpinned by a rebound after the economy was fully reopened and pandemic measures were lifted in August 2022 (Table 2.5.8). The expansion in construction, hotels and restaurants, and transport will fade in FY2024 due partly to base effects and the economy returning to normal levels of activity. The FSM's high dependence on imports and its exposure to international commodity price volatility remain the key risks to the outlook in the short term. In addition, the reopening of international borders may spur out-migration and exacerbate capacity constraints that hinder growth.

Table 2.5.8 Selected Economic Indicators in the Federated States of Micronesia, %

The economy is expected to rebound this year as it recovers from the pandemic before moderating to more normal growth next year.

	2022	2023		2024	
		Apr	Sep	Apr	Sep
GDP growth	2.0	4.1	4.1	0.5	0.5
Inflation	5.0	3.6	3.6	0.4	0.4

GDP = gross domestic product.
Note: Years are fiscal years ending on 30 September of that year.
Source: Asian Development Bank estimates.

Inflation forecasts are unchanged from *ADO April 2023*'s projections. Inflation is expected to decelerate in line with modest decreases in the prices of key commodities. Nonetheless, the outlook is far from certain given that imports account for 68.2% of the consumer price index and international commodity markets remain volatile and vulnerable to geopolitical risks, as well as the potential impact of weather-related developments, such as El Niño, on food prices. In the first quarter of FY2023, a steady acceleration in the transport, food and beverages, and housing and utilities sub-indices drove a 6.9% increase in consumer prices.

The fiscal surplus is projected to steadily increase after declining during the pandemic. At the equivalent of 4.4% of GDP, the fiscal surplus in FY2022 was the lowest since FY2013 due to pandemic spending and the impact of the economic downturn on revenues. The reversal of these factors should see the surplus increasing to 5.4% in FY2023 and 7.4% in FY2024. Moreover, the FSM stands to benefit from increased financial assistance under the proposed extension of its Compact of Free Association with the US, which is up for Congressional approval. This includes annual sector grants worth $140 million ($2.8 billion over 20 years) and a total infusion of $500 million to the FSM Trust Fund.

Marshall Islands

Growth forecasts are revised up. The economy is expected to expand faster than earlier forecast, driven largely by revived fisheries and construction output (Table 2.5.9). In May 2023 alone, the number of vessels calling at Majuro port was almost equal to that in January–April, indicating a pickup in fishing transshipments. Construction financed by development partners and preparations for the Micronesian Games in June 2024 are also spurring economic activity. El Niño poses a significant downside risk to the outlook as it could depress agriculture and fisheries output.

Table 2.5.9 Selected Economic Indicators in the Marshall Islands, %

Faster economic growth is expected, driven by fisheries and construction output.

	2022	2023		2024	
		Apr	Sep	Apr	Sep
GDP growth	−0.9	1.5	2.2	2.0	2.5
Inflation	3.3	3.7	3.7	3.5	3.5

GDP = gross domestic product.
Note: Years are fiscal years ending on 30 September of that year.
Source: Asian Development Bank estimates.

Inflation projections are retained from *ADO April 2023*'s projections. The impact of lower international fuel prices is expected to be offset by domestic factors, such as revived business activity and increased power tariffs in the urban centers of Majuro and Ebeye during FY2023. Furthermore, the suspension of the country's sole air cargo carrier between February and June 2023 resulted in supply chain disruptions. Demand from the Micronesian Games and the potential impact of El Niño on food prices are expected to keep inflation elevated in FY2024 relative to past years.

A fiscal deficit equivalent to 2.9% of GDP is still expected for both the current and next fiscal year. Government spending is still seen growing faster than revenues, especially given higher prices, preparations for the Micronesian Games, and El Niño's possible impact on revenues from fishing license fees. An upside risk is the increased likelihood that a new Compact of Free Association with the US will be signed, although this is unlikely to happen before the current agreement expires on 30 September. The new agreement would substantially increase financial assistance, as well as continue postal, weather, aviation, and disaster assistance services provided by the US.

Palau

GDP growth forecasts are unchanged from *ADO April 2023*'s projections (Table 2.5.10). International arrivals increased by 234.1% yoy in the third quarter of FY2023, but the year-to-date total still represents only 24.1% of FY2019's level. Tourist arrivals from Taipei,China and the People's Republic of China (PRC) have grown rapidly. In FY2022, tourist arrivals from Palau's top source markets prior to the pandemic—Taipei,China, Japan, the Republic of Korea, and the PRC—remained low as direct flights had not been fully restored. Still, latest data show signs of catch-up with the resumption of scheduled flights by United Airlines and chartered flights by Taipei,China's flag carrier, as well as a new Air Niugini connection from Port Moresby. Given the challenging economic environments in major source markets and competition from other travel destinations, the pace of recovery in tourism remains uncertain.

Table 2.5.10 Selected Economic Indicators in Palau, %

A sharp rise in inflation expected this year on tax and tariff increases.

	2022	2023		2024	
		Apr	Sep	Apr	Sep
GDP growth	–1.0	3.8	3.8	6.5	6.5
Inflation	10.2	5.0	8.0	5.5	5.0

GDP = gross domestic product.
Note: Years are fiscal years ending on 30 September of that year.
Source: Asian Development Bank estimates.

The inflation forecast for FY2023 is considerably higher than *ADO April 2023*'s due to recent tax and tariff developments. The introduction of value-added taxes in January 2023 pushed up food and fuel prices, and increases in electricity and wastewater tariffs raised household utility costs. Because of the resulting higher base, FY2024's inflation forecast is slightly lower than the earlier projection. Palau remains vulnerable to volatility in international prices because of its dependence on imported commodities. Although oil prices have declined faster than expected, they will likely rise over the rest of the year and into 2024. Further shocks to fuel or food prices from the Russian invasion of Ukraine or El Niño on agriculture are upside risks to inflation.

Fiscal gaps remain despite the prospect of increased financial resources. Revenues are expected to recover only gradually in line with the positive growth outlook, although economic activity will likely remain well below pre-pandemic levels over the forecast horizon. Thus, the country is still expected to run fiscal deficits equivalent to 9.5% of GDP in FY2023 and 10.2% in FY2024. Tax reforms coinciding with already elevated inflation may dampen consumption and constrain revenue growth in the near term. The main upside risk to the fiscal outlook for FY2024 is the enhanced financial assistance package under Palau's renewed Compact of Free Association with the US, which is pending Congressional approval. However, absorptive capacity remains a constraint to maximizing the uptake of increased fiscal resources.

South Pacific Economies

The Cook Islands, Niue, Samoa, and Tonga continue to recover faster than expected. But visitor arrivals and flight access to the Cook Islands and Niue are still below pre-pandemic levels. Inflation is a growing challenge in all four countries, with higher-than-expected results for fiscal year 2023 (FY2023, ended 30 June 2023 for all four) due to domestic and imported price pressures. Labor constraints are becoming increasingly prominent in these countries and may be a drag on future growth if not mitigated through active interventions in skills training, immigration, and labor force participation.

Cook Islands

Growth was stronger than expected in FY2023 (Table 2.5.11). After a full year of open borders, growth was driven by tourist arrivals that, at 116% of FY2022's level and 70% of FY2019's, exceeded expectations earlier in the year. New Zealand, as the primary tourism market, accounted for 80.5% of arrivals. Natural hazards and acute labor shortages are downside risks to the recovery, although the active recruitment of foreign workers should somewhat mitigate labor shortages.

Inflation over FY2023 was higher than projected in *ADO April 2023*, but is expected to fall back to trend in FY2024. Global supply disruptions escalated international fuel prices and transportation costs, which raised commodity prices, particularly for electricity and food. This increased the cost of living in the Cook Islands and reduced the purchasing power of consumers. However, inflation is expected to decelerate as imported fuel and food prices normalize, and the forecast for FY2024 is unchanged.

Table 2.5.11 Selected Economic Indicators in the Cook Islands, %

GDP growth rebounded stronger than expected in 2023.

	2022	2023		2024	
		Apr	Sep	Apr	Sep
GDP growth	10.5	11.2	14.5	9.1	9.1
Inflation	4.2	7.7	13.0	2.3	2.3

GDP = gross domestic product.
Note: Years are fiscal years ending on 30 June of that year.
Source: Asian Development Bank estimates.

A small fiscal surplus is now estimated for FY2023. *ADO April 2023* forecast a fiscal deficit, but the outturn was a surplus equivalent to 1.5% of GDP, driven by a 22.2% rise in tax revenue, mainly from value-added taxes, and 18.0% lower expenditure yoy due to underspending on capital projects. This update forecasts a fiscal deficit of 1.5% of GDP in FY2024, assuming public investment spending achieves its targets. Public debt equaled 45.6% of GDP in FY2023, and is expected to decline to 38.1% in FY2024.

Samoa

Growth for FY2023 is revised up on a stronger-than-expected rebound (Table 2.5.12). Visitor arrivals and domestic demand supported a recovery in tourism, commerce, and services through to the March quarter of 2023 and visitor arrivals in the June quarter recovered to near pre-pandemic levels. This momentum is forecast to continue into FY2024, with these sectors getting an additional lift from the increased mobilization of public spending, which has so far been subdued. Labor turnover has been significant, especially in tourism services. Continued growth in labor participation, as well as attracting former residents and overseas workers back to the domestic market, will be required to support growth.

Table 2.5.12 Selected Economic Indicators in Samoa, %

The recovery in 2023 accelerated faster than expected, but so did inflation.

	2022	2023		2024	
		Apr	Sep	Apr	Sep
GDP growth	–5.3	4.8	6.0	2.5	4.2
Inflation	8.8	10.2	12.0	2.0	5.3

GDP = gross domestic product.
Note: Years are fiscal years ending on 30 June of that year.
Source: Asian Development Bank estimates.

Inflation in FY2023 was higher than earlier forecast because of persistent increases in import prices. *ADO April 2023* forecast inflation reaching its highest level since FY2009, but the final result exceeded that estimate. Increases in the prices of local and imported food were the largest contributors to inflation, with most other categories posting declines or modest increases. Domestic inflationary pressure is expected to persist because the impact of international prices has not yet been fully felt, prompting the inflation forecast for FY2024 to be revised up.

This update estimates a fiscal surplus for FY2023, equivalent to 2.4% of GDP, on strong revenue growth. This is considerably higher than the 0.8% surplus forecast in April. Revenue growth was due to improved collection, higher-than-expected economic output, and the impact of inflation on consumption taxes. Although these factors are expected to continue to support the fiscal position in FY2024, expenditure for the District Development Plan and preparations for the Commonwealth Heads of Government meeting will likely result in a fiscal deficit of 3.5% of GDP, unchanged from April's projection.

Tonga

An earlier-than-expected recovery in visitor arrivals improved economic activity in FY2023, but growth in FY2024 is expected to be lower than was projected in April (Table 2.5.13). Competition from other international destinations and limited domestic air capacity are expected to slow growth in visitor arrivals. This will make it harder to attract much-needed reinvestment in tourism following the destruction of several properties from disasters in 2022 and 2020.

Table 2.5.13 Selected Economic Indicators in Tonga, %

The faster recovery in visitor arrivals and GDP growth in 2023 will slow in 2024.

	2022	2023		2024	
		Apr	Sep	Apr	Sep
GDP growth	-2.2	2.5	2.8	3.2	2.6
Inflation	8.5	9.4	10.3	1.5	4.5

GDP = gross domestic product.
Note: Years are fiscal years ending on 30 June of that year.
Source: Asian Development Bank estimates.

Capacity constraints in carrying out capital projects will weigh on future growth, due in large part to labor shortages.

Inflation in FY2023 accelerated faster than was projected in *ADO April 2023*. Increases in consumer prices were initially driven by higher import prices, but domestic prices quickly caught up due to local supply constraints and the surging costs of local food items. Inflation has accelerated since May 2023. Despite a recovery in domestic agriculture and the prospect of softer international commodity prices, inflationary pressures are expected to remain and the inflation forecast for FY2024 is therefore revised up.

Post-disaster reconstruction will put downward pressure on fiscal balances. While financing needs for post-disaster reconstruction remain large, this will be offset by significant funding from development partners. As a result, a slight fiscal surplus equivalent to 0.4% of GDP is estimated for FY2023 (0.3% in *ADO April 2023*), and a modest surplus of 1.9% of GDP is forecast for FY2024. Consequently, external debt is expected to fall by more than was projected in April. The debt-to-GDP ratio is estimated at 31.7% in FY2023 and forecast to be 28.7% in FY2024.

Niue

The economy is likely to perform slightly better in FY2024 if expectations of a doubling in visitor arrivals starting this November are on the mark. The economy contracted by 4.7% in FY2020 and 6.2% in FY2021 as prolonged border closures stalled tourism and slowed public investment spending. Having just a single weekly flight since borders reopened in June 2022 has hindered a quick recovery in the tourism industry. Although visitor arrivals in the first quarter of 2023 were higher than in the same period of last year, they remained well below pre-2019 levels.

The budget balance is expected to be in line with *ADO April 2023*'s forecast. FY2023's fiscal deficit is estimated at 26.4% of FY2021's GDP (21.4% of FY2019's) as expenditure grew faster than revenue. Donor grants declined by 24.7%. An expected sharp increase in tourism arrivals from November 2023, when a second weekly flight is to be introduced, bodes well for fiscal outcomes.

Inflation is likely to remain elevated over the near term in line with higher prices in New Zealand, Niue's main trading partner. Annual average inflation in New Zealand was 6.8% from July 2022 to June 2023, with food prices increasing by 10.6%.

3

STATISTICAL APPENDIX

STATISTICAL NOTES AND TABLES

This statistical appendix presents economic indicators for the 46 developing member economies in the Asian Development Bank (ADB) in three tables: gross domestic product (GDP) growth, inflation, and current account balance as a percentage of GDP. The economies are grouped into five subregions: the Caucasus and Central Asia, East Asia, South Asia, Southeast Asia, and the Pacific. The tables contain forecasts for 2023–2024 and historical data for GDP and inflation from 2020 and for the current account balance from 2018. Updated historical data are lacking for Niue, which precludes forecasts.

The data are standardized to the degree possible to allow comparability over time and across economies, but differences in statistical methodology, definitions, coverage, and practice make full comparability impossible. National income accounts are based on the United Nations System of National Accounts, while data on the balance of payments use International Monetary Fund (IMF) accounting standards. Historical data are variously based on official sources, statistical publications and databases, and documents from ADB, the IMF, and the World Bank. Projections for 2023 and 2024 are generally ADB estimates based on quarterly or monthly data as available, though some projections are from governments.

Most economies report by calendar year. The following report all variables by fiscal year: Afghanistan, Bangladesh, Bhutan, India, Nepal, and Pakistan in South Asia; Myanmar in Southeast Asia; and the Cook Islands, the Federated States of Micronesia, the Marshall Islands, Nauru, Palau, Samoa, and Tonga in the Pacific.

Regional and subregional averages are provided in the three tables. Averages are weighted by purchasing power parity (PPP) GDP in current international dollars. PPP GDP data for 2020–2021 were obtained from the IMF World Economic Outlook Database, October 2022 edition. Weights for 2021 are carried over to 2024.

The following paragraphs discuss the three tables in greater detail.

Table A1: Growth Rate of GDP (% per year). The table shows annual growth rates of GDP valued at constant market prices, factor costs, or basic prices. GDP at market prices is the aggregate value added by all resident producers at producers' prices including taxes less subsidies on imports plus all nondeductible value-added or similar taxes. Most economies use constant market price valuation. Pakistan uses constant factor costs, and Fiji basic prices. Some historical data for Turkmenistan are not presented for lack of uniformity. A fluid situation permits no data and forecasts for 2022–2024 for Afghanistan.

Table A2: Inflation (% per year). Data on inflation rates are period averages. Inflation rates are based on consumer price indexes. The consumer price indexes of the following economies are for a given city only: Cambodia is for Phnom Penh, the Marshall Islands for Majuro, and Sri Lanka for Colombo. Data on Afghanistan in 2022 were collected from international sources, but a fluid situation permits no forecasts for 2023–2024.

Table A3: Current Account Balance (% of GDP). The current account balance is the sum of the balance of trade in merchandise, net trade in services and factor income, and net transfers. The values reported are divided by GDP at current prices in US dollars. Some historical data for Turkmenistan are not presented for lack of uniformity. A fluid situation permits no data for 2021–2022 for Afghanistan.

Table A1 Growth Rate of GDP, % per Year

	2020	2021	2022	2023 Apr	2023 Sep	2024 Apr	2024 Sep
Developing Asia	**-0.6**	**7.2**	**4.3**	**4.8**	**4.7**	**4.8**	**4.8**
Developing Asia excluding the PRC	**-3.2**	**6.1**	**5.5**	**4.6**	**4.5**	**5.1**	**5.0**
Caucasus and Central Asia	**-1.9**	**5.8**	**5.1**	**4.4**	**4.6**	**4.6**	**4.7**
Armenia	-7.2	5.8	12.6	6.5	7.0	5.5	5.5
Azerbaijan	-4.3	5.6	4.6	3.5	2.2	3.8	2.6
Georgia	-6.8	10.5	10.1	4.5	6.0	5.0	5.0
Kazakhstan	-2.5	4.3	3.2	3.7	4.1	4.1	4.3
Kyrgyz Republic	-7.1	5.5	6.3	4.5	3.8	4.0	4.0
Tajikistan	4.5	9.2	8.0	5.5	6.5	6.5	7.0
Turkmenistan	...	5.0	6.2	6.5	6.2	6.0	6.0
Uzbekistan	2.0	7.4	5.7	5.0	5.5	5.0	5.5
East Asia	**1.8**	**7.9**	**2.8**	**4.6**	**4.4**	**4.2**	**4.2**
Hong Kong, China	-6.5	6.4	-3.5	3.6	4.3	3.7	3.3
Mongolia	-4.6	1.6	5.0	5.4	5.7	6.1	5.9
People's Republic of China	2.1	8.4	3.0	5.0	4.9	4.5	4.5
Republic of Korea	-0.7	4.3	2.6	1.5	1.3	2.2	2.2
Taipei,China	3.4	6.5	2.4	2.0	1.2	2.6	2.7
South Asia	**-4.4**	**8.4**	**6.7**	**5.5**	**5.4**	**6.1**	**6.0**
Afghanistan	-2.4	-20.7	...	...	...	...	...
Bangladesh	3.4	6.9	7.1	5.3	6.0	6.5	6.5
Bhutan	-10.0	4.1	4.7	4.6	4.3	4.2	4.4
India	-5.8	9.1	7.2	6.4	6.3	6.7	6.7
Maldives	-33.5	41.7	13.9	7.1	7.1	6.9	6.9
Nepal	-2.4	4.8	5.6	4.1	1.9	5.0	4.3
Pakistan	-0.9	5.8	6.1	0.6	0.3	2.0	1.9
Sri Lanka	-4.6	3.5	-7.8	-3.0	-3.0	1.3	1.3
Southeast Asia	**-3.2**	**3.5**	**5.6**	**4.7**	**4.6**	**5.0**	**4.8**
Brunei Darussalam	1.1	-1.6	-1.6	2.5	2.8	2.8	2.5
Cambodia	-3.1	3.0	5.2	5.5	5.3	6.0	6.0
Indonesia	-2.1	3.7	5.3	4.8	5.0	5.0	5.0
Lao People's Democratic Republic	-0.5	2.3	2.5	4.0	3.7	4.0	4.0
Malaysia	-5.5	3.1	8.7	4.7	4.5	4.9	4.9
Myanmar	3.2	-5.9	2.0	2.8	2.8	3.2	3.2
Philippines	-9.5	5.7	7.6	6.0	5.7	6.2	6.2
Singapore	-3.9	8.9	3.6	2.0	1.0	3.0	2.5
Thailand	-6.1	1.5	2.6	3.3	3.5	3.7	3.7
Timor-Leste	-8.3	2.9	3.2	3.1	2.8	3.0	2.9
Viet Nam	2.9	2.6	8.0	6.5	5.8	6.8	6.0
The Pacific	**-6.2**	**-1.3**	**6.1**	**3.3**	**3.5**	**2.8**	**2.9**
Cook Islands	-15.7	-25.5	10.5	11.2	14.5	9.1	9.1
Federated States of Micronesia	-3.6	-1.3	2.0	4.1	4.1	0.5	0.5
Fiji	-17.0	-4.9	20.0	6.3	8.3	3.0	3.7
Kiribati	-1.4	7.9	1.8	2.3	2.3	2.8	2.8
Marshall Islands	-1.8	1.1	-0.9	1.5	2.2	2.0	2.5
Nauru	4.2	3.3	2.8	1.8	1.6	2.2	1.6
Niue	-4.7	-6.2	...	...	...	...	...
Palau	-9.7	-17.1	-1.0	3.8	3.8	6.5	6.5
Papua New Guinea	-3.2	0.1	3.2	2.4	2.0	2.6	2.6
Samoa	-3.1	-7.1	-5.3	4.8	6.0	2.5	4.2
Solomon Islands	-3.4	-0.5	-4.2	3.0	3.0	2.5	2.5
Tonga	0.4	-2.7	-2.2	2.5	2.8	3.2	2.6
Tuvalu	-4.3	1.8	0.7	2.5	3.0	2.0	2.5
Vanuatu	-5.0	1.0	2.0	1.0	1.0	4.2	4.2

... = not available, GDP = gross domestic product, PRC= People's Republic of China.

Note: The current uncertain situation permits no estimates or forecasts for Afghanistan in 2022–2024.

Table A2 Inflation, % per Year

	2020	2021	2022	2023 Apr	2023 Sep	2024 Apr	2024 Sep
Developing Asia	**3.2**	**2.6**	**4.4**	**4.2**	**3.6**	**3.3**	**3.5**
Developing Asia excluding the PRC	**3.9**	**4.2**	**6.7**	**6.2**	**6.3**	**4.4**	**4.9**
Caucasus and Central Asia	**7.7**	**9.0**	**12.9**	**10.3**	**10.6**	**7.5**	**8.0**
Armenia	1.2	7.2	8.6	7.0	4.0	6.2	5.5
Azerbaijan	2.8	6.7	13.9	7.0	10.0	6.5	8.5
Georgia	5.2	9.6	11.9	6.0	3.0	4.0	3.5
Kazakhstan	6.8	8.0	15.0	11.8	12.7	6.4	7.6
Kyrgyz Republic	6.3	11.9	13.9	12.0	12.0	8.6	8.6
Tajikistan	9.4	8.0	4.2	7.0	5.5	6.5	6.0
Turkmenistan	10.0	12.5	10.0	10.0	8.0	10.0	8.0
Uzbekistan	12.9	10.7	11.4	11.0	11.0	10.0	10.0
East Asia	**2.2**	**1.1**	**2.3**	**2.3**	**1.0**	**2.0**	**2.1**
Hong Kong, China	0.3	1.6	1.9	2.3	2.5	2.1	2.1
Mongolia	3.7	7.3	15.2	10.9	10.5	8.7	8.6
People's Republic of China	2.5	0.9	2.0	2.2	0.7	2.0	2.0
Republic of Korea	0.5	2.5	5.1	3.2	3.3	2.0	2.2
Taipei,China	−0.2	2.0	2.9	2.0	2.0	2.0	2.0
South Asia	**6.5**	**5.8**	**8.2**	**8.1**	**8.6**	**5.8**	**6.6**
Afghanistan	5.6	5.2	13.8	...	...	...	...
Bangladesh	5.7	5.6	6.2	8.7	9.0	6.6	6.6
Bhutan	5.6	7.3	5.6	5.5	4.1	5.1	5.1
India	6.2	5.5	6.7	5.0	5.5	4.5	4.2
Maldives	−1.4	0.5	2.3	4.5	3.5	2.0	2.5
Nepal	6.2	3.6	6.3	7.4	7.7	6.2	6.2
Pakistan	10.7	8.9	12.2	27.5	29.2	15.0	25.0
Sri Lanka	4.6	6.0	46.4	24.6	18.7	5.5	5.5
Southeast Asia	**1.5**	**2.0**	**5.1**	**4.4**	**4.2**	**3.3**	**3.3**
Brunei Darussalam	1.9	1.7	3.7	2.0	1.5	1.6	1.4
Cambodia	2.9	2.9	5.3	3.0	3.0	4.0	4.0
Indonesia	2.0	1.6	4.2	4.2	3.6	3.0	3.0
Lao People's Democratic Republic	5.1	3.8	23.0	16.0	28.0	5.0	10.0
Malaysia	−1.1	2.5	3.4	3.1	3.0	2.8	2.7
Myanmar	5.7	3.7	18.4	10.5	14.0	8.2	8.2
Philippines	2.4	3.9	5.8	6.2	6.2	4.0	4.0
Singapore	−0.2	2.3	6.1	5.0	5.0	2.0	3.0
Thailand	−0.8	1.2	6.1	2.9	2.5	2.3	2.3
Timor-Leste	0.5	3.8	7.0	5.5	5.8	2.8	3.3
Viet Nam	3.2	1.8	3.2	4.5	3.8	4.2	4.0
The Pacific	**2.9**	**3.1**	**5.2**	**5.0**	**4.9**	**4.4**	**4.5**
Cook Islands	0.7	1.8	4.2	7.7	13.0	2.3	2.3
Federated States of Micronesia	1.0	1.8	5.0	3.6	3.6	0.4	0.4
Fiji	−2.6	0.2	4.3	4.2	3.0	3.5	3.0
Kiribati	2.5	2.1	5.0	3.7	6.0	3.0	3.0
Marshall Islands	−0.7	2.2	3.3	3.7	3.7	3.5	3.5
Nauru	5.3	2.0	1.0	2.5	5.5	1.9	4.2
Niue	2.6	...	...	...	...	...	...
Palau	0.7	0.5	10.2	5.0	8.0	5.5	5.0
Papua New Guinea	4.9	4.5	5.3	5.0	5.0	5.0	5.0
Samoa	1.5	−3.0	8.8	10.2	12.0	2.0	5.3
Solomon Islands	2.7	−0.1	5.5	4.5	5.5	3.7	3.7
Tonga	0.2	1.4	8.5	9.4	10.3	1.5	4.5
Tuvalu	1.6	6.7	12.2	3.3	6.2	2.8	3.3
Vanuatu	5.3	2.3	6.7	4.0	9.0	3.0	5.0

... = not available, PRC= People's Republic of China.
Note: The current uncertain situation permits no forecasts for Afghanistan in 2023–2024.

Table A3 Current Account Balance, % of GDP

	2018	2019	2020	2021	2022
Developing Asia	**0.1**	**0.8**	**2.0**	**1.5**	**1.2**
Caucasus and Central Asia	**-1.5**	**-2.9**	**-4.8**	**-0.8**	**4.3**
Armenia	-7.2	-7.1	-4.0	-3.5	0.8
Azerbaijan	12.8	9.1	-0.5	15.1	30.0
Georgia	-6.8	-5.5	-12.4	-10.4	-4.1
Kazakhstan	-1.0	-3.9	-6.4	-1.3	3.5
Kyrgyz Republic	-12.1	-12.1	4.5	-8.0	-43.7
Tajikistan	-4.4	-2.2	4.1	8.4	3.3
Turkmenistan	...	...	...	0.6	6.0
Uzbekistan	-7.1	-5.6	-5.0	-7.0	-0.6
East Asia	**1.1**	**1.5**	**2.6**	**2.9**	**2.8**
Hong Kong, China	3.7	5.9	7.0	11.8	10.5
Mongolia	-16.7	-15.2	-5.1	-13.8	-15.8
People's Republic of China	0.2	0.7	1.7	2.0	2.2
Republic of Korea	4.5	3.6	4.6	4.7	1.8
Taipei,China	11.6	10.9	14.4	15.2	13.3
South Asia	**-2.5**	**-1.3**	**0.4**	**-1.3**	**-2.6**
Afghanistan	12.2	11.7	11.2	...	...
Bangladesh	-3.0	-1.3	-1.3	-1.1	-4.1
Bhutan	-20.9	-13.9	-13.7	-21.9	-34.3
India	-2.1	-0.9	0.9	-1.2	-2.0
Maldives	-28.4	-26.6	-35.6	-8.4	-16.6
Nepal	-7.1	-6.9	-0.9	-7.7	-12.6
Pakistan	-5.4	-4.2	-1.5	-0.8	-4.7
Sri Lanka	-3.0	-2.1	-1.4	-3.7	-1.9
Southeast Asia	**0.7**	**1.7**	**2.8**	**0.7**	**0.6**
Brunei Darussalam	6.9	6.6	4.3	11.2	9.0
Cambodia	-11.8	-10.8	-3.4	-40.4	-25.3
Indonesia	-2.9	-2.7	-0.4	0.3	1.0
Lao People's Democratic Republic	-13.1	-12.2	-6.0	-2.4	-1.7
Malaysia	2.2	3.5	4.2	3.8	2.6
Myanmar	-4.7	0.4	-2.5	-1.3	-4.0
Philippines	-2.6	-0.8	3.2	-1.5	-4.4
Singapore	15.7	16.2	16.5	18.0	19.3
Thailand	5.6	7.0	4.2	-2.1	-3.5
Timor-Leste	-12.2	7.9	-12.8	-24.2	-21.9
Viet Nam	1.9	3.6	4.3	-2.0	-0.3
The Pacific	**7.0**	**8.9**	**6.6**	**5.4**	**12.0**
Cook Islands	37.6	31.7	9.6	-16.1	-7.0
Federated States of Micronesia	20.4	31.3	12.2	-3.6	-13.9
Fiji	-7.2	-4.9	-13.4	-12.5	-17.3
Kiribati	38.9	49.5	20.0	28.4	32.6
Marshall Islands	0.7	-27.8	19.4	25.1	...
Nauru	7.6	4.6	2.4	4.8	-0.5
Niue	14.5	...	...	...	...
Palau	-15.6	-31.1	-48.2	-55.9	-67.9
Papua New Guinea	12.9	14.8	14.1	12.6	24.6
Samoa	0.9	3.1	0.0	-17.8	-13.4
Solomon Islands	-3.0	-9.5	-1.6	-4.8	-13.6
Tonga	-6.3	-4.0	-7.5	-6.2	-6.2
Tuvalu	60.9	-22.2	16.3	24.1	4.6
Vanuatu	8.7	23.0	6.7	0.2	-14.7

... = not available, GDP = gross domestic product.

www.ingramcontent.com/pod-product-compliance
Lightning Source LLC
Chambersburg PA
CBHW050043220326
41599CB00045B/7260